SECOND CALIFORNIA EDITION

The
Conservatorship
Book

BY LISA GOLDOFTAS & ATTORNEY CAROLYN FARREN

NOLO PRESS BERKELEY

YOUR RESPONSIBILITY WHEN USING A SELF-HELP LAW BOOK

We've done our best to give you useful and accurate information in this book. But laws and procedures change frequently and are subject to differing interpretations. If you want legal advice backed by a guarantee, see a lawyer. If you use this book, it's your responsibility to make sure that the facts and general advice contained in it are applicable to your situation.

KEEPING UP-TO-DATE

To keep its books up to date, Nolo Press issues new printings and new editions periodically. New printings reflect minor legal changes and technical corrections. New editions contain major legal changes, major text additions or major reorganizations. To find out if a later printing or edition of any Nolo book is available, call Nolo Press at (510) 549-1976 or check the catalog in the *Nolo News,* our quarterly newspaper.

To stay current, follow the "Update" service in the *Nolo News*. You can get the paper free by sending us the registration card in the back of the book. In another effort to help you use Nolo's latest materials, we offer a 25% discount off the purchase of any new Nolo book if you turn in any earlier printing or edition. (See the "Recycle Offer" in the back of the book.)

This book was last revised in: **July 1994.**

SECOND EDITION	July 1994
BOOK DESIGN	Jackie Clark
	Terri Hearsh
COVER DESIGN	Amy Ihara
PROOFREADING	Anne Hayes
INDEX	Sayre Van Young
PRINTING	Delta Lithograph

Goldoftas, Lisa,
    The conservatorship book / by Lisa Goldoftas & Carolyn Farren. --
2nd national ed.
      p.   cm.
    Includes index.
    ISBN 0-87337-272-7 :
    1. Conservatorships--United States--Popular works.   I. Farren,
Carolyn,   II. Title.
KFC112.Z9G65   1994
346.79401'8—dc20   94-429655
[347.940618]   CIP

Printed on recycled paper

DEDICATION

To Barbara, Marcia and Neil, for your support and encouragement.

—LSG

To my loving daughter, Janna, whose patience with me and my schedule allowed me to complete this book. Also, to my friend, Carson, for his invaluable support.

—CMF

ACKNOWLEDGMENTS

The authors extend their thanks to the many people who generously contributed to this book:

Private conservator Debra Dolch (San Francisco), for her example of how a conservator can make a difference in other people's lives.

Attorney Bruce Feder (of Kato & Feder in San Francisco), for his detailed reading of the manuscript. His thorough understanding of conservatorship law added to the quality of this book.

Probate Paralegal Eryka Fraczek for contributing her time, expertise and experience.

Dr. Marcia Goldoft, for providing information about medicine and life.

James Kaspar, Chief Court Investigator (San Mateo County), for reviewing the manuscript and giving excellent suggestions.

Attorney John P. Kelley (of Greene, Kelley, Tobriner & Farren in San Francisco), for sharing his knowledge and expertise.

Jack McKay, consultant in gerontology (San Francisco), whose vast knowledge and keen perceptions added immensely to this book.

Attorney Gary L. Motsenbocker (of Cone & Motsenbocker in Fresno), for his analysis of financial accounts and fine review of the manuscript.

The wonderful people at Nolo, whose enthusiasm and endurance helped this book make its appearance. Special thanks to Terri Hearsh and Jackie Clark, for producing such a fine-looking book.

And last—but not least—Barbara Kate Repa, for patiently enduring the prolonged adolescence of this book.

CONTENTS

CHAPTER 1

INTRODUCTION TO CONSERVATORSHIPS

ADULTS SUFFERING FROM SEVERE physical or mental illnesses or recovering from serious accidents often need help from their relatives, lovers or friends. They may require assistance with preparing meals, finding a place to live and obtaining health care. They might need help depositing checks in the bank and paying bills or managing and investing their finances.

If an adult cannot manage alone, a court may give the responsibility to another person—a conservator. The adult must be so seriously incapacitated that he cannot take care of his basic personal needs or handle his own finances. He is usually too debilitated to sign documents allowing someone else to take over. Often conservatorships are established for people who are in comas, suffer from advanced stages of Alzheimer's disease or have other serious illnesses. A conservatorship is one way to ensure that someone will be responsible for taking care of an incapacitated adult.

Example: Heidi has Alzheimer's disease, and is confused and disoriented most of the time. One rainy day, her sister finds her sitting outside, wet and shivering, but Heidi doesn't seem to notice her own discomfort. Her sister discovers that Heidi frequently leaves her windows unlocked and front door wide open at night. Heidi eats when she is given food by her sister, and picks at leftovers which she leaves unrefrigerated for days at a time. Heidi does not open her mail or pay bills, her utilities have been cut off and her landlord is about to evict her. Because Heidi is unable to manage her personal and financial needs, her sister is appointed conservator by a judge.

LEGAL CITATIONS

Throughout the book you will see references to California law, called legal citations. If you are interested in tracking down specific laws that are mentioned, you can look up these citations. (Legal research is discussed in more detail in Chapter 17, Section D.) These are the citations you'll see:

- Civil Code
- Code of Civil Procedure
- California Rules of Court
- Probate Code
- Welfare & Institutions Code
- United States Code

This book explains the effects of establishing a conservatorship in California and discusses some alternatives. The role of a conservator is explained, along with a number of considerations to help you evaluate whether to accept those duties and responsibilities. Where a conservatorship is necessary, this book gives instructions for establishing, maintaining and ending one.

A.   What Is a Conservatorship?

A CONSERVATORSHIP IS A LEGAL ARRANGEMENT in which an adult oversees the personal care or financial matters of another adult considered incapable of managing alone. The incapacitated person is the "conservatee." The person who takes over is the "conservator."

A California conservatorship must be formally established and ended by a court. To set up a conservatorship, an adult must file documents with a court, have copies given to the proposed conservatee and mailed to the proposed conservatee's close relatives. A court investigator talks to the proposed conservatee and others who may know something about the situation. A hearing date is set up, and there a judge decides whether to appoint a conservator.

A conservatorship is, above all, intended to "protect the rights of persons who are placed under conservatorship" (Probate Code §1800). As a matter of course, conservatees are encouraged to maintain as much independence as possible.

The legal system assumes that even a well-meaning person may find the responsibilities of serving as conservator difficult if he has access to a large sum of money or becomes emotionally and physically drained by caring for a needy or demanding incapacitated person. So once a conservatorship is established, the court plays a role in monitoring the conservator's actions. One year after the conservatorship is established and every two years after that, a judge will evaluate whether the conservator is doing the job right.

While a conservatorship is in place, periodic court investigations are conducted to verify that it is needed and the conservatee is receiving appropriate care. If a conservator is handling the conservatee's finances, a financial guarantee called a "bond" must usually be posted. The conservator must follow certain guidelines when investing and selling the conservatee's assets. The conservator must provide special detailed accounts every year or two that list all assets and expenditures and explain how the conservatee's estate was handled. The conservator may

also need to prepare periodic status reports, which tell how the conservatee is doing and how the conservator is handling the required duties.

Even though a legal conservatorship is aimed to protect everyone involved, it is also very time consuming and usually uses up some of the conservatee's money for court fees and related costs. A conservatorship also limits the legal rights of the conservatee, which can be psychologically harmful. Depending on the type of conservatorship, the conservatee may not be permitted to make decisions about how his money is managed or spent. The conservatee could be denied the right to make all medical decisions for himself, vote or have access to a car. (See Chapter 2, Section A for more information about the legal effects of a conservatorship.)

This book covers three types of California conservatorships: conservatorship of the person, conservatorship of the estate and conservatorship of the person and estate.

1.   Conservatorship of the Person

A conservator of the person is responsible for making sure that the conservatee has proper food, clothing, shelter and health care. The conservator must attend to personal needs, including social contact with family and friends and other sources of enjoyment such as books or music. Depending on the conservatee's ability to understand and make decisions, the conservator may need to make important medical choices for her.

The conservatee may live with the conservator or elsewhere, such as in a private residence, board and care home or nursing facility in California. Before permanently moving the conservatee out of California, a conservator first must obtain a court order.

2.   Conservatorship of the Estate

A conservator of the estate handles the finances of someone who cannot manage them alone, or is susceptible to being taken advantage of financially by others.[1] However, a conservatorship of the estate may not be needed if there are only isolated incidents of mishandling money. For example, a conservator of the estate would probably not be needed for someone who only once impulsively donates a large sum of money to a local charity. But a conservatorship would likely be needed for someone who gives away his Social Security checks each month and doesn't have any money to pay bills.

A conservator of the estate must use the conservatee's money and other assets to support and educate the conservatee and any dependents (Probate Code §2420). Legal guidelines require a conservator of the estate to invest and handle the conservatee's funds carefully, and to obtain court approval before undertaking any potentially risky transactions. Courts require periodic accounting reports to make sure the conservator does not mismanage or steal any money.

3. Conservatorship of the Person and Estate

If a conservatorship is needed for both the person and estate, only one court proceeding is required to establish both types of conservatorships.

B. When You Need a Lawyer's Help

THIS BOOK PROVIDES all the help most California residents will need to obtain a legal conservatorship of someone else who lives in this state, but it does not cover every possible situation. This section guides you on when to seek the help of a lawyer. (Information on how to find and hire lawyers is contained in Chapter 17.)

1. Complicated Situation

Consult a lawyer if:

- Someone else has filed or plans to file court papers seeking conservatorship of the same person—even if one conservatorship is for the person and the other is for the estate.[2]

- The proposed conservatee has nominated someone else as conservator in writing and that person is willing and able to serve.

- There are conflicts or serious differences of opinion between you and family members or people who stand to inherit from the proposed conservatee. These conflicts may include how the estate will be managed, where the proposed conservatee will live or what kind of medical treatment she will receive.

- You and the proposed conservatee have differing beliefs about what forms of medical treatment should be used, and you would find it difficult to advocate the proposed conservatee's choices. For example, the proposed conservatee might believe in healing by prayer alone, while you advocate using western medicine.

- The proposed conservatee has already signed durable power of attorney documents giving someone else authority to make health care or financial decisions, and you want to take over making those decisions.

- Anyone objects to (contests) the conservatorship by filing papers in court, or tries to have you removed from your position after you are appointed conservator.

- You want to be the conservator for two or more people—such as a husband and wife.[3]

- You are seeking a conservatorship on behalf of a non-profit charitable corporation, state or local public entity or agency, officer or employer, or you are a

---

[1] With a special court order, a conservator of the estate may manage a conservatee's business matters as well as the conservatee's personal finances. This is beyond the scope of this book.

[2] Two or more people can serve as co-conservators or someone can be appointed conservator of the person and someone else conservator of the estate. Because this can be complicated, a lawyer's help is suggested.

[3] One conservatorship can be established for two or more conservatees (Probate Code §2106(a)). This might be appropriate where both members of a married couple need conservators. Due to complications involved in this type of conservatorship, an attorney's help may be needed.

professional private conservator or creditor of the proposed conservatee.[4]

2. Complications With Proposed Conservatee

Consult a lawyer if:

- The proposed conservatee does not want a conservatorship or does not want you to serve as conservator—regardless of whether he is fully able to understand the situation.

- The proposed conservatee is institutionalized in or on leave from a state mental health facility, or you expect the proposed conservatee will require hospitalization in a mental health treatment facility. (See Section B5a, below.)

- The proposed conservatee is developmentally disabled. (See Section B5b, below.)

- The proposed conservatee is an American Indian. Courts must enforce federal law in this area, which is beyond the scope of this book.

- You want to manage the finances of someone who is "missing" and presumed dead, or who was a member of the uniformed services or an employee of the U.S. government or agency, and is considered an "absentee" by a government authority.

3. Complex Conservatorship Estate

Consult a lawyer if:

- The proposed conservatee's estate includes assets that will require your special or discretionary management, including making investments, purchasing real estate, exercising stock options or handling trusts on behalf of the conservatee or someone else.

- You don't have the expertise to handle the proposed conservatee's estate, probably because it is very large or complicated.

- The proposed conservatee's estate has a value of $600,000 or more; complicated federal inheritance tax laws will affect how the conservatorship is set up and handled.

- You anticipate selling major assets belonging to the proposed conservatee, such as personal property with a value of $5,000 or more or any real estate. Although you may obtain the conservatorship yourself, you will need an attorney's help with the sale.

- The proposed conservatee owns real estate or other significant assets outside of California.

- The proposed conservatee is married and her spouse either already has a conservator of the estate or doesn't have a conservator, but is incapacitated and unable to handle financial matters.

- The proposed conservatee owns a sole proprietorship, partnership or other business. Sometimes a small business may be managed by a conservator or his spouse. But an existing contract between owners of the business could complicate matters and even supersede that authority.

4. If You Need a Conservatorship Right Away

If you need a conservatorship in less than six to eight weeks, a special temporary conservatorship can be established, usually within five days. This entails completing all the documents required for a regular conservatorship, as well as additional documents for a temporary conservatorship. Judges are reluctant to grant temporary conservatorships unless there is an urgent reason. To obtain a temporary conservatorship, you will need to do your own research or obtain the help of an attorney. (See Chapter 17.)

---

[4]As a creditor, you are not eligible to petition for the conservatorship unless you are also the proposed conservatee's spouse or relative (Probate Code §1820(c)).

5. Special Conservatorships Not Covered in This Book

Two special types of conservatorships require that the proposed conservatee be represented by a private lawyer or the county's own attorney, such as the public defender. These kinds of conservatorships are beyond the scope of this book.

SPECIAL CONSIDERATIONS FOR CONSERVATORSHIPS OF THE ESTATE

A conservatorship of the estate can become complicated in a hurry if the conservatee co-owns property with anyone, owns a business or is responsible for supporting a spouse, ex-spouse or children. While hiring a lawyer is not mandatory, it is often recommended in these circumstances:

- *Married Conservatee:* The spouse who is not under a conservatorship usually has the legal right to control community property and the responsibility to financially support the conservatee. Under some circumstances, community property may be divided, or the spouse can agree to have a portion or all community property included in the estate. This can prevent the spouse from mismanaging the property, and keep the conservatee from being liable for the spouse's debts. Dividing community property may also be advisable if there is a possibility of either spouse going into a nursing home, since community property assets could be quickly used up. (Community property is covered in more detail in Chapter 2, Section B2d and Chapter 12, Section C2b.)

- *Dependents:* A conservator is responsible for the support and education of the conservatee's dependents. Large educational or living expenses may be problematic or impossible, given the size of the conservatorship estate. Matters may be even more complex if a divorced conservatee is responsible for paying child or spousal support.

- *Property Owned With Others:* Real estate, bank accounts and vehicles are commonly co-owned in a form of ownership called "joint tenancy." Joint tenants can manage their share of these assets regardless of the conservatorship. It is difficult for a conservator to monitor how a joint tenant manages property. For example, if a joint tenant removes money from an account, damages the property or injures others, the conservator could be held liable.

a. Mental Health (LPS) Conservatorships

A special type of conservatorship of the person may be established for someone who has a mental disorder or is impaired by chronic alcoholism. The person must be a danger to himself or others or be "gravely disabled"—unable to take care of his basic personal needs such as food, shelter and clothing.

Under the Lanterman-Petris-Short (LPS) Mental Health Services Act, a conservatorship of the person may be set up to assure that a gravely disabled individual is provided with individualized mental health treatment and services. LPS conservatees, either adults or minors, are sometimes hospitalized in mental health treatment facilities or placed in board and care homes.

LPS conservatorships last only one year, with a one-year renewal available upon court approval. Such conservatorships are recommended by professionals in mental health facilities, and special investigations are conducted to assure that the LPS conservatorship is appropriate. Petitions are filed by the county's district attorney or county counsel, not by private citizens. They are generally initiated by the Department of Social Services or Welfare Department, often after someone has been confined in a hospital's acute psychiatric ward.

 Even if an LPS conservatorship is established, a regular conservatorship of the person—which is covered in this book—may be needed at the same time. An attorney can help sort this out.

b. Conservatorships for Developmentally Disabled Adults

For developmentally disabled adults, a special type of conservatorship—called a "limited conservatorship"—may be needed. Those who are "developmentally disabled" have a condition that is not solely physical, originated before age 18 and is expected to last indefinitely. Examples of developmental disabilities include mental retardation, cerebral palsy, epilepsy and autism.

Limited conservatorships are specially tailored by the courts to encourage developmentally disabled adults to be self-reliant and independent.[5] Depending on local policy, a limited conservatorship may be mandatory for a developmentally disabled adult, or either a limited or regular conservatorship might be allowed.

C. Answers to Common Questions About Conservatorships

Q: *What is the difference between a conservatorship and a guardianship?*

A: In California, a conservatorship may be established for adults and in some instances married or divorced minors—people under the age of 18. Guardianships are only available for minors. The source of some historical confusion is that until 1981, it was possible to establish a guardianship for an adult.

Q: *Could I become a conservator without letting anyone know about it?*

A: No. The proposed conservatee and close relatives are legally entitled to be notified about the conservatorship hearing beforehand. A judge is unlikely to waive any of these notice requirements unless there is an extremely good reason, such as when a relative cannot be located.

Q: *Can I change my mind after I've been appointed as conservator?*

A: Once you are appointed conservator, you are obligated to serve until the court issues an order relieving you of your responsibilities. If you become unable or unwilling to handle the responsibility, the court may allow you to resign as conservator. However, to protect the conservatee, a judge might decide not to allow you to resign or, more likely, may prolong your role as conservator until someone else can be found to take over.

Q: *As conservator of the estate, may I use estate money for myself?*

A: The estate must only be used for the benefit of the conservatee and any dependents. Your money and the estate's money must always be kept separate. This is true even if you are the only person who will inherit from the conservatee. If you believe you should be financially compensated for time you spent on the conservatorship, you must formally ask the court to allow payment. Without a court order, you cannot take any money for yourself.

Q: *If I'm appointed conservator of the person, will I have to live with and care for the conservatee?*

A: You must see that the conservatee receives adequate care, but you are not responsible for providing a home and caring for the conservatee. Some conservatees live in the same household as their conservators, especially when it is a close-knit family situation. But often, conservatees live in their own homes and receive professional care, or live in nursing facilities where their needs can best be met.

Q: *As conservator, am I personally liable for everything the conservatee does?*

A: No. As conservator you are not responsible for any civil or criminal misconduct committed by the conservatee unless it was caused by your own negligence. You are also not personally liable for the conservatee's debts, property or any obligations under contracts. You are, however, responsible for how you handle your job as conservator. (These duties are discussed more thoroughly in Chapters 11 and 12.)

Q: *Can I get financial help for the conservatee, such as welfare, Social Security or Medi-Cal?*

A: Yes. It is a conservator's duty to apply for all benefits to which the conservatee may be entitled. You should seek and be able to receive benefits on the conservatee's behalf. However, it is not always necessary to obtain a conservatorship if your sole reason is to receive financial benefits for another adult. (See Chapter 2, Section B.)

Q: *How long does a conservatorship last?*

A: A conservatorship may end when the conservatee dies or when the conservatee can resume caring for herself or her finances. A court must approve the ending of a conservatorship.

---

[5]Regular probate conservatorships may also be designed to give the conservatee specific rights. But those are not considered "limited conservatorships," which are available only for developmentally disabled adults.

DECIDING WHETHER TO SEEK A CONSERVATORSHIP

CONSERVATORSHIPS ARE TIME CONSUMING and relatively costly and require filling out a mound of paperwork and appearing in court—mostly unpleasant prospects.

Although a conservatorship might be necessary, other excellent and more appropriate alternatives may exist. By law, before a conservatorship is established, you must give information about what alternatives you considered and why they're not available (Probate Code §1821(a)(3)). This chapter will help you analyze your situation and decide whether seeking a conservatorship is the best option.

A. Legal Consequences of a Conservatorship

A CONSERVATORSHIP IS AN EXTREME MEASURE and should not be taken lightly. It limits an individual's legal ability to make his own decisions, and deprives him of many legal rights others take for granted. A conservatorship also places a great deal of legal, emotional and ethical responsibility on the conservator.

How the conservatee and conservator are affected depends in part on what type of conservatorship is established. If you are unclear about the distinctions between a conservatorship of the person, estate or person and estate, review Chapter 1, Section A, before going on.

1. Possible Effects on Proposed Conservatee

It may be upsetting for a person to learn that a court determined he cannot handle his own finances, or needs someone else to make sure he has food, clothing, shelter and medical care. Depending on the decision of a judge, the conservatee may also lose his right to vote.

For someone who takes pride in his independence, a conservatorship can be psychologically devastating. It may not be a good solution for someone who is surrounded by supportive family members and excellent community resources. That person may get all the help he needs without the stress of a court proceeding.

On the other hand, the proposed conservatee might find it a relief that someone else is stepping in to take over matters she cannot handle. Of course, if the proposed conservatee does not have the capacity to understand the effects of a conservatorship, the loss of independence associated with the conservatorship should not affect her at all.

A proposed conservatee has the legal right to oppose the conservatorship and request a jury trial, regardless of her ability to understand the proceedings (Probate Code §1827). She has the right to an attorney to represent her in the conservatorship case, and if she cannot afford a lawyer, the court will appoint one to represent her (Probate Code §1471). Even if a proposed conservatee doesn't object to the conservatorship, the court may appoint a lawyer to represent her—usually at the estate's expense. This usually happens if there are any questions raised about the need for a conservatorship, the choice of conservator or the proposed conservatee's willingness to be under a conservatorship.

Once a conservatorship is established, the conservatee retains the right to vote, marry, seek legal separation, divorce or annulment, unless there is a court order forbidding it. The conservatee always retains the right to be represented by an attorney. If the conservatee is able, she generally may make a will—but under no circumstances may a conservator create a will on the conservatee's behalf.

a. Conservatorship of the Person

When a conservatorship of the person is established, the conservator decides where the conservatee will live, and makes arrangements for his personal care. The conservatee must go along with those decisions, although he retains the right to object in court.[1]

Unless a court determines otherwise, the conservatee may consent to or refuse medical treatment, and may override the medical decisions of a conservator except in the case of a medical emergency. However, a court could take away the conservatee's right to make his own medical decisions if it determines that he is incapable of making those choices. If the conservatee created a valid durable power of attorney for health care or living will before conservatorship was established, that document remains valid.

Only the conservatee may decide whether he wants to take experimental drugs, undergo convulsive treatment (shock therapy) or be committed to a mental health facility.[2]

b. Conservatorship of the Estate

When a conservatorship of the estate is established, the conservatee loses some basic legal rights unless a special court order states otherwise. Generally, the conservatee loses all control over his and anyone else's finances, with the exception of the right to any wages he earns and the right to take steps to support himself, his spouse and minor children—such as to sign contracts or incur debts (Probate Code §1871(d)).

Otherwise, the conservatee cannot sign contracts, make gifts, incur debts or serve as a fiduciary. He cannot choose to waive rights—such as the right to receive or inherit property, and cannot delegate a power—for example, by creating a financial power of attorney. The conservatee may not make transactions involving real estate—such as buying, selling, transferring or encumbering property. Only with a court order may the conservatee receive and spend a personal allowance.

---

[1] The conservator may not mistreat, abuse or unnecessarily restrict the conservatee. However, the conservator may make decisions that affect the conservatee's lifestyle, regardless of whether the conservatee likes those decisions.

[2] A special type of mental health conservatorship—called an LPS conservatorship—may be established to allow these medical treatments if the conservatee has a mental disorder or suffers from chronic alcoholism. (An explanation of LPS conservatorships is contained in Chapter 1, Section B5a.)

2. Potential Effects on Proposed Conservator

Conservatorships follow technical legal procedures and involve considerable time and paperwork to set up. A conservatorship is an ongoing responsibility which usually lasts from the time a court establishes it until the conservatee dies. A conservator must notify the court when he or the conservatee moves to a new residence, and must get court approval before stepping down from the position. A conservator who causes damages by failing to perform legal duties may be held liable in court.

Example: Virginia is conservator of the person of Franklin, who has a habit of throwing lit cigarette butts out his bedroom window, onto the garage next door. The neighbors have complained and asked Virginia to lock the windows overlooking their property. But even though Virginia agrees that locking the windows would solve the problem, she never gets around to taking that precaution. If the garage catches on fire due to Franklin's actions, Virginia could be held legally liable. Or the next door neighbors could sue her personally for allowing Franklin to keep throwing burning cigarette butts on their property.

Example: Gretchen is conservator of the estate of Shane. Gretchen is careless with the estate's money, and leaves most of it in an uninsured bank account, figuring nothing will happen to it. If the bank goes

under, Gretchen will be personally liable for the amount lost.

Being a conservator can be time-consuming and a real source of stress. You should understand what the position involves before taking on that job. (Read Chapter 11 for information about a conservatorship of the person and Chapters 12 and 13 for information about a conservatorship of the estate.)

A conservator of the person assumes responsibility for making personal care decisions the conservatee would make if she were able—about food, clothing, shelter and medical care. Sometimes a conservator has sole authority to make medical decisions for the conservatee—a weighty responsibility if any decisions must be made in sensitive situations. Most commonly, the conservatee retains authority to make her own medical decisions or override the conservator's medical decisions. A conservator chooses where the conservatee lives, which can be trying if he needs to change the residence of someone whose health is deteriorating. The conservator must obtain court approval before moving the conservatee out of California or stepping down from his role.

A conservator of the estate must devote the time and planning necessary to handle the conservatee's assets wisely. This includes seeing that bills are paid, property is adequately insured and maintained and that the conservatee and any dependents (spouse and minor children) are supported.

The conservator of the estate must have non-cash estate items appraised by a probate referee, file documents with the court itemizing the estate and periodically complete financial accounts for the court. The conservator must return to court and obtain permission for any but the most conservative financial transactions. When it is time to end the conservatorship, the conservator must prepare documents requesting that the conservatorship be allowed to end.

Although a conservator's job can be very time consuming and difficult, it is extremely important. There is also satisfaction in providing an invaluable service for someone who cannot take care of critical personal and financial needs. A conservator can be secure that he is making the best possible decisions for a friend or family member, rather than passing the responsibility to an agency or outsider.

B. Alternatives to Conservatorships

BEFORE PROCEEDING WITH A CONSERVATORSHIP, look into alternate ways of meeting the proposed conservatee's needs. If you decide to seek a conservatorship, the court will require information about other options and why they aren't appropriate. (The form used to explain this information to the court is contained in Chapter 4, Section C.)

Alternatives are often appropriate in congenial, stable family situations where there are no conflicts about inheritance or money, and everyone agrees about the handling of personal and health care matters.

> ## WHEN ALTERNATIVES TO CONSERVATORSHIPS ARE AVAILABLE
>
> For good reason, conservatorships are often considered only as a last resort, since they are time-consuming, relatively expensive and are overseen by California courts. It's likely that alternatives to conservatorships may be pursued if:
>
> * The proposed conservatee is only temporarily unable to care for herself or her finances.
> * The proposed conservatee has signed—or is able to understand and is willing to sign—legal documents giving someone else authority to make medical or financial decisions for her.
> * The proposed conservatee is not at risk of being taken advantage of financially or being abused physically or emotionally.
> * All close family and friends are in agreement about who will serve as caretaker for the proposed conservatee and handle her finances.

1. Alternate Ways of Handling Medical and Personal Care Decisions

If an adult cannot make his own medical care decisions, someone else must be given legal authority to make them. These decisions can range from relatively minor concerns to serious choices about types of medical treatment, major surgery and the use of life support systems. It is sensible to plan ahead, since people become incapacitated for reasons ranging from old age to automobile accidents.

Informal documents, handwritten letters or oral requests instructing physicians or giving someone authority to make medical decisions are generally not legally binding on anyone. Normally, the most efficient method of giving another person authority to make medical care decisions for another adult is by use of a durable power of attorney along with a health care declaration, formerly called a living will, described in Sections B1a and B1b, below.

a   Durable Power of Attorney for Health Care

A durable power of attorney for health care is a document authorizing someone to make health care decisions if the person signing the document cannot make those decisions due to future incapacity. This document can only be created by someone who is of sound mind and capable of deciding what medical treatments she wants provided, withdrawn or withheld.

The document is generally drafted so it only takes effect if the person signing it becomes incapacitated and cannot consent to or refuse a particular medical treatment (Civil Code §2434(a)).

The document can specify how an individual wants medical treatment handled—for example, it is possible to request that life support systems be used if a patient becomes unconscious, or that blood transfusions be administered if the need arises. In California, a durable power of attorney cannot give another person the power to commit or place the person signing it into a mental health treatment facility, authorize convulsive treatment, psychosurgery, sterilization or abortion (Civil Code §2435).

For many people, a power of attorney for health care can help avoid the need for a legal conservatorship. In the unlikely event that a conservatorship is necessary, a durable power of attorney allows the person signing it to choose someone in advance to serve as conservator. A judge must appoint the named person as conservator unless there is a good reason not to do so.

b.   Health Care Directive

A declaration is a document individuals can use to express their right to have specific medical treatment provided or withheld if they become permanently comatose or are diagnosed to have a terminal condition. The document is interchangeably called a "declaration," "directive," and a "directive to physicians."[3] Directives are specifically binding on doctors—unlike durable powers of attorney for health care which give another person authority to make medical decisions. If possible, a directive should be used in conjunction with, and be consistent with, a durable power of attorney for health care, explained in Section B1a, above.[4] But it's not always possible to find someone who is able and willing to see that an individual's medical wishes are carried out. In that case, a directive is very important.

A directive can specify what medical care should be provided or withheld if an individual becomes unable to communicate those wishes. Directives are typically used to specify that an individual wishes to have life-sustaining treatment withheld or withdrawn—including artificially administered food and water. However directives may be used much more broadly. In 1990, the U.S. Supreme Court ruled that everyone has a constitutional right to control his or her own medical care. The Court stated that "clear and convincing evidence" of an individual's wishes for medical care must be followed—even if they conflict with the wishes of close family members or friends (*Cruzan v. Director, Missouri Dept of Health*, 497 U.S. 261). The best evidence of medical care wishes is a written document, so a growing number of people are rejecting the declaration form commonly provided and tailoring their declarations to reflect their specific wishes. All written health care directives should be signed by the person making them and by two witnesses who are not the individual's health care providers. It is also essential for the attending physicians to be notified that the document exists.

c. Informal Personal Care Arrangements

Often a family member or friend takes charge of an incapacitated person without obtaining any legal documentation. In these instances the incapacitated person's needs—food, clothing, shelter, personal and medical care—are handled informally. Local agencies may be able to help with meals, home health care, transportation or housekeeping. (For information on locating an agency, check with your local senior information and referral line. Also see Appendix A.)

Informal arrangements often work well, especially where a family is close, no serious medical decisions are made and money is not a problem.[5]

d. Court Authorization for Medical Treatment

If an adult patient cannot consent to treatment for a medical condition, a petition can be filed in the superior court requesting that a specific medical treatment be allowed and someone else—such as a family member, friend or doctor—be entitled to authorize that treatment. This is generally done only if a nonimmediate treatment is required to save a life or prevent further injury. For example, this might include eye surgery or a bone marrow or organ transplant. An attorney must represent the incapacitated person. These procedures are beyond the scope of this book. (See Probate Code §§3200-3211.)

2. Alternate Ways of Handling Financial Decisions

Alternatives to a conservatorship of the estate are commonly used when family members are close and there is no dispute about the incapacitated person's finances by family or people who will inherit, since whoever acts on behalf of the incapacitated person is not supervised by a court.[6]

If possible, it is best to plan ahead for financial matters, taking into account that a person who becomes

---

[3] This document, formerly referred to as a living will, is called a directive or declaration in California. But there is still a great deal of confusion about its name.

[4] Information on health care directives and computer-generated forms are contained in WillMaker computer program published by Nolo Press.

[5] *Beat the Nursing Home Trap*, by Joseph Matthews (Nolo Press) provides an overview of alternatives for selecting long-term care, both in the home and in care facilities. The book also gives information on financial planning for long-term care.

[6] Special procedures apply for someone who is a member of the uniformed services or an employee of the U.S. government or agency, and is considered an "absentee" by the government. If the absentee's property isn't worth more than $20,000, it may be turned over to the absentee's family after a court hearing (Probate Code §3701). If the absentee's property is worth $5,000 or less and doesn't include real estate, a court proceeding is not necessary (Probate Code §3710). These procedures are beyond the scope of this book.

incapacitated will die someday. Even the best methods of handling financial matters generally end when the incapacitated person dies.

a.   Financial Durable Power of Attorney

A financial durable power of attorney authorizes someone to make decisions in the event the person signing it cannot. The document usually goes into effect only if the person signing it becomes incapacitated—which allows the person signing to retain full control over his finances as long as he is able. A financial durable power of attorney automatically ends when the person creating it dies. It can be created only if the person signing it is of sound mind.

A financial durable power of attorney allows an adult to choose who she wants to handle her finances without the need for a court-supervised conservatorship. If a conservatorship becomes necessary—for example, in the unlikely event that a financial institution won't accept the power of attorney—the conservator can be specified in the document.[7] It may authorize the specified person to sign checks, make bank deposits, sell property and handle the incapacitated individual's assets. It's also easy to place restrictions in the durable power of attorney for financial matters, such as preventing authority to sell or encumber real estate.[8]

b.   Financial Benefits

Most government agencies allow financial benefits to be received and monitored by someone other than the person entitled to those benefits. The money must always be spent for the person it was intended to benefit. Benefits include:

- Social Security;
- Medical coverage and insurance such as Medi-Cal and Medicare;
- Veterans' Administration benefits;
- Disability benefits;
- Public Assistance such as Subsidized (Section 8) Housing and food stamps; and
- Supplemental Security Income (SSI).

To receive and monitor benefits, contact each agency and follow its procedures. If the agency requires periodic accountings to show how money was spent, you must comply.[9]

USING A NON-DURABLE POWER OF ATTORNEY

Unless a power of attorney document clearly specifies that it is a durable power of attorney—intended to last even if the person signing it becomes incapacitated—by definition it automatically terminates upon incapacity of the person creating it.

A non-durable power of attorney may be created by someone who is of sound mind and able to understand and sign legal documents. A non-durable power of attorney authorizes another person to handle financial matters on behalf of the person creating it. This may include handling bank accounts, paying bills and receiving pensions or investment dividends. Some institutions have their own form documents.

A non-durable power of attorney is designed to give another person the right to completely or partially manage one's financial affairs. This flexible document may be drafted to be valid for a specified or open-ended time period. A non-durable power of attorney may:

- give authority for all financial transactions; or
- restrict authority to one or several specific transactions.

A non-durable power of attorney is not appropriate for handling health or medical care decisions because it becomes ineffective if the person signing it becomes incapacitated.

Nolo's Law Form Kit: Power of Attorney provides forms and instructions for creating non-durable power of attorney documents.

---

[7]Laws require that a judge appoint the named person as conservator unless there is a good reason not to do so.

[8]All the instructions and the forms you'll need to create a durable power of attorney for financial matters are contained in *Who Will Handle Your Finances if You Can't?*, by Denis Clifford and Mary Randolph. (Nolo Press). The book also provides instructions on creating conventional powers of attorney.

[9]Chapter 10 gives information about obtaining benefits and coverage after a conservatorship is established, but much of the material in that chapter is relevant to someone receiving benefits without a conservatorship.

c.   Living Trusts (Inter Vivos Trusts)

In a typical living trust—also called a revocable inter vivos trust—the creator of the trust also serves as trustee and beneficiary.[10]

A living trust is an estate planning method by which someone can maintain control over his assets until he either becomes incapacitated or dies. At that time, the successor trustee whom he chose when he set up the trust automatically manages the trust. Living trusts do not save on death taxes.

With a living trust, there is no need for court involvement or other administrative action. The trust can also specify how different people—such as the adult creating the trust and his children—are to be cared for, even while the creator of the trust is alive.[11]

MEDI-CAL AND OTHER IRREVOCABLE TRUSTS

Certain types of "irrevocable" trusts can help avoid death taxes and protect assets. However, the person creating the trust loses control over all assets placed in them. Unlike a living trust, the trustee managing the irrevocable trust cannot be the person creating it. Common types of irrevocable trusts include:

- *Medi-Cal trusts,* set up to prevent assets from being used to pay for nursing facility costs. Assets in a Medi-Cal trust that is established more than 30 months before the person creating it enters a nursing facility are not counted in determining Medi-Cal eligibility.

- *Special needs trusts,* set up to assist in supporting someone who is physically disabled or emotionally disadvantaged, while not affecting the person's government assistance benefits such as SSI.

- *Marital life estate trusts,* established to save on death taxes, and usually used if a couple's combined estate exceeds $600,000. The couple does not have to be married. The person creating the trust manages it during his lifetime, and leaves the trust property for his surviving partner to use—but not own—until her death, when property is distributed as specified in the trust. The trust property is irrevocable once the person creating it dies.

To set up irrevocable trusts, the proposed conservatee must be of sound mind and able to make arrangements. A lawyer's help is usually required.

---

[10]There are other types of trusts, many of which are used to minimize or avoid the need to probate an estate, to minimize death taxes or to ensure that a beneficiary does not receive substantial assets until he is mature enough to handle them. Trusts are usually created only where the amount in the trust is at least $60,000. For more about trusts, including living trusts, see *Make Your Own Living Trust,* by Denis Clifford and *Nolo's Living Trust* software, both published by Nolo Press.

[11]If the estate is relatively small but a conservatorship is required because the proposed conservatee is unable to sign legal documents, you may be able to set up a living trust once the conservatorship is established, and then have the conservatorship terminated. This requires the help of an attorney.

d. Spouse's Management of Community Property

If one spouse becomes incapacitated, the other spouse generally may manage the community property fully. If a married couple's real estate and property with title are all community property, it will probably not be necessary to have a court proceeding to set up management for it unless the spouse with capacity is rolling over T-bills, selling stock, mortgaging or selling a house or subsequently becomes incapacitated. (For details on a spouse's role after a conservatorship is established, see Chapter 12, Section C2b.)

Instead of a conservatorship, a special court procedure may be followed to authorize transactions that ordinarily would require the consent of both spouses. As long as one spouse is competent, a court hearing can be set to:

- determine whether the incapacitated spouse is capable of authorizing the transaction;

- authorize one or more specific transactions; and

- decide whether property is community property or separate property (Probate Code §3101).

   Example: Millie wants to take out a second deed of trust on the home she and her husband, Bert, own. Bert is disabled and cannot fully understand or sign legal documents. However, because Millie can take care of him and he values his independence, she wants to avoid a conservatorship. With the help of a lawyer, Millie gets a court order allowing the second deed of trust with only her signature.

 Seek the help of a lawyer if you want to undertake this court procedure. Also see a lawyer if both spouses are incapacitated or if one already has a conservator.

CHANGE IN PROPERTY OWNERSHIP NOT AN ALTERNATIVE TO CONSERVATORSHIP

Personal property and real estate may be owned by one or more people. Changing the way title to property is held in itself will not necessarily avoid or delay the need for a conservatorship. For example, if you sell or refinance property, the signatures of all owners—or someone authorized to sign for them—will be required.

Changing ownership may also result in serious tax consequences when an owner dies. Or it could mean the loss or gain of Medi-Cal or other benefits. If you want to change the method of ownership, it is wise to consult with an attorney experienced in tax and estate planning. Here's how property may be owned in California.

- *Community Property:* Only applies to married couples. Generally consists of property the spouses accumulate by their earnings during marriage. Included are wages, personal and real property bought with the spouses' income, rents and profits from community assets and sometimes pensions.

- *Joint Tenancy:* Property equally owned by two or more people, where surviving owners automatically inherit the share of an owner who dies. Bank accounts, real estate and personal property with title documents, such as cars, are examples of property often held in joint tenancy. Each joint tenant has control over property and is not obligated to turn it over to the other owner's heirs when the other owner dies.

- *Tenancy in Common:* A form of shared ownership where surviving owners don't automatically inherit the share of the deceased owner—each owner can give his share to whomever he chooses.

C. What Type of Conservatorship Is Needed?

DEPENDING ON THE PROPOSED CONSERVATEE'S situation, you may need a conservatorship of the person, estate, or both person and estate.

1. Conservatorship of the Person

You will need a conservatorship only of the person if the proposed conservatee:

- needs to be cared for personally but can manage his finances and business matters;

- has made arrangements for financial matters, such as by creating a durable power of attorney for finances; or

- only receives money from agency benefits and the agency does not require a conservatorship.

> *Example:* Before Darren became sick with a degenerative illness, he executed a durable power of attorney for financial matters, authorizing Victor to make financial decisions if he cannot. Darren now requires periodic hospitalization, medical treatment and prescription drugs, and he does not have the mental ability to make medical choices for himself. Victor uses the durable power of attorney to take care of Darren's financial matters. Victor goes to court and obtains a conservatorship of the person to make personal and medical decisions for Darren.

2. Conservatorship of the Estate

You will need a conservatorship only of the estate if the proposed conservatee is unable to manage assets she owns now or is going to receive in the future, but can make her own personal and health care decisions or has made other arrangements for medical decisions, such as a durable power of attorney for health care.

> *Example:* Sandy undergoes a serious operation that leaves him almost entirely paralyzed. He is able to make medical decisions by nodding or shaking his head, but he cannot understand complicated financial matters, and he cannot speak or sign legal documents. Cathy obtains a conservatorship of the estate to handle his financial affairs.

3. Conservatorship of the Person and Estate

The most typical conservatorship is one of both the person and estate. This type of conservatorship is needed when someone cannot take care of herself and her finances and no advance arrangements were made. (See Sections C1 and C2, just above.)

> *Example:* Yvonne is in an automobile accident, suffers irreparable brain damage and goes into a coma. Before the accident she had not signed any durable power of attorney or created a living trust. Because someone must make ongoing medical decisions for Yvonne, obtain benefits and manage her assets, Joan goes to court and is appointed conservator of Yvonne's person and estate.

D. Should You Be the Conservator?

A CONSERVATORSHIP IS an ongoing responsibility which usually lasts from the time a court establishes it until the conservatee dies—although a court can relieve a conservator from his job earlier. It can be time consuming and stressful, so thoroughly consider the possible difficulties of the job before deciding to become a conservator. (The appointed conservator's duties and responsibilities are covered in more detail in Chapters 11, 12 and 13.)

It is sensible to consider your other options carefully before going through with the conservatorship procedure. Before you take the plunge, be sure to take a realistic look at your expected role as conservator. After honestly answering the following questions, you may want to pursue some of the options listed in Section B of this chapter, or look into the possibility of someone else serving as conservator.

1. Do You Want to Be Conservator?

An obvious but extremely important question to ask yourself before you take any steps to establish a conservatorship is: Do you want to be the conservator? When you consider taking on the job of conservator, count on the conservatee being dependent on you until she dies. This could require a great deal of time and energy, and, although not required by law, you may decide to assist the conservatee financially.

In a close family situation, it may be easy to agree to be the conservator. You may be taking care of a loved one who has always been there for you, and to whom you are glad to return the favor. The job can be challenging, and can provide a wonderful service to someone who lacks the ability to care of herself. On the other hand, you may want to think long and hard about the decision if you feel obliged to take care of someone with whom you don't get along or don't have strong ties. It may be especially difficult to serve as conservator if there are ill feelings between family members, especially when the incapacitated person's estate is a point of contention.

Take into account the kind of personal relationship you have with the proposed conservatee. A conservator must make important decisions—including serious medical decisions for a conservatorship of the person. If you are either very close or have personal problems with the proposed conservatee, it may be difficult to make these types of decisions.

If you anticipate problems with the proposed conservatee's relatives, your job as conservator can be problematic. Perhaps relatives are hostile to you because of personal differences or because they don't approve of you being the proposed conservatee's partner. Or maybe a number of family members all want a share of the proposed conservatee's assets. If you expect problems, be aware that a contested conservatorship situation can be costly, time consuming and will require the help of a lawyer.

2. Are You Qualified to Be Conservator?

Carefully read about a conservator's responsibilities. (See Chapter 11 for information about the role of a conservator of the person and Chapters 12 and 13 for information about the role of a conservator of the estate.) To decide if you are a good choice as conservator, take into consideration your own family, health, job, age and other factors which may change over time.

Examine whether there are any reasons you shouldn't be conservator. A court might consider you to be an improper choice if you have been convicted of a felony, have had other run-ins with the law, or if there is any well-known undesirable information about your personal life—for example, alcohol, drug or gambling problems. You should not serve as conservator if you have been charged with neglecting or abusing anyone.

For conservatorships of the estate, be certain that you do not have problems managing money. If you have difficulty budgeting, or have personal financial difficulties, you should not serve as conservator of the estate. Especially if the proposed conservatee has a lot of money and you have very little, you could have difficulty managing the estate. Or you might feel resentment at having to take care of an estate which does not belong to you. If you might feel tempted to use the estate's money or want to make sure you'll inherit something, you are not a suitable choice for conservator.

3. Should Someone Else Serve as Conservator?

Even if you don't personally know someone able to take on the role, there are many sources for finding conservators. People available to serve may include the county's public conservator or guardian, certain nonprofit organizations, professional conservators—often individuals with a background in social work—and people who have handled the proposed conservatee's finances in the past.

Whoever serves as conservator may legally obtain some money as compensation for the time and work. With permission from the court, these fees may be paid out of the conservatee's estate. Seek the help of a lawyer, who can locate potential conservators, check into their backgrounds and help determine whether they are a good choice.

It is up to a judge or court commissioner to determine who will be appointed as conservator but, by law, there is an order of preference as shown in the accompanying sidebar. However, this system is flexible and gives a judge discretion to choose one conservatorship candidate over another. Generally, judges prefer to appoint a close family member as conservator and are hesitant to allow a neighbor or acquaintance to fill the role. Often there is only one person willing and able to assume the conservatorship role, unless there is a conflict over the proposed conservatee's estate.

WHO WILL BE APPOINTED CONSERVATOR?
(Probate Code §§1810-1812)

According to legal guidelines, the court should give preference when appointing a conservator first to the conservatee's own choice, if it was made in writing, as long as the conservatee had the capacity to make that decision. Then the proposed conservatee's spouse, adult child, parent or adult sibling may be appointed. If any of these relatives is an unsuitable conservator but nominates another, that choice usually takes their place in the court's preference list.

In deciding whether to appoint you conservator of the estate, a judge should consider your ability to manage and preserve the estate's assets, as well as your concern for the conservatee. A judge may consider your own financial situation and your ability to manage or hire people to handle relatively large sums of money.

It's possible that the proposed conservatee needs a conservator of the person and estate, but you're only qualified for one position. For example, you may be a close relative who spends time with the proposed conservatee, understands his personal care needs and would be well qualified to serve as conservator of the person. But if you are poor at managing money, it wouldn't be a good idea for you to take on the responsibilities of a conservator of the estate. Either a different conservator could be appointed as conservator of the estate, or two or more people can share the responsibility by serving as co-conservators. Because of complications, such as co-conservators having differences of opinion or one co-conservator being out of California when an important decision must be made, you'll need a lawyer's help.

GETTING STARTED

IF, AFTER READING CHAPTERS 1 AND 2, you conclude that a conservatorship is necessary, you must take steps to get the legal process underway. You'll need to gather documents and information and discuss the conservatorship with the proposed conservatee, her doctor and close relatives.

A. Getting Organized

YOU WILL ACCUMULATE MANY PAPERS in the process of establishing a conservatorship. Now is a good time to set up a system to keep all of these documents organized in a safe place. It may be helpful to go into an office supply or large stationery store to see what's available to organize your paperwork. File folders or large manila envelopes are a good start; even better is a card board accordion file with a top flap that can be tied securely. You might want to keep several file folders in an expandable file which are separated by category—such as court papers, correspondence, financial documents.

B. Talk With Proposed Conservatee

IT IS BEST TO INCLUDE the proposed conservatee in your plans to file for a conservatorship. By law, the proposed conservatee is entitled to know about the proceeding. If she does not want a conservatorship or would rather have someone else appointed conservator, the proposed conservatee has the right both to a lawyer and a jury trial.

If you haven't already discussed the possibility of a conservatorship, bring it up in a way that is respectful of the proposed conservatee's wishes and feelings. Explain what a conservatorship is, and what type you think is needed. Say why you wish to be conservator, and how you think it will be best for her. For example, if she cannot manage paying the bills and shopping for food, tell her you'll be legally authorized to do that. Let the proposed conservatee know that you want to do what's best for her.

Do not try to change the proposed conservatee's mind or talk her into going along with the conservatorship. After all, she has a legal right to contest the conservatorship—even if she doesn't have the mental capacity to understand the proceeding. If she is not in favor of the conservatorship—or does not want you to serve as conservator—seriously reconsider whether a conservatorship is necessary and whether you are the best choice of conservator. Explore the options set out in Chapter 2.

 If you plan to pursue a conservatorship despite the proposed conservatee's opposition, a lawyer's help will be needed. (See Chapter 17 for information on hiring and dealing with lawyers.)

C. Talk With Proposed Conservatee's Doctor

WHENEVER POSSIBLE, it is wise to consult with the proposed conservatee's doctor before initiating a conservatorship proceeding. Medical records are confidential, so you'll probably need the proposed conservatee's consent.

It's best if you and the proposed conservatee visit the doctor together. If the proposed conservatee belongs to a religion that espouses healing by prayer alone, consult with an accredited practitioner of that religion who has been providing treatment. If the proposed conservatee is too sick to go to the doctor with you, contact the doctor by phone.

When you talk or meet with the doctor, explain that you are planning to file a conservatorship proceeding and find out whether:

- the proposed conservatee's condition is expected to change, enabling him to take care of his finances or personal and medical needs;

- the proposed conservatee's condition could change with proper medical care such as a new medication or changed dosage;

- the proposed conservatee's symptoms are caused by emotional stress or trauma—for example, someone who recently lost a loved one may only temporarily appear disoriented;

- a psychiatric worker's opinion should be sought;

- the proposed conservatee is unable to make *all* medical decisions for himself—and if so, whether the doctor would be willing to sign documents to that effect; and

- the proposed conservatee is too physically sick to attend a court hearing.

If the proposed conservatee is unable to make all medical decisions or is too sick to attend the court hearing, let the doctor know you'll need her medical opinion in writing. If she's unwilling to give that opinion, you'll need to contact another physician.

D. Talk with Relatives of Proposed Conservatee

IN CLOSE FAMILIES, everyone may agree with the conservatorship. But sometimes conservatorship proceedings cause conflict, especially if money is involved and certain relatives are wary about who handles those finances. The proposed conservatee's close relatives are entitled by law to know in advance about the conservatorship proceeding, and they have the right to contest it.

In Section F of this chapter, you will complete a Conservatorship Worksheet, listing the names and addresses of the proposed conservatee's close relatives. All of them must receive documents about the proposed conservatorship. If you haven't already told these relatives about the conservatorship, it's now time to think about doing this. But don't put down this book and contact them yet. This section gives you an overview of why you'll be talking to the relatives, and what you might say.

Although you aren't required to talk about the conservatorship with any of the proposed conservatee's relatives, it's a good idea. It's possible that talking about a conservatorship will bring up ideas about less drastic ways to handle the situation. If a relative opposes either the conservatorship or having you appointed as conservator, you'll have time to prepare yourself for a possible challenge by consulting with a lawyer before the hearing date.

How you approach the proposed conservatee's relatives is extremely important. Call them on the telephone or get together in person. Reassure them that you are seeking a conservatorship because you believe it's best for the proposed conservatee. However you decide to bring up the conservatorship, do it in an open and friendly way, and follow these guidelines:

- Be prepared. Know what a conservatorship is, and how you get one. If the relatives ask you questions, answer them as best you can. It might help to show them this book, as it may address their concerns.

- Carefully and respectfully explain why a conservatorship would be best for the proposed conservatee. You may want to talk about some of the alternatives outlined in Chapter 2 and why you concluded that a conservatorship is the best option.

- Talk over any concerns the relatives have. For example, they might be worried about your ability to manage the proposed conservatee's finances, or they might want to make sure they have a right to keep in contact with the proposed conservatee.

E. Collect Documents and Information

COLLECT THE FOLLOWING INFORMATION and documents:

- Full name, home address and telephone number of the proposed conservatee. If she is permanently living in a nursing facility, board and care home, or other facility, obtain that name, address and telephone number. If she is temporarily staying in a hospital or some other place, also acquire the full name, address and telephone number.

- Any original documents signed by the proposed conservatee which name you or anyone else as conservator. This may be a durable power of attorney or a nomination of conservator.[1]

- Names, addresses and telephone numbers of the proposed conservatee's treating physicians, including medical doctor and psychiatrist.

- Copies of any papers having to do with the proposed conservatee's competency or need for a conservatorship. Obtain copies of court documents if there were prior legal proceedings to establish a regular or LPS conservatorship.

F. Complete Conservatorship Worksheet

COMPLETING THE FOLLOWING Conservatorship Worksheet is simple, and it provides an easy way to keep track of who must get copies of conservatorship papers you file with the court.

You may not be able to fill in all the requested information, but do the best you can. If a relative is dead, write in the word "deceased." If you don't know the name or location of a relative, write "unknown." If you don't know the whereabouts of all those who must be notified, you must go through a special procedure to attempt to locate

---

[1]Sometimes different people serve as conservator of the person and conservator of the estate. If someone else has been named one type of conservator and you have been named another, consult a lawyer. (See Chapter 17.)

them. (Chapter 6, Section F, contains detailed information about that process.)

1. Conservatorship Worksheet: Part 1

In Part 1 of the Conservatorship Worksheet, fill in the names and home addresses of these relatives of the proposed conservatee:

- Spouse;
- Children;
- Grandchildren;
- Sisters and brothers;
- Parents; and
- Grandparents.

2. Conservatorship Worksheet: Part 2

Few people will need to complete Part 2 of the worksheet. It is only for the unusual situation where you do not know of any of the close relatives listed in Part 1. If so, in Part 2, fill in the names and addresses of all of these relatives of the proposed conservatee:

- Spouse of a parent who is deceased;
- Children of a spouse who is deceased;
- Aunts and uncles—if none, then first cousins; and
- Nieces and nephews.

If you complete Part 2 of the Conservatorship Worksheet, throughout this book, these people will all be referred to as the proposed conservatee's "relatives" (Probate Code §1821).

G. Obtain Information From Probate Clerk

IN CALIFORNIA, conservatorships are handled in the Probate Division of the Superior Court, referred to in this book as the probate court. A conservatorship is usually filed in the probate court in the county where the proposed conservatee lives.[2] However, the conservatorship may be filed in any county which is "in the best interests" of the proposed conservatee (Probate Code §2201(b)). For example, a conservatorship of the estate might be filed in the county in which a proposed conservatee owns most of her property, even if she doesn't live there. Or, while less common, it could even be filed in the county where the proposed conservator lives.

The probate court is usually located in the largest city in the county. Some of the larger counties have additional branch courts in cities other than the county seat. If there is a branch court close to where the proposed conservatee lives, local court rules probably will require that you file the conservatorship there.

To find the probate court in your county, check the telephone directory in the county government listings for the Superior Court. In larger counties you should find a separate listing for the Probate Division of the Superior Court; in smaller counties you may need to call the general number listed for the Superior Court.

1. Call Probate Clerk

Telephone the probate court clerk and ask for this information you'll need to complete forms for filing a conservatorship:

- The proper branch of the court for filing your conservatorship papers. If you're filing in the county where the proposed conservatee lives, tell the clerk in what city or town the proposed conservatee lives.
- Mailing address of the court.
- Street address of the court—if it is different from the mailing address.
- Fee for filing a petition for a conservatorship. (If you cannot afford the fees, you may be able to get them waived. See Chapter 5, Section B.)

---

[2] This book does not cover situations in which either the proposed conservatee or proposed conservator are not residents of California.

CONSERVATOR WORKSHEET

Part 1: Close Relatives of Proposed Conservatee

RELATIONSHIP AND NAME	RESIDENCE ADDRESS
Spouse (husband or wife):	
Children:	
Grandchildren:	
Sisters and brothers:	
Parents:	
Grandparents (parents of both the proposed conservatee's mother and father):	

CONSERVATOR WORKSHEET

Part 2: Other Relatives of Proposed Conservatee

Important: Only complete this part if NONE of the close relatives listed in Part 1 are known to you. Then obtain the names and addresses of each of these relatives of the proposed conservatee:

RELATIONSHIP AND NAME	RESIDENCE ADDRESS
Spouse of a deceased parent:	
Children of proposed conservatee's deceased spouse:	
Aunts and uncles (brothers and sisters of proposed conservatee's parents)—if none are living, then natural and adoptive first cousins (children of aunts and uncles):	
Nieces and nephews (natural and adoptive children of proposed conservatee's brothers and sisters):	

2. Obtain Probate Policy Manual

All California probate courts follow the same basic proce-dures for conservatorships. But courts in different counties, especially those with large populations, commonly have a number of their own procedural rules. Most counties have these court rules printed in small pamphlets called probate policy manuals or memoranda. Some of these individual county rules are referred to in this book, but it is impos-sible to identify every one.

Check with the clerk at the probate court to find out how to obtain a copy. It may be free, or it may be available through the court for a reasonable fee (approximately $6 to $15). If you can't conveniently get a copy through the court, you'll find it easier to read or photocopy it at the county law library. (Chapter 17, Section D gives more information about probate policy manuals and legal research.)

RULES, RULES, RULES

In addition to each county's probate policy manual, other special rules may apply. You probably won't need to look into these rules unless you are specifically referred to them by someone at the court. If so, copies will be at the local law library:

- *California Rules of Court:* These rules govern many aspects of the preparation, filing and procedures involved in California courts. A special section covers superior courts, and all probate courts follow these rules.

- *Local Rules for the Superior Court:* Some superior courts have extra rules which supplement the California Rules of Court. Because the probate court is a division of the superior court, any local superior court rules would apply. Generally, a conservator won't need to consult these rules unless the case involves litigation, which requires an attorney's help.

H. Court Documents

TO SET UP A CONSERVATORSHIP, you'll need to prepare and file a number of papers with the court. Many documents will be in a standardized, fill-in-the-blanks format. Others must be completed with a typewriter or word processor on lined legal paper.

1. Preprinted Forms

There are several kinds of preprinted forms. Most of the ones you'll need are provided in Appendix B in the back of the book.

a. Judicial Council Forms

Most of the forms you'll use are standard "Judicial Council forms," approved for use in all California courts. Each Judicial Council form has a title in bold print at the bottom of the page, and information in the lower left-hand corner that will help you identify the form and determine whether it is up-to-date. The number in the lower left-hand corner is the Judicial Council's way of identifying the form. For example, the Notice of Hearing number is "GC-020(81)."[3]

Near the identifying number is the date the form was last revised. The forms were current when this book was published. However, Judicial Council forms are subject to change approximately once a year, although many of them stay current for years. To be safe, if you use this book more than a year after it was last printed (see the printing history at the beginning of the book), call the court clerk and find out if the forms are still current. The clerk will need to know the name and number of the forms.

If the form you need is outdated, or if you accidentally used your original form, new Judicial Council forms are available from the clerk of the Superior Court either free or for a small fee. Or you can visit a law library where there are several sources for obtaining Judicial Council forms to photocopy. (See Chapter 17, Section D2.)

b. Local Court Forms

Many courts have their own forms which must be used in addition to the forms in this book. Wherever possible,

---

[3]Some forms also refer to California law. For instance, the Petition for Appointment of Probate Conservator has a notation in the lower right-hand corner which reads "Probate Code, §§1820, 1821" meaning that the form was designed according to those statutes.

these local forms are mentioned. This book later discusses when and how to check with the court clerk to see if additional local court forms are required.

c.   Forms to Fill the Gaps

In some instances, a form is desirable but the Judicial Council does not provide one. To solve this problem, we have provided forms which are specially designed to fill this gap. These forms are designated in the lower left-hand corner by "NP" (an abbreviation for "Nolo Press").

2.   How to Complete Preprinted Forms

As you fill in the conservatorship forms, you'll find they follow a standardized, check-the-boxes, fill-in-the-blanks format. With a little experience, you'll quickly get comfortable with them. Throughout the book, there is specific information about every item on each form.

a   Tips for Using Forms in Book

Here are some general tips on how to use the forms in this book. Following these suggestions can save you a lot of time and trouble.

- Before you fill out any of the tear-out forms provided in Appendix B at the back of this book, make several photocopies of each. This will save you many worried moments if you make a mistake or misplace a form. Also, note that many forms have printing on both sides. If the form is two-sided, make sure you copy both sides. You can copy each side on a separate piece of paper and staple the pages together before filing the form with the court or you can make two-sided copies.

- All forms should be completed carefully and neatly, preferably using a typewriter. It is best to use the larger type size (called "pica" or "10-pitch" type). Some courts may refuse to accept forms with smaller type (called "elite" or "12-pitch" type). If you do not have access to a typewriter, check with the court, library or local office supply store to find out if there are typewriters provided for public use or rental. In many places, typing and paralegal services will prepare forms

for you at a reasonable cost. (See Chapter 17, Section B.)[4]

- Use blue ink (or any color other than black) whenever you sign a form. Otherwise, the clerk may think it is a photocopy and send it back to you without filing it.

b.   How to Complete the Caption

Most forms have a heading of several boxes with blank spaces, which is referred to as a "caption." The caption is completed the same way on almost every form. Here is how to do it.

Attorney or Party Without Attorney: You are a "Party Without Attorney." In capital letters, fill in your full name. Use whatever name is listed on your identification and that you use for official matters. Then insert your mailing address and telephone number. If possible, give a number where you can be reached during the day or one with an answering machine or answering service. Probate courts are notorious for calling with picky questions before a hearing, and delaying the hearing if they can't get through.

Attorney for (Name)—In Pro Per: Here the court is asking for the name of the person you are representing. Fill in the words "In Pro Per." This means that you are representing yourself in the proceeding.

Superior Court of California, County of: In capital letters, fill in the county in which you are filing the conservatorship.

Court Address: Fill in the court's street address, mailing address, and city and zip code. Also fill in the branch name, if there is one.

---

[4]Depending on the court's policies, handwritten forms may be accepted if you print clearly and neatly. If you want to submit handwritten forms, call the filing clerk beforehand to make sure they'll be accepted and to find out if the court has any requirements on how handwritten papers should be prepared.

ATTORNEY OR PARTY WITHOUT ATTORNEY *(Name and Address)* :	TELEPHONE NO.:	*FOR COURT USE ONLY*

ATTORNEY FOR *(Name)* :

SUPERIOR COURT OF CALIFORNIA, COUNTY OF

STREET ADDRESS:

MAILING ADDRESS:

CITY AND ZIP CODE:

BRANCH NAME:

CONSERVATORSHIP OF (NAME):

PROPOSED CONSERVATEE

CASE NUMBER:

PETITION FOR APPOINTMENT OF PROBATE CONSERVATOR OF THE
☐ **PERSON**   ☐ **ESTATE**   ☐ **Limited Conservatorship**

S A M P L E   C A P T I O N

Conservatorship of (Name): In capital letters, fill in the complete first and last names of the proposed conservatee. Make sure that the name is complete and correctly spelled. If the conservatee is known by any former names, middle names or nicknames, include them as well, especially if those names may be used on official documents. For example, you might insert the words: "William Shakespeare, also known as Bill Shakespeare and Billy Shakespeare."

Type of Conservatorship: Depending on the form, this part of the caption may vary a little bit. Different types of conservatorships are covered in Chapter 1, Section A. Check any boxes that apply:

☐ **Person:** Check this box if the conservatorship is for the person or person and estate.

☐ **Estate:** Check this box if the conservatorship is for the estate or person and estate.

Case Number: When you complete your first court papers, leave this space blank, since you won't have a case number yet. The first time you file papers with the court, you will be assigned a case number which will be stamped or written on the conservatorship documents. From then on, always fill in that case number by copying it carefully from your filed papers.

c. Declarations (Oaths)

On some documents you will need to sign a Declaration Under Penalty of Perjury. This declaration has the same effect as an oath or sworn statement, which means that you could be prosecuted under California law if you lie in it. The declaration usually has the wording, "I declare under penalty of perjury under the laws of the State of California that the foregoing is true and correct."[5]

To complete the declaration, fill in the date, type or print your name and sign the declaration. If there is space for the city and the state—which should be California— fill these in as well.

If at any time you need to submit an additional declaration either by itself or attached to another form, prepare it on lined paper following the format of the Due Diligence Declaration in Chapter 6, Section F2a.

---

[5]A few forms may have slightly different wording, which could mean that if you sign the declaration outside of California it must be notarized. Some—but not all—forms use the language listed above, which is valid for declarations signed either inside or outside of California.

d. Verification

Some documents require that the person signing them must "verify" the document under penalty of perjury. When verification is necessary, add these words to the end of the document, and sign where indicated:

VERIFICATION

I declare that: I am the [*"proposed"*] conservator of the [*"person," "estate" or "person and estate"*] of [*conservatee's name*]. I have read the foregoing [*exact title of document*] and know its contents. It is true of my own knowledge, except as to the matters that are stated on information and belief, and as to those matters I believe it to be true. I declare under penalty of perjury under the laws of the State of California that the foregoing is true and correct.

Dated: [*today's date*]   _____

[*your name*]

e. Attachment Pages

When you fill in some forms, you may need more room to complete a particular item. Most courts will accept a blank piece of typing paper, but others are sticklers and prefer legal paper, provided in Appendix B. If you use lined legal paper, make several blank copies before you use it, and save the original.

At the top of each additional page, type in the title of the conservatorship with the full name of the conservatee and the case number, once it has been assigned. Next, label the page an "Attachment," and indicate the item number and form you are continuing. For example, "Attachment 7 to Petition for Appointment of Conservator." Then type your text using double-spacing. Use a new page for each new item number you continue. At the bottom of the page, number the pages you're adding to the form. Here's a sample of an attachment heading.

1	Conservatorship of [*proposed conservatee's name*] Case No. _____
2	
3	ATTACHMENT 7 TO PETITION FOR APPOINTMENT OF
4	PROBATE CONSERVATOR
5	
6	[*Start typing a few lines down from the heading using double spacing*]

SAMPLE ATTACHMENT PAGE HEADING

3. Preparing Your Own Pleadings

When no form is available for a document, you'll need to prepare it from scratch following the guidelines in this book. Either purchase lined, numbered paper from an office supply store, or make copies of the lined paper contained in Appendix B.

Documents prepared on lined paper are referred to as "pleadings." They must be double-spaced, except for captions, legal descriptions and listings on schedules. Number the pages of each document at the bottom.

On the first page of each pleading, fill in your name, address and phone number at the top left. Starting on line 8, center the title of the court in capital letters. Place the caption and case number several lines below. If there is a hearing date, time and location, include these under the document title.

The samples in this book are intended as a guide, and instructions should not be copied word-for-word into your document. On the following page is a sample of what a pleading should look like.

 Some courts, such as Los Angeles, require "bluebacks" for all pleadings. Bluebacks are simply blue paper stapled to the backs of court documents which identify the people involved in the legal action, the court and the document being filed. Bluebacks can be obtained from most large office supply stores.

I. Amending Documents

IF, AFTER YOU FILE conservatorship papers, you need to make changes to a document you already filed, you must prepare an "amended" document to take the place of the incorrect one. You might need to amend a document if:

- The facts or situation stated change substantially after you file the document with the court—for example, the proposed conservatee's physical and mental condition deteriorates suddenly and he is now unable to attend the conservatorship hearing; or

- You discover a serious error on the document after it is filed—for example, you forgot to list the names and addresses of several relatives. You shouldn't need to amend a document if you made a minor typographical error.

To amend a document, use the same title as the original document, but put the word "AMENDED" before the name of the document. If you are using a preprinted form, print or type the word "AMENDED" both before the form's printed name in the caption and on the bottom of the page, and redo the form so it is correct. If you are correcting a document typed on lined paper, you must designate the pages and lines of the document being amended (Calif. Rules of Court 327(b)).

Once you've completed the amended document, make photocopies and file the original and copies of the amended document with the court. Have copies served by mail on everyone who was served with the original, incorrect document.

1	[YOUR NAME in caps]
	[your street address]
2	[your city, state and zip]
	[your phone number, including area code]
3	
4	Conservator In Pro Per
5	
6	
7	

SUPERIOR COURT OF CALIFORNIA

COUNTY OF [COUNTY in caps]

10	In the matter of the conser- vatorship of the ["person," "estate" or	) Case No. [case number]
11	"person and estate"] of:	))
12	[CONSERVATEE'S NAME in caps],	) [DOCUMENT NAME in caps])
13	Conservatee.	) [if a hearing is scheduled, add:]) DATE: [hearing date]
14	_____	) TIME: [hearing time]) DEPT: [department]

15 [Start typing here; double-spaced, except for legal descriptions and listings on account

16 schedules.]

17

18 [most documents end with your signature and the date:]

19 Dated: [today's date]

20   _____

                                                     [your name]

21   Conservator In Pro Per

22 [some documents end with room for the judge to sign:]

23 Dated: [today's date]   _____

24   Judge of the Superior Court

25

26

27

28

SAMPLE PLEADING

CHAPTER 4

PREPARING THE FORMS TO FILE
FOR A CONSERVATORSHIP

AFTER READING introductory Chapters 1, 2 and 3, you're now ready to complete the paperwork required to file for a conservatorship. You'll need to fill in a number of legal forms to obtain a conservatorship, but you can usually complete the process by yourself. Forms are provided in Appendix B. The step-by-step instructions here will take you through each form and help you complete each procedure. As long as you're patient, and willing to spend a little time preparing and double-checking your work, you shouldn't have any trouble.

You will need to complete some or possibly all of these forms to file for a legal conservatorship:

- **Petition for Appointment of Probate Conservator.** In this form, you request appointment as conservator of the person, estate, or both.

- **Declaration of Medical or Accredited Practitioner (Attachment 6c to Petition for Appointment of Probate Conservator).** This form is required if the proposed conservatee is physically unable to attend the hearing.

- **Confidential Supplemental Information.** Here you give reasons why the conservatorship is needed and why alternatives to a conservatorship are not appropriate.

- **(Proposed) Order Appointing Court Investigator.** In this form, you give information to the court investigator, who will conduct a routine investigation of the proposed conservatee.

- **Notice of Hearing.** This form lists information about when and where the conservatorship hearing will take place.

- **Citation for Conservatorship.** This form gives information to the proposed conservatee about how the conservatorship will affect her.

- **(Proposed) Order Appointing Probate Conservator.** This form gives information about the duties and responsibilities the conservator will be taking on.

- **Additional documents** may be required by your local court. A list and samples of some of these documents are contained in Section H.

Generally, a conservatorship is not established for at least four to six weeks from the time you file your papers. If you need a conservatorship before then, you'll need to hire an attorney or do your own legal research to obtain a temporary conservatorship.

Judicial Council forms are periodically updated, and old forms rendered obsolete. You may want to check with the court clerk before using the forms contained in Appendix B. If new forms have been issued, obtain copies from the court clerk or the law library. (See Chapter 17, Section D.)

A. Petition for Appointment of Probate Conservator

TO BEGIN CONSERVATORSHIP PROCEEDINGS, a "petition" must be filed with the court. The Petition for Appointment of Probate Conservator is the document in which you summarize why you should be appointed conservator. Since you are the person filing this petition, you are referred to as the "petitioner" in the proceedings. Have handy the information and documents you collected in Chapter 3, Sections E and F.

CAPTION: PETITION FOR APPOINTMENT OF PROBATE CONSERVATOR

- Fill in the caption following the general instructions in Chapter 3, Section H2b.
- At the bottom of the caption, check the boxes to indicate whether you are seeking conservatorship of the person, estate or both. Make sure you know exactly what type of conservatorship you are seeking. This is discussed in detail in Chapter 1, Section A.
- Leave the box entitled "Limited Conservatorship" blank. That is beyond the scope of this book. (See Chapter 1, Section B5b.)

Item 1: You are the person who is filing for the conservatorship. After the words "Petitioner (name)" fill in your full name.[1] If you're known by more than one name—such as a nickname or married name, fill in the name you use on important documents, such as a driver's license. Use the same form of the name consistently in the conservatorship documents.

Item 1a: Complete this item only if you are seeking conservatorship of the person or person and estate. In the space provided fill in your full name, followed by your address and telephone number. This indicates that you want to be appointed conservator of the person. Then check the box before the word "conservator."

Item 1b: Complete this item only if you are seeking conservatorship of the conservatee's estate or person and estate. In the space provided fill in your full name, followed by your address and telephone number. This indicates that you are the proposed conservator of the conservatee's estate. Then check the box before the word "conservator."

Item 1c: This entire item deals with the requirement that a conservator of an estate post a "bond." If you are only seeking conservatorship of the person, go on to Item 1c(1). If you are seeking conservatorship of the estate or person and estate, you'll need some information to understand and complete this item. First turn to Chapter 14, and read Sections A through D, which describe when bond is required, how to figure the amount and when bond may be reduced or waived.

Item 1c(1): This item always applies if you are only seeking conservatorship of the person. It might apply if you are seeking conservatorship of the estate or person and estate and do not want to post bond.

---

[1] Throughout this book, the instructions refer to only one petitioner. Two or more people can serve as conservators for the same person, but that can get complicated if one conservator is outside of California or unavailable when an important decision must be made or conservators disagree about how to handle a given matter. If you want to be appointed co-conservator with someone else, seek the help of an attorney.

ATTORNEY OR PARTY WITHOUT ATTORNEY *(Name and Address)*:	TELEPHONE NO.:	FOR COURT USE ONLY

MARIE SMITH   (415) 555-1212
64313 Kildare Street
San Francisco, CA 94111

ATTORNEY FOR *(Name)*: In Pro Per

SUPERIOR COURT OF CALIFORNIA, COUNTY OF San Francisco
STREET ADDRESS: Room 317, City Hall
MAILING ADDRESS: 400 Van Ness Ave.
CITY AND ZIP CODE: San Francisco, CA 94102
BRANCH NAME:

CONSERVATORSHIP OF (NAME):
RICHARD SHAPIRO

PROPOSED CONSERVATEE

PETITION FOR APPOINTMENT OF PROBATE CONSERVATOR OF THE
[X] **PERSON** [X] **ESTATE** [ ] **Limited Conservatorship**

CASE NUMBER:

1. **PETITIONER** *(name)*:   MARIE SMITH   **REQUESTS THAT**

a. *(name and address)*:
     MARIE SMITH   *(telephone)*:   (415) 555-1212
     64313 Kildare Street
     San Francisco, CA 94111

be appointed [X] conservator [ ] limited conservator of the PERSON of the proposed conservatee and Letters issue upon qualification.

b. *(name and address)*:
     MARIE SMITH   *(telephone)*:   (415) 555-1212
     64313 Kildare Street
     San Francisco, CA 94111

be appointed [X] conservator [ ] limited conservator of the ESTATE of the proposed conservatee and Letters issue upon qualification.

c. (1) [ ]   bond not be required for the reasons stated in Attachment 1c.
    (2) [X]   bond be fixed at: $ 54,000   to be furnished by an authorized surety company or as otherwise provided by law. *(Specify reasons if the amount is different from the minimum required by section 2320 of the Probate Code.)*
    (3) [ ]   deposits at *(specify institution)*:
        in the amount of: $ be allowed. Receipts will be filed.

d. [ ]   authorization be granted under section 2590 of the Probate Code to exercise independently the powers specified in Attachment 7.

e. [ ]   orders relating to the capacity of the proposed conservatee under sections 1873 or 1901 of the Probate Code be granted. *(Specify orders, facts, and reasons in Attachment 1e.)*

f. [ ]   orders relating to the powers and duties of the proposed conservator of the person under sections 2351-2358 of the Probate Code be granted. *(Specify orders, facts, and reasons in Attachment 1f.)*

g. [ ]   the proposed conservatee be adjudged to lack the capacity to give informed consent for medical treatment or healing by prayer and that the proposed conservator of the person be granted the powers specified in section 2355 of the Probate Code.

h. [ ]   *(for limited conservatorship only)* orders relating to the powers and duties of the proposed limited conservator of the person under section 2351.5 of the Probate Code be granted. *(Specify powers and duties in Attachment 1h.)*

i. [ ]   *(for limited conservatorship only)* orders relating to the powers and duties of the proposed limited conservator of the estate under section 1830(b) of the Probate Code be granted. *(Specify powers and duties in Attachment 1i.)*

j. [ ]   *(for limited conservatorship only)* orders limiting the civil and legal rights of the proposed limited conservatee be granted. *(Specify limitations in Attachment 1j.)*

k. [X]   other orders be granted. *(Specify in Attachment 1k.)*

(Continued on reverse)   Page one of four

Form Approved by the
Judicial Council of California
GC-310 (Rev. July 1, 1990)   **PETITION FOR APPOINTMENT OF PROBATE CONSERVATOR**   Do NOT use this form for a temporary conservatorship.

Probate Code, §§ 1820, 1821

Check this box if you are only seeking conservatorship of the person. Then cross off the words "for the reasons stated in Attachment 1c," and fill in the words "pursuant to Probate Code Section 2322." This code section says that a conservator of the person does not have to file a bond unless the court specifically requires it.[2]

If you are seeking conservatorship of the estate or person and estate and, after reading Chapter 14, Sections A through D, believe bond should be waived, check this box. Then prepare an "Attachment 1c" following the instructions in Chapter 3, Section H2e. Explain briefly and simply why you think bond should not be required, and document your reasons.

For example, if the proposed conservatee nominated you in a durable power of attorney and requested that bond be waived, you might type: "The proposed conservatee, Richard Stone, has nominated me conservator in a financial durable power of attorney dated March 11, 19__ and requested that no bond be required. A copy of the original nomination follows this attachment." If the proposed conservatee is of sound mind, understands the bond requirement, and has not yet nominated you but is willing to do so, prepare an Attachment 1c using the accompanying sample as a guide.

ATTACHMENT 1C TO PETITION

[Use lined paper and prepare the heading following the Sample Attachment Page in Chapter 3, Section H2e.]

NOMINATION OF CONSERVATOR
AND WAIVER OF BOND

I, *[proposed conservatee's name]* nominate *[your name]* to serve as conservator of my *["person and"]* estate. I waive a bond because it would be an unnecessary expense to the estate. I trust the proposed conservator to manage my funds, since *[briefly specify why, such as "she has been my best friend for over 20 years," or "he is my son and only heir of my estate. He has been informally handling my finances for the last two years."]*. Also, in my opinion, the proposed conservator is a stable and economically sound citizen.

I declare under penalty of perjury under the laws of the State of California that the foregoing is true and correct.

Dated: *[today's date]*   _____

                                               [proposed conservatee's name]

If the proposed conservatee owns less than $5,000 worth of assets, excluding a home, receives public benefits and no more than an additional $300 per month, bond may be waived. Use the accompanying sample as a guide to prepare Attachment 1c.

If you checked Item 1c(1), skip to Item 1d.

ATTACHMENT 1C TO PETITION

[Use lined paper and prepare the heading following the Sample Attachment Page in Chapter 3, Section H2e.]

1. Petitioner is or will be receiving the following public benefit payments on behalf of the proposed conservatee:

[ ] General Assistance from

_____ County.

[ ] Supplemental Security Income and State
     Supplemental Program (SSI/SSP) benefits
     paid through the Social Security
     Administration.
[ ] Aid to Families with Dependent Children
     (AFDC).
2. The proposed conservatee receives:
[ ] less than $300 per month in addition to
     these benefits; or
[ ] no additional money per month in
     addition to these benefits.
   3. The entire amount of assets belonging to
the proposed conservatee does not exceed
$5,000, excluding the residence of the proposed
conservatee.
   4. Any money petitioner will receive on
behalf of the proposed conservatee will be
spent for his/her benefit.
   5. Bond may be waived pursuant to Probate
Code Section 2323, as it appears the estate
will satisfy the conditions of Probate Code
Section 2628.

Item 1c(2): If you are seeking conservatorship of the estate or person and estate and, after reading Chapter 14, Sections A through D, believe bond is necessary, check this box. Follow the instructions in Chapter 14, Section D, for figuring out the amount of bond, and fill in that figure. If you plan to deposit some funds or assets in blocked accounts, deduct that sum from the amount of bond required. If you're planning to use personal sureties, fill in double the amount required when a surety company is used and prepare an Attachment 1c following the instructions in Chapter 3, Section H2e. In Attachment 1c, specify that "Bond will be furnished by personal sureties. As provided in Probate Code Section 2320(b), the amount of bond is for twice the amount required for a bond given by a surety company."

Item 1c(3): If you are seeking conservatorship of the estate or person and estate and, after reading Chapter 14, Sections A through D, plan to place money or assets in a blocked account during the conservatorship, check this box. Fill in the name of the financial institution after the words "(specify institution)," and enter the amount to be deposited in blocked accounts. If you will need to use the interest or dividends to support the conservatee, you may request permission to have access to it. After the words "Receipts will be filed," type in the words "Withdrawal of _["interest" or "dividends," depending on the type of assets being placed in a blocked account]_ does not require a court order."

 If assets are already held in a financial institution, fill in the name of that institution. If you specify a different institution from where the assets now are located, you may not be able to transfer them unless you are already an authorized signer on the current account.[3]

Item 1d: Skip this item. It is used only when a proposed conservator of the estate wants broad authority to handle complex estate matters without returning to court for specific authorization. This authority is known as "independent powers" (Probate Code §§2590, 2591). Judges are usually reluctant to grant independent powers, and usually also increase the amount of bond. Conservators who expect to engage in sophisticated investing—for example, operating a farm, selling and purchasing other investment property, borrowing money against the conservatee's property for investment, lending money or exercising stock options—should consult an attorney. (See Chapter 17.)

Item 1e: Do not check this box. This item pertains to situations where the conservator seeks an order that allows the conservatee to enter into certain types of transactions that bind him or the conservatorship estate (Probate Code §1873), or that determine the conservatee does not have the capacity to marry (Probate Code §1901).[4] These are beyond the scope of this book and would require an attorney's help.

Item 1f: Skip this item. It pertains only to special conditions that a conservator of the person must follow. This is beyond the scope of this book and requires the help of an attorney.

---

[3]In that case, you would need to return to court to get a judge's approval to open a blocked account in the current institution. Then you would need to get a court order allowing the transfer. You can avoid the hassle by keeping assets where they are.

[4]Unless the court orders otherwise, the appointment of a conservator does not affect the capacity of the conservatee to marry (Probate Code §1900).

Item 1g: Skip this item if you are seeking conservatorship of estate only.

For proposed conservators of the person or person and estate, this item is not commonly checked, since it takes away *all* medical decision-making authority from the proposed conservatee. Typically, a conservator of the person may make medical decisions for the conservatee—but the conservatee retains the right to make her own medical choices, agree with or override medical decisions made by the conservator.[5] Check this item only if:

- The proposed conservatee lacks legal capacity to make *any* medical decisions for herself; and

- A medical doctor is willing and able to provide you with written confirmation of this lack of legal capacity.

Because of the power this takes away from the proposed conservatee, some courts may also require that you indicate that you have discussed the matter with the proposed conservatee. Check your local rules.

Items 1h-j. Skip these items. They apply to limited conservatorships, which are beyond the scope of this book.

Item 1k: Skip this item if you are seeking conservatorship of the person only. Check this box only if you are seeking conservatorship of the estate or person and estate, and want to:

- provide the conservatee with a nominal personal allowance for his own use; or

- request a waiver of court accounts for a conservatee who owns less than $5,000 worth of assets—excluding a home—receives public assistance benefits and no more than an additional $300 per month.

If so, prepare an Attachment 1k following the instructions in Chapter 3, Section H2e, and use the accompanying sample as a guide.

---

[5]A conservator of the person may authorize medical treatment for a conservatee in an emergency, if treatment is needed to alleviate severe pain, or if the conservatee is in a life-threatening situation and would die or become seriously disabled without the treatment. (See Chapter 11, Section D.)

ATTACHMENT 1K TO PETITION

[Use lined paper and prepare the heading following the Sample Attachment Page in Chapter 3, Section H2e.]

[ ]   REQUEST FOR ORDER GRANTING ALLOWANCE

Petitioner requests that an order be granted authorizing petitioner to pay the conservatee an allowance of $_____ on a *[weekly/monthly]* basis. It would be in the best interests of the conservatee for these reasons: *[State reasons, such as: "The proposed conservatee wishes to maintain a small checking account for personal expenses such as cosmetics, perfume and inexpensive costume jewelry. An allowance would allow the proposed conservatee to maintain a degree of independence which is extremely important to her."]*. The proposed conservatee is able to handle small amounts of money as shown by: *[State reasons, such as: "The proposed conservatee has been handling a weekly allowance of $10 for the last six months. She has used the money to purchase personal items. Over three months, she successfully saved $25 of her allowance to buy a purse she wanted. She is able to count and keep track of small amounts of money."]*.

[ ]   REQUEST FOR ORDER WAIVING ACCOUNTS
       (Probate Code §2628)
1. Petitioner is or will be receiving the following public benefit payments on behalf of the proposed conservatee:
   [ ]   General Assistance from
          _____ County.
   [ ]   Supplemental Security Income and State
          Supplemental Program (SSI/SSP)
          benefits paid through the Social
          Security Administration.
   [ ]   Aid to Families with Dependent
          Children (AFDC).
2. The proposed conservatee receives:
   [ ]   less than $300 per month in addition
          to these benefits; or
   [ ]   no additional money per month in
          addition to these benefits.
3. The entire amount of assets belonging to the proposed conservatee does not exceed

$5,000, excluding the residence of the proposed conservatee.

   4. Any money petitioner will receive on behalf of the proposed conservatee will be spent for his/her benefit.

   5. It would be an unnecessary inconvenience to complete accounts for the conservatorship, and such accounts should be waived pursuant to Probate Code Section 2628.

CAPTION: PAGE 2 OF THE PETITION FOR APPOINTMENT OF PROBATE CONSERVATOR

After the words "CONSERVATORSHIP OF (Name)," in capital letters fill in the proposed conservatee's full name.

Item 2: Fill in the proposed conservatee's name, current street address (not post office box), city, state, zip code and telephone number (including the area code) in the spaces indicated. If the proposed conservatee lives in an institution or rest home, include the name of that institution.

Item 3a: In this item you state that the proposed conservatee doesn't already have a conservator in California, and give additional information about the proposed conservatee.

Item 3a(1): Skip this item if the proposed conservatee is not a resident of California. If this is your situation, you will need the help of an attorney.

Check the first box if the proposed conservatee is a California resident. Also check the second box if the proposed conservatee lives in the county in which you are filing the conservatorship.

Check the second box if the county where you are filing the conservatorship is different from the county where the proposed conservatee lives. You will then need to prepare an Attachment 3a following the instructions in Chapter 3, Section H2e, and explain briefly why it is best to file the conservatorship in this county. For example, if you are seeking conservatorship of the estate only and the conservatee's assets are in a different county from where he lives, you might type: "Gordon Gold presently lives in Los Angeles County with his daughter Katherine Silver and her family. Gordon Gold used to live in San Mateo County and his assets are located here, including a house, rental apartment building, bank accounts and personal property. Because I live in San Mateo County, it would be convenient and in the best interests of the proposed conservatee for the conservatorship to be commenced in San Mateo County where I can smoothly manage the property."

Item 3a(2): Skip this entire item. If the proposed conservatee is not a California resident, you will need the help of a lawyer.

Item 3b: In this item you state whether you or the proposed conservatee owe one another money.

Item 3b(1): Check only one box in this item. Check the first box if the proposed conservatee owes you any money. If the proposed conservatee owes you money, you cannot file to be conservator unless you are also the proposed conservatee's spouse or relative (Probate Code §1820). Or check the second box if the proposed conservatee does not owe you any money.

Item 3b(2): Check only one box in this item. Check the first box if you owe the proposed conservatee any money. Or check the second box if you do not owe the proposed conservatee any money.

Item 3c: You will check one or two boxes in this item.

Item 3c(1): Check this box if the proposed conservatee or her close relative nominated you in writing to be the conservator. Then attach a copy of the written nomination as "Attachment 3c." This could be a copy of a durable power of attorney signed by the proposed conservatee, a letter or any other document signed by the conservatee or her close relative that names you conservator.

CONSERVATORSHIP OF *(NAME)*:	CASE NUMBER:
RICHARD SHAPIRO PROPOSED CONSERVATEE	

2. Proposed conservatee is *(name)*:
(present address):

RICHARD SHAPIRO   (415) 555-1212
4545 Pebble Ave.   *(telephone)*:
San Francisco, CA 94118

3. a. JURISDICTIONAL FACTS The proposed conservatee has no conservator within California and is a

   (1) [X] resident of California and

       [X] a resident of this county.

       [ ] not a resident of this county but commencement of the conservatorship in this county is in the best interests of the proposed conservatee. *(Specify reasons in Attachment 3a.)*

   (2) [ ] nonresident of California but

       [ ] is temporarily living in this county, or

       [ ] has property in this county, or

       [ ] commencement of the conservatorship in this county is in the best interests of the proposed conservatee. *(Specify reasons in Attachment 3a.)*

b. Petitioner

   (1) [ ] is [X] is not a **creditor** or agent of a creditor of the proposed conservatee.

   (2) [ ] is [X] is not a **debtor** or agent of a debtor of the proposed conservatee.

c. Proposed conservator is

   (1) [ ] a nominee. *(Affix nomination as Attachment 3c.)*

   (2) [X] related to proposed conservatee as *(specify)*: Daughter of proposed conservatee

   (3) [ ] a private professional conservator as defined in Probate Code section 2341 who has filed with the county clerk the information statement required by Probate Code section 2342.

   (4) [ ] other *(specify)*:

d. Petitioner is

   (1) [ ] the proposed conservatee.

   (2) [ ] the spouse of the proposed conservatee.

   (3) [X] a relative of the proposed conservatee *(specify relationship)*: Daughter of proposed conservatee

   (4) [ ] a state or local public entity, officer, or employee.

   (5) [ ] a bank [ ] other entity authorized to conduct the business of a trust company.

   (6) [ ] an interested person or friend of the proposed conservatee.

   (7) [ ] a private professional conservator who has filed the information statement (Prob. Code, § 2342).

   (8) [ ] the guardian of the proposed conservatee.

e. Character and estimated value of the property of the estate

   (1) Personal property: .... $ 15,000

   (2) Annual gross income from

      (i) [X] real property: .... $ 11,000

      (ii) [ ] personal property: .... $ 1,000

             Total: .... $ 27,000

   (3) Real Property: $ 325,000

4. Proposed conservatee

  a. Proposed conservatee [X] is not [ ] is a patient in or on leave of absence from a state institution under the jurisdiction of the State Department of Mental Health or the State Department of Developmental Services *(specify state institution)*:

  b. Proposed conservatee [X] is neither receiving nor entitled to receive [ ] is receiving or entitled to receive benefits from the Veterans Administration *(estimate amount of monthly benefit payable)*: $

  c. Proposed conservatee [X] is [ ] is not able to complete an affidavit of voter registration.

(Continued on next page)

GC-310 [Rev. July 1, 1990]   **PETITION FOR APPOINTMENT OF**   Page two of four
                                  PROBATE CONSERVATOR

Item 3c(2): Check this box if you are a relative of the proposed conservatee by blood or marriage, and list the relationship.

Item 3c(3): Leave this item blank. It only applies to people who are professional conservators, which is beyond the scope of this book.

Item 3c(4): Check this box if you're not a relative of the proposed conservatee. Then, after the words "other (specify)," briefly describe your relationship with the proposed conservatee. This might be "friend of proposed conservatee," "next door neighbor of proposed conservatee" or, if you are presently serving as the legal guardian of a minor who will soon reach age 18 and needs a conservatorship, "legal guardian of the [*"person," "estate" or person and estate*]."

Item 3d(1): Leave this item blank. It is only checked where the conservatee is filing to have a conservatorship established for himself.

Item 3d(2): Check this box if you are presently married to the proposed conservatee. If you are in the process of legal separation or divorce, indicate that after the words "the spouse of the proposed conservatee." For example, you might type: "Filed for divorce March 9, 19___, Marin County Superior Court Case No. 123."

Item 3d(3): Check this box if you are a relative of the proposed conservatee by blood or marriage, and list the relationship.

Item 3d(4): Skip this item. It applies to a situation where an agency seeks a conservatorship, which is beyond the scope of this book.

Item 3d(5): Leave this item blank. It only applies to banks or other financial institutions, which is beyond the scope of this book.

Item 3d(6): Check this box if you are a friend, neighbor or acquaintance of the proposed conservatee, but are not related by blood or marriage.

Item 3d(7): Leave this item blank. It only applies to people who are professional conservators, which is beyond the scope of this book.

Item 3d(8): Check this box if you are seeking conservatorship of a minor for whom you are presently the court-appointed legal guardian.

Items 3e(1)-(3): Complete this item only if you are seeking conservatorship of the estate or person and estate.

In Chapter 14, Section D, are instructions for completing a Worksheet for Calculating Bond. You'll notice that the information requested in this item is the same as that requested in the worksheet. Check the appropriate boxes and copy the figures from that worksheet. The figures listed in the "Total" must correspond with the amount of bond requested in Item 1c, excluding real property and blocked accounts, if you are using a surety company or making deposits with the court clerk. If personal sureties are used, the bond requested in Item 1c will be double the amount listed in this "Total."

 Do not list personal property which has value only to the proposed conservatee—such as old clothes or toiletries. Also, do not have any real or personal property appraised yet.

Item 4a: This item asks if the proposed conservatee is either a patient of or on leave from an institution which is operated by the California Department of Mental Health or the State Department of Developmental Services. Check the first box before the words "is not," if the proposed conservatee is not a patient in an institution for the mentally disabled or severely disabled. If the proposed conservatee is a patient in such an institution, or on leave from one, you will need to see an attorney. (See Chapter 17.)

Item 4b: Veterans of the U.S. armed services and their immediate families may be eligible or may be receiving Veterans' Administration benefits. Check the first box before the words "is neither," if the proposed conservatee is neither receiving nor entitled to receive benefits from the Veterans' Administration. Check the second box next to the word "is" if the proposed conservatee is receiving or is entitled to receive benefits from the Veterans' Administration. Then list the monthly amount in the space indicated.

If you don't know whether the proposed conservatee is receiving or eligible to receive Veterans' Administration benefits, check the first box. Then type in the words: "It is unknown at this time whether the proposed conservatee is eligible for or receiving Veterans' Administration benefits."

Item 4c: In this box you state whether the proposed conservatee is capable of filling in a voter registration form by himself. That form requires information about where he lives, his birthdate, occupation and whether he has previously registered to vote. Check the first box if you believe the proposed conservatee is able to complete such a form. Check the second box if you think the proposed conservatee cannot fill out such a form.

> **CAPTION:** PAGE 3 OF THE PETITION FOR APPOINTMENT OF PROBATE CONSERVATOR
>
> After the words "CONSERVATORSHIP OF (Name)," in capital letters fill in the proposed conservatee's full name.

Item 5a(1): Check this box if the proposed conservatee is 18 years of age or older.

Item 5a(2): Check this box if you are seeking conservatorship of a person who is under age 18 but will turn 18 by the time you are appointed conservator.[6]

Item 5a(3): Check this box if the proposed conservatee is younger than 18 years of age and is also married.

Item 5a(4): Check this box if the proposed conservatee is younger than 18 years of age, has been married and divorced. Do not check this box if the marriage was annulled.[7] If the minor is divorced, type in the words: "The proposed conservatee is divorced."

Item 5b(1): Complete this item only if you are seeking conservatorship of the person or person and estate. Here you give a brief explanation of why a conservatorship of the person is needed. For sake of the proposed conservatee's privacy, do not go into detail in this item. You will provide more information in a Confidential Supplemental Information form provided in Section C of this chapter that will not be made part of the public court record.

Check the box before the words "as follows," and explain why a conservatorship is needed. State facts, not your own conclusions.

Example: Jack Black, the proposed conservatee, was diagnosed with progressive senile dementia. He refuses or is unable to communicate medical and personal decisions. Jack Black must have constant care and attention at the rest home or he does not take care of his physical needs. A detailed explanation is contained in the Confidential Supplemental Information form filed with this petition.

Example: The proposed conservatee, Olivia Johnson, has Lou Gehrig's disease and is unable to speak or move about. She cannot make any personal and medical care decisions for herself. A detailed explanation is contained in the Confidential Supplemental Information form filed with this petition.

Note for Los Angeles County: If you are filing for a conservatorship in Los Angeles County, you must state whether the proposed conservatee already has an LPS conservator, which is explained in Chapter 1, Section B5a. In Item 5b(1), add these words: "The proposed conservatee does not have a conservator appointed under the Lanterman-Petris-Short Act."[8]

Item 5b(2): Complete this item only if you are seeking conservatorship of the estate or person and estate. Here you give a brief explanation of why a conservatorship of the estate is needed. For sake of the proposed conservatee's privacy, do not go into detail in this item. You will provide more information in a Confidential Supplemental Information form, provided in Section C of this chapter.

---

[6]A court-appointed guardian can petition for a conservatorship to take over once the minor reaches age 18, if management of the person or estate is still needed (Probate Code §1820(b)).

[7]You can only obtain conservatorship of a minor's person if the minor is or has been married, as long as that marriage was not annulled. If the marriage was annulled, you would need to seek a guardianship. See *The Guardianship Book,* by Lisa Goldoftas and David Brown (Nolo Press).

[8]You'll need a lawyer's help if the proposed conservatee has an LPS conservator. (See Chapter 17.)

CONSERVATORSHIP OF *(NAME)*:		CASE NUMBER:
RICHARD SHAPIRO	PROPOSED CONSERVATEE	

5. a. **Proposed conservatee**

(1) [X] is an adult.

(2) [ ] will be an adult on the effective date of the order *(date)*:

(3) [ ] is a married minor.

(4) [ ] is a minor whose marriage has been dissolved.

b. **Proposed conservatee** requires a conservator and is

(1) [X] unable properly to provide for his or her personal needs for physical health, food, clothing, or shelter.
  Supporting facts are [ ] specified in Attachment 5b(1) [X] as follows:

  Richard Shapiro was diagnosed with progressive senile dementia. He refuses or is unable to communicate medical and personal decisions. A detailed explanation is contained in the Confidential Supplemental Information form filed with this petition.

(2) [X] substantially unable to manage his or her financial resources or resist fraud or undue influence.
  Supporting facts are [ ] specified in Attachment 5b(2) [X] as follows:

  Richard Shapiro was diagnosed with progressive senile dementia. He is not paying his bills or opening his mail. He is unable to manage his own finances without assistance. A detailed explanation is contained in the Confidential Supplemental Information form filed with this petition.

c. [ ] **Proposed conservatee** voluntarily requests the appointment of a conservator. *(Specify facts showing good cause in Attachment 5(c).)*

d. [X] **Confidential Supplement Information** *(Judicial Council form GC-312)* is filed with this petition. *(All petitioners must file this form except banks and other entities authorized to do business as a trust company.)*

e. **Proposed conservatee** [ ] is [X] is not developmentally disabled as defined in section 1420 of the Probate Code *(specify the nature and degree of the alleged disability in Attachment 5e).* Petitioner is aware of the requirements of section 1827.5 of the Probate Code.

(Continued on reverse)

GC-310 [Rev. July 1, 1990]   **PETITION FOR APPOINTMENT OF**
                                   PROBATE CONSERVATOR   Page three of four

Check the box before the words "as follows," and explain why a conservatorship of the estate is needed. State facts, not your own conclusions. Here are some examples:

Example: My father, Harry Wood, was diagnosed with Korsakoff's syndrome, a neurological disorder with symptoms of memory loss. He is not paying his bills or opening his mail. He is unable to manage his own finances without assistance. A detailed explanation is contained in the Confidential Supplemental Information form filed with this petition.

Example: The proposed conservatee, Donald Price, lives in a nursing home, where he is completely disabled from multiple sclerosis. He needs a conservator to handle his finances. A detailed explanation is contained in the Confidential Supplemental Information form filed with this petition.

Example: Marilyn Noble, the proposed conservatee, was diagnosed with Huntington Chorea, a neurological disorder. She cannot manage her money without assistance. A detailed explanation is contained in the Confidential Supplemental Information form filed with this petition.

Note for Los Angeles County: If you are filing for a conservatorship in Los Angeles County, you must state whether the proposed conservatee already has an LPS conservator, which is beyond the scope of this book—see Chapter 1, Section B5a. In Item 5b(2), add these words: "The proposed conservatee does not have a conservator appointed under the Lanterman-Petris-Short Act."[9]

Item 5c: Skip this item. It is only used when a proposed conservatee is also the petitioner, which is beyond the scope of this book.

Item 5d: Check this box. You will prepare the Confidential Supplemental Information in Section C of this chapter.

Item 5e: Check the second box before the word "is not," indicating that the proposed conservatee is not developmentally disabled. If the proposed conservatee is developmentally disabled, you will need the assistance of an attorney. (See Chapter 17.)

---

[9]You'll need a lawyer's help if the proposed conservatee has an LPS conservator. (See Chapter 17.)

CAPTION: PAGE 4 OF THE PETITION FOR APPOINTMENT OF PROBATE CONSERVATOR

After the words "CONSERVATORSHIP OF (Name)," fill in the proposed conservatee's full name in capital letters.

Item 6: In this item you state whether or not the proposed conservatee will attend a court hearing at which a judge will decide whether to grant the conservatorship. She must attend unless:

- She is not willing to attend the hearing and a court investigator has spoken with her and determined that she does not object to you being appointed conservator (investigations are covered in Chapter 7); or
- She cannot attend because of medical reasons. These must be substantiated by a doctor's statement. (This is covered in Section B of this chapter.)[10]

Item 6a: Check the first box if the proposed conservatee will attend the hearing. Also check the box before the words "is not the petitioner." If the proposed conservatee nominated you conservator in writing, check the box before the word "has." If the proposed conservatee did not nominate you conservator, check the box before the words "has not."

Item 6b: Check this item only if the proposed conservatee is able to, but does not plan to attend the hearing. Also check the box before the words "does not wish to contest the establishment of a conservatorship," and before the words "does not object to the proposed conservator." If the proposed conservatee objects to the conservatorship or wants someone else to serve as conservator, you'll need a lawyer.[11]

---

[10]The proposed conservatee does not need to attend if she was not in California at the time she was provided with notice of the conservatorship. That is beyond the scope of this book.

[11]A court investigator will interview the proposed conservatee if she is able but unwilling to attend the hearing. Investigations are covered in Chapter 7.

CONSERVATORSHIP OF (NAME):		CASE NUMBER:
RICHARD SHAPIRO	PROPOSED CONSERVATEE	

6. ATTENDANCE AT HEARING   Proposed conservatee

a. [X] will attend the hearing   AND [ ] is the petitioner [X] is not the petitioner
AND [X] has [ ] has not   nominated the proposed conservator.

b. [ ] is able but unwilling to attend the hearing   AND [ ] does [ ] does not   wish to contest the establishment of a conservatorship   AND [ ] does [ ] does not   object to the proposed conservator
AND [ ] does [ ] does not   prefer that another person act as conservator.

c. [ ] is unable to attend the hearing because of medical inability. An affidavit or certificate of a licensed medical practitioner or an accredited religious practitioner is affixed as Attachment 6c.

d. [ ] is not the petitioner, is out of state, and will not attend the hearing.

7. [ ] Granting the proposed conservator of the estate powers to be exercised independently under section 2590 of the Probate Code would be to the advantage and benefit and in the best interest of the conservatorship estate. Powers and reasons are specified in Attachment 7.

8. [ ] a. There is no form of medical treatment for which the proposed conservatee has the capacity to give an informed consent.

b. Attached to this petition is a declaration executed by a licensed physician stating that the proposed conservatee lacks the capacity to give informed consent for any form of medical treatment and giving reasons and the factual basis for this conclusion. (Label as Attachment 8.)

c. Proposed conservatee [ ] is [ ] is not   an adherent of a religion that relies on prayer alone for healing as defined in section 2355(b) of the Probate Code.

9. [ ] Filed with this petition is a Petition for Appointment of Temporary Conservator (Judicial Council form GC-110).

10. [X] The names, residence addresses, and relationships of the spouse and all relatives within the second degree of the proposed conservatee so far as known to petitioner are

a. [X] listed below [ ] listed in Attachment 10

b. [ ] not known, so relatives under Probate Code section 1821(b)(1)-(4) are [ ] listed below [ ] listed in Attachment 10.

RELATIONSHIP AND NAME	RESIDENCE ADDRESS
(1) Spouse: PETUNIA SMITH, deceased	---
(2) Daughter: MARIE SMITH	64313 Kildare St., San Francisco, CA 94111
(3) Son: JEROME SHAPIRO	2076 Prospect Ave., Macomb, MI 48065
(4) Sister: FRANCES RYAN	60 East 306, Cleveland, OH 44132
(5) Niece: JANE RYAN	266A Tilden, Cleveland, OH 44108
(6) Grandson: JASON RYAN	266A Tilden, Cleveland, OH 44108

11. [X] Filed with this petition is a proposed Order Appointing Court Investigator (see Judicial Council form GC-330).

12. [X] Number of pages attached: __4__

Date: April 10, 19__

► *Marie Smith*
(SIGNATURE OF PETITIONER)

I declare under penalty of perjury under the laws of the State of California that the foregoing is true and correct.

Date: April 10, 19__

.....MARIE SMITH.....................
(TYPE OR PRINT NAME)

► *Marie Smith*
(SIGNATURE OF PETITIONER)

GC-310 [Rev. July 1, 1990]   **PETITION FOR APPOINTMENT OF PROBATE CONSERVATOR**   Page four of four

Item 6c: Check this item only if the proposed conservatee cannot attend the hearing because of medical reasons. These reasons may not be because of emotional or psychological instability, but must be physical. If you check this box, you must prepare an Attachment 6c and have it completed and signed by a medical practitioner. This attachment is a separate form which is contained in Appendix B. You will fill out the form referred to in this item later, in Section B of this chapter. For now, go on to the next item on this form.

Item 6d: Skip this item, which pertains to an out-of-state proposed conservatee, which is beyond the scope of this book.

Item 7: Skip this item unless you checked the box in Item 1d. If you completed Item 1d, also check this item.

Items 8a-c: Skip these items unless you checked Item 1g, above, because the proposed conservatee is not capable of making *any* medical decisions for himself. If you checked Item 1g, above, check the first box. If the proposed conservatee is a member of a religion that relies on prayer as the *only* method of healing, check the box in Item 8c before the word "is." Or check the box before the words "is not" if the proposed conservatee's religion does not limit healing to prayer alone.

If you check Item 8, you must provide a declaration from a licensed physician stating that the proposed conservatee is not capable of making *any* medical decisions for himself, and giving facts to support that conclusion. Some courts have specific requirements for what must be contained in the doctor's declaration, while others may accept a signed letter from a doctor as long as it ends with a declaration under penalty of perjury, as set out in Chapter 3, Section H2e. Check your local probate policy manual, then follow the instructions in Chapter 3, Section H2e, to prepare and attach a declaration of a medical doctor as Attachment 8.

Item 9: Skip this item unless you need to obtain a conservatorship in less than six to eight weeks. If so, you'll need to hire a lawyer or do your own research. (See Chapter 17.)

Item 10: Check this box. You will list the close relatives of the proposed conservatee—including yourself, if you are closely related. It is essential that you list all known names and addresses. If you know the name or address of any relatives but do not list them, any of them may later claim the conservatorship was not properly obtained and ask the court to end it. Refer to the Conservatorship Worksheet you completed in Chapter 3, Section F, to fill in this item.

Item 10a: Look at the worksheet to see how many relatives you will list. If there is enough room on the petition to list all the relatives' names and addresses, check the box before the words "listed below." If there is not enough room on the petition to list all the relatives' names and addresses, check the box before the words "listed in Attachment 10."

Item 10b: Skip this item if you completed Part 1 of the Conservatorship Worksheet. If you completed Part 2 of the worksheet—because none of the proposed conservatee's close relatives are known or living—check the box before the words "not known." If there is enough room on the petition to list all the relatives' names and addresses, check the box before the words "listed below." If there is not enough room on the petition to list all the relatives' names and addresses, check the box before the words "listed in Attachment 10."

Item 10(1): After the word "Spouse," list the proposed conservatee's spouse's name. If the proposed conservatee is divorced or unmarried, fill in the word "none." If the spouse is dead, fill in the spouse's name, followed by the word "deceased." At the right, under the words "RESIDENCE ADDRESS," fill in the spouse's address, or the word "unknown," if that information is not available.

Item 10(2): Beginning with the blank Item 10(2), list all of the conservatee's living relatives in the same format as Item 10(1), listing the name and relationship of each relative after a separate number item (2, 3, 4 and so on). If you need additional space, prepare an Attachment 10 following the instructions in Chapter 3, Section H2e. At the top left of the page, type in the words "Relationship and Name," and at the top right type in "Residence Address." Then continue listing the names and addresses of each living relative. If a relative has died, fill in the relative's name, followed by the word "deceased." If you do not know a name or address for a particular relative, fill in the word "unknown."

Item 11: Check this box. You will later complete the Order Appointing Court Investigator form in Section D of this chapter.

Item 12: Check this box. If you are not attaching any additional pages, fill in the word "None." Otherwise, count up and enter the number of total pages to be attached. A checklist of possible attachments follows. All attachments should be stapled (in numerical order) to the Petition for Appointment of Probate Conservator before you file it with the court.

 If the proposed conservatee will not attend the hearing because of medical reasons, prepare an Attachment 6c following the instructions in Section B of this chapter. Have a doctor or medical practitioner complete it, then count the number of attached pages.

Date and Signature: Finally, fill in today's date in the two spaces provided at the bottom of the last page. To the left of the second signature line, type or clearly print your name in capital letters, and sign your name in the two spaces provided. You're now ready to prepare the next form.

CHECKLIST OF POSSIBLE ATTACHMENTS TO PETITION FOR APPOINTMENT OF PROBATE CONSERVATOR*

☐ Attachment 1c: Information on bond requirements.

☐ *Attachment 1e: Information on orders relating to the capacity of the proposed conservatee. (This material is beyond the scope of this book.)*

☐ *Attachment 1f: Information on special orders for conservatorship of the person. (This material is beyond the scope of this book.)*

☐ *Attachments 1h-1j: Information about a proposed conservatee who is developmentally disabled. (This material is beyond the scope of this book.)*

☐ Attachment 1k: Request for additional orders.

☐ Attachment 3a: Information about filing conservatorship in a county other than where the proposed conservatee lives.

☐ Attachment 3c: Nomination of proposed conservator.

☐ Attachment 5b(1): Facts specifying why a conservatorship of the person is needed for the proposed conservatee (if there is not enough space in the petition or if supporting documentation is attached).

☐ Attachment 5b(2): Facts specifying why a conservatorship of the estate is needed for the proposed conservatee (if there is not enough space in the petition or if supporting documentation is attached).

☐ *Attachment 5c: Facts specifying why petitioner who is also proposed conservatee requests appointment of conservator. (This material is beyond the scope of this book.)*

☐ *Attachment 5e: Information about a proposed conservatee who is developmentally disabled. (This material is beyond the scope of this book.)*

☐ Attachment 6c: Information about a proposed conservatee who is unable to attend the conservatorship hearing because of medical inability. (Instructions for completing this form are contained in Section B of this chapter.)

☐ *Attachment 7: Information on additional powers for conservatorship of the estate. (This material is beyond the scope of this book.)*

☐ Attachment 8: Declaration of a licensed physician stating that the proposed conservatee is not capable of making any medical decisions for himself.

☐ Attachment 10: Additional names and addresses of conservatee's relatives (if there is not enough space in the petition).

*Some or possibly all of these attachments may be required. See the instructions for each item number. Attachments in the checklist which are italicized are for situations beyond the scope of this book, and you probably will need to consult an attorney if you need to include any of them.

B. Declaration of Medical or Accredited Practitioner (Attachment 6c to Petition)

SKIP THIS ENTIRE SECTION if the proposed conservatee will attend the conservatorship hearing. If she is unable to attend because of physical infirmity, make sure you have checked Item 6c of the petition. You will need to have this form completed and signed by the proposed conservatee's licensed medical doctor or if the proposed conservatee follows a religion which believes in healing by prayer only, by an accredited practitioner of that religion. This form will be attached to the petition as Attachment 6c.

The Declaration of Medical or Accredited Practitioner gives information about why the proposed conservatee cannot attend the hearing. As indicated in the instructions to Item 6c of the petition, these reasons may not be because of emotional or psychological instability; they must be physical.

To complete this form, you will need to contact the proposed conservatee's medical doctor or religious practitioner to discuss the conservatorship. (See Chapter 3, Section C, for information about discussing the conservatorship with the doctor.) If you haven't already spoken with the proposed conservatee's medical or religious practitioner, first explain that you are planning to seek a conservatorship. Tell him that you need a signed statement indicating that the proposed conservatee is physically unable to attend the conservatorship hearing, and find out if he is willing to sign such a document. If he will not sign the statement, you have two choices:

- Provided that the proposed conservatee truly is *physically* unable to attend the hearing, locate another doctor or religious practitioner who is presently treating or will treat the proposed conservatee and is willing to sign such a statement; or

- Change Item 6 of the petition. Remove your check mark from Item 6c. Then check either Item 6a—if the proposed conservatee is able and willing to attend the hearing, or check Item 6b—if the proposed conservatee is able but declines to attend the hearing. Instructions for completing both items are contained in Section A of this chapter.

CAPTION: DECLARATION OF MEDICAL OR ACCREDITED PRACTITIONER

- At the top of the form fill in the words "Attachment 6c to Petition for Appointment of Probate Conservator."
- Fill in the caption following the general instructions in Chapter 3, Section H2b.

After the words "I, (name)," fill in the name of the licensed medical doctor or religious practitioner who will be completing the form.

Item 1a: Skip this item if this form will be signed by an accredited practitioner of a religion which calls for healing by prayer only, and go on to Item 1b. If a licensed medical practitioner will be signing the form, check this box. Then fill in the office address of the medical practitioner.

Item 1b: Skip this item if you completed Item 1a, and go on to Item 2. If an accredited practitioner of a religion which calls for healing by prayer only will be signing the form, check this box. Then fill in the office address of the religious practitioner.

Item 2: Cross off the words "set for (date)," and insert the words "specified in Notice of Hearing." Leave the rest of this item blank.

You have completed your portion of this form. The rest must be filled in by the medical or religious practitioner.

Take or send the form to the proposed conservatee's medical or religious practitioner and ask her to complete the rest of Item 2 and date and sign the form.

 If you send the form to the practitioner, specify a date by which you need it returned. You may need to follow up by calling, writing or visiting the practitioner's office, since it is part of the Petition for Appointment of Probate Conservator which you need to file with the court.

In Item 2, the practitioner will specify an approximate date when the proposed conservatee will be well enough to attend a hearing, or indicate that the proposed conservatee won't be able to attend a hearing in the foreseeable future. The practitioner will tell why the

ATTORNEY OR PARTY WITHOUT ATTORNEY (Name and Address):	TELEPHONE NO.:	FOR COURT USE ONLY
RONALD DAPHNE 55 West Hill Street Los Angeles, CA 90012	(213) 555-1212	

ATTORNEY FOR (Name):   In Pro Per

SUPERIOR COURT OF CALIFORNIA, COUNTY OF Los Angeles

STREET ADDRESS 111 North Hill Street
MAILING ADDRESS P.O. Box 151
CITY AND ZIP CODE Los Angeles, CA 90053
BRANCH NAME

CONSERVATORSHIP OF THE [X] PERSON [X] ESTATE OF (NAME):

MATILDE DAPHNE   Proposed Conservatee

DECLARATION OF MEDICAL OR ACCREDITED PRACTITIONER

CASE NUMBER:

I, (name):   JANE McGEE, M.D.   , hereby state:

1. a. [X] I am a duly licensed medical practitioner, and the proposed conservatee is under my treatment. My office
is located at (address):

> 144 Hollywood Blvd.
> Los Angeles, CA 90027

b. [ ] I am an accredited practitioner of a religion whose tenets and practices call for reliance on prayer alone
for healing, which religion is adhered to by the proposed conservatee. The proposed conservatee is under
my treatment. My office is located at (address):

2. The proposed conservatee is unable to attend the court hearing on the petition for appointment of a conservator
~~set for (date):~~ specified in Notice of Hearing   and will continue to be unable to attend a court hearing
[ ] until (date):   [X] for the foreseeable future because of medical inability. Supporting
facts are [ ] stated below [X] stated in attachment 2.

I declare under penalty of perjury under the laws of the State of California that the foregoing is true and correct
and that this declaration is executed on (date): June ___, 19__ at (place): Los Angeles, CA . . . .

_____
(Signature of declarant)

Emotional or psychological instability shall not be considered good cause for the absence unless, by reason of the instability, attendance at the hearing
is likely to cause serious and immediate physiological damage to the proposed conservatee.

Form Approved by the
Judicial Council of California
Revised Effective January 1, 1981
GC-335(81)

**DECLARATION OF MEDICAL OR
ACCREDITED PRACTITIONER**

proposed conservatee is physically unable to attend the hearing. Supporting documents, such as medical reports, may be attached to the declaration as Attachment 2, and should be labeled "Attachment 2 to Declaration of Medical or Accredited Practitioner" and numbered. Have the practitioner fill in the date and sign her name in the spaces provided.

Finally, attach this document to the Petition for Appointment of Probate Conservator as Attachment 6c. Make sure you have listed the correct number of attachment pages in Item 12 of the petition.

C. Confidential Supplemental Information

IN THE CONFIDENTIAL SUPPLEMENTAL information form, you provide personal information about the conservatee and his needs. The form is designed to help a judge determine whether a conservatorship is necessary, while simultaneously keeping personal—and often embarrassing—information out of the public court record.

The completed document is available only to those people who are entitled to notice of the conservatorship or those who have appeared in the proceeding. The court has discretion to release the document to anyone else, and may only do so if it is in the conservatee's interest (Probate Code §1821(a)).

If you do not know the information required in this form, other people who do may provide declarations. The declarations should be stapled to this document. (See Chapter 3, Section H2c, for information on preparing declarations.)

 Do not attach this form to the Petition for Appointment of Probate Conservator. The petition is a public court record, while the Confidential Supplemental Information form is not.

CAPTION: CONFIDENTIAL SUPPLEMENTAL INFORMATION

- Fill in the caption following the general instructions in Chapter 3, Section H2b.
- Leave the boxes requesting information about the hearing date blank. The clerk will provide them.

Item 1a: Fill in the proposed conservatee's name exactly as it appears in the petition.

Item 1b: Fill in the proposed conservatee's date of birth, including the year.

Item 1c: Fill in the proposed conservatee's Social Security number.

Item 2: Complete this item only if you are seeking conservatorship of the person or person and estate. If so, check the first box. Then in your own words, explain why the proposed conservatee cannot take care of his personal and physical needs. If there is enough room on the form to provide an explanation, fill it in there. Otherwise, check the box before the words "Specified in Attachment 2" and prepare an Attachment 2 following the instructions in Chapter 3, Section H2e.

Include detailed information about the proposed conservatee's inability to provide for his physical health, food, clothing and shelter. Use specific examples from the proposed conservatee's daily life and state facts, not your own conclusions. If you have documents that support your position, they should be attached.

Example: Jack Black, the proposed conservatee, is 84 years old. He has been diagnosed as having progressive senile dementia, which has gotten noticeably worse in the last three months. He has been living in Sunnyside Rest Home for one year. Jack Black must have constant care and attention at the rest home or he does not take care of his physical needs such as getting out of bed, dressing, eating and using the toilet. He does not appear to understand or remember what he is told. He answers "No" to any question he is asked, even if his answers are contradictory. For example, on January 18, 19__, his physician, Dr. Jane Smith, gave him a package of cough drops. The next day, she asked him if he had taken any and he replied, "No."

CONFIDENTIAL (DO NOT ATTACH TO PETITION)

ATTORNEY OR PARTY WITHOUT ATTORNEY *(Name and Address)*:	TELEPHONE NO.:	FOR COURT USE ONLY
ANTONIA COREZONE 1721 49th Ave. Bakersfield, CA 93304	(805)555-1212	

ATTORNEY FOR *(Name)*: In Pro Per

SUPERIOR COURT OF CALIFORNIA, COUNTY OF Kern

STREET ADDRESS: 1415 Truxton Ave.

MAILING ADDRESS: Bakersfield, CA 93301

CITY AND ZIP CODE:

BRANCH NAME:

CONSERVATORSHIP OF (NAME):

DORTHEA JOHNSON

PROPOSED CONSERVATEE

CONFIDENTIAL SUPPLEMENTAL INFORMATION (Probate Conservatorship)	CASE NUMBER:
Conservatorship of [X] Person [X] Estate [ ] Limited Conservatorship	HEARING DATE:

1. a. Proposed conservatee *(name)*: DORTHEA JOHNSON
   b. Date of birth: 2/14/14
   c. Social Security No.: 999-99-9999

DEPT.:   TIME:

2. [X] UNABLE TO PROVIDE FOR PERSONAL NEEDS* The following facts support petitioner's allegation that the proposed conservatee is unable to provide properly for his or her needs for physical health, food, clothing, and shelter *(specify in detail. Enlarge upon the reasons stated in the petition. Provide specific examples from the proposed conservatee's daily life showing significant behavior patterns)*: [X] Specified in Attachment 2.

The proposed conservatee, Dorthea Johnson, was in an automobile accident on May 4, 19__. She is in an irreversible coma. She lives in a nursing home where she receives round-the-clock care. She cannot communicate, speak or write. She cannot feed, clothe or bathe herself and she is incontinent. She needs a conservator to make all personal and medical care decisions for her. A declaration by her physician, Dr. Pat Patterson, is attached as Attachment 2.

(Continued on reverse)   Page one of four

She then asked if he understood her question and he said, "No." She asked if he had any cough drops left or whether he had taken them all, and he again answered, "No." She asked several more questions and got "No" as the answer each time. A copy of the medical report by his physician, Dr. Jane Smith, is attached as Attachment 2.

Example: The proposed conservatee, Olivia Johnson, lives in her own home. There she receives round-the-clock nursing and home care. She has Lou Gehrig's disease and is unable to speak or move about. She cannot feed, clothe or bathe herself and she is incontinent. Olivia Johnson needs a conservator to make all personal and medical care decisions for her. A copy of the medical report by her physician, Dr. Kyle Kramer, is attached as Attachment 2.

CAPTION: PAGE 2 OF THE CONFIDENTIAL SUPPLEMENTAL INFORMATION

- After the words "CONSERVATORSHIP OF (Name)," in capital letters fill in the proposed conservatee's full name.

Item 3: Complete this item only if you are seeking conservatorship of the conservatee's estate or person and estate. If so, check the first box. If there is enough room on the form to provide an explanation, fill it in there. Otherwise, check the box before the words "Specified in Attachment 3" and prepare an Attachment 3 following the instructions in Chapter 3, Section H2e.

In your own words, explain why the proposed conservatee cannot handle his finances or resist fraud or undue influence. Use specific examples from the proposed conservatee's daily life and state facts, not your own conclusions. If you have documents that support your position, they should be attached.

Example: My father, Harry Wood, was diagnosed with Korsakoff's syndrome, a neurological disorder with symptoms of memory loss. A copy of the medical report by his physician, Dr. Carmen Wilson, is attached as Attachment 3. My father lives alone in his home, and is responsible for paying his bills and managing his house. For approximately the last six months I have received phone calls from PG&E (on January 16, 19__, April 14, 19__ and July 1, 19__) threatening to shut off his service because he didn't pay. On each of these instances, I wrote a check for my father and he later reimbursed me. He stated that he didn't remember getting any bills. Last week, Harry Wood's phone service was disconnected. I went to his house and found a stack of unopened mail which included all of his PG&E and telephone bills as well as several Social Security and Veterans' Administration checks. On July 15, 19__, I made phone calls and arranged to pay all his overdue bills, including the mortgage, utilities and insurance. Harry Wood is unable to manage his own finances without assistance.

CONFIDENTIAL

CONSERVATORSHIP OF *(NAME)*:		CASE NUMBER:
DORTHEA JOHNSON	PROPOSED CONSERVATEE	

3. [X] UNABLE TO MANAGE FINANCIAL RESOURCES* The following facts support petitioner's allegation that the proposed conservatee is substantially unable to manage his or her financial resources or to resist fraud or undue influence *(specify in detail. Enlarge upon the reasons stated in the petition. Provide specific examples from the proposed conservatee's daily life showing significant behavior patterns.)*: [X] Specified in Attachment 3.

      The proposed conservatee, Dorthea Johnson, was in an automobile accident on May 4, 19__. She is in an irreversible coma. She cannot communicate, speak or write, so needs a conservator to handle her finances. A declaration by her physician, Dr. Pat Patterson, is attached as Attachment 3.

4. RESIDENCE *("Residence" means the place usually described as "home"; for example, owned real property or long-term rental)*
   a. The proposed conservatee is **located** at *(street address, city, state)*:

      1721 49th Ave.
      Bakersfield, CA 93304

   b. The proposed conservatee's **residence** is* [X] the address in item 4a [ ] other *(street address, city, state)*:

(Continued on next page)

Example: The proposed conservatee, Donald Price, lives in a nursing home, where he is completely disabled from multiple sclerosis. He is unable to speak, communicate or write, so needs a conservator to handle his finances. A copy of the medical report by his physician, Dr. Sharon Gross, is attached as Attachment 3.

Example: Marilyn Noble, the proposed conservatee, was diagnosed with Huntington Chorea, a neurological disorder. She now lives in Halfway Home in Daly City, California. She has problems managing her money. In July and August 19__, she cashed and then gave away the entire amount of her SSI checks to others living in Halfway Home. At the end of September 19__, she told me that she hadn't received an SSI check that month, then admitted that she gave the entire amount to a stranger on the street. Her psychiatrist, Dr. Andrew White, believes that she is not capable of making rational decisions for her financial well-being. A copy of her doctor's statement is attached as Attachment 3.

Item 4a: Give the full address where the proposed conservatee is presently staying, even if she doesn't plan to live there. For example, this might be a hospital, nursing facility, relative's house or the proposed conservatee's own home.

Item 4b: Complete this item only if the proposed conservatee has a regular residence—a house, apartment or condominium that she rents or owns or shares with you or others. Check the first box if the proposed conservatee's regular residence is the same address as listed in Item 4a. Check the second box if her regular residence address is not listed in Item 4a. Then fill in her full address in the space provided.

CAPTION: PAGE 3 OF THE CONFIDENTIAL SUPPLEMENTAL INFORMATION

- After the words "CONSERVATORSHIP OF (Name)," in capital letters fill in the proposed conservatee's full name.

Item 4c(1): Check this box if the proposed conservatee is living in her permanent residence. Then check one of the following boxes.

Item 4c(1)(i): Check this box if the present plan is for the proposed conservatee to keep living in her home.

Item 4c(1)(ii): Check this box if you expect the proposed conservatee will need to be moved to a different place. You must also complete Item 4c(3).

Item 4c(1)(iii): Check this box if you did not check Item 4c(1)(i) or 4c(1)(ii). For example, you may be unsure about whether the proposed conservatee will keep living in her home or expect she will only live there temporarily. If you check this box, you must also complete Item 4c(3).

Item 4c(2): Check this box if the proposed conservatee is not living in her permanent residence. Then check the following boxes that apply.

Item 4c(2)(i): Check this box if you expect the proposed conservatee to return to her home. Fill in the date by which you expect this to occur. For example, this might apply if the proposed conservatee is temporarily in a hospital or nursing facility.

Item 4c(2)(ii): Check this box if you do not expect the proposed conservatee to return to her home. If you check this box, you must also complete Item 4c(3).

CONFIDENTIAL

CONSERVATORSHIP OF (NAME):		CASE NUMBER:
DORTHEA JOHNSON	PROPOSED CONSERVATEE	

4. RESIDENCE (continued)

c. **Ability to live in residence***   The proposed conservatee is

(1) [X] living in his or her residence and

    (i) [X] will continue to live there unless circumstances change.

    (ii) [ ] will need to be moved after a conservator is appointed (specify supporting facts below in 4c(3)).

    (iii) [ ] other (specify and give supporting facts below in 4c(3)).

(2) [ ] not living in his or her residence and

    (i) [ ] will return by (date):   (specify supporting facts below in 4c(3)).

    (ii) [ ] will not return to live there (specify supporting facts below).

    (iii) [ ] other (specify and give supporting facts below in 4c(3)).

(3) [ ] Supporting facts (specify if required):   [ ] Specified in Attachment 4.

5. ALTERNATIVES TO CONSERVATORSHIP*   Petitioner has considered the following alternatives to conservatorship and found them to be unsuitable or unavailable to the proposed conservatee (specify alternatives considered and reasons each is unsuitable or unavailable):   [ ] Reasons specified in Attachment 5.

a. Voluntary acceptance of informal or formal assistance (reason unsuitable or unavailable):

    Proposed conservatee is in a coma and unable to authorize anyone to handle her finances or make health care decisions for her.

b. Special or limited power of attorney (reason unsuitable or unavailable):

    Proposed conservatee is in a coma and is unable to sign legal documents.

c. General power of attorney (reason unsuitable or unavailable):

    See Item 5b above.

d. Durable power of attorney for [X] health care [X] estate management (reason unsuitable or unavailable):

    See Item 5b above.

e. Trust (reason unsuitable or unavailable):

    See Item 5b above.

f. Other alternatives considered (specify and give reason each is unsuitable or unavailable):

(Continued on reverse)

CONFIDENTIAL SUPPLEMENTAL INFORMATION
(Probate Conservatorship)

*If this item is not applicable, complete item 8.
Page three of four

Item 4c(2)(iii): Check this box if the proposed conservatee is not living in her permanent residence and you did not check Item 4c(2)(i) or 4c(2)(ii). For example, you may be unsure about whether the proposed conservatee will return to live in her home or expect she will return there temporarily. If you check this box, you must also complete Item 4c(3).

Item 4c(3): Check this box if you are providing any supporting facts for Items 4c(1) or 4c(2). If there is enough room on the form to provide an explanation, fill it in there. Otherwise, check the box before the words "Specified in Attachment 4" and prepare an Attachment 4 following the instructions in Chapter 3, Section H2e.

Item 5: Review Chapter 2, Section B, to complete this item. You may check the box before the words "Reasons specified in Attachment 5" and prepare an Attachment 5 following the instructions in Chapter 3, Section H2e. Or, if there is enough room on the form, fill in Items 5a through 5f there. For each item, state in your own words why the alternative is unsuitable or unavailable. For example, the proposed conservatee may be unable or unwilling to sign legal documents delegating authority to anyone else.

Item 5a: See Chapter 2, Section B.

Items 5b-c: See Chapter 2, Section B2a.

Item 5d: See Chapter 2, Sections B1a and B2a.

Item 5e: See Chapter 2, Section B2d.

Item 5f: See Chapter 2, Section B.

CAPTION: PAGE 4 OF THE CONFIDENTIAL SUPPLEMENTAL INFORMATION

- After the words "CONSERVATORSHIP OF (Name)," in capital letters fill in the proposed conservatee's full name.

Item 6a: Check this item only if you know what health services, social services or help with financial management the proposed conservatee received last year.

Items 6a(1)-(3): Complete all items that apply. Check the first box if the proposed conservatee received services listed in the item during the last year. Or check the second box if those services were not provided. If there is not room in the space below to explain the services or

why they were not provided, check the box before the words "Explained in Attachment …" and prepare an attachment following the instructions in Chapter 3, Section H2e.

Item 6b: Check this box only if you don't know all the services that were provided to the proposed conservatee during the last year. Then check the box before each category of which you have no knowledge.

Items 7a-f: Here you refer to the sources of information you relied upon to complete Items 1 through 6 of this form. For each item, check the box to indicate whether the facts are based on your own knowledge or someone else's declaration—which must be attached to the form.

Item 8: You may have skipped some items in this form because you are only seeking one type of conservatorship (person or estate), or because some of the items do not apply. Check the box to indicate any items you left blank. Then either indicate the reasons in the space provided or check the box before the words "Reasons specified in Attachment 8" and prepare an attachment following the instructions in Chapter 3, Section H2e.

Item 9: Check this box. If you are not attaching any additional pages, fill in the word "None." Otherwise, count up and enter the total number of pages to be attached.

Item 10: Leave this item blank.

Date and Signature: Fill in today's date at the bottom of the page. To the left of the signature line, type or clearly print your name in capital letters, and sign your name in the space provided.

CONFIDENTIAL

CONSERVATORSHIP OF (NAME):	CASE NUMBER:
DORTHEA JOHNSON PROPOSED CONSERVATEE	

6. SERVICES PROVIDED* (complete a or b, or both a and b)

   a. [X] During the year before this petition was filed,

      (1) **health services** [X] were provided [ ] were not provided to the proposed conservatee (explain):
        [X] Explained in Attachment 6a(1).

      (2) **social services** [ ] were provided [X] were not provided to the proposed conservatee (explain):
        [ ] Explained in Attachment 6a(2).

      (3) **estate management assistance** [ ] was provided [X] was not provided to the proposed conservatee (explain):
        [ ] Explained in Attachment 6a(3).

   b. [ ] Petitioner has **no knowledge** of what [ ] social services [ ] health services [ ] estate management assistance were provided to the proposed conservatee during the year before this petition was filed. Petitioner has no reasonable means of determining what services were provided.

7. SUPPORTING FACTS (AFFIDAVITS) The information provided above is stated

   a. Item 1: [X] on petitioner's own knowledge [ ] in an affidavit (declaration) by another person attached as Attachment 1a.
   b. Item 2: [X] on petitioner's own knowledge [X] in an affidavit (declaration) by another person attached as Attachment 2a.
   c. Item 3: [X] on petitioner's own knowledge [X] in an affidavit (declaration) by another person attached as Attachment 3a.
   d. Item 4: [X] on petitioner's own knowledge [ ] in an affidavit (declaration) by another person attached as Attachment 4a.
   e. Item 5: [X] on petitioner's own knowledge [ ] in an affidavit (declaration) by another person attached as Attachment 5a.
   f. Item 6: [X] on petitioner's own knowledge [ ] in an affidavit (declaration) by another person attached as Attachment 6a.

8. ITEMS NOT APPLICABLE The following items on this form were not applicable to the proposed conservatee:

   [ ] 2 [ ] 3 [ ] 4b [ ] 4c [ ] 5 [ ] 6 (specify reasons each item is not applicable):
   [ ] Reasons specified in Attachment 8.

9. [X] Number of pages attached: ___3___

10. DECLARATION   I declare under penalty of perjury under the laws of the State of California that the foregoing is true and correct.

Date: August 10, 19__

ANTONIA COREZONE
. . . .
      (TYPE OR PRINT NAME)

▶ *Antonia Corezone*
      (SIGNATURE OF PETITIONER)

GC-312 (New July 1, 1990)   **CONFIDENTIAL SUPPLEMENTAL INFORMATION**   *If this item is not applicable, complete item 8.
(Probate Conservatorship)   Page four of four

D. (Proposed) Order Appointing Court Investigator

THIS FORM GIVES DIRECTIONS to a court investigator to interview the proposed conservatee and determine whether he approves of the conservatorship. The investigator will also talk to the proposed conservatee periodically after the conservatorship has been established. The guidelines for the court investigator are set out by California law (Probate Code §§1825(a)(3), 1826, 1850-1852) and are covered in Chapter 7.

 Some courts use a short local form for the court investigator and do not require this form. Check with your court.

CAPTION: ORDER APPOINTING COURT INVESTIGATOR

- Fill in the caption following the general instructions in Chapter 3, Section H2b.
- After the words "Order Appointing Court Investigator," check the box just before the word "Conservatorship." Do not check the box before the words "Limited Conservatorship"—that is beyond the scope of this book.

After the words "TO (name)," leave the space blank. This will be completed by the clerk when you file your papers.

Item 1: Check the box. Then read the entire item so you will understand what is being requested of the court investigator.

Item 1e(1): After the words "the attorney, if any, for the petitioner," type in your name and the words "In Pro Per." Then go to Item 2.

Item 2: Skip this entire item unless you completed Item 1g of the petition, because the proposed conservatee is unable to make any medical decisions for his own treatment.

Check the first box if you checked Item 1g of the petition and are requesting the authority to make all medical decisions for the proposed conservatee. Then read Items 2a through 2d so you understand exactly what is being requested of the court investigator.

Skip the second box, which applies to temporary conservatorships where the proposed conservator wants to change the proposed conservatee's residence. This is beyond the scope of this book.

CAPTION: PAGE 2 OF THE ORDER APPOINTING COURT INVESTIGATOR

- After the words "CONSERVATORSHIP OF (Name)," in capital letters fill in the proposed conservatee's full name. Check the box before the words "proposed conservatee."

Item 2d(1): After the words "the attorney, if any, for the petitioner," type in your name and the words "In Pro Per." Now go on to Item 3.

Item 3: Check this box.

Items 3a-g: Read these items so you will understand what is being requested of the court investigator.

Items 3h-m: Skip all of these items.

Item 4: If you are not attaching any additional pages, fill in the word "None." Otherwise, count up and enter the number of total pages to be attached.

The form is now complete. Do not fill in the date or signature line. The judge will complete these when she signs the order.

ATTORNEY OR PARTY WITHOUT ATTORNEY *(Name and Address)*:	TELEPHONE NO.:	FOR COURT USE ONLY

ESTHER GOLDSTEIN   (916) 555-1212
23 Z Street
Sacramento, CA 95842

ATTORNEY FOR *(Name)*:   In Pro Per

SUPERIOR COURT OF CALIFORNIA, COUNTY OF   Sacramento
STREET ADDRESS: 720 Ninth Street
MAILING ADDRESS:
CITY AND ZIP CODE: Sacramento, CA 95814
BRANCH NAME:

CONSERVATORSHIP OF THE [ ] **PERSON** [X] **ESTATE OF** *(NAME)*:

HERMAN STONE

[ ] CONSERVATEE [X] PROPOSED CONSERVATEE

ORDER APPOINTING COURT INVESTIGATOR
[X] Conservatorship [ ] Limited Conservatorship

CASE NUMBER:

TO *(name)*:

You are hereby appointed Court Investigator in the matter entitled above.

1. [X] **Prior to appointment of a conservator** YOU ARE DIRECTED TO
   a. personally interview and inform the proposed conservatee of the contents of the citation, the nature, purpose, and effect of the proceedings, and of the right to oppose the proceeding, attend the hearing, have the matter tried by jury, be represented by counsel, and have legal counsel appointed by the court if unable to retain an attorney.
   b. determine
      (1) whether it appears that the proposed conservatee is unable or unwilling to attend the hearing.
      (2) whether the proposed conservatee wishes to contest the establishment of the conservatorship; and whether the proposed conservatee objects to the proposed conservator, or whether he or she prefers another person to act as conservator.
      (3) whether the proposed conservatee wishes to be represented by counsel, and if so, whether counsel has been retained, and if not, the name of an attorney the proposed conservatee wishes to retain.
      (4) whether the proposed conservatee desires the court to appoint legal counsel if the proposed conservatee has not retained an attorney.
      (5) whether the appointment of legal counsel would be helpful to the resolution of the matter or is necessary to protect the interests of the proposed conservatee if the proposed conservatee does not plan to retain legal counsel and has not requested the court to appoint legal counsel.
      (6) whether the proposed conservatee is capable of completing an affidavit of voter registration.
   c. review (i) the allegations of the petition as to why the appointment of a conservator is required and (ii) the statements in the **Confidential Supplemental Information** *(form No. GC-312)* and refer to the supplemental information in making your determinations.
   d. at least five days before the hearing, report your findings in writing to the court, including in your report the proposed conservatee's express communications concerning the following:
      (1) representation by legal counsel;
      (2) whether the proposed conservatee is not willing to attend the hearing, does not wish to contest the establishment of the conservatorship, and does not object to the proposed conservator or prefer that another person act as conservator.
   e. at least five days before the date set for hearing, mail a copy of your report to all of the following:
      (1) the attorney, if any, for the petitioner;   ESTHER GOLDSTEIN/In Pro Per
      (2) the attorney, if any, for the proposed conservatee;
      (3) [ ] other persons ordered by the court *(specify names and addresses in Attachment 1e)*.
   f. [ ] other *(specify in Attachment 1f)*.

2. [X] **Before the court grants an order relating to medical consent under section 1880 of the Probate Code**
   [ ] **Before the court grants an order under section 2253 of the Probate Code authorizing the temporary conservator to change the residence of the temporary conservatee**
   YOU ARE DIRECTED TO
   a. personally interview and inform the conservatee of the contents of the petition, the nature, purpose, and effect of the proceedings, and of the right to oppose the petition, attend the hearing, and be represented by legal counsel.

(Continued on reverse)

Form Approved by the
Judicial Council of California
GC-330 [Rev. July 1, 1990]

ORDER APPOINTING COURT INVESTIGATOR
(Probate Conservatorship)

Probate Code. §§ 1454,
1826, 1851

CONSERVATORSHIP OF *(NAME)*:		CASE NUMBER:
HERMAN STONE ☐ CONSERVATEE ☒ PROPOSED CONSERVATEE		

2. *(continued)*
b. determine
   (1) whether it appears that the conservatee is unable or unwilling to attend the hearing.
   (2) whether the conservatee wishes to contest the petition.
   (3) whether the conservatee wishes to be represented by counsel, and if so, whether counsel has been retained, and if not, the name of an attorney the conservatee wishes to retain.
   (4) whether the conservatee desires the court to appoint legal counsel if the conservatee has not retained an attorney.
   (5) whether the appointment of legal counsel would be helpful to the resolution of the matter or is necessary to protect the interests of the conservatee if the conservatee does not plan to retain legal counsel and has not requested the court to appoint legal counsel.
   (6) *(for change of residence only)* determine whether the proposed change of place of residence is required to prevent irreparable harm to the conservatee and whether no means less restrictive of the conservatee's liberty will suffice to prevent the harm.
c. at least five days before the hearing on medical consent or at least two days before the hearing on change of residence, report your findings in writing to the court, including in your report the conservatee's express communications concerning representation by legal counsel and whether the conservatee is not willing to attend the hearing and does not wish to contest the petition.
d. at least five days before the date set for hearing on medical consent or at least two days before the hearing on change of residence, mail a copy of your report to all of the following:
   (1) the attorney, if any, for the petitioner;   ESTHER GOLDSTEIN/In Pro Per
   (2) the attorney, if any, for the conservatee;
   (3) ☐ other persons ordered by the court *(specify names and addresses in Attachment 2d).*
e. ☐ other *(specify in Attachment 2e).*

3. ☒ **Duties after appointment of conservator** YOU ARE DIRECTED TO
a. visit and personally inform the conservatee that he or she is under a conservatorship and of the name of the conservator.
b. determine whether the conservatee wishes to petition the court for termination of the conservatorship.
c. determine whether the conservatee is still in need of the conservatorship.
d. determine whether the conservatee is capable of completing an affidavit of voter registration.
e. determine whether the conservator is acting in the best interests of the conservatee.
f. inform the court immediately if you are unable at any time to locate the conservatee.
g. as may be necessary, visit personally with the conservator and other persons to determine whether the conservator is acting in the best interest of the conservatee.
h. ☐ *(for conservatorships existing on December 31, 1980, in which the conservatee has not been adjudged incompetent)* determine whether an order should be made under section 1873 of the Probate Code broadening the capacity of the conservatee.
i. ☐ determine whether the present condition of the conservatee is such that the terms of the court order under sections 1873 or 1901 of the Probate Code should be modified or that the order should be revoked.
j. ☐ determine whether the conservatee still lacks the capacity to give informed consent for any form of medical treatment.
k. ☐ *(for limited conservatorship only)* make a recommendation regarding the continuation or termination of the limited conservatorship.
l. mail at the same time your report is certified to the court a copy to the conservator, to the attorneys of record for the conservator and conservatee, and to any other persons as ordered by the court *(specify names and addresses in Attachment 3l).*
m. ☐ other *(specify in Attachment 3m).*
The visit and investigation under item 3 shall be so conducted that it is completed and your findings are certified in writing to the court not less than 15 days before the expiration of one year from the date the conservator was appointed. Visits and investigations shall be made biennially thereafter, with written findings certified to the court not less than 15 days before the date of biennial court review.

4. Number of pages attached: <u>None</u>

Date: _____   _____
                                                   JUDGE OF THE SUPERIOR COURT

GC-330 (Rev. July 1, 1990)   **ORDER APPOINTING COURT INVESTIGATOR**   Page two
                                         (Probate Conservatorship)

E. (Proposed) Order Appointing Probate Conservator

BEFORE YOU CAN BECOME A CONSERVATOR, a judge must sign an order appointing you and defining the scope of your authority. You must prepare the order for the judge to sign.

> **CAPTION:** ORDER APPOINTING PROBATE CONSERVATOR
>
> - Fill in the caption following the general instructions in Chapter 3, Section H2b.
> - Do not check the box before the words "Limited Conservatorship." That is beyond the scope of this book.

Item 1: Give information about when the hearing will be held, and who will attend. If there are any changes or additions, they may be filled in at the hearing by the judge or clerk.

Item 1a: Leave this item blank. It will be completed at the hearing.

Item 1b: This item may be left blank. It will be completed at the hearing.

Item 1c: Check this box. Then fill in your full name.

Item 1d: Check this box. Then after the words "Attorney for petitioner (name)," fill in your full name, followed by the words "In Pro Per."

Item 1e: Leave this item blank. It is for situations where the proposed conservatee is being represented by his own attorney. If he is, you'll need the help of a lawyer. (See Chapter 17.)

Item 1f: Check only one box in this item, depending on whether the proposed conservatee will attend the hearing. If he will attend, check the box before the word "present." If he cannot attend because of medical inability, check the box before the words "unable to attend." If he knows about the conservatorship but is not willing to attend, check the box before the words "able but unwilling to attend." Leave the last box, entitled "out of state," blank—it is beyond the scope of this book.

Item 2a: Leave this item blank.

Item 2b: After the word "(Name)," fill in the full name of the proposed conservatee listed in the petition.

Items 2b(1)-(3): You may need to check more than one box in this item. Check Item 2b(1) if you are seeking conservatorship of the person or person and estate. Check Item 2b(2) if you are seeking conservatorship of the estate or person and estate. Check Item 2b(3) if the proposed conservatee signed a document nominating you as conservator. (See the instructions for Items 1c and 3c(1) of the petition in Section A.)

Item 2c(1): Check this box if the proposed conservatee is at least 18 years of age.

Items 2c(2)-(4): Skip these items unless the proposed conservatee is under 18 years of age. Check Item 2c(2) if you want the conservatorship to go into effect when the proposed conservatee turns 18—a likely situation if you are now serving as legal guardian of a minor who will need further care. Check Item 2c(3) if the proposed conservatee is under 18 years of age and is married. Check Item 2c(4) if the proposed conservatee is under 18 years of age and is divorced.

Item 2d: To complete this item, look at Item 1g of the Petition for Appointment of Probate Conservator. Check this box if you checked Item 1g in the petition, meaning that you believe the proposed conservatee does not have the capacity to consent to any form of medical treatment. Then check the second box only if the proposed conservatee belongs to a religion which professes healing by prayer alone.

Item 2e: Skip this item. Like Item 1d of the Petition for Appointment of Probate Conservator, it is beyond the scope of this book.

Item 2f: Leave this item blank.

Item 2g: Skip this item. It is for situations where the proposed conservatee is being represented by his own attorney or a court-appointed attorney. If he is, you'll need to hire a lawyer.

Items 2h-k: Leave these items blank.

ATTORNEY OR PARTY WITHOUT ATTORNEY *(Name and Address)*:	TELEPHONE NO.:	FOR COURT USE ONLY
JESUS GONZALES 2020 College Ave. East Santa Rosa, CA 95401	(707) 555-1212	

ATTORNEY FOR *(Name)*: In Pro Per

SUPERIOR COURT OF CALIFORNIA, COUNTY OF SONOMA

STREET ADDRESS: Hall of Justice, Room 100-J

MAILING ADDRESS: P.O. Box 11187

CITY AND ZIP CODE: Santa Rosa, CA 95406

BRANCH NAME:

CONSERVATORSHIP OF THE [X] **PERSON** [X] **ESTATE OF** *(NAME)*:

CLARITA GONZALES

CONSERVATEE

ORDER APPOINTING PROBATE CONSERVATOR
[ ] **Limited Conservatorship**

CASE NUMBER:

1. The petition for appointment of conservator came on for hearing as follows *(check boxes c, d, e, and f to indicate **personal presence**)*:
   a. Judge *(name)*:

   b. Hearing date: Time: [ ] Dept.: [ ] Room:
   c. [X] Petitioner *(name)*: JESUS GONZALES
   d. [X] Attorney for petitioner *(name)*: JESUS GONZALES/In Pro Per
   e. [ ] Attorney for person cited *(name, address, and telephone)*:

   f. Person cited was [ ] present [ ] unable to attend [x] able but unwilling to attend [ ] out of state.

2. THE COURT FINDS
   a. All notices required by law have been given.
   b. *(Name)*: CLARITA GONZALES
      (1) [X] is unable properly to provide for his or her personal needs for physical health, food, clothing, or shelter.
      (2) [ ] is substantially unable to manage his or her financial resources or to resist fraud or undue influence.
      (3) [X] has voluntarily requested appointment of a conservator and good cause has been shown for the appointment.
   c. Conservatee
      (1) [X] is an adult.
      (2) [ ] will be an adult on the effective date of this order.
      (3) [ ] is a married minor.
      (4) [ ] is a minor whose marriage has been dissolved.
   d. [ ] There is no form of medical treatment for which the conservatee has the capacity to give an informed consent.
      [ ] Conservatee is an adherent of a religion defined in section 2355(b) of the Probate Code.
   e. [ ] Granting the conservator powers to be exercised independently under section 2590 of the Probate Code is to the advantage and benefit and in the best interest of the conservatorship estate.
   f. [ ] Conservatee is not capable of completing an affidavit of voter registration.
   g. [ ] Attorney *(name)*: has been appointed by the court as legal counsel to represent the conservatee in these proceedings. The cost for representation is: $
      The conservatee has the ability to pay [ ] all [ ] none [ ] a portion of this sum *(specify)*: $
   h. [ ] Conservatee need not attend the hearing.
   i. [ ] The appointed court investigator is *(name, address, and telephone)*:

   j. [ ] *(for limited conservatorship only)* The limited conservatee is developmentally disabled as defined in section 1420 of the Probate Code.
   k. [ ] The conservator is a private professional conservator as defined by Probate Code section 2341 who has filed with the county clerk the confidential statement required by Probate Code section 2342.

(Continued on reverse)

Form Approved by the Judicial Council of California GC-340 [Rev. July 1, 1990]	**ORDER APPOINTING** **PROBATE CONSERVATOR** **(Probate Conservatorship)**	Do NOT use this form for a temporary conservatorship. Probate Code, § 1830

CONSERVATORSHIP OF *(NAME)*:

CLARITA GONZALES   CONSERVATEE

CASE NUMBER:

3. THE COURT ORDERS

   a. *(Name)*:   JESUS GONZALES
      (Address): 2020 College Ave. East   *(Telephone)*:   (707) 555-1212
                Santa Rosa, CA 95401

       is appointed [X] conservator [ ] limited conservator of the PERSON of *(name)*:   CLARITA GONZALES
       and Letters shall issue upon qualification.

   b. *(Name)*:   JESUS GONZALES
      (Address): 2020 College Ave. East   *(Telephone)*:   (707) 555-1212
                Santa Rosa, CA 95401

       is appointed [X] conservator [ ] limited conservator of the ESTATE of *(name)*:   CLARITA GONZALES
       and Letters shall issue upon qualification.

   c. [X] Conservatee need not attend the hearing.

   d. (1) [ ] Bond is not required.
       (2) [X] Bond is fixed at: $ 30,000   to be furnished by an authorized surety company or as otherwise
            provided by law.
       (3) [X] Deposits shall be made at *(specify institution)*:   Bank of the World, Santa Rosa, CA
            in the amount of: $ 65,000   and receipts filed.

   e. [ ] For legal services rendered, [ ] conservatee [ ] conservatee's estate [ ] parents of the minor [ ] minor's
       estate   shall pay to *(name)*:   the sum of: $
            [ ] forthwith [ ] as follows *(specify terms, including any combination of payors)*:

   f. [ ] Conservatee is disqualified from voting.

   g. [ ] Conservatee lacks the capacity to give informed consent for medical treatment and the conservator of the person is granted
       the powers specified in section 2355 of the Probate Code. [ ] The treatment shall be performed by an accredited
       practitioner of the religion defined in section 2355(b) of the Probate Code.

   h. [ ] The conservator of the estate is granted authorization under section 2590 of the Probate Code to exercise independently
       the powers specified in Attachment 3h [ ] subject to the conditions provided.

   i. [ ] Orders relating to the capacity of the conservatee under sections 1873 or 1901 of the Probate Code as specified in At-
       tachment 3i are granted.

   j. [ ] Orders relating to the powers and duties of the conservator of the person under sections 2351-2358 of the Probate Code
       as specified in Attachment 3j are granted.

   k. [ ] Orders relating to the conditions imposed under section 2402 of the Probate Code upon the conservator of the estate
       as specified in Attachment 3k are granted.

   l. [ ] Other orders as specified in Attachment 3l are granted.

   m. [ ] The inheritance tax referee appointed is *(name and address)*:

   n. [ ] *(for limited conservatorship only)* Orders relating to the powers and duties of the limited conservator of the person under
       section 2351.5 of the Probate Code as specified in Attachment 3n are granted.

   o. [ ] *(for limited conservatorship only)* Orders relating to the powers and duties of the limited conservator of the estate under
       section 1830(b) of the Probate Code as specified in Attachment 3o are granted.

   p. [ ] *(for limited conservatorship only)* Orders limiting the civil and legal rights of the limited conservatee as specified in At-
       tachment 3p are granted.

   q. [X] This order is effective on the [X] date signed [ ] date minor attains majority *(date)*:

4. Number of boxes checked in item 3: _____ 7

5. [X] Number of pages attached: _____ None

Date: _____
                                                 JUDGE OF THE SUPERIOR COURT
                                               [ ] SIGNATURE FOLLOWS LAST ATTACHMENT.

GC-340 (Rev. July 1, 1990)   **ORDER APPOINTING**   Page two
                        PROBATE CONSERVATOR
                        (Probate Conservatorship)

CAPTION: PAGE 2 OF THE ORDER
APPOINTING PROBATE CONSERVATOR

- After the words "CONSERVATORSHIP OF (Name)," in capital letters fill in the proposed conservatee's complete name.

Item 3a: If you are only seeking conservatorship of the estate, skip this item. If you are seeking conservatorship of the person or person and estate, fill in your complete name, address and telephone number in the spaces provided. Check the box between the words "is appointed" and "conservator." Then, after the words "of the person of (name)," fill in the complete name of the proposed conservatee listed in the petition.

Item 3b: If you are only seeking conservatorship of the person, skip this item. If you are seeking conservatorship of the estate or person and estate, fill in your full name, address and telephone number in the spaces provided. Check the box between the words "is appointed" and "conservator." Then, after the words "of the estate of (name)," fill in the full name of the proposed conservatee listed in the petition.

Item 3c: Leave this item blank.

Item 3d: To complete this item, you will need to look at Item 1c of the Petition for Appointment of Probate Conservator.

Item 3d(1): Check this box if you checked Item 1c(1) of the petition.

Item 3d(2): Check this box if you checked Item 1c(2) of the petition. Then fill in the amount of bond requested in Item 1c(2) of the petition.

Item 3d(3): Check this box if you checked Item 1c(3) of the petition. Then fill in the name of the financial institution and the amount of money or property to be deposited, as indicated in Item 1c(3) of the petition. If you want to use the interest or dividends to support the proposed conservatee, type in the words, "Withdrawal of *["interest" or "dividends" depending on the type of assets being placed in a blocked account]* does not require a court order."

Item 3e: Leave this item blank.

Item 3f: Skip this item.

Item 3g: Skip this item unless you checked Item 2d of this form. If you checked Item 2d, also check the first box

in this item. If the proposed conservatee follows a religion which believes in healing by prayer only, also check the second box in this item.

Item 3h: Skip this item.

Item 3i: Skip this item.

Item 3j: Skip this item.

Item 3k: Skip this item.

Item 3l: Skip this item unless you completed Item 1k of the Petition for Appointment of Probate Conservator. If so, prepare an Attachment 3l following the instructions in Chapter 3, Section H2e, and use the accompanying sample as a guide.

ATTACHMENT 3L TO ORDER

[Use lined paper and prepare the heading following the Sample Attachment Page in Chapter 3, Section H2e.]

[ ] ORDER GRANTING ALLOWANCE

The court orders that *[your name]*, conservator of the *["estate" or "person and estate"]* of *[name of proposed conservatee]* pay the conservatee an allowance of $_____ per *[week/month]* .

[ ] ORDER WAIVING ACCOUNTS

Accounts for the conservatorship of the *["estate" or "person and estate"]* of *[name of proposed conservatee]* are waived pursuant to Probate Code Section 2628.

Item 3m: Leave this item blank.

Items 3n-p. Skip these items. They pertain to limited conservatorships, which are beyond the scope of this book.

Item 3q: Check the first box. If you are seeking conservatorship of an adult (someone over age 18), check the box before the words "date signed," and go on to the next item. If you are seeking conservatorship of a minor (someone under the age of 18), check the box before the words "date minor attains majority (date)," and fill in the date the minor will turn 18.

Item 4: Count all of the boxes you checked in Item 3, and fill in that number.

Item 5: Check the box. If you are not attaching any additional pages, fill in the word "None," and leave the date and signature line blank. They will be completed at the hearing by the judge. If you are adding any attachment pages, fill in the number. If so, cross out the date and judge's signature line on the second page of the form and check the box before the words "signature follows last attachment." Then type in a date and judge's signature line—identical to the one you crossed off—at the bottom of the very last page attached.

F. Citation for Conservatorship

BY LAW, THE PROPOSED CONSERVATEE must be notified of the conservatorship unless she is the one petitioning for it (Probate Code §1823(a)). The Citation for Conservatorship gives information to the proposed conservatee about how the conservatorship will affect her life.

> **CAPTION:** CITATION FOR CONSERVATORSHIP
>
> - Fill in the caption following the general instructions in Chapter 3, Section H2b.
> - Do not check the box next to the words "Limited Conservatorship." That is beyond the scope of this book.

After the words "TO (name)," fill in the full name of the proposed conservatee in capital letters.

Item 1: Leave the long rectangular box blank for now. This is the space for the time and place of the hearing that you will obtain from the clerk when you file your papers with the court.

Immediately below the box in Item 1, after the words "located at (street address and city)," fill in the court's street address again, even though it's already listed in the caption at the top of the form. Then check all the boxes that apply:

- If you are seeking conservatorship of the person, check the box before the words "unable to provide for your personal needs."

- If you are seeking conservatorship of the estate, check the box before the words "unable to manage your financial resources."

- Check the box before the word "conservator." Do not check the box before the words "limited conservator."

- Depending on the type of conservatorship you are seeking, check the boxes before the words "person," "estate," or both.

Finally, after the word "(name)," fill in your full name in capital letters.

Item 2: Leave this item blank, but read it to find out what information the proposed conservatee is being given.

Item 3: Depending on the type of conservatorship you are seeking, check the boxes before the words "person," "estate," or both. Also read the rest of the item.

Item 4: Leave this item blank, but read it.

Item 5: Leave this item blank.

Leave the rest of the front of the form blank. When you file the Citation for Conservatorship with the court, the clerk will date the form, sign on the line after the words "Clerk, by," and stamp the court's seal in the box in the lower left corner.

Also leave the back of the form blank for now. The back of the form is a proof of service, which indicates that the proposed conservatee was given papers telling him about the conservatorship. You will complete the proof of service later, after filing your papers with the court and having the proposed conservatee served. But make sure that you photocopy the back of the form when you make copies.

ATTORNEY OR PARTY WITHOUT ATTORNEY (NAME AND ADDRESS):	TELEPHONE NO.:	FOR COURT USE ONLY
ANANDABAI HARI 123 Main Street San Diego, CA 92131	(619) 555-1212	

ATTORNEY FOR (NAME): In Pro Per

SUPERIOR COURT OF CALIFORNIA, COUNTY OF San Diego

STREET ADDRESS: 220 West Broadway
MAILING ADDRESS: P.O. Box 128
CITY AND ZIP CODE: San Diego, CA 92112-4104
BRANCH NAME:

CONSERVATORSHIP OF THE [X] PERSON [X] ESTATE OF (NAME):

DJUNA JOSHEE   Proposed Conservatee

CITATION FOR CONSERVATORSHIP ☐ **Limited Conservatorship**	CASE NUMBER:

THE PEOPLE OF THE STATE OF CALIFORNIA,

To (name):   DJUNA JOSHEE

1. You are hereby cited and required to appear at a hearing in this court

on (date):	at (time):	in ☐ Dept:	☐ Div:	☐ Rm.:

located at (street address and city):   220 West Broadway, San Diego, CA 92112

and to give any legal reason why, according to the verified petition filed with this court, you should not be found to be [X] unable to provide for your personal needs [X] unable to manage your financial resources and by reason thereof, why the following person should not be appointed [X] conservator ☐ limited conservator of your [X] person [X] estate (name):   ANANDABAI HARI

2. A conservatorship of the person may be created for a person who is unable properly to provide for his or her personal needs for physical health, food, clothing or shelter. A conservatorship of the property (estate) may be created for a person who is unable to resist fraud or undue influence, or who is substantially unable to manage his or her own financial resources. "Substantial inability" may not be proved solely by isolated incidents of negligence or improvidence.

3. At the hearing a conservator may be appointed for your [X] person [X] estate. The appointment may affect or transfer to the conservator your right to contract, to manage and control your property, to give informed consent for medical treatment, to fix your place of residence, and to marry. You may also be disqualified from voting if you are found to be incapable of completing an affidavit of voter registration. The judge or the court investigator will explain to you the nature, purpose, and effect of the proceedings and answer questions concerning the explanation.

4. You have the right to appear at the hearing and oppose the petition. You have the right to hire an attorney of your choice to represent you. The court will appoint an attorney to represent you if you are unable to retain one. You must pay the cost of that attorney if you are able. You have the right to a jury trial if you wish.

5. *(for limited conservatorship only)* You have the right to oppose the petition in part by objecting to any or all of the requested duties or powers of the limited conservator.

Dated: . . . . Clerk, by _____ _____ _____ , Deputy

SEAL	
	(Proof of service on reverse)

Form Approved by the
Judicial Council of California
Revised Effective January 1, 1981
GC-320(81)

CITATION FOR CONSERVATORSHIP
AND PROOF OF SERVICE

G.   Notice of Hearing

THIS FORM TELLS EVERYONE entitled to notice when and where the conservatorship petition will be heard in court. When you file your papers with the court, the clerk will give you a hearing date and place. This information will be written or stamped on the Notice of Hearing form.

CAPTION: NOTICE OF HEARING

- Fill in the caption following the general instructions in Chapter 3, Section H2b.
- After the words "NOTICE OF HEARING," check the box just before the word "Conservatorship."

Item 1: After the words "NOTICE is given that (name)," fill in your full name in capital letters exactly as you entered them on the Petition for Appointment of Probate Conservator. Just below, after the words "(representative capacity, if any)," enter the words that apply: "proposed conservator of the person," or "proposed conservator of the estate," or "proposed conservator of the person and estate." Just below this, after the words "has filed (specify)," enter the words "Petition for Appointment of Probate Conservator of the" followed by the words "person," "estate," or "person and estate" as appropriate.

Item 2: Skip this item

Item 3: Leave the rectangular box blank for now. This is the space for specific information on the time and place of the hearing that you will obtain from the clerk. As noted, the clerk will fill in this part of the form when you file it, listing the hearing date and time as well as the courtroom in which the hearing will be held, by checking the box next to "Dept.," "Div.," or "Rm.," depending on how the court refers to its courtrooms.

Immediately below Item 3, fill in the court's street address again, even though it's already listed in the caption at the top of the form.

Below the court's street address is a space for the date. Leave this blank for now—the court clerk will later stamp it in. Check the box before the words "Clerk, by" to indicate that the clerk will be signing the original Notice of Hearing. Do not check the box before the word "Attorney," since only a licensed attorney or a court clerk can sign the original.

Leave the rest of the front side of the form blank. When you file the Notice of Hearing with the court, the clerk will date the form and sign on the line after the words "Clerk, by."

Also leave the back of the form blank for now. The back of the form is a proof of service, which tells how documents were mailed to people entitled to notice of the conservatorship. You will complete the proof of service later, after you file your papers with the court and have people served. But make sure you also photocopy the back of the form when you make copies.

ATTORNEY OR PARTY WITHOUT ATTORNEY (NAME AND ADDRESS):	TELEPHONE NO.:	FOR COURT USE ONLY
WINSTON GREEN 20 Any Street Martinez, CA 95607	(415) 555-1212	

ATTORNEY FOR (NAME):   In Pro Per

SUPERIOR COURT OF CALIFORNIA, COUNTY OF   Contra Costa
STREET ADDRESS: 725 Court Street
MAILING ADDRESS: P.O. Box 911
CITY AND ZIP CODE: Martinez, CA 94553
BRANCH NAME:

☐ GUARDIANSHIP ☒ CONSERVATORSHIP OF THE ☒ PERSON ☒ ESTATE OF
(NAME):
      JOHN GREEN

☐ Minor ☒ Conservatee

CASE NUMBER:

NOTICE OF HEARING
☐ Guardianship ☒ Conservatorship ☐ Limited Conservatorship

This notice is required by law. This notice does not require you to appear in court, but you may attend the hearing if you wish.

1. NOTICE is given that (name):   WINSTON GREEN
   (representative capacity, if any):   Proposed conservator of the person and estate
   has filed (specify):   Petition for Appointment of Probate Conservator of the
                           person and estate

   reference to which is made for further particulars.

2. ☐ The petition includes an application for the independent exercise of powers under section 2590 of the Probate
   Code. Powers requested are ☐ specified below ☐ specified in attachment 2.

3. A hearing on the matter will be held

on (date):	at (time):	in ☐ Dept:	☐ Div:	☐ Rm.:

   located at (address of court):   725 Court Street
                                     Martinez, CA 94553

Dated: . . . .   ☒ Clerk, by _____ , Deputy

                                              ☐ Attorney _____
                                                              (Signature)

This notice was mailed on (date): . . . . , at (place): . . . ., California.

(Continued on reverse)

Form Approved by the
Judicial Council of California
Revised Effective January 1, 1981
GC-020(81)
**NOTICE OF HEARING
GUARDIANSHIP OR CONSERVATORSHIP**

H. Additional Documents Required by Local Rule

DEPENDING ON YOUR SITUATION and the court in which you are filing, you may need to prepare one or a number of additional local court forms. Copies of local forms are not supplied in this book, so you must contact your court to arrange to obtain copies. Here is information about some—but not all—local forms. Check with your local court to find out its requirements.

1. Declaration for Filing and Assignment

In some counties, a special form is required if you want your case to be filed in a branch court—which may be closer and more convenient—rather than the main court. Branch courts are discussed in Chapter 3, Section G, along with information about where to file your papers. If you will be filing in a branch court, call the court clerk and ask if there is a local declaration for filing and assignment form, and find out how to obtain a copy. If you don't complete the form, there may be some confusion about where your case is filed, and that can create problems for you later. These forms are self-explanatory and easy to complete.

2. Address Information

You may need to complete a form that gives the current addresses of the proposed conservator and conservatee. The form may be a notification to the court or a referral form for the probate court investigator.

The form in Appendix B in the back of the book entitled Notification to Court of Address of Conservator and Conservatee contains substantially the same information as most local court forms. However, many courts require that you use their forms, so to be on the safe side, check with the court and find out its requirements.

 An easy-to-use form such as the Notification to Court of Address of Conservator and Conservatee should be used to notify the court within 30 days of the date you or the conservatee moves. Remember to make extra copies before you fill it out; you or the conservatee might move again.

CAPTION: NOTIFICATION TO COURT OF ADDRESS OF CONSERVATOR AND CONSERVATEE

- Fill in the caption following the general instructions in Chapter 3, Section H2b.

Item 1: In the spaces provided, fill in your name. Then enter your current street and mailing address (if different from your street address), your city, state, zip code and telephone number.

Item 2: Fill in the conservatee's name. Next, enter the conservatee's current street and mailing address (if different from the street address), city, state, zip code and telephone number.

Item 3: You will be filling in most of the same information here as requested in Item 1. In the first space, fill in your name. In the second space, fill in your capacity in the conservatorship. This would be (proposed) conservator of the person, (proposed) conservator of the estate, or (proposed) conservator of the person and estate. Next enter your street and mailing address (if different from your street address), your city, state, zip code and telephone number. Then fill in the date the form was completed. In the spaces indicated, fill in and sign your name.

3. Private Professional Conservators

People who are in the business of serving as conservators are called "private professional conservators." People are usually considered private professional conservators if they have at least two conservatees who are unrelated by blood or marriage. However, the court can require someone with only one conservatee who is not related by blood or marriage to comply with the requirements of private professional conservators (Probate Code §§2341). Private professional conservators must file several extra documents with the court, comply with a background fingerprint check and pay an annual fee (Probate Code §§2340-2343). If the court requires you to comply with the procedures of private professional conservators, you'll need to do your own research or hire a lawyer. (See Chapter 17.)

PARTY WITHOUT AN ATTORNEY *(Name and Address):*	TELEPHONE NO:	FOR COURT USE ONLY
TAKITA YU 5303 104th Avenue Berkeley, CA 94704 *In Pro Per*	(415) 555-1212	

NAME OF COURT:	ALAMEDA SUPERIOR COURT
STREET ADDRESS:	Courthouse
MAILING ADDRESS:	1225 Fallon, Room 105
CITY AND ZIP CODE:	Oakland, CA 94612
BRANCH NAME:	Northern

CONSERVATORSHIP OF THE ☒ PERSON ☐ ESTATE OF (NAME):

    CH'IU CHIN

                                CONSERVATEE

NOTIFICATION TO COURT OF ADDRESS OF CONSERVATOR AND CONSERVATEE	CASE NUMBER

1. **INFORMATION ABOUT CONSERVATOR**

    NAME OF CONSERVATOR: TAKITA YU

    STREET ADDRESS: 5303 104th Avenue

    CITY: Berkeley   STATE: CA   ZIP: 94710

    MAILING ADDRESS (If different):   ---

    CITY: STATE: ZIP:

    PHONE NUMBER (Include area code):   (415)   555-1212

2. **INFORMATION ABOUT CONSERVATEE**

    NAME OF CONSERVATEE: CH'IU CHIN

    STREET ADDRESS: 20½ Stargate Street

    CITY: Oakland   STATE: CA   ZIP: 94612

    MAILING ADDRESS (If different):   ---

    CITY: STATE: ZIP:

    PHONE NUMBER (Include area code):   (415)   555-1212

3. **INFORMATION ABOUT COMPLETION OF THIS FORM:**

    NAME: TAKITA YU

    CAPACITY (e.g., Conservator):   Conservator of estate

    STREET ADDRESS: 5303 104th Avenue

    CITY: Berkeley   STATE: CA   ZIP: 94710

    MAILING ADDRESS (If different):   ---

    CITY: STATE: ZIP:

    PHONE NUMBER (Include area code):   (415)   555-1212

Date: August 10, 19__

TAKITA YU
....
          (TYPE OR PRINT NAME)

Takita Yu
          (SIGNATURE OF PERSON WHO SERVED PAPERS)

NP   **NOTIFICATION TO COURT OF ADDRESS (CONSERVATORSHIP)**

FILING YOUR PAPERS WITH THE COURT

AFTER YOU HAVE FILLED IN and signed the initial conservatorship documents following the instructions in Chapter 4, review them carefully. Make sure any additional pages are numbered and stapled to the appropriate documents. Be sure that all the proper boxes are checked, everyone's name is spelled correctly and any necessary signatures have been obtained.

A. Check Local Filing Rules

SOME COURTS HAVE SPECIAL LOCAL RULES about how papers must be prepared and filed there. Many of these rules don't seem logical or even sensible, but if you use a court which has them, you have no choice but to comply.

1. Obtain Information From Clerk

When you have completed your documents, call the probate court. Tell the clerk that you have prepared the Judicial Council forms for a conservatorship, and want to know if any local forms are required.[1]

---

[1] The clerk might not give you this information, claiming it's giving legal advice. If so, you can check a copy of the court's probate policy manual. (See Chapter 17, Section D2.)

If any additional forms are mandated by the court's local rules, they'll probably have to do with the required court investigation. Arrange to get copies. You usually can get forms either by going to court, or through the mail by sending a letter to the court explaining what forms you want, and enclosing a self-addressed, stamped envelope. There may be a charge for these additional forms; if so, it will be only a slight one.

Ask the clerk for this information you'll need to photocopy, prepare and file your papers with the court:

- How many copies of each document are required, and if that number includes a copy for the court investigator. Some courts require only the original, others require one or two extra copies.

- Whether documents must be two-hole punched at the top. Some courts prefer this, and other courts require it.

- Whether documents may be folded. Although it may seem ridiculous, a few courts have policies not to accept folded documents.

- Whether original documents must be marked with the word "original" and copies must be marked with the word "copy." Some courts prefer this, and others require it.

- Whether "bluebacks" are required. Bluebacks are simply blue paper stapled to the backs of court documents which identify the people involved in the legal action, the court and the document being filed. Courts that require bluebacks, such as those in Los Angeles, usually require them only for papers that are not preprinted forms. Bluebacks can be obtained from most large office supply stores.

B. Filing Fees and Court Costs

WHEN YOU FILE your conservatorship documents, you will be required to pay a filing fee of $182. In some counties, you may be required to purchase a *Handbook for Conservators* at a cost of $20 at the time you file your papers. Some counties also require that investigator's fees be paid when the conservatorship is filed. (See Chapter 7, Section E.)

For conservatorships of the estate, if you use your own money for filing fees, you may reimburse yourself from the conservatee's estate once you are appointed conservator.

If you have a very low income, you do not have to pay court fees and costs if you obtain court approval. People currently receiving AFDC, Food Stamps, County Relief, General Relief, General Assistance, SSI or SSP should have no problem qualifying for a fee waiver. You'll need to complete two easy forms, available from the clerk's office, where you give information about your financial situation and request that fees be waived:

- Application for Waiver of Court Fees and Costs; and
- Order on Application for Waiver of Court Fees and Costs.

If you are petitioning for conservatorship of the estate and have a very low income, you can still apply to have court fees and costs waived. However, once you are appointed conservator, you will need to reimburse the court using money from the estate.

C. Photocopy Documents

YOU'RE NOW READY to photocopy all the documents you've prepared. In addition to any extra copies the court may require, you'll need at least two for your own files— one to leave at home when you mail or take the documents to court in case the papers are lost or misplaced, and one to be file-stamped and returned to you. The documents and number of copies needed are set out in the accompanying chart.

You'll need extra copies of the Petition for Appointment of Probate Conservator—including all attachments—and the Notice of Hearing for each relative listed in the Conservatorship Worksheet as well as the court investigator. And if the proposed conservatee is entitled to receive Veterans' Administration benefits, you'll need an extra copy for the Veterans' Administration.

You can make all the copies of completed forms before you file them with the court, and have each copy file-stamped, or you can file your papers with the court and then make photocopies of the file-stamped papers, whichever is more convenient. Many of the forms have printing on both sides; either make single-sided copies and staple the pages together before filing them with the court, or make two-sided copies. After the copies are made, comply with any requirements your court may have for two-hole punching, folding, or marking the papers as originals or copies. Always staple together the pages of any documents consisting of two or more pages.

 Do not staple the Confidential Supplemental Information to the Petition for Appointment of Probate Conservator. It must be filed separately.

CONSERVATORSHIP DOCUMENTS TO BE FILED WITH THE COURT

Depending on your situation, you may be filing all or just some of these documents:

YOU MUST FILE	NUMBER OF COPIES NEEDED*
Petition for Appointment of Probate Conservator—if you completed a **Declaration of Medical or Accredited Practitioner**, it should be attached to the petition as Attachment 6c (Chapter 4, Sections A and B)	Original + 3 + one copy for the investigator, if required by local rules + one copy for each relative listed in the Conservatorship Worksheet + one copy for the Veterans' Administration, if the proposed conservatee is eligible for VA benefits
Confidential Supplemental Information (Chapter 4, Section C)	Original + 3
Notice of Hearing (Chapter 4, Section G)	Original + 3 + one copy for each relative listed in the Conservatorship Worksheet + one copy for the Veterans' Administration, if the proposed conservatee is eligible for VA benefits
Citation for Conservatorship (Chapter 4, Section F)	Original + 3
(Proposed) Order Appointing Probate Conservator (Chapter 4, Section E)	Original + 3

YOU MAY FILE	NUMBER OF COPIES NEEDED*
(Proposed) Order Appointing Court Investigator (Chapter 4, Section D)	Original + 2
Fee waiver documents, if you have a very low income and are applying for a waiver of court fees and costs (Section B of this chapter)	Original + 2
Declaration for Filing and Assignment (Chapter 4, Section H1)	Original + 2
Notification to Court of Address of Conservator and Conservatee (Chapter 4, Section H2)	Original + 2

*The number of copies listed include one which you leave at home when you take or send your papers to the court. You may need one or two additional copies of all documents if required by the court's local rules.

D. Filing Papers With the Court

WHAT HAPPENS WHEN YOU FILE your papers might be a mystery to you, especially if you've never gone to court before. Fortunately, it's really quite simple. When you first deliver the papers to the court, your conservatorship case will be assigned a case number and a new file will be opened. Each time you deliver an additional document to the court, the clerk will file it and make it part of the official record of your case.

1. Take or Mail Papers to the Court

You file documents simply by mailing them to the court or handing them across the counter at the court clerk's office. When the clerk receives your papers, he will file the original, which goes in your conservatorship case file, and may also keep one or two photocopies, depending on the local policy. You will get back any extra copies with rubber-stamped information in the upper right-hand corner, showing the date and often the time that the original was filed and indicating that the copy is a file-stamped copy.

When you first file your papers with the court, the clerk assigns the case a number. This will either be written or stamped in the caption part of the form. Once the case number has been assigned, put that number on all court papers you later complete. The case number is the court's system of keeping track of cases, and it will be printed on a file folder which is kept at the courthouse and contains your filed papers and notations of any court action on the case. If you ever need to get information about your case over the telephone, you must tell the clerk your case number.

You may choose to go to the court to file your papers in person, to make sure you haven't made a mistake or in case you want more information from the clerk. If you file your papers in person, give the filing clerk the required filing fee, the original documents and photocopies. The filing clerk will either file-stamp and return the copies to you or, in some of the larger courts, the clerk will have you stamp the copies.

If going to the courthouse is inconvenient, you can mail your documents to the court. Write a short letter to the clerk at the probate court and include your documents for filing along with the filing fee and a self-addressed, stamped envelope with the correct amount of postage. Ask the clerk to file the original documents, assign a hearing date and send extra date-stamped copies back to you.

APPLYING FOR A WAIVER OF COURT FEES AND COSTS

If you have a very low income and are applying to have court fees and costs waived, you must prepare documents requesting a fee waiver for filing with the court. (See Section B.) By law, you may file your conservatorship papers at the same time as the fee waiver request, without paying a filing fee. Some clerks may tell you that you'll have to wait a few days for a judge to grant the fee waiver before you can file your papers. If this happens, be polite but firm. Tell the clerk that you are entitled to file your papers under Rule 985 of the California Rules of Court. If for some reason the clerk still will not file your papers, ask to speak with a supervisor, and give the supervisor the same information.

If you file your documents in person, you may have to take the fee waiver documents to be reviewed and filed by a clerk in a different department or courtroom from the probate court's filing desk. To find out the procedure, ask the filing clerk where to file fee waiver documents.

Once your fee waiver documents have been filed, the court must decide whether to grant the request within five days. If the court doesn't deny your request within that time, your fees and costs are automatically waived (Calif. Rules of Court 985(e)). If your fee waiver request is granted, the court might send you a document indicating that your request was granted, but in the real world, courts usually don't send out anything. However, if your fee waiver request is denied, the Order on Waiver of Court Fees and Costs will be marked to indicate this. You will then have to pay court fees and costs within 10 days. If you don't get any notification from the court within a week after you file your fee waiver documents, call the clerk to find out whether your fees were waived.

a   Get a Hearing Date

The filing clerk will give you a date and time when you will appear in court before a judge or probate commissioner who decides whether to grant the conservatorship. This court appearance is called a "hearing." You must appear in court, even if it seems unnecessary because everyone involved is in favor of the conservatorship.

Generally, the filing clerk automatically assigns you a hearing date unless you ask to choose your own. If you make it clear from the start that you want to select a date, you'll probably have better luck getting a convenient date and time. If you select the date, choose one at least four weeks from the date you file your papers with the court. That way you will have enough time to have everyone served with papers at least 20 days before the hearing.

The clerk will need to complete information about the date, time and location of the hearing in boxes provided for this purpose in two forms:

- Notice of Hearing (Item 3); and
- Citation for Conservatorship (Item 1).

The clerk should date and sign the two documents in the spaces provided for this purpose. The clerk will also imprint the court's seal in the lower left-hand corner of the Citation for Conservatorship.

Sometimes clerks will only fill in the information on the original document, and ask you to "conform" the rest of the copies, meaning that you must write in the same information on additional copies of forms. Some courts may require you to fill out a simple local form specifically requesting a hearing date.

b. Original Documents Clerk Returns

Most courts do not file the original Notice of Hearing and Citation for Conservatorship until everyone entitled to notice has been served. After you file your initial papers with the court, make sure that you have the original signed Notice of Hearing and Citation for Conservatorship. You can tell which are the originals because they are signed by the clerk, while the copies should be stamped with the clerk's name. If you're not sure whether you have the originals, ask the clerk. If the clerk gives original documents back to you, make sure you keep them in a safe place. You will need to file them with the court along with proofs of service after everyone entitled to notice has been served.

 Make sure the hearing date, place and time are completed by the clerk on the Notice of Hearing and Citation for Conservatorship.

c. (Proposed) Orders Are Not Returned

When you give your papers to the court clerk, he will stamp and return most of them. However, certain documents require a judge's authorization first, and will not be returned to you. At a hearing, the judge will decide whether to sign the orders. Once she does, you will get copies of the signed papers as long as you submitted extra photocopies. To alert you to these papers, they are flagged by the word "(proposed)," indicating that you won't get them back from the court until a judge has reviewed and approved their contents.

2. Follow Local Court Procedures

Some local court rules require that you complete additional forms at the time of filing or after you file the initial conservatorship papers. These additional local court forms usually pertain to the court investigation. (See Chapter 7 for more information about investigations.)

If the filing clerk gives you more forms to complete, look at them carefully before leaving the court. The forms probably will be self-explanatory, but if you are confused by something, you might be able to get additional information from the clerk. However, understand that court clerks can't answer every question you might have. By law, they're forbidden to direct you in any way that might be considered giving legal advice—only lawyers can do that. If you need more help, the court clerk might refer you to a local service that gives free or low-cost legal assistance. (Or see Chapter 17 for information about doing your own research or finding a lawyer.)

Make sure you understand when all forms are due back at the court, and follow those deadlines carefully. For example, if a form must be completed and returned within 10 days and you don't get it back for 11 or 12, you may lose your scheduled hearing date. That could mean a lot of extra work, since you'd have to obtain a new hearing date and have those entitled to notice served again.

CHAPTER 6

SERVING THE
CONSERVATORSHIP PAPERS

AT LEAST TWENTY DAYS before the date of the hearing at which a judge or commissioner will decide whether to grant the conservatorship, certain people must be notified of the conservatorship proceeding through a procedure called "service of process."

A. What Is "Service of Process"?

SERVICE OF PROCESS takes place when someone personally delivers or sends legal documents by mail. The person who receives the documents is "served." There are specific rules about how documents must be served for the service to be legally valid. Having documents properly served is an essential part of the process of obtaining a conservatorship. The proposed conservatee must be served personally unless he is able and willing to sign a document acknowledging receipt of the papers. Everyone else may be served by regular U.S. mail.

The reason for requiring this formal notice is simple: anyone affected by the conservatorship has a legal right to be notified of the proceedings. Anyone notified may then contest your appointment as conservator by filing papers with the court or appearing before the judge at the hearing. Before you can have a court hearing on the conservatorship, the court must be assured that everyone entitled to know about the hearing was given notice or cannot be located.

If you don't follow service rules to the letter, you may have to start over—rescheduling your case for a new hearing date and having everyone served all over again—even if only one person was served incorrectly.

B. Service Requirements

LEGAL NOTICE OF THE CONSERVATORSHIP must be served on the proposed conservatee, his relatives and possibly agencies entitled to notice at least 20 days before the hearing date.[1] Documents served by mail must be **mailed** at least 20 days before the hearing date. Documents personally served must be **received** at least 20 days before the hearing date. If you don't know the name or address of some of the proposed conservatee's relatives, you will need to follow a special procedure for locating them. (That is covered in Section F of this chapter.)

The law forbids you, the person filing for the conservatorship, from serving the papers yourself. But service can be carried out by any other person 18 years of age or older, as long as they're not listed anywhere on the Petition for Appointment of Probate Conservator.

The accompanying chart summarizes what documents everyone must receive, and what type of service is required.[2] If you do not comply with these requirements, the conservatorship will not be heard on the scheduled hearing date. To be safe, have the papers served immediately after you file them with the court.

C. How to Serve Proposed Conservatee

REGARDLESS OF WHETHER the proposed conservatee wants the conservatorship or even understands it, at least 20 days before the hearing date he must be served with three documents:

- Citation for Conservatorship;
- Petition for Appointment of Probate Conservator— including all of the attachments; and
- Notice of Hearing.

---

[1] Although only 15 days notice is required for service by mail, we advise you to give at least 20 days notice. The hearing date is listed in the Notice of Hearing in the box in Item 3.

[2] Special service is required if the proposed conservatee is a patient of or on leave from a state mental hospital, or if the proposed conservatee is developmentally disabled (Probate Code §§1461, 1461.4). Both situations are beyond the scope of this book and require the help of an attorney. (See Chapter 17.)

The proposed conservatee may be served in one of two ways—either personally or by Notice and Acknowledgment of Receipt. Read Sections C1 and C2, below, and select the method most convenient for you. Once documents are served, you must complete a form stating that service was completed and have the process server sign it.

 If neither type of service is possible—perhaps because the conservatee is out of California—consult a lawyer. (See Chapter 17.)

1. Personal Service

For personal service, copies of the documents must be handed to or left for the proposed conservatee by a process server. You can have a friend or family member who isn't involved in the conservatorship case deliver the papers. Or you can hire either a professional process server or marshal or sheriff's deputy. Hiring a professional for process serving should only be necessary if the proposed conservatee doesn't live nearby and you don't know anyone who can serve him with papers. Bear in mind that the proposed conservatee may be upset by an unfamiliar person delivering legal papers, so if possible, arrange to have a friend or family member hand them to him. Let the proposed conservatee know in advance that someone other than you will be giving him legal documents about the conservatorship, so he knows what to expect.[3]

If you have documents served by a relative, neighbor or friend, give careful instructions about how to do it. The server must give copies of the legal papers to the proposed conservatee. This, of course, means that the server must actually see and be able to talk to him. If the server does not know the proposed conservatee, she should make sure she has the right person by asking before handing him the papers.

---

[3] This book covers conservatorship situations where the proposed conservatee agrees with or does not object to the conservatorship. If the proposed conservatee does not want the conservatorship, consult a lawyer. (See Chapter 17.)

SERVICE REQUIREMENTS		
WHO MUST BE SERVED	DOCUMENTS SERVED	TYPE OF SERVICE
Proposed conservatee	• **Petition for Appointment of Probate Conservator**—including all attachments • **Notice of Hearing** • **Citation for Conservatorship**	Personal (Section C1) or by Notice and Acknowledgment of Receipt (Section C2)*
Relatives of proposed conservatee (from Conservatorship Worksheet—see Chapter 3, Section F)	• **Petition** • **Notice of Hearing**	Mail (Section D)
Veterans' Administration (if required—see Section D1b)	• **Petition** • **Notice of Hearing**	Mail (Section D)
Court Investigator (if required by local rule—see Section D1c of this chapter)	• **Petition** • **Notice of Hearing** • **Order Appointing Court Investigator** (or local forms for court investigation)	Mail (Section D)
*If neither type of service is possible—perhaps because the conservatee is out of California—consult a lawyer. (See Chapter 17.)		

If the proposed conservatee does not take the papers—perhaps because he is in a coma or is too sick or weak to respond—the proposed conservatee can still be served. The server should put the papers on the ground or as close to the proposed conservatee's feet as possible and say something like, "This is for you" or "You have been served."

The server should never pick the papers up once they have been served in this manner. If she does, the service will be invalidated and will have to be done again. The server should never try to force the proposed conservatee to take the papers—that may subject the process server (or even you) to a lawsuit for battery. Your server should understand that personal service is not complete if she simply leaves the papers with someone other than the proposed conservatee, on the porch or in the mailbox (which is illegal under Postal Service regulations).

If you decide instead to use a process serving firm, get a recommendation from a paralegal or attorney, if you know one. Or check the Yellow Pages for process servers.

Since the firm will charge for serving—usually a set fee plus mileage—you may want to shop around. You will need to provide copies of the papers to be served, and the date by which service must be completed. Since the process server won't be familiar with the person she's serving, you'll need to help out by providing as much detailed information as possible, such as the best hours to find the proposed conservatee at home, and a detailed physical description. It's even better if you can provide a recent photograph of the proposed conservatee.

If you choose to have a marshal or deputy serve the papers, call the marshal's office or civil division of the county sheriff's office to find out who serves court papers in your county. You then send or take to that office copies of the papers to be served, pay a fee (usually around $20), and fill out a form giving information such as the physical description of the person to be served and the best hours to find him at home or work.

2. Service by Notice and Acknowledgment of Receipt

If the proposed conservatee is willing and able to cooper-ate, you can satisfy the legal requirements for personal service by mailing her the required papers along with one extra Notice and Acknowledgment of Receipt form which she must sign and return to you within 20 days. If you mail documents to the proposed conservatee, you might not have enough time before the hearing date to accomplish this type of personal service, since she must be served 20 days before the hearing date.[4] However, if you'll be visit-ing with the proposed conservatee before then, she can return the signed Notice and Acknowledgment of Receipt to you.

a   Notice and Acknowledgment of Receipt

Prepare this document on lined pleading paper following the instructions in Chapter 3, Section H3, using the accompanying sample as a guide. Or obtain a preprinted copy of the Judicial Council Notice and Acknowledgment of Receipt form, available from your county clerk's office or local law library. Note that the Acknowledgment of Receipt portion of the form should be left blank for the conservatee to date and sign the form before returning it to you.

---

[4] By law, only 15 days notice is required for service by mail, but we suggest you send this 30 days before the hearing date to give the proposed conservatee time to get the documents back to you.

[Use lined paper and prepare the caption following the Sample Pleading in Chapter 3, Section H3.]

NOTICE AND ACKNOWLEDGMENT OF RECEIPT

To *[conservatee's name]*:

The documents indicated below are being served pursuant to Section 415.30 of the California Code of Civil Procedure. Your fail-ure to complete this form and return it to me within 20 days may subject you to liability for the payment of any expenses incurred in serving these documents on you in any other manner permitted by law.

This form must be signed by you personally or by a person authorized by you to acknowledge receipt of these documents. Section 415.30 provides that these documents are deemed served on the date you sign the Acknowledgment of Receipt below, if you return this form to me.

Dated: *[today's date]*   _____
                              [your name]

ACKNOWLEDGMENT OF RECEIPT

This acknowledges receipt of: *[list the full title of each document being served]*.

(To be completed by recipient):

Date of receipt: _____
(Signature of person acknowledging receipt)

Date this form is signed: _____

_____
(Type or print your name)

b. Copy and Have Notice Sent

Make two copies of the Notice and Acknowledgment of Receipt, and keep one for your records. Then put the following in an envelope addressed to the proposed conservatee, with the correct amount of postage affixed:

- Signed original and one copy of the Notice and Acknowledgment of Receipt;
- A self-addressed, stamped envelope; and
- One copy of each of the documents you listed in the Acknowledgment of Receipt section of the form.

After you have gathered all of the above documents and made sure that you have an extra copy of everything for your files, have someone else mail them. The person who mails the papers must be at least 18 years old, must not be involved in the conservatorship case, and must live or work in the county where the mailing occurs. The server should simply put the envelope, with correct postage attached, in a U.S. mailbox. Let the proposed conservatee know the documents have been mailed so she can expect them.

Do not have the papers served by certified or registered mail, since someone must sign for this kind of mail before it is delivered. If the proposed conservatee isn't home when the envelope arrives, she must make a special trip to the post office—an inconvenience that could lead to further delays.

3. Proof of Service

Once service has taken place, complete a proof of service form. This form is a declaration by someone (other than you) stating how and when the documents were served. After the form is filled in, the person who serves the papers must sign it. The proof of service is located on the second page of the original Citation for Conservatorship.

CAPTION: PAGE 2 OF THE CITATION FOR CONSERVATORSHIP

- In the space provided, fill in the proposed conservatee's name. Also fill in the case number.

Item 1a: Fill in the full name of the proposed conservatee.

Item 1b: Fill in the full name of the person served—almost always the proposed conservatee.

Item 1c: Check this box if the proposed conservatee was personally served, and check the box before the word "home" or "business," depending on where he was served. If the proposed conservatee was served by Notice and Acknowledgment of Receipt, skip this item and go on to Item 1d.

Item 1c(1): Fill in the date the person was served.

Item 1c(2): Fill in the time the person was served.

Item 1c(3): Fill in the address where the person was served.

Item 1d: Check this box if the person was served by Notice and Acknowledgment of Receipt. If the proposed conservatee was personally served, skip this item and go on to Item 2.

Item 1d(1): Fill in the date the documents were mailed.

Item 1d(2): Fill in the city and state where the documents were mailed. Note that this must be in the county where the person mailing them either lives or works.

Item 2: Check only one box in this item.

Item 2(a): Check this box if the proposed conservatee was personally served.

Item 2(b): Check this box if the proposed conservatee was sent documents by mail along with a Notice and Acknowledgment of Receipt. Attach the original Notice and Acknowledgment of Receipt signed both by the sender and the person who received the documents.

Item 2(c): Leave this box blank. It is beyond the scope of this book.

Item 2(d): Leave this box blank. It is beyond the scope of this book.

CONSERVATORSHIP OF (NAME):		CASE NUMBER:
HARLEY DAVIS	Proposed Conservatee	127

PROOF OF SERVICE
(Citation for Conservatorship)   Page 2

1. I served the citation and petition as follows:

   a. Person cited (name):   HARLEY DAVIS

   b. Person served (name):   HARLEY DAVIS

   c. [X] By delivery at [x] home ☐ business   (1) date: March 18, 19__
      (2) time: 2:30 P.M.   (3) address: 8407 Tamara Lane
                                                               Palm Springs, CA 92262

   d. ☐ By mailing (1) date:
              (2) place:

2. Manner of service (check proper box)
   a. [X] **Personal service.** By personally delivering copies to the person served. (CCP 415.10)
   b. ☐ **Mail and acknowledgment service.** By mailing (by first-class or airmail) copies to the person served, together with two copies of the form of notice and acknowledgment and a return envelope, postage prepaid, addressed to the sender. (CCP 415.30) **(Attach completed acknowledgment of receipt.)**
   c. ☐ **Service on person outside state** (CCP 415.40) (specify manner of service):
   d. ☐ **Other manner authorized by court** ☐ specified below ☐ specified in attachment 2d.

3. At the time of service I was at least 18 years of age and not a party to this proceeding.

4. Fee for service: $ -0-

5. Person serving
   a. [X] Not a registered California process server.
   b. ☐ Registered California process server.
   c. ☐ Employee or independent contractor of a registered California process server.
   d. ☐ Exempt from registration under Bus. & Prof. Code 22350(b).

   e. ☐ California sheriff, marshal, or constable.
   f. Name, address and telephone number and, if applicable, county of registration and number:

      Emma Frand
      950 Mystreet
      Anycity, CA 94382

I declare under penalty of perjury under the laws of the State of California that the foregoing is true and correct and that this declaration is executed on (date): . . . . .
. . June 24, 19__ . . . .
at (place): . Anycity, California . . . .

_____
(Signature)

(For California sheriff, marshal or constable use only)
I certify that the forgoing is true and correct and that this certificate is executed on (date): . . . .
at (place): . . . ., California.

_____
(Signature)

Item 3: Leave this item blank. It simply states that the person who served the documents is at least 18 years old and not involved in the conservatorship action.

Item 4: If the process server charged a fee, fill in the amount paid.

Item 5: Check only one box in Items 5(a-e), then complete Item 5(f). If a professional process server or sheriff, marshal or constable served papers, he will complete this item.

Item 5(a): Check this box if the person who served the papers was not a registered California process server—for example, a friend or relative.

Item 5(b): If a professional process server served papers, he will complete this item.

Item 5(c): If a professional process server served papers, he will complete this item.

Item 5(d): Leave this item blank.

Item 5(e): If a sheriff, marshal or constable served the papers, she will complete this item.

Item 5(f): If a professional process server or sheriff, marshal or constable served papers, he will complete this item. Otherwise, fill in the business or residence address and telephone number of the person who served the documents. If the documents were served by mail along with a Notice and Acknowledgment of Receipt, make sure this address is in the same county where the mailing occurred.

Finally, have the person who served the documents fill in the date, city and state where the form was signed and sign the form on the signature line provided. Instructions on how to file proofs of service with the court are covered in Section E in this chapter.

D. How to Serve Relatives and Agencies

AT LEAST 20 DAYS before the hearing date the proposed conservatee's relatives and possibly some agencies must be sent two documents by regular mail:

- Petition for Appointment of Probate Conservator— including all of the attachments; and

- Notice of Hearing.[5]

1. Who Must Be Served?

Carefully read this section and note who is entitled to receive notice of the conservatorship proceeding.

a. Which Relatives Must be Served?

All of the proposed conservatee's close relatives must be served. Look at the Conservatorship Worksheet you completed in Chapter 3, Section F. In Part 1 you filled in the names and home addresses of these relatives who are entitled to service: the proposed conservatee's spouse, children, grandchildren, sisters and brothers, parents and grandparents.

In the rare situation where *none* of the above relatives are known, the relatives listed in Part 2 of the Conservatorship Worksheet must be served instead: spouse of a parent who is deceased, children of a spouse who is deceased, nieces and nephews (all children of proposed conservatee's brothers and sisters, including any who were adopted), and aunts and uncles. If no aunts and uncles are known or living, then you must serve the natural and adoptive first cousins (all children of proposed conservatee's aunts and uncles, including any who were adopted).

b. Veterans' Administration

Look at the Petition for Appointment of Probate Conservator you filed with the court. If you answered yes to Item 4b (checked the second box), you must serve the office of the Veterans' Administration (Probate Code §§1822, 1461.5). If you're not sure whether the proposed conservatee receives or is entitled to receive benefits, serve the Veterans' Administration.

There are several regional Veterans' Administration offices for California. To find the one closest to the court in which you filed the conservatorship, look in the government section of the telephone book. Call that number to obtain the correct address.

---

[5]You may need to send additional documents to the court investigator, as explained in Section D1c, below.

c. Court Investigator

Depending on local rules, you may need to have the court investigator served by mail with notice of the conservatorship proceeding. Some courts require that you file extra copies of all documents, which the court then forwards to the court investigator. Other courts require that you send copies of court documents directly to the court investigator.

If you're not *positive* that the court will forward copies of the conservatorship documents to the court investigator, have him served by mail. The court investigator should be served with copies of the Petition, Notice of Hearing and Order Appointing Court Investigator. If you completed any local forms pertaining to the investigation, also include copies. (Additional information on conservatorship investigations is contained in Chapter 7.)

2. Service by Mail

You cannot serve papers yourself, as you're involved in the conservatorship proceeding. You may, however, get the papers ready to be mailed and have someone else drop the envelopes in a mail box. Here's how to do that.

Write or type on envelopes the names and addresses of every person and agency who must be served. Prepare a separate envelope for each person, even if more than one lives at the same address.

Look at the first page of the Notice of Hearing. At the bottom of the page are the words "This notice was mailed on (date)." Fill in the date documents are being served. After the words "at (place)," fill in the city where they are being mailed.

Place one copy of the Petition for Appointment of Probate Conservator and Notice of Hearing in each envelope and seal the envelopes. Put on the amount of postage required for regular U.S. mail, unless someone lives outside of the United States, when it is better to use air mail service. Do not have the papers sent by certified or registered mail. It's an unnecessary expense, and can create delays if no one is home to sign for the mail.

Have someone mail the envelopes for you at least 20 days before the hearing date. The server must be at least 18 years old, must not be involved in the conservatorship proceeding and must live or work in the county where the mailing occurs. It's fine to ask a friend or relative to do it. There's no reason to pay a professional to mail your papers.

3. Proof of Service by Mail

Once service has taken place, complete the Proof of Service by Mail form located on the second page of the original Notice of Hearing. This form is a declaration by someone (other than you) stating how and when the documents were served. After the form is filled in, the person who served the papers must sign it.

Instructions for filling out a Proof of Service by Mail form that can be used for any documents being served by mail are contained in Chapter 9, Section E4b.

> **CAPTION:** PAGE 2 OF THE NOTICE OF HEARING
>
> • Check the boxes before the words "CONSERVATORSHIP" and "CONSERVATEE," and fill in the proposed conservatee's name after the words "CONSERVATORSHIP OF (Name)." Also fill in the case number.

Skip the first part of the form entitled "Clerk's Certificate of Posting/Mailing."[6] About a third of the way down the page are the words "Proof of Service by Mail." After the words "My residence or business address is," fill in the server's home or business address.

Check the box before the words "with a copy of the petition (title)." Then in the space provided, fill in the full name of the petition—for example, "Petition for Appointment of Probate Conservator."

Item (1): Fill in the date the documents were mailed.

Item (2): Fill in the city and state where the documents were mailed.

In the spaces indicated, fill in the date, city and state where this form will be signed by the server. Then fill in the server's name.

---

[6]In a few counties, the clerks will mail documents for you if requested.

☐ GUARDIANSHIP ☒ CONSERVATORSHIP OF (NAME): BERTHA SMITH ☐ Minor ☒ Conservatee	CASE NUMBER: 140

NOTICE OF HEARING—GUARDIANSHIP OR CONSERVATORSHIP
CLERK'S CERTIFICATE OF ☐ POSTING ☐ MAILING

Page 2

I certify that I am not a party to this cause and that a true copy of the foregoing Notice of Hearing—Guardianship or Conservatorship

1. ☐ (for sales under section 2543(c) of the Probate Code only) was posted at (address):

2. ☐ was mailed, first class, postage fully prepaid, ☐ with a copy of the petition (title):

in a sealed envelope addressed to each person whose name and address is given below.
I certify that the notice was posted or mailed and this certificate was executed on (date): . . . .
at (place): . . . . , California.

Clerk, by _____ , Deputy

PROOF OF SERVICE BY MAIL

I am over the age of 18 and not a party to this cause. I am a resident of or employed in the county where the mailing occurred. My residence or business address is: 1447 College Street, San Jose, CA 95112

I served the foregoing Notice of Hearing—Guardianship or Conservatorship ☒ with a copy of the petition (title):
Petition for Appointment of Probate Conservator
by enclosing a true copy in a sealed envelope addressed to each person whose name and address is given below and depositing the envelope in the United States mail with the postage fully prepaid.

(1) Date of deposit: Sept. 27, 19___ (2) Place of deposit (city and state): San Jose, CA

I declare under penalty of perjury under the laws of the State of California that the foregoing is true and correct and that this declaration is executed on (date): Sept. 27, 19___ at (place): San Jose, CA . . . . . .

. . . . JOHN SMITH . . . .   _____
(Type or print name)   (Signature of declarant)

NAME AND ADDRESS OF EACH PERSON TO WHOM NOTICE WAS MAILED

DAMIEN SMITH   2731 Oxford Dr.   Sunnyvale, CA 94089

MARTHA RODREGIEZ   233 Palos Lane   Stockton, CA 95209

CONCHA CREBES   807D Dolores   Thousand Oaks, CA 91362

HECTOR SMITH   9137 Sutter St. West   Sunnyvale, CA 94089

☐ List of names and addresses continued on attachment.

Complete the section entitled "Name and Address of Each Person to Whom Notice was Mailed." Fill in all the names and addresses of everyone to whom papers were mailed, following the guidelines of Section D1, above. If you need more room, check the box at the bottom of the page before the words "List of names and addresses continued on attachment." Then prepare an attachment entitled "Attachment to Notice of Hearing," following the instructions in Chapter 3, Section H2e. List the names and addresses of any additional people served.

Have the process server or court clerk sign on the appropriate line. Finally, turn to the first page of the Notice of Hearing. In the blanks provided on the last line of that page, make sure the date, city and state where the notice was mailed are filled in.

E. Copy and File Original Documents

YOU'RE NOW READY TO PHOTOCOPY the signed proofs of service located on the second pages of the original issued Citation for Conservatorship and the original signed Notice of Hearing. These papers should be filed at least five days before the hearing date, not including weekends or holidays.

Make at least two or three copies of both sides of the original Citation for Conservatorship and Notice of Hearing, if you have them. Otherwise, attach the original proofs of service to photocopies of those documents. Then file them with the court, following the instructions in Chapter 5, Section D. Obtain a date-stamped copy of each paper from the court. If you mail documents to the court, keep extra copies at home in case they are lost in the mail or misplaced at the court.

F. Unknown or Missing Relatives

IF YOU HAVE THE NAMES AND ADDRESSES of all living relatives listed on the Conservatorship Worksheet, skip this section. But you may be in the unlucky position of not knowing the names or addresses of all of the proposed conservatee's relatives who are entitled to notice. This means you will need to put in some time and effort trying to track down these relatives *before* the hearing date.

There is no legal requirement that you notify a person who simply can't be located. You must, however, do your very best to find and give that person notice. If, after doing everything reasonably within your power, you still can't locate the relative, a judge can allow for that relative not to be served. The judge has the right to decide what is reasonable, however, and may require that you try harder than you already have. There are no hard and fast rules about what an individual judge will require, but in general, courts are reluctant to dispense with notice to immediate family of a proposed conservatee.

This section gives a summary of some of the most stringent requirements in California for searching for relatives who are required to get notice of a conservatorship. Your county may be more lenient, depending on which relatives cannot be located, and on the attitude of the particular judge. Some judges expect you to spend at least three hours in the search for a close relative. It is best to follow all suggestions in this section when attempting to find the proposed conservatee's missing relatives. In your attempts to locate a missing relative:

- *Keep an accurate written record of your activities.* Write down the date of each attempt, and a simple explanation of what happened. For example: "September 1, 19___: Called Directory Assistance in Sacramento, California, requested telephone numbers and addresses for John Xerox, and there were no listings."

- *Keep copies of correspondence.* If you have mailed letters trying to track down missing relatives, keep copies of the letters and returned correspondence. If someone else conducts the search for missing relatives for you, have that person keep accurate records of those attempts. Follow up any leads you get.

- *Be discreet.* When checking with friends or employers who may know the missing relative, simply say that you are trying to contact the person. Don't volunteer information about the conservatorship or say that the person may have something to do with a court proceeding.

1. How to Locate Relatives

If you need to look for a missing relative, you may conduct the search yourself or get help from others, such as adult friends or relatives. Here are some sources to contact:

- *Telephone Company.* Check telephone directories and Directory Assistance in cities where the missing relative has lived recently. Most public libraries carry copies of telephone directories for many large cities, including areas outside of California.

- *Friends, Relatives and Former Employers.* Contact the missing relative's friends and relatives to see if they have leads on his whereabouts. If you know where the missing relative used to work, contact former employers to find out if they have an address, telephone number, or the name of someone else who might know how to locate the missing relative.

- *Last Known Address.* If the missing relative has moved and left a forwarding address, you can obtain it from the U.S. Post Office. Send a post card or envelope to the last known address with the words "Address Correction Requested" printed next to the old address, and list your return address on the envelope. You might check with the people living at the missing relative's last known address and the neighbors on both sides. If the last known address is a mental or penal institution, find out whether the institution's records are confidential or if you can obtain the missing relative's current address.

- *Voter Registration Records.* In California, you can find listings for registered voters which include their names, addresses and phone numbers. To look at these records, contact the registrar of voters for the county where you believe the relative lives. If the missing relative has moved within the same county, the registrar may have the new address.

- *Department of Motor Vehicles.* If the missing relative lives outside of California, contact the motor vehicle department in that state to find out how to obtain information on registered vehicles and drivers. If the missing relative lives in California, the California Department of Motor Vehicles (DMV) will not release address information without first contacting the person about whom information is sought (Vehicle Code §1808.21). Contact your local DMV office or write to the DMV, Division of Driver's Licenses, P.O. Box 2590, Sacramento, CA 95812.

- *Military Services.* If you think the missing relative is a member of the military, write to the personnel records branch of the appropriate military branch in Washington, D.C. You'll need to pay a fee (approximately $15), and request information as to whether or not the missing relative is on active duty in that branch of the military service.

2. Complete Documents for Missing Relatives

If, after carefully following the instructions in Section F1 of this chapter, you still can't find all of their names and addresses, you must prepare these documents to be submitted to the court:

- **Due Diligence Declaration** for each missing relative, which tells how you conducted the search; and

- **Order Dispensing Notice**, which asks a judge to waive notice requirements for any missing relatives.

a. Due Diligence Declaration

For each missing relative, you must prepare a separate document called a Due Diligence Declaration, which tells what steps you took to find the missing relative. If anyone helped you search, prepare a separate Due Diligence

Declaration for each relative that person tried to find. Use the accompanying sample as a guide, and give detailed descriptions of all attempts made to locate the missing relative.

[Use lined paper and prepare the caption following the Sample Pleading in Chapter 3, Section H3.]

DUE DILIGENCE DECLARATION

I, *[your name or name of person who searched for missing relative]*, declare that I am *[if you, "the petitioner and proposed conservator" or state relationship, such as "the sister of the proposed conservatee and friend of the petitioner"]*. I have made the following attempts to locate *[name of missing relative]*, who is the proposed conservatee's *[state relationship]*, but to date my efforts have been unsuccessful.

1. I checked in telephone directories for listings. The details of my attempts are: *[list the date each attempt was made, the city of the telephone directory and the results of the search, such as no one was listed under that name, or you called and it was the wrong person]*.

2. I checked with directory assistance. The details of my attempts are: *[list the date each attempt was made, the city or area code that was called and the results of the search, such as no one was listed under that name, or you called and it was the wrong person]*.

3. I checked with friends and relatives. The details of my attempts are: *[list the date each attempt was made, the name and relationship to the missing relative of each person who was contacted and the results of the search, such as a friend didn't know the whereabouts of the missing relative, or a brother gave a telephone number for the missing relative which had been disconnected]*.

4. I checked with former employers. The details of my attempts are: *[list the date each attempt was made, the name of each former employer who was contacted and the results of the search, such as the former employer had fired the missing relative and didn't know where he'd gone, or the former employer had the forwarding address of a business which went bankrupt two years ago]*.

5. I checked the last known residence address. The details of my attempts are: *[list the date each attempt was made and the results of the search, such as you went to the house and the missing relative was no longer living there and the tenant didn't know where he had moved, or the post office did not have a forwarding address on file]*.

6. I checked with voter registration records. The details of my attempts are: *[list the date each attempt was made, the county and state of each registrar of voters that was contacted and the results of the search, such as the missing relative was not registered to vote, or was no longer at the address listed with the registrar of voters]*.

7. I checked with the motor vehicles department. The details of my attempts are: *[list the date each attempt was made, the state in which the motor vehicles department was contacted and the results of the search, such as the missing relative was not registered with the motor vehicles department, the California DMV would not release address information or there was no current address listed]*.

8. *[If the person conducting the search contacted any other source, list the date each attempt was made and a detailed description of the results of the search, such as you checked with the army and there was no forwarding address on file, or you checked with the court where the missing relative had filed a divorce and there was not a current address listed in the court's files]*.

I declare under penalty of perjury under the laws of the State of California that the foregoing is true and correct.

Dated: *[today's date]*   _____
                              [your name]
                              Petitioner In Pro Per

b. (Proposed) Order Dispensing Notice

To get permission from a judge to waive notice for relatives, you must prepare an Order Dispensing Notice form. Before you begin filling out this form, have handy the Conservatorship Worksheet and all completed copies of the Due Diligence Declaration you completed in Section F2a, above. You will need to refer to these forms.

> **CAPTION:** ORDER DISPENSING NOTICE
>
> - Fill in the caption following the general instructions in Chapter 3, Section H2b.
> - Do not check the boxes before the words "GUARDIANSHIP" or "Minor," as these boxes only are used in guardianship proceedings.

Item 1: After the words "THE COURT FINDS that a petition for (specify)," fill in the words "conservatorship of the person," "conservatorship of the estate," or "conservatorship of the person and estate" depending on the type of conservatorship you are seeking.

Item 1a: Leave this item blank.

Item 1b: Leave this item blank. It applies to guardianships only.

Item 1c: Leave this item blank. It applies to guardianships only.

Item 1d: Leave this item blank.

Item 1e: Check this box if you cannot find certain of the proposed conservatee's relatives. Fill in the words, "There is good cause for dispensing with notice to the following people referred to in Section 1822 of the Probate Code, as they cannot with reasonable diligence be given notice" Then list all of the missing relatives and their relationships to the proposed conservatee.

Item 2: After the words "THE COURT ORDERS that notice of hearing on the petition for (specify)," enter the words "Petition for Appointment of Probate Conservator of the" followed by the words "person," "estate," or "person and estate" as appropriate.

Item 2a: Leave this item blank.

Item 2b: Check this box and again list the names of all of the conservatee's relatives you cannot locate. You may copy this from Item 1e.

The form is now complete. Leave the date and signature line blank. The judge will fill these in if and when she signs the order. Depending on your thoroughness in searching for missing relatives, and how close they are to the proposed conservatee, a judge may or may not sign the Order Dispensing Notice.

3. Obtain Signed Order Dispensing Notice

Call the probate court at least five days before the hearing date and explain that you could not find everyone entitled to notice of the conservatorship proceeding. Ask whether you should submit an Order Dispensing Notice and supporting declarations before the hearing date or bring them to the hearing. If you need to submit documents beforehand, make sure you know exactly where to take the papers. Your file may be in a special room where a probate clerk or examiner is reviewing it.

Some courts will want to review your papers and decide whether to waive notice before the hearing. Others will want them at the hearing itself. Once a judge has agreed that you don't need to serve a particular individual, she will sign the Order Dispensing Notice. Obtain copies of the signed order from the clerk.

 It's possible that a judge may want you to conduct a more thorough search before signing the Order Dispensing Notice. If so, the hearing could be continued to a later date to give you time to search. (See Chapter 8, Section C.)

ATTORNEY OR PARTY WITHOUT ATTORNEY (NAME AND ADDRESS):	TELEPHONE NO.:	FOR COURT USE ONLY
SUDDAM ASSAD 50 River Road Chico, CA 95926	(916) 555-1212	

ATTORNEY FOR (NAME):   In Pro Per

SUPERIOR COURT OF CALIFORNIA, COUNTY OF   Butte

STREET ADDRESS: 25 County Center Dr.

MAILING ADDRESS: Oroville, CA 95965-3373

CITY AND ZIP CODE:

BRANCH NAME:

☐ GUARDIANSHIP ☒ CONSERVATORSHIP OF (NAME):

ARMAD MOHAMMAD   ☐ Minor ☒ Conservatee

ORDER DISPENSING NOTICE

CASE NUMBER:

1. THE COURT FINDS that a petition for (specify):   Conservatorship of the person and estate
   has been filed and

   a. ☐ all persons entitled to notice of hearing have ☐ waived notice ☐ consented to the appointment of the
      proposed ☐ guardian ☐ conservator.

   b. ☐ (for guardianship only) the following persons cannot with reasonable diligence be given notice (names):

   c. ☐ (for guardianship only) the giving of notice to the following persons is contrary to the interest of justice
      (names):

   d. ☐ good cause exists for dispensing with notice to the following persons referred to in section 1460(b) of the
      Probate Code (names):

   e. ☒ other (specify):   There is good cause for dispensing with notice to
      the following people referred to in Section 1822 of the Probate
      Code, as they cannot with reasonable diligence be given notice:
      SAHID MOHAMMAD (brother); BUTEE BARRI (niece).

2. THE COURT ORDERS that notice of hearing on the petition for (specify):   Petition for Appointment
   of Probate Conservator of the Person and Estate
   a. ☐ is not required except to persons requesting special notice under section 2700 of the Probate Code.
   b. ☒ is dispensed with to the following persons (names):   SAHID MOHAMMAD (brother)
                                                                BUTEE BARRI (niece)

Dated: . . . .   _____
                                                          Judge of the Superior Court

Form Approved by the
Judicial Council of California
Effective January 1, 1981
GC-021(81)

ORDER DISPENSING WITH NOTICE
GUARDIANSHIP OR CONSERVATORSHIP

CONSERVATORSHIP INVESTIGATIONS

BECAUSE A CONSERVATORSHIP is such a serious measure, the court requires periodic investigations to make sure the arrangement is suitable. The word "investigation" might sound intimidating, but it isn't anything to worry about. This chapter gives an overview of conservatorship investigations, but each court has its own procedures. How the investigation proceeds depends both on local court rules and the particular case.

rules for the procedure you should follow. Some courts require that you complete a form giving information to the investigator, often due when you first file your conservatorship papers. (See Chapter 4, Section D.) Some courts require that you file an extra copy of all initial conservatorship papers with the court which the court forwards to the investigator. Others require that you have copies sent directly to the investigator. (See Chapter 6, Section D1c.)

A. The Court Investigator

INVESTIGATIONS ARE CONDUCTED by a person with training and experience in conservatorships. Depending on the county, the court investigator may play a very active role in conservatorships, and examine all documents filed in the case, including financial accounts. But in some counties, the court investigator's duties are limited to conducting periodic investigations and preparing reports of her findings.

1. Notifying the Investigator

To initiate an investigation, the court investigator must know that conservatorship papers were filed. Check local

B. Investigation Required Before Hearing

BY LAW, INVESTIGATIONS MUST BE CONDUCTED before the appointment hearing (Probate Code §1826).[1] The court investigator meets with the proposed conservatee, usually several weeks before the scheduled hearing date.

At that meeting, the court investigator explains the effect of a conservatorship and informs the proposed conservatee of his legal right to oppose the proceeding, attend the hearing and have the matter tried by a jury.

---

[1] If the proposed conservatee nominated a conservator in writing, an investigation is not mandatory if she plans to attend the hearing (Probate Code §1826(o)). However, local rules may require an investigation.

She tells the proposed conservatee that he may hire a lawyer or have one appointed by the court if he is unable to hire one (Probate Code §1826(b)).[2] She reviews the Confidential Supplemental Information form and assesses your reasons why the conservatorship is necessary (Probate Code §1826(d)).

The court investigator finds out if the proposed conservatee wants a conservatorship established and whether he prefers someone other than you to fill the role of conservator. Even if the proposed conservatee doesn't oppose the conservatorship, the court investigator determines if a lawyer should be appointed to protect the proposed conservatee's interests. For example, this might happen if the investigator thinks you are trying to coerce the proposed conservatee into a conservatorship, or if she is concerned about possible abuse.

The court investigator determines if the proposed conservatee is unwilling or medically unable to attend the hearing. Finally, she finds out whether he is able to complete an affidavit of voter registration—if not, he will be ineligible to vote.

Some court investigators allow you or another person to attend the meeting. Others discourage it because they want to make sure no one influences the proposed conservatee. If the proposed conservatee is confused or easily frightened, unable to communicate intelligibly, has problems understanding English or would have other difficulties meeting with a stranger, special arrangements may be made.

If the proposed conservatee is living in a care facility, the court investigator will probably contact a few of its employees. If an agency is providing at-home care, she might contact that agency. The court investigator may legally obtain medical information about the proposed conservatee from his health care providers if the proposed conservatee is unable to consent (Civil Code §56.10(c)(12)).

1. Investigator May Contact You

You will probably be contacted by the court investigator for a routine interview. The court investigator may want more information about your plans to care for the proposed conservatee or handle his estate. The court investigator may also wish to check on why alternatives to a conservatorship are not suitable. Interviews of proposed conservators are often conducted by phone, but the court investigator might want to meet with you in person.

Bear in mind that both you and the court investigator want what's best for the proposed conservatee, and she is not looking for ways to trick you. The best approach during the interview is to be honest, relaxed and do your best to answer all the questions. If you are seeking conservatorship of the person, the court investigator may want to make sure you are in a position to adequately provide or oversee care for the conservatee. For a conservatorship of the estate, the court investigator may want information about your experience with managing finances, and possibly to learn more about your own financial situation.

2. Investigator's Report

The court investigator must submit a written report to the court at least five days before the hearing. Copies must be sent to the proposed conservatee and his attorney—if he has one—and to you, the proposed conservator (Probate Code §1826(l)).[3] The report discusses why a conservatorship is necessary, and summarizes the court investigator's findings. The report explains whether the proposed conservatee is willing to attend the hearing, whether he wants to be represented by a lawyer and whether he is in favor of having you appointed conservator or would prefer someone else.

If the court investigator thinks the proposed conservatee should be represented by a lawyer—even if he didn't request it—she will put that information in the report. Finally, the court investigator usually makes a recommendation about whether the conservatorship

---

[2] The court investigator's duties are set out in Probate Code §1826.

[3] By law, the report is to be sent to your attorney (Probate Code §1826(l)(1)). Since you are representing yourself, you should get a copy.

should be granted. Judges almost always follow the court investigator's recommendation.

If you haven't received a copy of the investigator's report at least two days before the hearing date, call the court investigator and make sure you've been sent a copy. The report is confidential, and is only available to those involved in the conservatorship case.[4] You have the legal right to see the report (Probate Code §1826(n)). If you weren't sent a copy, arrive at the hearing a little early so you can look at the report before the hearing begins.

3. If Investigator Recommends Against Conservatorship

It's likely that the court investigator will recommend that you be appointed conservator. But the court investigator may be hesitant to make an affirmative recommendation if the proposed conservatee says he doesn't want you to be appointed, if there is dissension among family members, or if the court investigator has doubts about your qualifications or intentions. If the investigator gives a negative report, seek assistance from a lawyer. (See Chapter 17.)

Occasionally, a court investigator will refrain from making a recommendation because she isn't sure if a conservatorship should be established. The judge then has to make her own decision at the hearing, or choose to continue the case to obtain more information.

C. General Plan May Be Required

IN SOME COUNTIES, a conservator must prepare and file a general plan with the court and send copies to the court investigator. Depending on local rules, the conservator usually has 60–90 days following appointment to do so. The court investigator is responsible for reviewing the general plan. (See Chapter 9, Section E.)

---

[4]The court investigator may at her discretion forward a copy to the public conservator, interested public agencies and a long-term care ombudsman (Probate Code §1826(m)).

D. First-year and Bi-yearly Investigations

ADDITIONAL INVESTIGATIONS are periodically conducted to make sure the conservatee and his estate are being well cared for, and that the conservatee does not want the conservatorship ended. An investigation is conducted one year after the conservatorship is established and usually every two years after that. There may be more frequent investigations if there is a problem with the conservatorship—for example, if the conservatee or someone else complained about the way the conservator is handling the job or the type of care the conservatee is receiving.

The court investigator visits the conservatee to conduct these follow-up interviews. These interviews are similar to the initial investigation, but if the conservatorship has specifically limited or granted any of the conservatee's rights or responsibilities, the investigator assesses the scope of the conservatorship.

The court investigator may contact you. Some court investigators only contact the conservator if they have questions about the care the conservatee and his estate are receiving. Some court investigators interview the conservatee's friends and relatives, caretakers, medical providers and others who are around him.

At least 15 days before the one-year or biannual review date, the court investigator must prepare and provide a copy of the report of her findings to the court, you (the conservator) and the conservatee's attorney, if he has one (Probate Code §1851(b)). The report is confidential and available only to those people who were entitled to notice of the conservatorship or those who appeared in the proceeding. The court has discretion to release the document to anyone else if it is in the conservatee's interest (Probate Code §18251(e)).

Usually the report will confirm that the conservatorship is running smoothly. But you'll need the help of a lawyer if:

- the court investigator recommends you be removed from your position as conservator; or
- the court investigator recommends the conservatorship end, unless you agree with this assessment.[5]

---

[5]You may end a conservatorship following the instructions in Chapter 16.

E. Fees for Investigations

INVESTIGATION COSTS VARY from county to county, and are typically between $300 and $450 for each investigation. Fees for investigations are to be paid by the conservatorship estate, if there is one (Probate Code §1851.5(a)). If the estate cannot afford to pay costs of the investigations, the county may waive all or a portion of the costs. The county must waive costs if the conservator is receiving public assistance, such as welfare and food stamps (Government Code §6102). Some counties also waive fees for investigations if only a conservatorship of the person is established. If you or the conservator can't afford the fees, check with the court to find out its procedures for obtaining a waiver of investigation fees due to hardship.

Methods for handling the payment of fees depend on local policy. Investigators' fees are assessed annually, but it's important that you check with your court to find out how payments of investigators' fees are handled. Some courts may require that investigators' fees be paid at the time you file the petition (unless fees are waived). Other courts require proof of payment before Letters of Conservatorship will be issued or when the Inventory and Appraisement is filed with the court 90 days after the conservatorship is established. (See Chapter 13, Section C3.)

CHAPTER 8

THE APPOINTMENT HEARING

THIS CHAPTER DISCUSSES the court hearing at which a judge decides whether to appoint you as conservator. Going to a hearing in a courtroom may sound scary at first, but it can be quite easy. If you follow this chapter's guidelines and instructions, you shouldn't have trouble handling the hearing yourself.

It's a good idea for you to read or reread this chapter at least two weeks before the hearing date. That way, you won't be scrambling around just before the hearing, trying to gather papers and figure out procedures. If you have any reason to believe the conservatee or anyone else will come to the hearing to object, see a lawyer well before the hearing date. (Chapter 17 discusses how to find a lawyer.)

Before you go to court for the conservatorship hearing, make sure you have:

- completed all documents in Chapter 4 and filed them with the court, including a proposed Order Appointing Probate Conservator form for the judge to sign;[1] and

- had everyone entitled to notice served and filed proofs of service with the court as discussed in Chapter 6.[2] If you could not locate all relatives entitled to notice, you should have prepared a Due Diligence Declaration and Order Dispensing Notice following the instructions in Chapter 6, Section F2.

A. Get Ready for the Hearing

SEVERAL DAYS BEFORE THE HEARING, review all the documents you've filed with the court—especially the Petition for Appointment of Probate Conservator—so that you're familiar with the facts the judge will have in front of him. Be ready to answer the judge's questions about why the conservatorship is necessary and your ability to provide care for the proposed conservatee or manage her assets.

1. Gather Documents

Bring to the hearing copies of all of the papers you've filed. You might not need any of them, but if you don't have copies with you, it could mean a delay of the conservatorship. Organize the documents so you can quickly find any one of them. The documents you'll need are:

- Copies of all conservatorship papers you filed with the court, including proofs of service;

- Two extra copies of the unsigned proposed Order Appointing Probate Conservator (Chapter 4, Section E);

- Two blank copies of the Duties of Conservator form (you can fill this out after the hearing following the instructions in Section F3, below); and

- If you could not locate all relatives entitled to notice, and your court requires that you bring these documents to the hearing, the original and two copies of a Due Diligence Declaration and Order Dispensing Notice. (See Chapter 6, Section F2, for a discussion of the procedures.)

2. Arrange for the Proposed Conservatee to Attend

The proposed conservatee must attend the hearing unless you stated in your petition that she is unwilling to attend but wants you to be appointed conservator, or is unable to attend because of medical reasons.[3] Occasionally, a proposed conservatee planned to attend and when the hearing date arrives cannot either because she is suddenly unwilling or medically unable to attend. (If that happens, see Sections C and E3 of this chapter.)

Talk to the proposed conservatee about the hearing, and answer any questions he may have. If he is anxious or confused about the hearing, reassure him by letting him know that you will be there with him throughout it. You

---

[1] Some courts will refuse to hear your case if they don't have a proposed Order Appointing Probate Conservator in the file at least five days before the hearing date. If for some reason you haven't already sent the proposed order to the court, call the probate clerk and find out if you can bring it to the hearing with you. If the probate clerk tells you to bring it to the court, find out exactly where you should take it. Your file will probably be in the office of the probate examiner or commissioner, and the documents will not get to the file on time unless you take it to that office. (If you must continue the case, see Section C of this chapter.)

[2] If for some reason you have not filed the proofs of service with the court in advance of the hearing date, you might be able to bring the originals—along with copies for your files—to the hearing. Call the probate clerk and find out. If the probate clerk tells you to bring it to the court, find out exactly where you should take it—your file may already be in the office of the probate examiner or commissioner.

[3] See Item 6 of the Petition for Appointment of Conservator. Medical reasons must be substantiated by a written statement of a doctor or accredited practitioner of a religion which calls for healing by prayer alone. Emotional difficulties or psychological instability are not considered sufficient "medical reasons" unless the proposed conservatee would suffer physical harm by attending.

might be in court several hours waiting for your case to be called, but your own hearing won't last long. If all your papers are in order and the conservatorship is uncontested, the hearing should take less than ten minutes.

If the proposed conservatee is disabled, in a wheelchair or has mobility difficulties, call the court ahead of time. Find out about wheelchair accessibility, parking, elevators and any other particulars that will make it convenient for the proposed conservatee to get to court.

B. Make Sure Your Hearing Is on the Court Calendar

THE HEARING DATE, time and location are listed on the Notice of Hearing. Call the court clerk a few days before the hearing and ask her to confirm that the case is still "on calendar," meaning it is scheduled to take place as planned. If you don't know where the courtroom is located, get this information. Find out as much information as possible over the phone about where and when you should arrive, so you won't be harried on the day of the hearing.

If your conservatorship case is not on calendar, you can't go into court and have it heard by a judge. If the clerk says your case isn't on calendar, give the case number and name of the case, and ask him to locate the file.[4] If the documents you completed in Chapter 4 are in the file,

the case should be set for hearing. If all your paperwork is in order, ask the clerk to add the matter to the court's list of cases to be heard. You may need to be persistent with the clerk, and ask to speak to his supervisor if he seems unreasonably uncooperative.

But if all your papers aren't in the file or aren't filled out correctly, find out what went wrong. You may have made a mistake in completing or serving the papers, or maybe you forgot to send in a required document. Make sure you understand exactly what you need to fix. If necessary, go to the clerk's office to look at the case file and see what's missing or incorrect. In the rare situation where you took or sent documents to the court and they never made it to the file, you may be able to get your case put on calendar by going into the court and showing the court clerk your file-stamped copies of documents or by providing duplicates.

If your case is not scheduled and you can't track down what went wrong, you will need to contact the court clerk about getting a hearing date, following the instructions in Chapter 5, Section D1a. Refile and reserve any necessary documents following the instructions in Chapters 4, 5 and 6.

C. Continuing (Postponing) Hearing Date

IF YOU WANT THE HEARING DATE RESCHEDULED— called "continued" in legalese—carefully read this section. If you don't follow your court's local procedures, you could end up having to file another petition—and pay the expensive filing fees all over again.

There are several reasons why you might need to postpone the hearing date once it has been set:

- It's impossible for you to appear in court on that date (usually because some urgent matter has come up);

- The proposed conservatee cannot appear in court on that date but will be able to attend at a later date; or

- Someone objects to the conservatorship, and you need time to find a lawyer.

If you need to postpone the hearing date, call the probate clerk. Explain that you want to continue the conservatorship hearing and get a new date. Local proce-

---

[4]In larger counties, the file may be in the office of the probate examiner or commissioner who is reviewing it.

dures vary, and this book does not cover them in detail. For example, you may need to appear on the scheduled date and request a hearing or you may have to serve everyone with an amended Notice of Hearing. Continuances should be outlined in the court's probate policy manual and local rules.

D.   Attend the Hearing

BEING WELL PREPARED for the hearing should help everything go smoothly. Discuss the hearing in detail with the proposed conservatee if she will be attending.

1.   Before You Leave Home

Appearances might count, so dress cleanly and neatly. If you own any, wear business-type clothing. Arrive at least half an hour before the scheduled hearing time if you know where you're going, and give yourself even more time if you're not familiar with the building.

Double-check that you have ready all the documents listed in Section A1, above. Also remember to bring along a checkbook or cash to obtain a required conservatorship handbook or court instructions, which will cost $20 or less.

If you are taking the proposed conservatee with you to the hearing, make sure you allow enough time—especially if she is disabled or has mobility difficulties. If possible, have a family member or friend attend along with you, in case you need to do some extra walking.

2.   Find the Courtroom

In most counties, you go straight to the assigned courtroom for your hearing. In some of the larger counties, you may need to go to a special department (often called a "master calendar department") to find out in which courtroom your case will be heard. Usually you'll find a list of cases to be heard that day posted outside the assigned courtroom. If you can't find a list, go to the clerk's office and ask to see a copy of the calendar for any conservatorship or probate cases scheduled.

When you get to the proper courtroom for your hearing, tell the clerk or bailiff you are there. You may be required to sign in, or to fill out an additional form listing your name and the name of the conservatorship case. Before the judge arrives, the clerk may call roll to find out who is present.

Video Viewing Required: Many courts—for example, those in San Francisco and Alameda—require that all proposed conservators come to court early to watch a video that explains a conservator's duties and responsibilities.

3.   Appearing Before the Judge

When the judge enters the courtroom, everyone will be asked to rise. You might have an opportunity to see other conservatorship cases take place before yours. Depending on the court schedule, you may even have to wait several hours before your case is called. If your papers are in order, an uncontested hearing should take less than ten minutes.

When your case is called, stand up and answer: "Ready, your Honor." You and the proposed conservatee will probably go up to a table in front of the judge's bench. You may be sworn in by the bailiff who will ask you to promise to tell the truth. Relax, and take time to get comfortable and arrange your papers.

Always call the judge "Your Honor." Speak slowly and clearly, and loud enough for the courtroom reporter to hear. He will be typing a record of the hearing. Identify yourself by giving your name and saying that you are the petitioner and proposed conservator. Then identify the proposed conservatee, and indicate that he is the one for whom you're seeking the conservatorship. You will probably need to spell out your name and the proposed conservatee's.

Many judges will ask you questions to get the information they want. The judge may have some questions about service of the conservatorship papers, or want more information about your search for relatives if you claim that certain relatives can't be located. When the judge asks questions, it is only to become better informed and satisfied that the best legal solution is reached. Try to stay relaxed—and just briefly answer exactly what is asked.

If the judge simply wants you to start, state your relationship to the proposed conservatee, explain why the conservatorship is needed and tell how you plan to handle your duties as conservator. If you're seeking conservatorship of the estate, briefly summarize the assets, why the proposed conservatee is unable to manage them and that you are willing and able to do so.

The judge should talk with the proposed conservatee to be sure that she understands the effects of a conservatorship, and agrees with your appointment as conservator. The judge must tell the proposed conservatee that she has a right to oppose the conservatorship, she may be represented by a lawyer and have a jury trial. If she does, the case will be continued to a later date, which will give you time to consult an attorney.

When the judge has no more questions, he will announce the orders being made in your case. He may complete and sign the original Order Appointing Probate Conservator right there. Or he may sign the order later, usually the same day. If you submitted an Order Dispensing Notice, he should also sign that, unless he believes you didn't try hard enough to locate the proposed conservatee's relatives. If that's the situation, the judge will probably continue the case to a later date, and give you more time to look for the missing relatives.

At the close of your hearing, the judge may schedule additional hearing dates. Generally, documents are due then, but no one is required to attend an actual court hearing. For example, a general plan for the conservatorship may be set for hearing approximately 90 days away. For a conservatorship of the estate, hearing dates may be set for dates when various documents are due at the court—usually the Inventory and Appraisement (three months after the appointment date) and the First Account (one year after the appointment date). Make sure you take note of the dates, whether you are required to appear at any scheduled hearing and whether any papers are due. These dates may also be listed in the Order Appointing Probate Conservator.

4. Obtain Copies of Orders

If the judge signed any orders, the clerk should give you stamped copies, provided you submitted extra copies when you filed your papers with the court. Before you leave the courtroom, make sure you either receive copies of the Order Appointing Probate Conservator, or find out when they'll be available and how to get copies.

If you could not locate a given relative, also obtain copies of the Order Dispensing Notice. If the judge signed an order but didn't give copies back to you, check with the bailiff or clerk before you leave. He should be able to locate them in your file.

If the judge made any changes to either of those orders, make sure these changes are on all the copies. If they haven't been made, write in those same changes on your copies.

 Check the Order Appointing Probate Conservator carefully. If any hearing dates or filing dates are listed, you'll need to comply with those deadlines or you'll be in contempt of court. You could even be arrested for failing to file documents on time if they're required by court order.

E. Handling Problems at the Hearing

USUALLY YOU WILL NOT HAVE TROUBLE with the conservatorship hearing. However, it will probably make you feel better if you have a little information about what to do if something does go wrong.

1. Before the Hearing

Sometimes court personnel are less than helpful to people who are representing themselves in court. If a judge is rude or refuses to help you, do your best to keep your composure. Start by calmly trying to get to the root of the problem. It may be a simple issue you can correct.

If the person you're dealing with can't help you, seek assistance from someone else, such as another clerk or a supervisor. Keep in mind that your goal should be simply to correct the problem. Double-check everything with the help of this book.

2.   During the Hearing

If the judge won't grant the conservatorship yet, it may be because you left out something important in your paperwork. Politely ask the judge to explain; it's quite likely that you can provide additional information that will resolve the matter.

If you can't figure out what the problem is, or you feel you can't handle the situation, you can ask for a continuance. A continuance simply postpones the hearing to a later date. Pause for a moment to collect your thoughts. Then politely tell the judge: "Your Honor, I request that this matter be continued two weeks [or longer if you need additional time], to give me time to seek legal advice." During the next recess (when the court is not in session), see if the clerk or bailiff can help you. If you are able to figure out what went wrong and how to correct it, you'll need to arrange to appear at another hearing to be held on a new "continued" date.

If the judge is very difficult, it's possible that he might not grant a continuance, which means that you'll have to start the process all over again. If that happens, seek the help of a lawyer so you don't end up in the same situation. (See Chapter 17.)

If the judge continues the case, you will not have to serve new notices of hearing unless the problem is that not everyone was properly served. If everyone was correctly served, they either will be there to hear the judge set the new court date, or by not appearing, have given up the right to be told about it.

3.   If Proposed Conservatee Unexpectedly Doesn't Attend

Occasionally, a proposed conservatee who was supposed to appear at the hearing does not attend because of an accident or unexpected illness, or simply because she suddenly changes her mind and refuses to attend.

In such a situation, go to the hearing anyhow. When your case is called, let the judge know the proposed conservatee is not present, and explain why. It's possible that the judge will appoint you to be conservator anyhow, particularly if she has nominated you conservator or the court investigator recommended you be appointed. Or the judge may continue the case to a later date, when the proposed conservatee will be able to attend, or a court investigator can look into the circumstances and make a recommendation. Sometimes the court will appoint a lawyer to represent the proposed conservatee and make sure he agrees with the conservatorship.

4.   If the Conservatorship Is Contested

You could arrive in court on the day of the hearing and unexpectedly find yourself face-to-face with someone who opposes the conservatorship. The proposed conservatee could even change her mind at the last minute and decide she doesn't want a conservatorship or wants to be represented by a lawyer. If you're in any of these uncomfortable situations, it's unlikely that the judge will decide whether to grant the conservatorship that day. The matter will be decided later, and in the meantime, you will need the help of a lawyer. (See Chapter 17.)

5.   Temporary Conservatorships

Occasionally, a judge with questions about granting a conservatorship will want a more thorough investigation conducted or will want you to submit more information. In the meantime, he may grant a temporary conservatorship, to last up to 30 days.[5] If this happens, you will either need to do your own research or hire a lawyer.

---

[5]Temporary conservatorships may be extended for successive 30 day periods.

F.   Before Leaving the Courthouse

ONCE THE HEARING IS OVER, you will need to take care of several things before you leave.

1.   File Original Orders with Filing Clerk

Look carefully at any orders you received from the judge. If you have any original orders, they will be signed by the judge—rather than stamped with her name. Take them to the probate filing clerk for filing, and make sure you get back at least one file-stamped copy.

2.   Purchase Handbook for Conservators

By law, every county must provide conservators with written information about their rights, duties, limitations and responsibilities (Probate Code §1835). This information is contained in a *Handbook for Conservators*, which may be supplemented by information on community resources.

Before you leave the courthouse, obtain those written materials. The filing clerk will either provide you with copies or tell you where to obtain them. The court may not charge more than $20 for these written materials (Probate Code §1835(f)), and the cost may be reimbursed by the estate for conservatorships of the estate or person and estate. Keep a copy of the receipt. You may need to show proof of your purchase before you may obtain issued Letters of Conservatorship following the instructions in Chapter 9.

3.   Complete Duties of Conservator Form

The Duties of Conservator (and Acknowledgment of Receipt of Handbook) is a simple four-page form that summarizes your duties and obligations.

To complete this form, simply fill in the caption following the general instructions in Chapter 3, Section H2b. Then check each box that applies:

- II. Conservator of the Person (if you were appointed conservator of the person or person and estate); and
- III. Conservator of the Estate (if you were appointed conservator of the estate or person and estate.)

Fill in the name of the conservatee and the case number on pages 2, 3 and 4. Finally, check each of the boxes that applies on page 4. Then sign and date the form. If your Social Security number and driver's license number are required by local rules, supply these as well. If you have an extra copy of the Duties of Conservator form, file one signed copy with the court. If you only have one copy, take it with you when you leave the court. You will need to sign, photocopy and file it with the court as discussed in Chapter 9.

G.   Obtain Letters of Conservatorship

EVEN THOUGH THE JUDGE may sign an Order Appointing Conservator, you do not have the power to act as conservator until you obtain issued Letters of Conservatorship. Turn to Chapter 9, which tells you how.

TO COURT CLERK: This form is CONFIDENTIAL if local rule requires the Acknowledgment of Receipt to have a Social Security or driver's license number.

ATTORNEY OR PARTY WITHOUT ATTORNEY (Name and Address):	TELEPHONE NO.:	FOR COURT USE ONLY
ATTORNEY FOR (Name):		

SUPERIOR COURT OF CALIFORNIA, COUNTY OF

STREET ADDRESS:

MAILING ADDRESS:

CITY AND ZIP CODE:

BRANCH NAME:

CONSERVATORSHIP OF (NAME):

DUTIES OF CONSERVATOR and Acknowledgment of Receipt of Handbook	CASE NUMBER:

DUTIES OF CONSERVATOR

When you have been appointed by the court as a conservator, you become responsible to the court and assume certain duties and obligations. All of your actions as conservator are subject to review by the court. An attorney is best qualified to advise you about these matters. You should clearly understand the information on this form. You will find additional information in the **Judicial Council** *Handbook for Conservators*, which you are required by law to possess.

I.   THE CONSERVATEE'S RIGHTS

A conservatee does not lose all rights or all voice in important decisions affecting his or her way of life. All conservatees have the right to be treated with understanding and respect, the right to have their wishes considered, and the right to be well cared for by you. A conservatee generally keeps the right to (1) control his or her own salary, (2) make or change a will, (3) marry, (4) receive personal mail, (5) be represented by a lawyer, (6) ask a judge to change conservators, (7) ask a judge to end the conservatorship, (8) vote, unless a judge decides the conservatee isn't capable of exercising this right, (9) control personal spending money, if a judge has authorized an allowance, and (10) make his or her own medical decisions, unless a judge has taken away that right and given it to you. Ask your attorney what rights the conservatee does not have and consult your attorney when you are in doubt.

II.   ☐ CONSERVATOR OF THE PERSON

As conservator of the person, you will arrange for the conservatee's care and protection, decide where the conservatee will live, and make arrangements for the conservatee's health care, meals, clothing, personal care, housekeeping, transportation, and recreation.

1.   ASSESS THE CONSERVATEE'S NEEDS AND DEVELOP A GENERAL PLAN
You must assess the conservatee's needs and show how you plan to meet them in a *General Plan of Conservatorship* and file your plan with the court within 90 days after your appointment.

2.   DECIDE WHERE THE CONSERVATEE WILL LIVE
You may decide where the conservatee will live, but you must choose the ''least restrictive, appropriate'' living situation that is safe and comfortable and allows the conservatee as much independence as possible. You must not move the conservatee from the state or place the conservatee involuntarily in a mental health treatment facility without permission of the court. You must notify the court of each change of the conservatee's address and your address.

3.   PROVIDE MEDICAL CARE TO THE CONSERVATEE
You are responsible for ensuring the conservatee's health needs are met. You may not, however, give or withhold consent for medical treatment over the conservatee's objection *unless* the court has given you exclusive authority to consent because the conservatee has lost the ability to make sound medical choices.

4.   FILE A STATUS REPORT
If you are conservator of the estate as well as conservator of the person, you must file with the court a *Status Report* on the conservatee's condition one year after your appointment and at least every two years after that.

(Continued on reverse)

Page one of four

Form Adopted by the
Judicial Council of California
GC-348 [New January 1, 1992]

DUTIES OF CONSERVATOR
and Acknowledgment of Receipt of Handbook
(Probate Conservatorship)

Probate Code, § 1834

CONSERVATORSHIP OF *(NAME)*:	CASE NUMBER:

II. CONSERVATOR OF THE PERSON *(continued)*

5. WORK WITH THE CONSERVATOR OF THE ESTATE

If someone else is handling the conservatee's assets, the two of you must work together to be sure the conservatee can afford the care you arrange. Purchases you make for the conservatee must be approved by the conservator of the estate or you may not be reimbursed.

6. CONSULT YOUR ATTORNEY AND OTHER RESOURCES

Your attorney will advise you on your duties, the limits of your authority, the rights of the conservatee, and your dealings with the court. If you have legal questions, check with your attorney, not the court staff. Other questions may be answered better and less expensively by calling on local community resources. (To find these resources, see the *Handbook for Conservators* and the local supplement distributed by the court.)

III. ☐ CONSERVATOR OF THE ESTATE

As conservator of the estate, you will manage the conservatee's finances, protect the conservatee's income and assets, make an inventory of the conservatorship estate's assets, develop a *General Plan* to ensure the conservatee's needs are met, make sure the conservatee's bills are paid, invest the conservatee's money, see that the conservatee is receiving all the income and benefits he or she is entitled to, ensure that tax returns are filed on time, keep accurate financial records, and regularly report your financial accounts to the court. (NOTE: The assets and finances of the conservatee are known as ''the estate.'')

1. MANAGING THE ESTATE'S ASSETS

a. Prudent investments

You must manage the estate assets with the care of a prudent person dealing with someone else's property. This means you must be cautious and you may not make any speculative investments.

b. Keep estate assets separate from anyone else's

You must keep the money and property in this estate separate from anyone else's, including your own. When you open a bank account for the estate, the account name must indicate that it is a *conservatorship* account and not your personal account. Never deposit estate funds in your personal account or otherwise mix them with yours or anyone else's property, even for brief periods. Securities in the estate must be held in a name that shows they are estate property and not your personal property.

c. Interest-bearing accounts and other investments

Except for checking accounts intended for ordinary administration expenses, estate accounts must earn interest. You may deposit estate funds in insured accounts in financial institutions, but you should not put more than $100,000 in any one institution. Consult with an attorney before making other investments.

d. Other restrictions

There are many other restrictions on your authority to deal with estate assets. Without prior order of the court, you may not pay fees to yourself or to your attorney, make a gift of estate assets, or borrow from the estate. If you do not obtain the court's permission when it is required, you may be removed as conservator or you may be required to reimburse the estate from your own personal funds, or both. You should consult with an attorney concerning the legal requirements affecting sales, leases, mortgages, and investments of estate property.

2. INVENTORY OF ESTATE PROPERTY

a. Locate the estate's property

You must locate, take possession of, and protect all the conservatee's income and assets that will be administered in the estate. You should change the ownership of most assets into the conservatorship estate's name. For real estate, you must record a copy of your Letters with the county recorder in each county where the conservatee owns real property.

b. Determine the value of the property

You must arrange to have a court-appointed referee determine the value of the property unless the appointment is waived by the court. You, rather than the referee, must determine the value of certain ''cash items.'' An attorney can advise you about how to do this.

c. File an inventory and appraisal

Within 90 days after your appointment as conservator, you must file with the court an inventory and appraisal of all the assets in the estate.

(Continued on next page)

GC-348 [New January 1, 1992]   **DUTIES OF CONSERVATOR**   Page two of four
and Acknowledgment of Receipt of Handbook
(Probate Conservatorship)

CONSERVATORSHIP OF *(NAME)*:	CASE NUMBER:

III. CONSERVATOR OF THE ESTATE *(continued)*

3. GENERAL PLAN FOR THE CONSERVATORSHIP
Within 90 days after your appointment, you must file a detailed *General Plan* describing how you will manage the estate.

4. INSURANCE
You should determine that there is appropriate and adequate insurance covering the assets and risks of the estate. Maintain the insurance in force during the entire period of the administration (except for assets after they are sold).

5. RECORD KEEPING

a. Keep an accounting
You must keep complete and accurate records of each financial transaction affecting the estate. The checkbook for the conservatorship checking account is your indispensable tool for keeping records of income and expenditures. You will have to prepare an accounting of all money and property you have received, what you have spent, the date of each transaction, and its purpose. You must describe in detail what you have left after you pay the estate's expenses.

b. Court review of your records
You must file a petition requesting the court to review and approve your accounting one year after your appointment and at least every two years after that. Save your receipts because the court may ask to review them also. If you do not file your accountings as required, the court will order you to do so. You may be removed as conservator if you fail to comply.

6. CONSULTING AN ATTORNEY
Your attorney will advise you and help prepare your inventories, accountings, and petitions to the court. If you have questions, check with your attorney, not the court staff. You should cooperate with your attorney at all times. **When in doubt, contact your attorney.**

IV. ☐ LIMITED CONSERVATOR (for the developmentally disabled only)

1. AUTHORITY SPECIFIED IN YOUR LETTERS
As limited conservator, you have authority to take care of *ONLY* those aspects of the conservatee's life and financial affairs specified in your Letters of Conservatorship and the court's order appointing you. The conservatee retains all other legal and civil rights. Although most of the information in parts I–III of this form also applies to limited conservatorships (especially the duties of the conservator of the person), you should clarify with your attorney exactly which information applies in your case.

2. DUTY TO HELP CONSERVATEE DEVELOP SELF-RELIANCE
You must secure for the limited conservatee treatment, services, and opportunities that will assist him or her to develop maximum self-reliance and independence. This assistance may include training, education, medical and psychological services, social opportunities, vocational opportunities, and other appropriate help.

V. ☐ TEMPORARY CONSERVATOR

As temporary conservator, you have generally the same duties and authority as general conservators *except* the conservatorship will end on the date specified in your Letters of Temporary Conservatorship. Most of the information in parts I–III of this form also applies to temporary conservatorships, but you must consult your attorney about which duties you will *not* perform because of the limited time. A temporary conservator should avoid making long-term decisions or changes that could safely wait until a general conservator is appointed. As temporary conservator, however, you may not move a conservatee from his or her home or sell or give away the conservatee's home or any other assets without court approval.

> ## Sign the Acknowledgment of
> ## Receipt on the reverse.

(Continued on reverse)

GC-348 [New January 1, 1992]   **DUTIES OF CONSERVATOR**   Page three of four
and Acknowledgment of Receipt of Handbook
(Probate Conservatorship)

CONSERVATORSHIP OF *(NAME)*:	CASE NUMBER:

ACKNOWLEDGMENT OF RECEIPT
of Duties of Conservator and *Handbook for Conservators*
(Probate Code, § 1834)

1. A petition has been filed with the court requesting that I be appointed as a conservator.
2. I acknowledge that I have received the following:
    a. ☐ A copy of this statement of the duties and liabilities of the office of conservator *(Duties of Conservator form)*.
    b. ☐ The *Handbook for Conservators* adopted by the Judicial Council *(check one)*:
        (1) ☐ and the *local court supplement* to "How to Find and Use Community Resources."
        (2) ☐ no *local court supplement* is now available. I shall acquire a copy when it becomes available.

    I declare under penalty of perjury under the laws of the State of California that the foregoing acknowledgment is true and correct.

Date:

. . . .   ▶ _____
             (TYPE OR PRINT NAME)   (SIGNATURE OF PETITIONER)
*Social Security No.: _____   *Driver's License No.: _____

Date:

. . . .   ▶ _____
             (TYPE OR PRINT NAME)   (SIGNATURE OF PETITIONER)
*Social Security No.: _____   *Driver's License No.: _____

Date:

. . . .   ▶ _____
             (TYPE OR PRINT NAME)   (SIGNATURE OF PETITIONER)
*Social Security No.: _____   *Driver's License No.: _____

*Supply your Social Security number and driver's license number ONLY if required to do so by local court rule. The law requires the court to keep this information CONFIDENTIAL. (Probate Code, § 1834(b).)

NOTICE
This statement of duties and liabilities is a summary and is not a complete statement of the law. Your conduct as a conservator is governed by the law itself and not by this summary or by the Judicial Council *Handbook for Conservators*. When in doubt, consult your attorney.

GC-348 [New January 1, 1992]   **DUTIES OF CONSERVATOR**   Page four of four
           and Acknowledgment of Receipt of Handbook
           (Probate Conservatorship)

FINAL STEPS TO BECOME CONSERVATOR

AFTER A JUDGE HAS APPOINTED YOU conservator, you'll need to take several important steps before you have authorization to act in that capacity. Your badge of office will be a document called Letters of Conservatorship, in which you pledge to perform your duties as conservator.

Here's an overview of what you'll do. Each step is discussed in detail later in the chapter.

- *Service of Conservatee.* A copy of the Order Appointing Probate Conservator must be served by mail on the conservatee before you are issued Letters of Conservatorship. You'll need to complete a form that contains information about when and how service took place.

- *Special Requirements for Conservator of the Estate.* If you were appointed conservator of the estate, the order may have required you to obtain bond or set up a blocked account. You'll need to demonstrate that you have fulfilled those requirements.

- *Letters of Conservatorship.* This form shows that you have the court's authority to act as conservator. You'll need this document to open accounts, transact business or make health care decisions for the conservatee. Although it is an extremely important document, you'll find it very easy to prepare. Either mail or take

your documents to the court in person, pay a fee and obtain issued Letters of Conservatorship.

- *Report to Court Within 90 Days.* You must prepare and file a document with the court that outlines your plans to care for the conservatee, his estate or both. Those who were notified of the conservatorship must receive copies.

A. Conservatee Must Be Served

BECAUSE THE CONSERVATORSHIP can dramatically limit the conservatee's legal rights, you must have a copy of the Order Appointing Probate Conservator mailed to the conservatee (Probate Code §2312). You are required to do this even if the conservatee was at the hearing and already saw a copy of the order.

1. Proof of Service of Order

This document states that the Order Appointing Probate Conservator was served on the conservatee as required by law.

ATTORNEY OR PARTY WITHOUT ATTORNEY (NAME AND ADDRESS):	TELEPHONE NO.:	FOR COURT USE ONLY
RAY WEAVER 3901 Post Lane Fresno, CA 93703	(209) 555-1212	

ATTORNEY FOR (NAME): In Pro Per

SUPERIOR COURT OF CALIFORNIA, COUNTY OF Fresno
STREET ADDRESS: Room 401, Courthouse
MAILING ADDRESS: P.O. Box 1628
CITY AND ZIP CODE: Fresno, CA 93717
BRANCH NAME: ---

[ ] GUARDIANSHIP [X] CONSERVATORSHIP OF THE [X] PERSON [X] ESTATE
OF (NAME):
SOPHIA COREZONE   [ ] Minor [X] Conservatee

PROOF OF SERVICE BY MAIL OF **ORDER APPOINTING [ ] GUARDIAN [X] CONSERVATOR**	CASE NUMBER: 151

PROOF OF SERVICE BY MAIL
(Personal delivery also permitted. Probate Code, § 1466)

I am over the age of 18 and not a party to this cause. I am a resident of or employed in the county where the mailing occurred. My residence or business address is:

3901 Post Lane
Fresno, CA 93703

I served the Order Appointing [ ] Guardian [X] Conservator by enclosing a true copy in a sealed envelope addressed to each person whose name and address is given below and depositing the envelope in the United States mail with the postage fully prepaid.

(1) Date of deposit: Aug. 10, 19__ (2) Place of deposit (city and state): Fresno, CA

I declare under penalty of perjury under the laws of the State of California that the foregoing is true and correct and that this declaration is executed on (date): August 12, 19__ at (place): Fresno, CA . . . .

Joanne Weaver
. . . .   _Joanne Weaver_
          (Type or print name)   (Signature of declarant)

NAME AND ADDRESS OF EACH PERSON TO WHOM NOTICE WAS MAILED

a. [ ] Ward 14 years of age or older:

b. [X] Conservatee: SOPHIA COREZONE
                              27 Taurua Ct.
                              Fresno, CA 93702

c.

[ ] List of names and addresses continued in attachment.

Do NOT use this form for personal delivery permitted in lieu of mailing by section 1466 of the Probate Code.

Form Approved by the
Judicial Council of California
Revised Effective January 1, 1981
GC-030(81)

PROOF OF SERVICE BY MAIL
OF ORDER APPOINTING
GUARDIAN OR CONSERVATOR

CAPTION: PROOF OF SERVICE BY MAIL OF ORDER APPOINTING CONSERVATOR

- Fill in the caption following the general instructions in Chapter 3, Section H2b.
- Check the box entitled "CONSERVATORSHIP," as well as boxes next to the words "PERSON," "ESTATE," or both. Check the box next to the word "Conservatee."
- After the words "PROOF OF SERVICE BY MAIL OF ORDER APPOINTING," check the box before the word "CONSERVATOR."

After the words "My residence or business address is," fill in the business or residence address of the person who will mail the Order Appointing Probate Conservator. Remember that it can be anyone over age 18—but you cannot be the server. Just below the space for the address, check the box before the word "Conservator."

Item (1): Fill in the date the order will be mailed to the conservatee.

Item (2): Fill in the city and state where the order will be mailed to the conservatee.

Leave the declaration just below Item (2) blank. The person who mails the papers will complete it.

Item a: Leave this item blank. It pertains only to guardianships.

Item b: Check this box, and fill in the name and mailing address of the conservatee. Leave the rest of the form blank.

Make a copy of the unsigned Proof of Service By Mail of Order Appointing Conservator for service on the conservatee.

2. Have Documents Served

The following documents must be sent to the conservatee by regular mail:

- Unsigned copy of the Proof of Service By Mail of Order Appointing Conservator; and
- Copy of the Order Appointing Probate Conservator. If the judge made any changes to the Order Appointing Probate Conservator, make sure they're marked on the conservatee's copy.

Have a friend or relative over the age of 18 mail a copy of the documents to the conservatee.[1] (Instructions for having documents served by mail are in Chapter 6, Section D2.) Finally, have the person who sent the documents print his name and sign in the spaces provided. Then keep the Proof of Service By Mail of Order Appointing Conservator in a safe place. You will file it with the court later.

B. Special Steps for Conservators of the Estate

MANY CONSERVATORS OF THE ESTATE are required to obtain bond, make deposits with the court or set up blocked accounts before Letters of Conservatorship are issued. If you're not sure about these requirements, look at Item 3d of the Order Appointing Probate Conservator. There you will find information about whether and how much bond is required, and how much money must be placed in blocked accounts at specific financial institutions.

If you need to obtain bond or make deposits with the court, turn to Chapter 14, Sections E2 and E3. If you need to set up a blocked account, turn to Chapter 14, Section E1. After you accomplish those tasks, return to this chapter.

---

[1] The Order Appointing Probate Conservator may be served personally instead of mailed to the conservatee. If it is personally served, you will need to obtain a proof of service for personal service form from the court or library.

C. Letters of Conservatorship

THE COURT MUST ISSUE Letters of Conservatorship before you will have authority to act as conservator. This document lets others know you have been legally confirmed in the role.

CAPTION: LETTERS OF CONSERVATORSHIP

- Fill in the caption following the general instructions in Chapter 3, Section H2b.
- Check the box at the top where you fill in your name before the words "IF RECORDED RETURN TO."

After the words "STATE OF CALIFORNIA, COUNTY OF," fill in the county in which you filed the conservatorship action.

Item 1: Check the first box. In capital letters, after the word "(Name)," fill in your full name. Check the box before the word "conservator." Also check the box or boxes before the words "person," "estate," or both, depending on the type of conservatorship you are seeking. After the words "of (name)," fill in the conservatee's full name in capital letters. If you listed several names for the conservatee, include all of them.

Item 2: Skip this entire item.

Item 3: To complete this item, look at a copy of the Order Appointing Probate Conservator that was signed by the judge. Before checking the first box in this item, complete the item entirely to make sure that at least one of Items 3a through 3g applies.

Item 3a: Skip this item unless Item 3g of the signed Order Appointing Probate Conservator is checked. If so, check the first box in this item. If the proposed conservatee follows a religion that espouses healing by prayer only, also check the second box.

Items 3b-d: Skip these items.

Items 3e-f: Skip these items. They pertain to limited conservatorships, which are beyond the scope of this book.

Item 3g: Skip this item unless Item 3l of the signed Order Appointing Probate Conservator is checked. If so, check the box in this item and insert the words, "Other orders are specified in Attachment 3g." Then prepare an Attachment 3g, repeating the information listed in

Attachment 3l of the Order Appointing Probate Conservator.

If you checked the boxes in any of Items 3a through 3g, make sure you check the box next to Item 3.

Check the box at the bottom right before the words "Number of pages attached." If you are attaching any pages, count them and fill in that number. Otherwise, enter the word "none."

Leave the rest of the front side of the form blank, including the date and clerk's signature line, and proceed to the back of the form.

CAPTION: PAGE 2 OF LETTERS OF CONSERVATORSHIP

- After the words "CONSERVATORSHIP OF (NAME)," in capital letters fill in the conservatee's full name. Also fill in the case number.

Affirmation: Check the box before the word "conservator." Fill in the date, city and state where you complete the form. Then sign your name on the signature line. By signing here, you promise to fulfill the duties of a conservator. (These duties are covered in detail in Chapters 11, 12 and 13.)

Certification: Leave this entire item blank. The clerk will complete this item, which confirms that the document is a certified copy of the original Letters of Conservatorship in the court's file.

ATTORNEY OR PARTY WITHOUT ATTORNEY (Name and Address):

TELEPHONE NO.: (707) 555-1212

FOR COURT USE ONLY

[X] IF RECORDED RETURN TO: JENNIE MEDVED
10 Roanoak Rd.
Ukiah, CA 95482

ATTORNEY FOR (Name): In Pro Per

SUPERIOR COURT OF CALIFORNIA, COUNTY OF Mendocino

STREET ADDRESS: State and Perkins Streets
MAILING ADDRESS: P.O. Box 148
CITY AND ZIP CODE: Ukiah, CA 95482
BRANCH NAME: _ _ _

CONSERVATORSHIP OF (NAME):

JOSEPH MEDVED   Conservatee

LETTERS OF CONSERVATORSHIP
[X] **Person**   [X] **Estate**   [ ] **Limited Conservatorship**

CASE NUMBER: 118

FOR RECORDER'S USE ONLY

STATE OF CALIFORNIA, COUNTY OF   MENDOCINO

1. [X] (Name): JENNIE MEDVED   is the appointed
   [X] conservator [ ] limited conservator of the [X] person [X] estate of
   (name): JOSEPH MEDVED

2. [ ] *(for conservatorship that was on December 31, 1980, a guardianship of an adult or of the person of a married minor)* (name):
   was appointed the guardian of the [ ] person [ ] estate by order
   dated: and is now the conservator of the
   [ ] person [ ] estate of (name):

3. [X] Other powers have been granted or conditions imposed as follows:
   a. [ ] exclusive authority to give consent for and to require the conservatee to receive medical treatment that the conservator in good faith based on medical advice determines to be necessary even if the conservatee objects, subject to the limitations stated in section 2356 of the Probate Code.
      [ ] This treatment shall be performed by an accredited practitioner of the religion whose tenets and practices call for reliance on prayer alone for healing of which the conservatee was an adherent prior to the establishment of the conservatorship.
      [ ] *(applicable only if the court order limits the duration)* This medical authority terminates on (date):

   b. [ ] powers to be exercised independently under section 2590 of the Probate Code as specified in attachment 3b *(specify powers, restrictions, conditions, and limitations)*.
   c. [ ] conditions relating to the care and custody of the property under section 2402 of the Probate Code as specified in attachment 3c.
   d. [ ] conditions relating to the care, treatment, education, and welfare of the conservatee under section 2358 of the Probate Code as specified in attachment 3d.
   e. [ ] *(for limited conservatorship only)* powers of the limited conservator of the person under section 2351.5 of the Probate Code as specified in attachment 3e.
   f. [ ] *(for limited conservatorship only)* powers of the limited conservator of the estate under section 1830(b) of the Probate Code as specified in attachment 3f.
   g. [X] other *(specify):*   Other orders are specified in Attachment 3g.

SEAL

Dated: . . . .

Clerk, by _____ , Deputy
[X] Number of pages attached: 1
(Continued on reverse)

This form may be recorded as notice of the establishment of a conservatorship of the estate as provided in section 1875 of the Probate Code.

Form Approved by the
Judicial Council of California
Effective January 1, 1981
GC-350(81)

LETTERS OF CONSERVATORSHIP

CONSERVATORSHIP OF (NAME):	CASE NUMBER:
JOSEPH MEDVED Conservatee	118

LETTERS OF CONSERVATORSHIP   Page 2

AFFIRMATION

I solemnly affirm that I will perform the duties of ☒ conservator ☐ limited conservator according to law.

Executed on (date): . May 10, . 19 . . ., at (place) . . . .

_____
(Signature of appointee)

_____

CERTIFICATION

I certify that this document and any attachments is a correct copy of the original on file in my office, and that the letters issued to the person appointed above have not been revoked, annulled, or set aside, and are still in full force and effect.

Dated: . . . .   Clerk, by _____ , Deputy

SEAL

1. Obtain Issued Letters of Conservatorship

You are now ready to obtain issued Letters of Conservatorship. Make several photocopies of your documents. Depending on local rules, you must take or send to the filing clerk some or all of the following:

- Original signed Letters of Conservatorship and copies (five copies are recommended).

- A completed and signed Proof of Service By Mail of Order Appointing Conservator with a copy of the Order Appointing Probate Conservator stapled to it, along with one or two extra copies of both the proof of service and order.

- For conservatorships of the estate or person and estate, if bond is required or you are establishing a blocked account, written proof of bond or written proof of blocked account and one or two extra copies. (See Section B, above.)

- A document showing that you paid any assessed investigators' fees. (See Chapter 7, Section E.)

- Duties of Conservator (and Acknowledgment of Receipt of Handbook. (See Chapter 8, Sections F2 and F3.)

- A check or cash to pay for issued Letters of Conservatorship (the cost is about $3 per copy, depending on the number of pages).[2] If you mail a check, you may write "not to exceed $15" on a check payable to the court, and sign it. Or call the clerk ahead of time and find out exactly how much certified Letters of Conservatorship will cost. If you are conservator of the estate, these costs may be paid or reimbursed by the estate. Keep copies of all receipts.

If you mail your request to the court clerk, send along a self-addressed, stamped envelope and a cover letter explaining that you want the original documents filed, Letters of Conservatorship issued and certified copies returned to you along with file-stamped copies of all other documents.

---

[2] If your filing fees were waived by the court, you may request a waiver of the fees for certified copies by completing and filing an Application for Waiver of Additional Court Fees and Costs form. Contact the court to get a copy of the form.

D. Distribute Letters of Conservatorship

PROVIDE A COPY of the Letters of Conservatorship to anyone who requires verification of your authority to act as conservator. If you are making medical decisions for the conservatee, see that a certified copy of the Letters of Conservatorship are placed in her medical records. Naturally, if an agency or institution requires a conservatorship to distribute benefits or take some action, you should now take or send it a copy. You will also need a copy every time you open a new account or transact business with a new agency or company.

You could make photocopies of the Letters of Conservatorship, but you may have problems getting others to accept them as legal proof of the conservatorship, since photocopies are not considered official copies of court documents and could be altered. It's better to get certified copies from the court that are stamped with the court's seal. Keep extra certified copies of the Letters of Conservatorship in a convenient, safe place.

 For certain transactions, such as transferring bank accounts or corporate shares, you'll need Letters of Conservatorship that were certified no more than 60 days before the transfer. For those transactions, you can always get additional certified copies of the Letters of Conservatorship later.

E.   General Plan May Be Required

IN SOME COUNTIES, conservators must file a general plan with the court, typically within 60–90 days of the date the judge signs the Order Appointing Probate Conservator. The plan tells how the conservatee's personal and financial needs will be met. Check your probate policy manual to find out if local rules require a general plan.[3]

If a general plan is required, you'll need to address how you will handle the conservatee's personal and financial needs.

- *Residence:* whether you expect to move the conservatee, keep him at home or adapt his home to meet special needs, such as building a wheelchair ramp. Include the conservatee's address and telephone number.

- *Personal and Health Care Needs:* how these needs will be met. For example, you might plan to hire a part-time home care nurse or an aide to assist the conservatee with dressing, preparing meals and shopping.

- *Social Needs:* what arrangements for visits with family and friends will be made. Include your plans for visiting and caring for the conservatee and staying in contact with her family and friends.

- *Financial Resources:* what income, savings and assets will be available, how you intend to budget the money, and whether you anticipate selling the conservatee's property or getting rid of the conservatee's belongings, such as by donating unused furniture to a charitable organization.

- *Community Resources:* how you plan to use local resources to meet the conservatee's needs, such as having hot meals delivered to the home, using a telephone outreach service and taking the conservatee to a senior daycare program.

Think through and make notes about how you expect to handle each of the issues listed above. If you are serving only as conservator of the person or estate, but not both, some areas might be handled outside of the conservatorship. If so, briefly state how those matters will be

managed. Pay attention to any special needs the conservatee may have. For example, if he has physical disabilities, he may require extra supervision or at-home care.

1.   Prepare General Plan

If local preprinted forms are provided, use them. Otherwise, prepare your document on lined paper following instructions in Chapter 3, Section H3. Title the document "General Plan of Conservator." In your own words, explain how you will take care of each area. Include a verification at the end and sign and date the document.

2. Verification

Some documents require that the person signing them must "verify" the document under penalty of perjury. When verification is necessary, add these words to the end of the document, and sign where indicated:

```
              VERIFICATION
    I declare that: I am the ["proposed"]
conservator of the ["person," "estate" or "person and
estate"] of [conservatee's name]. I have read the
foregoing [exact title of document] and know its
contents. It is true of my own knowledge,
except as to the matters that are stated on
information and belief, and as to those matters
I believe it to be true. I declare under
penalty of perjury under the laws of the State
of California that the foregoing is true and
correct.

Dated: [today's date]     _____
                              [your name]
```

3.   File General Plan

Make three copies of the general plan, then file the original with the court. (Instructions for filing documents are found in Chapter 5, Section D.)

---

[3] The general plan was required for all conservators from July 1, 1990 through June 30, 1993. Currently, local rules govern whether or not a general plan is required.

4. Notice Requirements

Local rules will probably require that the court investigator be notified about the plan. You may also need to notify everyone listed in the Conservatorship Worksheet (see Chapter 3, Section F), as well as anyone who requested special notice (see Chapter 15, Section B4a). In that case, you need only send notice that a general plan was filed; you need not send a copy of the plan itself. These people may, however, go to court to review it.

a   Notice of Filing of General Plan

This document gives notice that the General Plan of Conservator was filed. Following the instructions in Chapter 3, Section H3, prepare a document on lined pleading paper using the accompanying sample as a guide.

[Use lined paper and prepare the caption following the Sample Pleading in Chapter 3, Section H3.]

```
          NOTICE OF FILING OF
          GENERAL PLAN
     Notice is given that [your name], conservator
of the ["person," "estate" or "person and estate"] filed a
General Plan of Conservator in the above
captioned case on [date document was filed in court]. You
have the right to review the General Plan at
the court, if requested.

Respectfully submitted,
Dated: [today's date]          _____
                              [your name]
                              Conservator In Pro Per
```

b. Proof of Service By Mail

This document lists everyone who was served with the Notice of Filing of General Plan. Prepare a Proof of Service By Mail, located in Appendix B. You may list everyone who was served by mail on one form, as long as the envelopes are mailed by one person at the same time.

> **CAPTION:** PROOF OF SERVICE BY MAIL
>
> • Fill in the caption following the general instructions in Chapter 3, Section H2b.

Items 1-2: Leave these items blank.

Item 3: Fill in the business or residence address of the person serving the documents.

Item 4: Fill in the words "Notice of Filing of General Plan (served on everyone listed in Item 5) and General Plan of Conservator (served on court investigator [*court investigator's name*] only)."

Item 5a: Fill in the date that the documents will be mailed.

Item 5b: Fill in the city and state where the documents will be mailed.

Item 6: In the blank space, fill in the name, title and address of the court investigator, everyone listed on the Conservatorship Worksheet and anyone who requested special notice. If you need additional space, check the box which reads "Additional names and addresses on reverse." Then at the top of the back of the form, type in the name and number of the conservatorship case. Beneath that, list additional names and addresses.

Finally, fill in the date and type or print the process server's full name on the line provided.

c. Have Documents Served

Make one photocopy of the Notice of Filing of General Plan and the unsigned Proof of Service By Mail for each person who is being served. Have a friend or relative over the age of 18 mail these two documents to everyone listed on the Proof of Service By Mail. Also have the server send a copy of the general plan to the court investigator. (Instructions for having documents served by mail are in Chapter 6, Section D2.) Once the papers have been mailed, have the server sign the document.

d. File Papers with the Court

Make two copies of the original Notice of Filing of General Plan and Proof of Service By Mail and file them with the court following the instructions in Chapter 5, Section D. If you listed additional people on the back of the Proof of Service By Mail, remember to photocopy both sides of the form.

Occasionally, someone you served may object to your plan, or the court may want more information. If so, a hearing on the particulars of the plan will be scheduled, which will be similar to the appointment hearing, except that the conservatee need not attend this hearing.

PARTY WITHOUT AN ATTORNEY ((Name and Address):

HECTOR RHODES
987 Island Avenue
Lodi, CA 95240

In Pro Per

TELEPHONE NO.: (209) 555-1212

FOR COURT USE ONLY

NAME OF COURT: SAN JOAQUIN SUPERIOR COURT
STREET ADDRESS: Courthouse, Room 302
MAILING ADDRESS: 222 East Weber Avenue
CITY AND ZIP CODE: Stockton, CA 95202
BRANCH NAME:

CONSERVATORSHIP OF THE ☒ PERSON ☒ ESTATE OF (NAME):

AMELIA RHODES
CONSERVATEE

PROOF OF SERVICE BY MAIL

CASE NUMBER: 181

I declare that:

1. At the time of service I was at least 18 years of age and not a party to this legal action.
2. I am a resident of or employed in the county where the mailing occurred.
3. My business or residence address is ___987 Island Ave., Lodi, CA 95240___

4. I served copies of the following paper(s) in the manner shown [list exact titles of paper(s)]: Notice of Filing of General Plan (served on everyone listed in Item 5); and General Plan of Conservator (served on court investigator Anthony Riccoti only).

5. Manner of service: by placing true copies in a sealed envelope addressed to each person whose name and address is given below and depositing the envelopes in the United States Mail with the postage fully prepaid.
   a. Date of deposit: ___February 13, 19___
   b. Place of deposit (city and state): ___Lodi, California___

6. Name and address of each person to whom documents were mailed:

ANTHONY RICCOTI, court investigator 222 E. Weber Ave. Stockton, CA
                                                                    95202

AMELIA RHODES   801 Ridgeway Grove   Lodi, CA 95240

RHODA RHODES   6201 Meadow Valley   Lodi, CA 95242

RICHARD RHODES   6201 Meadow Valley   Lodi, CA 95242

WILLIAM GEORGE   801 Ridgeway Grove   Lodi, CA 95242

☒ Additional names and addresses on reverse.

I declare under penalty of perjury under the laws of the State of California that the foregoing is true and correct.

Date: February 13, 19___

JAMES SMITH
·· (TYPE OR PRINT NAME)

James Smith
(SIGNATURE OF PERSON WHO SERVED PAPERS)

PROOF OF SERVICE BY MAIL

F. If a Hearing Is Required

Some counties may require that a hearing be set for the general plan or status report. Check with the court. If a hearing is scheduled, there's a good chance that you won't need to attend. Call the probate clerk's office to find out. Many courts have recorded information on the phone, often called "pre-grant" information.

If you must attend the hearing, plan to appear at the designated time and answer questions about how you expect to handle your job as conservator. Before the hearing, carefully review the general plan or status report and any written objections that were filed with the court. If the objections appear reasonable, look into ways you can improve the conservatee's care, and be prepared to discuss that at the hearing. If the objections seem unrealistic or don't take into account something you've planned, be ready to explain these factors. Bring a copy of the general plan or status report and any supplemental papers that support your plans, such as brochures from community service organizations you expect to use.

Seek a lawyer's help if objections to the general plan or status report are not resolved at the hearing.

G. Read Additional Chapters

DEPENDING ON THE TYPE of conservatorship established, read:

- Chapter 11 if you were appointed conservator of the person or person and estate; and

- Chapters 12 and 13 if you were appointed conservator of the estate or person and estate. You'll have to prepare additional documents for filing with the court within a couple weeks of the date you were appointed conservator.

CHAPTER 10

OBTAIN BENEFITS AND COVERAGE

THE CONSERVATEE MAY ALREADY receive medical and disability benefits, pensions, public assistance and other important coverage. But he might not be getting all coverage for which he qualifies, or he might not be aware that certain benefits are available. Once you're appointed conservator, you are obliged to apply for benefits and money to which the conservatee is entitled. You also may need to obtain insurance for the conservatee to cover future health care and nursing facility costs.

If the conservatee presently receives benefits, take or send a copy of the Letters of Conservatorship to the agency. Explain that you have been appointed conservator, and that all benefit checks should be sent to you. (See the sample letter in Chapter 12, Section C7.) Double-check the conservatee's benefits; because agency policies change, he may be eligible for more money or more extensive coverage. If the agency has its own requirements for accounting, follow those rules.

To sort out coverage and benefits, you'll need to match the conservatee's needs and condition with available benefits. After reviewing this chapter, contact appropriate organizations to find out what benefits are available and whether the conservatee is likely to qualify. Take time to learn about different benefits, and don't be put off by exclusions or bureaucrats' discouraging statements. To obtain benefits, you must complete a number of forms, appear at interviews and do a lot of waiting.

Unfortunately, you'll probably run into red tape in the process. To keep their own costs and time investment down, agencies often have unwritten policies of making it difficult for people to get through the qualification process. That way, some people will give up and fail to claim any benefits. Be patient and persevering. If all else fails, most agencies have appeals procedures that can be followed if the conservatee is denied benefits.

 Some benefit programs, notably Medi-Cal, are available only to people with few assets and little income. There may be ways to help the conservatee qualify for benefits without giving up everything she owns, but they generally require advance planning. And because of complex issues of eligibility, timing and title transfer, you should consult a lawyer for help when:

- the conservatee owns a house, regardless of whether title is held alone or with others; or

- the conservator or her spouse are in or will likely enter a nursing facility within a few years.

A. Community Resources

THIS CHAPTER GIVES A BRIEF OVERVIEW OF a number of financial benefits that may be available to the conservatee.[1] Don't overlook discounts available to the elderly and disabled through the local government or businesses. For example, there may be low rates for public transportation and certain grocery stores may give discounts to the elderly.

Local senior groups and other community organizations specializing in the concerns of the elderly and disabled often give excellent information about benefits and other local programs. Some offer free or low-cost assistance in completing required forms. (Also see Appendix A for more information on community organizations.)

B. Social Security

SOCIAL SECURITY PROVIDES A NUMBER of government-administered benefit programs for people who are retired or disabled and unable to work, and their depen-

---

[1] *Social Security, Medicare & Pensions: A Sourcebook for Older Americans* by Joseph Matthews with Dorothy Matthews Berman (Nolo Press) explains rules about government-funded income, disability and medical programs and private pensions.

dents or survivors. About 90% of all U.S. workers have jobs covered by Social Security—meaning that during their work lives, they pay into the Social Security system. Benefits are calculated according to the length of time worked, measured in quarter-years of work credit in employment from which Social Security taxes are paid.[2] The amount of benefits is generally determined by the average wages earned on jobs covered by Social Security, rather than by need.

There are three kinds of benefits available under the Social Security system:

- *Retirement Benefits:* A worker may choose to start receiving these benefits any time after reaching age 62, although the amount of the benefits increases each year the worker waits to retire. A "retired" worker may continue working while receiving these benefits, but the amount of benefits may be reduced if more than a prescribed amount of income is earned.

- *Disability Benefits:* People under the age of 65 who are considered "disabled" under the rules of the program may qualify for disability benefits. Generally, Social Security disability benefits are available to people with lasting physical or mental impairments preventing them from earning more than $500 a year.

- *Dependents' and Survivors' Benefits:* The spouse or dependent or disabled children of a retired, disabled, or deceased worker who would have qualified for retirement or disability benefits may be entitled to benefits based on the worker's earning record.

If you receive benefits on behalf of the conservatee, you will be referred to as the "representative payee," according to bureaucratic jargon. You must spend the money only for the conservatee's benefit, and fulfill Social Security's accounting requirements.

A conservatee may also become eligible for Social Security if his spouse was employed and contributed to the Social Security system. To contact the Social Security

---

[2] People who have worked for nonprofit organizations, the federal and some state and local governments may not have participated in the Social Security program. Many government agency employees are covered by civil service retirement systems. (See Section F of this chapter). Depending on the dates of employment and whether money was paid into the Social Security system, self-employed workers, domestic workers and farm workers might not be eligible for Social Security benefits.

Administration, look in the telephone book for a local office. Or call the toll-free California number: (800) 772-1213.

C. Supplemental Security Income (SSI)

THE SUPPLEMENTAL SECURITY INCOME (SSI) program is jointly administered by federal and state governments. SSI is intended to guarantee a minimum level of income to some financially-pressed people who are age 65 or over, blind or disabled. SSI benefits are based on financial need rather than work history. To be eligible, the conservatee's income must be under a monthly minimum set by the state, and her assets must not exceed $2,000 ($3,000 for a couple), although the value of a home, part of the value of a car, $2,000 worth of personal property and part of the value of life insurance are not included in this limit. Contact the Social Security Administration for more information. (See Section B, above.)

D. Medical Coverage

ALMOST ALL CONSERVATEES require frequent medical care and incur significant medical bills. As conservator, you will need to arrange for medical coverage through private insurance or public programs, and see that medical bills are paid.[3] (Also read Chapter 11, Section D, which discusses your role in making medical decisions for the conservatee.)

1. Medicare

Medicare is a federal government insurance program designed to assist people with their medical costs. It is run in cooperation with the Social Security Administration.

Medicare is available to some Americans who are 65 years of age or older, and some disabled people. Entitlement to Medicare is determined by contributions to the Social Security system through work time deductions rather than by need.

The Medicare program is divided into two parts.

- *Part A Hospital Insurance:* Covers some costs of doctor-prescribed stays in a hospital and of inpatient treatment. The care and cost must be medically necessary and reasonable, as determined by Medicare. For example, it does not pay for private duty nursing, private rooms—unless they're medically necessary—or conveniences such as a telephone or television. Some post-hospital nursing facilities are covered, as are some home health care and hospice care facilities. A yearly deductible must be paid.

- *Part B Medical Insurance:* Covers approximately 80% of the costs of doctors, outpatient hospital and laboratory work, medical equipment and supplies, home health care, therapy and other medical costs. A monthly premium must be paid.

Many medical expenses are not covered by Medicare. These include routine medical check-ups—although mammograms and PAP smears for women patients are now covered—dental care, most eye, ear and foot examinations and supplies (eyeglasses, contact lenses, hearing aids, orthopedic shoes), most immunizations, most long-term nursing home care, elective cosmetic surgery, extras in a hospital room (phone, television) and custodial care (services such as help with dressing, eating, bathing or moving around).[4]

---

[3] If you are only conservator of the person, arrangements should be made for the conservatee—if she is able—or someone else to pay the bills. You may need to supply copies of medical bills and receipts.

[4] What is and isn't covered falls into a gray area which sometimes results in disputes between Medicare and patients. How to appeal a denied claim is beyond the scope of this book. See *Social Security, Medicare & Pensions: A Sourcebook for Older Americans* by Joseph Matthews with Dorothy Matthews Berman (Nolo Press).

HEALTH INSURANCE COUNSELING ADVOCACY PROGRAMS

Every county is served by a state-sponsored Health Insurance Counseling Advocacy Program (HICAP). These agencies provide free information about Medicare coverage, filing claims for Medicare and private insurers, Medicare appeals, supplemental insurance and long-term medical care coverage. HICAP workers will also meet with you to help set up recordkeeping systems. Check in the white pages or call a local senior information line or Medicare number.

2. Medi-Cal (Medicaid)

Medicaid is a program established by the federal government and administered by individual states. In California, the program is called Medi-Cal. Medi-Cal provides low-income people with free or shared costs of medical and some dental care. This assistance is available to people who are over age 65, under age 21 and are blind, pregnant, permanently disabled or have dependent children under age 21. The conservatee's eligibility for Medi-Cal depends on income level, assets and financial resources. The conservatee would probably be eligible if he receives public assistance or SSI.[5] Medi-Cal generally covers hospital, clinic, home nursing, nursing facility and laboratory services. It also broadly covers diagnostic care and therapy, dental care, prosthetic devices and eyeglasses.

Even if the conservatee has financial resources that exceed public assistance standards, he may be eligible if he has relatively high medical bills. If the conservatee has private health insurance, he may still qualify for Medi-Cal if eligibility requirements are met. Some people who qualify for Medi-Cal may have higher incomes or assets than allowed for the regular Medi-Cal program. They may qualify for the Share of Costs Medi-Cal program, which includes an enrollment fee, monthly deductible and small co-payments for each doctor's visit (usually about $1).

California recently introduced special arrangements by which Medi-Cal and private insurance companies cooperate to offer long-term care policies protecting a greater measure of assets than are normally allowed when Medi-Cal covers long-term care.

Beware that the mere fact that these policies might protect some assets is not enough automatically to make them a good investment. All the other requirements for a good long-term care policy also apply to these asset-protection policies.

Those eligible may receive Medi-Cal benefits *in addition* to Medicare. (See Section D1, above.) Medi-Cal may pick up Medicare insurance deductibles or premiums, and cover a portion of reasonable charges that Medicare medical insurance doesn't cover for doctor bills and other outpatient care. Medi-Cal may also pay for prescription drugs, eyeglasses, dental care, and diagnostic and preventive care. Hospitals, doctors and other medical care providers accepting Medi-Cal patients must also accept Medi-Cal's payment of reasonable charges for services provided as payment in full. A Medi-Cal patient cannot be billed extra amounts for covered services.

Look in the white pages of the telephone book to find the nearest Medi-Cal office for information about eligibility and coverage.

3. Supplemental Health Insurance

Even if the conservatee receives medical coverage such as Medicare and Medi-Cal, it's extremely unlikely that all of her medical expenses will be covered under those plans. If the conservatee is only eligible for Medicare, a serious illness could wipe her out financially. A variety of additional insurance policies designed to cover long-term care may be available. Unfortunately, many such policies are expensive and virtually useless. They may duplicate Medicare coverage without providing for long-term custodial care. Most contain exclusions that keep the policy holder from qualifying for nursing facility care. If you are considering a supplemental policy, shop around

---

[5] If the conservatee is married, his spouse's income and assets may be taken into account when determining eligibility. If the conservatee is in a nursing home, the spouse's assets and income may not be counted in determining Medi-Cal eligibility.

carefully to find one that will provide the conservatee with the coverage she needs.[6]

FINDING LONG-TERM CARE INSURANCE

Information about long-term care policies may be obtained at no charge from the National Insurance Consumer Helpline, telephone (800) 942-4242. This organization provides free literature on long-term care insurance, Medicare supplemental insurance, companies marketing long-term care insurance, and information about disability and health insurance.

---

4. Other Sources for Health Insurance

If none of the sources discussed above provides sufficient information, you may need to spend some time and effort finding health insurance for the conservatee. Here are a few possibilities:

- If the conservatee became incapacitated suddenly, she may have health insurance coverage through her work which can be converted to a personal policy with similar coverage. Check with her former employer's health insurance or personnel office.

- You might be able to add the conservatee to your own medical insurance, particularly if she is a spouse or very close relative. Check with your own insurance company.

- Health Maintenance Organizations (HMOs) charge a monthly fee and provide basic medical services. Some HMOs have arrangements with Medicare to receive payments directly for services provided—although the Medicare patient is responsible for paying monthly HMO charges.

- Veterans may receive free or low-cost medical care at VA hospitals. (See Section E, below.)

- Depending on where you live, health care services may be provided for free or at low cost to elderly or disabled individuals. Check with local community clinics.

---

[6]Information on health insurance coverage can be found in *Beat the Nursing Home Trap*, by Joseph Matthews (Nolo Press).

E. Veterans' Administration Benefits

VETERANS AND THEIR CHILDREN or surviving spouses may be eligible for money, medical care and other benefits through the Veterans' Administration (VA). The type and amount of benefits available depend on the veteran's history of service, and whether he served in a war or during peacetime. Benefits available from the VA include pensions, disability compensation and medical treatment in VA hospitals. If the VA is paying benefits, it usually requires periodic accountings to monitor how the money is spent.

Look in the telephone book to find a local VA office to contact for information about eligibility and coverage.

F. Retirement, Pensions, Disability and Other Benefits

THE CONSERVATEE may be eligible for and receiving benefits from a former job. Or she may have become incapacitated before securing benefits to which she is entitled.[7] A brief sketch of different types of benefits follows.

1. Civil Service Retirement Benefits

To be eligible for money from the Civil Service Retirement System, a worker generally must be employed by the federal government for at least five years. Contributions may either be left in the Civil Service Retirement fund for a retirement pension, or may be removed in one lump sum.[8] Civil Service Retirement benefits are computed according to the number of years worked and the amount of money earned. A cost-of-living increase is added to the benefits.

---

[7]If you are conservator of the person only, you may be required to be appointed conservator of the estate as well before you may manage these assets. If the conservatee can manage her own finances, however, you may assist her in making arrangements to receive them.

[8] The money can be taken out in one lump sum up until 31 days after the date a person is eligible to receive a pension.

A federal worker may choose to receive maximum retirement benefits or reduced benefits so that her spouse will continue receiving some benefits upon her death. A surviving spouse or dependent child of a federal worker may be eligible for survivors' benefits if the worker was employed by the government for at least 18 months and died while still employed by the government.

2. Railroad Retirement System Benefits

Anyone who was employed for at least ten years in work directly connected to the operation of railroads—other than local or city rail and rapid transit systems—may be covered by the Railroad Retirement System.[9] These benefits are similar to those of Social Security. (See Section B, above.) Importantly, some retirees may be entitled to both Railroad Retirement and Social Security. For those who qualify, Railroad Retirement also provides a supplemental retirement annuity.

Railroad Retirement benefits are sometimes available to the surviving spouse or dependent children of a worker who dies while employed in the railroad industry.

3. Private and Government Pensions

If the conservatee or his spouse[10] worked for the government or a company with a private pension plan, contact that pension office and obtain a copy of the plan. As conservator, you may request a benefit statement which explains what benefits the conservatee has accrued and which of them has vested. The company must comply with your request only if you make it in writing and no more frequently than once a year.

If you can't get the information you need from the company, contact the Labor Management Services Administration. The local number should be listed in the United States Government section of the telephone book under the Department of Labor.

4. Disability Benefits

People who are ill or injured and unable to work may qualify for Social Security or SSI money benefits. (See Sections B and C in this chapter.) Each agency has its own definitions of what constitutes a "disability." Different businesses or government agencies may offer benefits to former employees. Disability benefits include:

- *State Disability Insurance (SDI).* People with medical disabilities that were not work-related may qualify for some financial assistance. SDI is funded by employee payroll deductions. For information, contact the California Employment Development Department.
- *Civil Service Disability Benefits.* Federal workers who were employed by the federal government for at least five years and become disabled by disease or injury before reaching retirement age may be eligible for Civil Service benefits.
- *Railroad Retirement Disability Benefits.* Former railroad workers may be entitled to disability benefits if they worked for the railroad for at least ten years or are at least 60 years of age, regardless of how many years they were employed. There are different eligibility requirements and types of disability benefits. Benefits also vary depending on the type and permanence of the disability.

5. Other Compensation

Some additional resources to contact for possible compensation for the conservatee include:

- *Unemployment Insurance.* The conservatee may be eligible if he became unemployed through no fault of his own within the last year and is still unemployed. California also offers disability benefits as part of its unemployment insurance program. Look in the government section of the telephone book for a local Unemployment Insurance office or the California Employment Development Department.

---

[9]Workers employed less than ten years will have credits to a regular Social Security retirement account.

[10]Some divorced conservatees may be eligible to receive pensions through an ex-spouse's pension plan, depending on the particular plan and whether the ex-spouse is still living.

- *Workers' Compensation.* The conservatee may be eligible if within the last year, he suffered or discovered a job-related injury or illness, or his spouse or child died from a job-related injury or illness. Look in the government section of the telephone book for a local Workers' Compensation office.

- *Compensation for Victims of Violent Crimes.* If the conservatee was the victim of a violent crime, he may be entitled to restitution from the person who committed the crime. Or a local victim/witness assistance program may provide help with expenses such as legal or medical bills, lost wages or loss of financial support. Contact your local victim/witness program, many of which are run by the district attorney or probation department. Or call the Victims of Crime Resource Center at (800) VICTIMS to obtain information.

- *Private Insurance.* The conservatee may hold disability policies, health, accident or crime victim's insurance, credit card insurance that pays credit card bills in case of disability, or other compensation benefits. Review any such policies and contact the insurance carrier. You'll need to provide the insurance company with documentation of all expenses and losses.

- *Veterans' Benefits.* There are programs that provide income to veterans of the U.S. military who become unable to work because of a disability, even if that disability is not a result of military service. The local Veterans' Administration office, listed in the federal government agency section of the telephone directory, can give you details.

- *Black Lung Benefits.* The Social Security Administration runs a special federal program that provides money benefits to victims of anthracosilicosis, an occupational disease often suffered by miners. Commonly known as black lung, the disease is caused by long exposure to coal particles in the air. It frequently leaves miners unable to work because they can't breath properly. The benefits under this program are also payable to dependents of black lung victims, so the best way to research the conservatee's eligibility for those benefits is to investigate details of the program at the local Social Security office.

G. Welfare Benefits

DEPENDING ON HER ASSETS and financial resources, the conservatee may be eligible for public assistance benefits to help pay the costs of food and housing. These benefits are distributed on the basis of need, so are available only to those who are very poor. Some eligible people don't apply because they feel embarrassed or too proud to accept the money. It's your job to make sure the conservatee receives all benefits to which she's entitled, so don't overlook this important source.

For information on home care, rehabilitation programs, General Assistance, Aid to Families with Dependent Children and other public assistance benefits, contact the local welfare office listed in the government section of the telephone book.

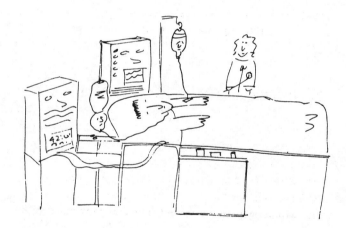

H. Food Stamps

The federal food stamp program is financed by the U.S. Department of Agriculture as a way of increasing the demand for food products. One doesn't have to be receiving welfare to qualify for food stamps. In fact, the eligibility formula for food stamps makes them available to many people who are not all that poor. If the conservatee has a relatively low income, check on whether she's eligible for food stamps. To locate the agency in your area that issues food stamps, look in county government offices listings in the telephone directory.

I. Subsidized (Section 8) Housing

SECTION 8 HOUSING is a housing program for low-income people subsidized by the government.[11] Eligibility requirements for subsidized housing vary from place to place, since funding comes from each city or county. If the conservatee has a low income, she may be eligible for Section 8 Housing, even if she is not now living in subsidized housing. If you qualify for Section 8 Housing and the conservatee is or will be living with you, it's likely that you will qualify for an additional bedroom. Contact the local Housing Authority for information.

---

[11]The program is called "Section 8" because it refers to subsidized housing covered in Section 8 of the Federal United States Housing Act (42 USC §1437f).

CHAPTER 11

YOUR ROLE AS CONSERVATOR
OF THE PERSON

AS CONSERVATOR OF THE PERSON, you are entrusted with the legal responsibility and authority to control many aspects of another person's life. This chapter gives an overview of your role and provides practical information for handling the job. Each person and situation is different, so this chapter cannot predict what will happen during your tenure as conservator. It does not tell you how to care for the conservatee, nor does it give advice about what choices to make. Your decisions will depend on the conservatee's health and temperament, your relationship with the conservatee, available community resources and family support.

The conservatee is probably someone who means a great deal to you, and to whom you have a strong commitment. It's likely that you have been helping the conservatee informally for some time. A conservatorship establishes your legal commitment to meet the conservatee's needs and make important personal and medical decisions on his behalf.

When a conservatorship is established, the conservatee's legal rights and daily decision-making abilities are limited. Remember that this set-up may be hard on the conservatee, since personal independence and self-esteem usually go hand-in-hand. When making decisions, be sensitive to the conservatee's needs and preferences. Talk to her about the conservatorship and your ideas, and find out what she wants. Help the conservatee maintain as much independence as possible. (A summary of the conservatee's legal rights is contained in Chapter 2, Section A1.)

You may also want to discuss your plans with the conservatee's family and close friends. Although you have legal authority to make decisions for the conservatee, there's no sense in creating conflicts between people who are all concerned about the conservatee's well-being. But sometimes people are too eager to give advice, so bear in mind that you'll need to follow your own good judgment.

If you need to make a particularly important decision, you can seek additional guidance from the court.[1]

 If you have not already made arrangements to obtain benefits and medical coverage for the conservatee, read Chapter 10.

THINGS YOU CAN DO TO MAKE LIFE EASIER

Whenever possible, help the conservatee maintain a lifestyle he enjoys and to which he is accustomed. Remember that little things add to the quality of life, so take the conservatee's preferences seriously.

- *Consult with Conservatee:* The conservatee is legally limited in the choices he may make about his own life, and this lack of control may be difficult. Seeking the conservatee's advice for even minor decisions can boost his morale. For example, before rearranging the furniture, check with the conservatee about how he wants it set up.

- *Habits and Preferences:* Try to keep up any routines the conservatee enjoys, such as periodic visits to a barber or beautician. If the conservatee is fond of certain belongings or cosmetics, make those available. Unless the items are valuable, see that the conservatee can get them without help—for example, a treasured photo album should be within reach, not on the top shelf of a hard-to-reach cabinet.

- *Social Contact:* Maintaining ties with others is very important. Encourage the conservatee's friends and family to stay in touch by phone or letter, and to take the conservatee out for visits, meals, concerts or other activities. Make sure you spend time with the conserva-tee. This will make your job more satisfying and give an emotional lift to the conservatee. If you are not living with the conservatee, you may choose to make frequent short phone calls or visits. Fit in time to go out with the conservatee for a meal, car ride, walk in the park or other pleasant event.

- *Pets:* If the conservatee owns a pet, see that it has enough food, water, exercise and is being properly treated. If the conservatee is fond of the pet, do your best to help them stay together.

- *Food and Nutrition:* Make sure the conservatee receives tasty, balanced meals. You may want to talk with a doctor or a nutritionist for help in setting up a meal plan. Keep the conservatee's preferences in mind—after all, there's no point in providing her with foods she doesn't like, just because they're part of a standard diet. If the conservatee can't cook for herself, you may be able to arrange to have some meals delivered. Some senior centers provide free or low-cost meals. (See Section B, for information on community resources.)

- *Entertainment:* If the conservatee is a music buff, see that she has access to a radio or sound system, and that any hearing aids are working correctly. If the conservatee enjoys magazines or books, arrange to have them available. The conservatee should always have good reading light and corrective lenses in the proper prescription. If she enjoys certain television shows, make sure a television is available. A remote control feature may be helpful for someone with mobility problems.

---

[1]The roles of the conservator of the person and conservator of the estate overlap in a variety of ways. For example, while you are responsible for deciding where the conservatee should live, the conservator of the estate must decide if the cost is suitable. Other areas such as budgeting, insurance and liability can be complicated, so get a lawyer's help if anyone else is conservator of the estate. (See Chapter 17.)

A. Conservator's Duties and Liabilities

YOU ARE RESPONSIBLE for seeing that the conservatee has adequate food, clothing, shelter and medical care. You will need to arrange for a great number of the conservatee's daily needs—which may include personal care, transportation, shopping, entertainment and visits with others. With some restrictions, you have authority to decide where the conservatee lives.[2] You may make medical decisions for a conservatee if he is unable to do so for himself. (Health care matters are covered in Section D of this chapter.)

 If the conservatee has not made estate planning arrangements, see Chapter 12, Section F4.

1. Responsibility to Protect and Control Conservatee

You must make arrangements to provide the conservatee with a safe and healthy environment. If the conservatee's home or apartment is a fire hazard or physically dangerous, change it. For example, if there are unsafe heaters or stacks of newspapers or other flammable material in the conservatee's residence, have them removed. (Also, see Section C of this chapter, which covers the conservatee's residence in more detail.)

If the conservatee damages other people or property and understands she is doing something wrong, the conservatee and her estate could be held liable. But if you are negligent and allow the conservatee to damage other people or property, you could be held personally liable. Physically controlling the conservatee can be touchy, since it is important to respect and encourage her independence. But if necessary, you must take steps to protect

others from harm. This should always be done in the least restrictive way. For example, if an emotionally volatile conservatee owns a cherished gun collection, remove ammunition from the weapons and the conservatee's home, and perhaps lock up the guns.

You may want to obtain insurance to protect yourself against possible liability to other people. However, these policies tend to be expensive and hard to find. (See Chapter 12, Section D3, for more information on insurance.)

 If the conservatee is violent and likely to injure himself or others, you may need the help of a mental health crisis worker. (See Section D2a of this chapter.)

VEHICLES AND DRIVING

If the conservatee owns or has access to a car, you must decide whether it is safe to let her drive. The conservatee should be permitted to drive only if she and the car are insured, her driver's license is current and she is able to drive competently. If you are also conservator of the estate, you may use money from the estate for insurance and license renewal. Or you may decide to sell the car. (See Chapter 12, Section C6 for details about a conservator of the estate's role when the conservatee owns a car and Chapter 12, Section D3 for information on obtaining insurance.)

---

2. If Conservatee Needs Financial Support

You are not legally obligated to support the conservatee financially unless he is your spouse, child or parent (Civil Code §242). If the conservatee needs financial help, apply for benefits on his behalf, such as Social Security or welfare. (See Chapter 10.) Although you may not be obligated to do so, the reality is that you may end up using some of your own money to cover the conservatee's needs. You may be able to claim the conservatee as a dependent on your tax returns, especially if you are closely related. Check with an accountant or tax advisor.

---

[2]You cannot move the conservatee to a new residence outside of California without court permission.

3. Contact with the Court

A conservator of the person handles the required conservatorship duties and maintains only limited contact with the court, such as filing documents or requesting court approval for a given action.

a. General Plan May Be Due Within 90 Days

See Chapter 9, Section E., If required, prepare a general plan following those guidelines. This typically must be done within 90 days of the date the judge signs the Order Appointing Probate Conservator.

b. Court Must Have Current Addresses

Promptly report any permanent change of address for you or the conservatee. To do so, complete a short form and file it with the court no more than thirty days after the move. (Instructions are contained in Chapter 4, Section H2.)

 If the court investigator cannot find the conservatee, the court can start proceedings to end the conservatorship (Probate Code §1853). So, if the conservatee will live in a different place for a few months, it's best to notify the court of the temporary change of address.

c. Periodic Investigations

One year after you are appointed conservator, and every two years after that, a court investigator will check to make sure the conservator is adequately handling the conservatee's needs. The investigator will meet with the conservator and will probably contact you and any other caretakers. An investigation may also be conducted if anyone brings a problem to the attention of the court—for example, if a doctor suspects the conservatee is being neglected or abused. (These investigations are covered in detail in Chapter 7.)

d. Seeking Help From the Court

You'll need to file documents with the court and obtain an order before you can:

- transfer the conservatorship to a different court (see Chapter 15, Section C4);

- step down as conservator or end the conservatorship altogether, usually because the conservatee dies or is able to take care of himself again (see Chapter 16); or

- obtain compensation for the time you spent on the conservatorship, if you are conservator of both the person and estate. Judges typically consider how much time you spent handling your duties and whether you performed tasks you would typically handle as a relative. (Compensation is covered in Chapter 12, Section H.)

4. When You Need an Attorney

Seek the help of an attorney if you want to:

- move the conservatee out of California for four or more months;

- make a controversial decision that anyone is likely to challenge—for example, placing the conservatee in a nursing facility against her wishes;

- make medical decisions that the conservatee is against, unless it is an emergency or the conservatee is legally disqualified from making all medical decisions;

- contest a petition filed by a medical facility or doctor compelling you to consent to a certain medical decision;

- authorize certain serious medical procedures such as shock therapy or experimental drugs; or

- prevent the conservatee from creating a will, marrying, seeking legal separation, divorcing or having a marriage annulled—or institute proceedings to have the conservatee's marriage annulled, seek separate maintenance, support or divorce.

B. Help from Community Resources

BEING A CONSERVATOR can be very demanding; it may come as a relief to find out that help is available. Many community organizations provide services ranging from hot meals at home to information and support groups for families of the terminally ill.

The available resources will vary. Most large communities and cities have a wide variety of free and moderately-priced services. These commonly include organizations that provide transportation for people with mobility problems, run senior centers, make daily social telephone calls to those who are house-bound and attend to the special needs of people with AIDS or other life-threatening illnesses. A number of agencies provide guidance on health care and insurance matters. Several give useful information on selecting a medical or long-term care facility.

If you're not familiar with your community's resources, and the conservatee is elderly, look up the local senior information and referral line in the government section of the white pages. Churches, synagogues, charitable organizations and government agencies may be able to assist you. Explain your situation, specify what kind of help you need, and obtain some phone numbers of available resources. (Also see Appendix A, which provides additional information about community resources.)

C.   The Conservatee's Residence

AS CONSERVATOR, you are responsible for deciding where in California the conservatee lives.[3] The conservatee must live in a place that is "the least restrictive appropriate setting" available (Probate Code §2352(a)(1)). This may be in the conservatee's own home or apartment, your home, a nursing facility, board and care home, convalescent hospital or other residence. You cannot move the conservatee out of California for longer than four months without first obtaining approval from the court.

1.   Keeping Conservatee at Home

It can be disruptive and disturbing to be uprooted to a new home. So avoid moving the conservatee unless her physical or mental situation changes dramatically, costs of maintaining the residence are too high or it would be dangerous for her to keep living there.

If the conservatee rents her apartment or house, contact the landlord about any needed repairs. Give the landlord your phone number and address, and let him know you are acting as conservator. If you are also conservator of the estate or are helping the conservatee with her financial matters, you will probably want to make arrangements to pay rent.[4]

If the conservatee owns her own home, look for unsafe features such as broken steps, loose handrailings, broken windows and doors and windows that don't close or lock properly. (If you are also conservator of the estate, see Chapter 12, Section G4 for information on paying for home repairs.) If there are building code violations, you must make the necessary changes. The home may also need to be altered to accommodate a wheelchair or additional handrailings.

Contact local utilities such as PG&E, water, garbage and the telephone company, and make sure the accounts are paid. If you're also handling the conservatee's finances, arrange for bills to be sent to you. You may request that utility companies contact you before shutting off any services because of nonpayment. If you're managing the conservatee's finances, make sure the mortgage or rent is paid on time.

If the conservatee lives alone or spends long periods of time alone, look into having a medical emergency response system installed. She could then get medical assistance simply by pushing a button located on a special necklace or bracelet. Obtain information about emergency response systems by contacting a hospital in your area. Or check with a company that specializes in these systems, such as Lifeline (800) 451-0525. Medi-Cal may cover part of the cost.

---

[3] If the court restricted your authority, the conservatee may make this decision (Probate Code §2352(d)). Check the Order Appointing Probate Conservator that was signed by a judge.

[4] If you have problems with the landlord—such as illegal rent increases in a rent-controlled community, unsuitable living conditions or a threatened eviction, contact a local tenant's organization. You may find useful information in *Tenant's Rights* by Myron Moskovitz and Ralph Warner (Nolo Press).

2. Living with Others

The conservatee may already live in your home or with other close friends or relatives. Or perhaps the conservatee was living on his own, but now needs a supervised housing arrangement. Shared housing may be a good way to provide the conservatee with the care and attention he needs. It may also be an excellent alternative to placing the conservatee in a long-term care facility. If the circumstances warrant it, look into obtaining in-home care. (See Section C3, below.)

If you're thinking about moving the conservatee in with others, discuss your plans with everyone involved—the conservatee and your spouse, children or other relatives or friends with whom he'd be living. Make sure there is ample space in the home, and that everyone is willing to devote the time and energy necessary to meet the conservatee's needs.

3. Using In-Home Care

Assistance with dressing, bathing, grooming and moving about may be the key to keeping the conservatee out of a long-term care facility. You—or a close family member or friend—may be able to help out. However, it's often sensible to hire someone to help take care of a conservatee, particularly if she is home alone for long periods. If you are conservator of the estate, expenses for in-home care may be paid from the estate.

There are many kinds of in-home care available, with services and fees that vary according to need. Home helpers may be hired to assist with routine chores and housecleaning. Attendants can help the conservatee with personal care and moving about. If the conservatee has a serious medical condition, it may be necessary to hire a registered nurse, licensed vocational nurse or physical therapist.

If you use an agency to find someone to provide in-home care, first make sure you're clear about what you need done and what qualifications the employee should have. You'll usually pay more for advanced degrees and skills, which is unnecessary when all that is needed are companionship and help with personal care. Discuss with the agency who will pay the employee's taxes and what

arrangements will be made if you're dissatisfied with the services provided.

If you hire someone directly rather than through an agency, you may need to conduct an interview and check references. If you hire someone, you are supposed to calculate and pay payroll taxes—including Social Security, disability and income taxes, and prepare various documents for government agencies. In reality, people often make informal hiring arrangements.[5]

4. Moving Conservatee to a Care Facility

If it is necessary to move a conservatee into a facility that provides constant care, select a place that best meets the conservatee's needs and is convenient for friends and family to visit. Seriously consider the conservatee's preferences and thoroughly research the available facilities, such as board and care residences or nursing homes. The level of care and services provided will vary in different facilities.[6]

Local senior information lines should be able to direct you to facilities in your area. Each county is covered by a local ombudsman program, funded by the Department on Aging. The local ombudsman keeps a record of citations filed against care facilities, and gives guidance on selecting a facility. To find your local ombudsman, call the Long Term Care Ombudsman at (800) 231-4024 or the Residential Care Complaint Hotline at (800) 422-5669.

Make sure the conservatee has personal items that are enjoyable or have sentimental value to her—such as special cosmetics, perfumes, clothing, photographs and jewelry. Of course, use your common sense when making valuable items available to the conservatee. For example,

---

[5]Detailed information on selecting and paying for home care services can be found in *Beat the Nursing Home Trap*, by Joseph Matthews (Nolo Press). Also see *Nolo's Law Form Kit: Hiring Child Care and Household Help* for instructions on hiring workers paying taxes and other legal details.

[6]*Beat the Nursing Home Trap*, by Joseph Matthews (Nolo Press) provides an overview of alternatives for selecting and financing long-term care, both in the home and in care facilities. The book also gives information on financial planning and protecting assets when someone is going to enter a care facility.

if she lives in a place where theft is a problem, it would not be advisable for her to keep expensive jewelry.

THE IMPORTANCE OF PLANNING

Care facilities are extremely expensive, and many people are forced into near poverty before funding such as Medi-Cal covers any of the costs. Planning can make a big difference, because certain assets are considered exempt by Medi-Cal and do not have to be used up before the agency will contribute funds. For example, if the conservatee owns her own home and enters a long-term care facility financed by Medi-Cal, it is essential that she sign a document—usually part of the application—stating that she plans to return to her home. If the conservatee cannot write, you may sign it for her as conservator. This will keep the home as an exempt asset, which allows her to keep the home and still qualify for Medi-Cal benefits.

D. Medical and Health Care Decisions

AS CONSERVATOR OF THE PERSON, you may need to make important, even life and death, medical decisions. You must always act in the best interests of the conservatee. You must make your decisions based on medical advice (Probate Code §2355(a)), although legally you're under no obligation to follow a doctor's recommendations—even in situations where life support may be withdrawn. A few forms of medical treatments are prohibited unless prior court approval is obtained. (See Sections D1 and D2, below.)

If the conservatee regularly sees medical doctors, dentists and other health care professionals, and is happy with their services, retain them when possible. And do your best to develop a good rapport with them. If you're not sure about any of their recommendations, don't hesitate to get a second or even a third opinion.

Learn about the probable effects of the conservatee's illness over time, since this will help you understand the need for certain types of medical care. Many organizations distribute valuable information about particular diseases such as Alzheimer's, cancer, AIDS and Parkinson's. (See Appendix A.)

If the conservatee is on Medicare or Medi-Cal, make sure the medical practitioners accept these payments. Keep good records of medical bills and documents received from doctors or other medical providers. You may need them later—for accounts or to give proof of medical expenses when applying for benefits.

While it may be uncomfortable to think about, now is a good time to consider what steps to take when the conservatee dies. If possible, find out his wishes about donating organs. (See Appendix A.)

1. Binding Decisions by Conservatee

The conservatee may have signed binding legal documents, such as a health care declaration or durable power of attorney for health care, specifying what medical treatment she wants or who is to make medical decisions. (These documents are discussed in detail in Chapter 2, Sections B1a and B1b.)

A durable power of attorney authorizes someone else to make health care decisions and can rarely be revoked or amended by a conservator (Civil Code §2402(a)).[7] If someone other than you was appointed to make decisions for the conservatee under a durable power of attorney for health care, that person—not you—has the right to make medical decisions for the conservatee. In that situation, you'll need to see an attorney.

A health care declaration, formerly called a living will, informs doctors about what medical treatment an individual wants provided, withdrawn or withheld. You and the conservatee's doctors must abide by the terms of the directive unless you obtain a court order that allows otherwise (Probate Code §2356(e)).

If the conservatee is able to communicate with you, find out her preferences for medical treatment, and do your best to follow them. If the conservatee is able to

---

[7]The exception is where the person appointed to make health care decisions under a durable power of attorney for health care has authorized something illegal or contrary to the conservatee's wishes or is not acting in the best interests of the conservatee. Then a separate court order may be sought seeking its termination (Civil Code §2412.5(d)). That is beyond the scope of this book.

write, get decisions about life-sustaining procedures and other urgent matters in writing.

2. Conservator's Guidelines for Medical Decisions

The court determines the scope of your authority to make medical decisions for the conservatee. When legally binding documents were prepared by the conservatee, they must be followed. (See Section D1 just above.)

Look at Item 3g of a copy of the Order Appointing Probate Conservator that was signed by the judge. If the judge didn't grant Item 3g of the order, you may authorize medical treatment only if the conservatee doesn't object. She retains the right to make her own medical choices, agree with your decisions, or override any medical decisions you make on her behalf.

If Item 3g is checked, the conservatee neither has legal capacity to make *any* medical decisions for herself nor to override the decisions you make for her. As long as you consent to treatment based on medical advice, you may authorize treatment the conservatee is opposed to, except if binding documents don't allow it (Probate Code §2355(a)).

If the conservatee lacks the capacity to consent to any medical treatment, and before the conservatorship was established followed a religion that professes healing by prayer alone, the conservatee must be treated by an accredited practitioner of that religion. Look at Item 3g of the Order Appointing Probate Conservator. If both the first and second boxes are checked (before the words "The treatment shall be performed by an accredited practitioner of the religion defined in section 2355(b) of the Probate Code"), the conservatee must be treated by an accredited practitioner of his religion. In these circumstances, you cannot authorize supplemental medical treatment without court approval, which would require the help of an attorney.

a   Prohibited Medical Treatment

You can neither consent to certain types of treatment nor obtain permission from the probate court to:

- authorize the conservatee to receive convulsive treatment (shock therapy or insulin coma treatment) or experimental drugs;
- place the conservatee in a locked mental health treatment facility against his will (Probate Code §2356(a), Welfare & Institutions Code §§5150, 5350);[8]
- authorize medical treatment that conflicts with binding documents created by the conservatee prior to the establishment of the conservatorship, such as a directive or durable power of attorney for health care; or
- make medical decisions for the conservatee if he already appointed someone else to make those decisions in a binding durable power of attorney for health care.

If you want to undertake these actions, you must first initiate a separate court proceeding. That is beyond the scope of this book. (See Chapter 17 for information on how to find a lawyer.)

---

[8] If the conservatee is an immediate danger to himself or others, call a mental health crisis hotline, listed in the front of the phone book. Workers there can assess the situation and get assistance, which can range from counseling to temporary placement in a supervised mental health treatment facility. If extended confinement is necessary, and the conservatee is against it, an LPS Conservatorship may be needed. (See Chapter 1, Section B5a.)

b. Medical Decisions Requiring Court Approval

(Look at Item 3g of the Order Appointing Probate Conservator that was signed by the judge to determine your authority to make medical decisions for the conservatee. You must first obtain a court order to:

- make *all* medical decisions for a conservatee if the court determined he was able to make medical decisions when the conservatorship was established;

- allow a conservatee to make medical decisions if the court determined he was unable to make all medical decisions when the conservatorship was established;

- authorize medical treatment against the conservatee's wishes or beliefs if the court determined he was able to make medical decisions when the conservatorship was established; or

- if the conservatee believes in healing by prayer alone, authorize medical treatment by someone other than an accredited practitioner of the conservatee's religion.

These situations are beyond the scope of this book and require the help of an attorney, since a lawyer will probably be appointed to represent the conservatee (Probate Code §2357(d)).

c. Controversial Medical Decisions

While not specifically required, you may choose to obtain court approval before making extremely difficult medical decisions such as:

- a nonemergency but major medical decision if everyone close to the conservatee is not in agreement about the choice (for example, chemotherapy or radical surgery);

- sterilizing the conservatee—unless required to prevent serious disability or death; or

- authorizing the withdrawal of life support systems, if there are any objections from the conservatee's family or doctors.[9]

See Chapter 15 for information on returning to court for instructions. Or consult with a lawyer. (See Chapter 17.)

3. Emergency Medical Decisions

In an emergency, a hospital or doctor may request the conservator's permission to go ahead with a medical procedure. The conservator is authorized to consent to medical treatment required to alleviate severe pain or necessary to treat a serious medical condition that would lead to serious disability or death. By law, the conservator must base the emergency decision on medical advice. If the conservatee believes in healing by prayer alone or has prepared binding documents such as a durable power of attorney for health care or living will, the conservator must follow those guidelines.

---

[9]A conservator may make a decision to withdraw life support systems—including nutrition and hydration—even if the conservatee didn't sign a document stating her wishes to have life support withdrawn. If the hospital is unwilling to remove life support, the conservatee may be transferred to a different facility.

CHAPTER 12

YOUR ROLE AS CONSERVATOR OF THE ESTATE

ONCE YOU HAVE FOLLOWED the instructions in Chapter 9 and been issued Letters of Conservatorship, you become legally responsible for managing the conservatee's finances. This chapter discusses your duties and liabilities as conservator of the estate. However, it does not give advice about making investment decisions or tell you how to manage the estate. If you need help in those areas, consult an accountant, financial advisor or attorney.

 You'll need to provide the court with papers giving information about the estate and its management. Read and follow the guidelines in Chapter 9, Section E, and Chapter 13 no more than two weeks after your appointment as conservator.

A. Overview of Duties and Liabilities

YOU MUST MANAGE and protect the conservatorship estate, which consists of the conservatee's income and assets. You are responsible for seeing that the conservatee's bills are paid, opening conservatorship bank accounts, insuring property and verifying that the conservatee receives all benefits to which she is entitled.

You must spend money from the estate only for the care and benefit of the conservatee and her dependents, taking into account the size of the estate and the conservatee's standard of living (Probate Code §2420).

You are required to manage the conservatee's assets prudently—even more cautiously than you handle your own property—and may not combine estate property with your own. You must first obtain court approval before taking any financial risks, such as speculative investing. If you do not handle the estate's assets prudently or do not seek court approval when required, you or the sureties on your bond could be held personally liable for money lost or debts incurred.

Example: As conservator of Donald's estate of $40,000, Greg doesn't pay attention to how much he spends to support Donald. He buys extravagant food, clothing and household items for Donald, and keeps poor financial records. At the end of a year, there is no money

left in the estate, and unpaid bills total $4,000. Greg could be liable for the unpaid bills.

Example: Alfred is conservator of Candy's estate of nearly $175,000 cash. Without first obtaining court approval, he invests all of her money in the stock of one company. The stock market plunges and Candy's money is lost. Alfred could be liable for the entire amount lost.

As conservator, you must also keep current paperwork—making an inventory of the assets in the estate and filing it with the court. You must also periodically report to the court about the conservatee's estate. (Chapter 13 gives instructions on court paperwork and appearances.) You are responsible for serving as conservator until you get a court order relieving you of your duties.

 The conservatee retains certain rights even after a conservatorship is established. A summary of the conservatee's legal rights is contained in Chapter 2, Section A1.

1. When to Seek Court Approval

A conservator is limited in what she may do without first getting permission from the court. These limitations protect both the conservator—from getting in over her head and then later being held liable for her actions, and the conservatee—from having his money mishandled. Court approval is required for:

- most real estate transactions (except as described in Sections B and G4 of this chapter);
- taking actions with estate property that are likely to be challenged by the conservatee's relatives or close friends;
- removing money from a blocked account (see Chapter 14, Section G and Chapter 15, Section C3);
- increasing or decreasing the amount of bond (see Chapter 14, Section F and Chapter 15, Section C2);
- obtaining financial compensation for your work (see Section H of this chapter);
- decisions which appear to be a conflict of interest for the conservator;

- hiring a lawyer;
- borrowing money; and
- any investment or transaction that is risky or complicated.

A conservator of the estate may ask the court to authorize or give instructions about an action she plans to take, or to approve or confirm an action she has already made. If in doubt, it is always preferable to obtain permission from the court before taking action. Although many matters requiring court approval are beyond the scope of this book, Chapter 15 provides valuable guidance on how to do it.

Example: Dorothy is conservator of Malcolm's estate. Malcolm's home is in need of major repairs, and Dorothy wants to hire her son, an experienced contractor, to do the work. First Dorothy gets several telephone estimates for the job, and obtains an estimate from her son—which is within the same range as the other estimates. Then she returns to court and obtains an order authorizing her to hire her son to do the work on Malcolm's house.

2. Hiring Outside Help

A financial advisor, bookkeeper or accountant may give helpful advice on how to handle the conservatorship estate. Before hiring anyone, compare prices and services.

If significant work will be required—such as auditing the conservatee's estate or another time-consuming, costly job—you'll need to obtain court approval first. (Follow the instructions for obtaining instructions from the court in Chapter 15, Section C1.)

 Seek the help of an attorney if:

- you want to handle complicated legal actions for the conservatee, including filing or defending lawsuits, bankruptcy petitions or other legal matters;
- someone else is serving as conservator of the person;
- the conservatee owes wages to employees—there are certain procedures for paying those wages;

- someone you've hired mismanages the estate's assets. By law, the conservatorship estate would be liable for damages caused and you or your sureties might be partially liable if you gave someone else too much power; or
- you were named attorney in fact in the conservatee's financial power of attorney and want to take actions using that authority.

B. Record Letters for Real Estate

THE CONSERVATEE MAY own partial or whole interest in real estate such as a home, apartment, condominium, business property or unimproved land in California. If so, you must record a certified copy of the Letters of Conservatorship in the County Recorder's office where the conservatee's real estate is located. This will protect you from liability by preventing the property from being mortgaged or sold unlawfully (Probate Code §1875).[1]

Recording costs vary from county to county and depend on the number of pages being recorded. It should cost about $7 if the Letters of Conservatorship are two pages, and those fees may be paid or reimbursed by the estate. Look in the telephone book for the County Recorder's office.

To record Letters of Conservatorship, you'll need an original certified copy of the document. Check the box at the top of the document before the words "If recorded return to." Then take or send the document along with one photocopy to the County Recorder's office in each county where the conservatee owns real estate.

If you mail the document, enclose a self-addressed, stamped envelope and request that the Letters of Conservatorship be recorded and returned to you. The County Recorder should first send back your copy, then the original certified Letters of Conservatorship, which usually takes at least several weeks. Keep these with your other conservatorship papers.

---

[1] If the conservatee owns property in another state, seek the help of an attorney.

C. Take Charge of Conservatorship Estate

IF THE CONSERVATEE is able, review his financial records with him. Find out what he owns, what insurance he holds and what debts are outstanding. If the conservatee is not capable of giving you this information, look through financial records such as his checkbook, account ledgers, deeds, current bank and broker statements, insurance policies and tax returns.

You may want to put through a change of address request with the Post Office asking it to forward the conservatee's mail to your address. That will give you valuable information about the conservatee's assets and alert you to problems that may arise—such as utility cutoff notices.

You'll need to let people and agencies know about the conservatorship, which probably will require a little legwork. Before most people will discuss the conservatee's finances or release any materials to you, you must provide them with a certified copy of the Letters of Conservatorship.

1. Locate Assets and Income

To manage the conservatorship estate, you'll obviously need to know what assets you will be responsible for managing. You'll also need this information to prepare documents required by the court approximately two months after the conservatorship is set up.[2] You also will need to know the exact balance in the conservatee's accounts at all financial institutions on the date the judge signed the Order Appointing Probate Conservator.

If other people or institutions have some of the conservatee's property, you may request that they turn it over to you. Provide them with a signed receipt acknowledging the specific property you receive. To obtain benefits or money owed the conservatee, let the agency or person know where those benefits or payments should be

sent. A sample letter is provided in Section C7, below. (See Chapter 10 for more information on financial benefits.)

---

[2]*Nolo's Personal Recordkeeper* by Carol Pladsen and Ralph Warner (Nolo Press), a software program, allows you to organize and keep track of personal and financial records, including insurance, bank records and other important items.

COMMON ASSETS AND INCOME

When you take over as conservator, you may have to spend some time going through the conservatee's papers, hunting down assets and organizing his finances. For example, it is common for people to own a number of bank accounts or bonds accumulated over many years. Here is a list to help you figure out what the conservatee may own:

- Cash (some might be kept or hidden in the conservatee's home)
- Uncashed checks, traveler's checks, and money orders payable to the conservatee, refunds (for example, tax, insurance premiums, utilities, magazine subscriptions, auto clubs, hospital reimbursements)
- Bank, savings and loan, credit union, trust accounts, certificates of deposit
- Stocks, bonds and securities
- Life or accident insurance policies
- Annuities, promissory notes and loans payable to the conservatee
- Disability and public benefits such as Social Security, Veterans' Administration benefits and welfare
- Retirement benefits or pension funds (such as IRA, Keogh, 401-k)
- Real estate including property held in joint tenancy or community property (house, condominium, burial plot) and deeds of trust, mobile home or houseboat, escrow payments and rental income
- Court-ordered spousal support
- Vehicles, boats and aircrafts
- Personal property held in a safe-deposit box, with a trust company or which the conservatee has lent to other people
- Coin, stamp, book or art collections, jewelry, furs, antiques and heirlooms
- Household items including furniture, musical instruments, computers, cameras, stereo equipment, appliances, power tools, firearms and sports equipment
- Valuable pets such as purebreds, show dogs or racehorses
- Patents, copyrights, trademarks, royalty contracts, court judgments in which the conservatee is the judgment creditor
- Business, joint venture or partnership interests
- Foreign investments

2. Identify Property That Is Not Part of Estate

You are responsible for handling most of the conservatee's property. But a few types of property are handled outside of the estate.

a. Conservatee's Wages

If the conservatee works, she has a right to keep and control her wages. They are not part of the conservatorship estate, and you are not accountable for how the conservatee handles them (Probate Code §2601).

If you want the conservatee's wages included in the estate, you could ask the court for such an order, but that is beyond the scope of this book.

b. Community Property

If the conservator is married, most of what she owns may be community property. Community property generally consists of property the spouses accumulate by their earnings during marriage—including wages, personal and real property, rents and profits from community assets and sometimes pensions.

The spouse of a married conservatee usually has the right to control the couple's community property without any accountability to the court, regardless of whether she's appointed conservator of his estate. By law, the spouse managing community property has a duty of good faith to the other spouse (Civil Code §5125(e)). The spouse must provide information about community property and debts if the conservatee or conservator requests it. The conservatee's spouse is also obligated to use community property to support the conservatee (Civil Code §242).[3]

---

[3]Should the conservatee's spouse fail to support the conservatee, an action may be filed in the conservatorship proceeding to enforce support or divide property as in a marital dissolution. That is beyond the scope of this book.

COMPLICATED COMMUNITY PROPERTY TRANSACTIONS REQUIRE A LAWYER'S HELP

When the spouse of a conservatee is handling community property, special procedures must be followed for certain transactions that are beyond the scope of this book. See a lawyer if:

- the conservatee's spouse becomes incapacitated, enters or is about to enter a nursing home, becomes a conservatee under a probate or LPS conservatorship or dies.

- any community property is held in a revocable living trust. The spouse does not have automatic rights to manage this property (Probate Code §3002).

- the conservator or the conservatee's spouse wants to divide community property and include all or a portion in the estate.

- the conservatee's spouse wants to encumber or get rid of community property, including real estate, furniture, furnishings, the conservatee's clothing or other personal items (Civil Code §§5125(b) and (c), 5127).

- the conservatee's spouse wants to lease, sell, convey or encumber all or a portion of real estate that is community property (Civil Code §5127).

- the conservatee's spouse wants to operate or manage a business that is mostly or all community property (Civil Code §5125(d)).

L. R. STEIN
ATTORNEY AT LAW

With either a court order or the other spouse's written consent filed with the court, all or part of the community property can be included in the estate. This might be a good idea if the non-conservatee spouse is likely to mismanage community property. Also, if either spouse is likely to enter a nursing home, community property assets would be quickly depleted, while dividing the property would allow the non–nursing home spouse to protect her portion.

Example: Harvey and Joyce are a married couple in their 60s. Harvey suffers from a stroke and is unable to handle any business or financial matters. Joyce is appointed conservator of his estate. The estate includes property Harvey owns separately—his family heirlooms, a vacation home he inherited and several bank accounts. Harvey's separate property is all under court supervision, but the majority of what Harvey and Joyce own is community property—their home, joint bank accounts, cars and household items. Joyce continues to handle the community property outside of the conservatorship; she need not file any documents with the court about it.

Example: Felicia and Manuel have been married for nearly 40 years when their daughter Elizabeth is appointed conservator of Felicia's estate. Felicia has a number of separate bank accounts and investments, as well as many community property assets. For a while, Elizabeth handles all the separate property while Manuel manages the community property outside of the conservatorship estate. But when Manuel totals the couple's car, Elizabeth becomes concerned that he may destroy or mismanage other community property. As conservator, she has the responsibility to protect Felicia's interests. With an attorney's help, she has the community property divided, and half comes under her management as part of the conservatorship estate.

3. Identify Jointly Owned Property

Financial accounts and property with title—such as real estate, vehicles, stocks and bonds—are often owned by more than one person. Check financial records and title documents to find out if the conservatee co-owns any

property. With the exception of community property (see discussion just above), you are responsible as conservator for managing the portion the conservatee owns. (Chapter 2, Section B2d, provides a description of different ways title may be held.)

To determine what portion of the asset the conservatee owns, you'll probably have to get copies of title documents.

 If there are conflicts over who owns jointly-held property or you want to divide property and include it in the conservatorship estate, consult a lawyer. (See Chapter 17.)

4. Change Name on Assets with Title

The title on assets other than real estate should be changed to your name, as conservator of the estate, to protect against them being mismanaged or sold improperly. This includes stocks, bonds, securities and mutual funds. (See Section B of this chapter for instructions on how to record Letters of Conservatorship when the conservatee owns real estate.)

Contact the title company, business or financial institution holding the assets and arrange to make the change. For example, title held in conservatee Samuel Suni's name would be transferred to "Cerisse Suni, Conservator of the Estate of Samuel Suni." The institution holding the assets will require you to provide certified Letters of Conservatorship. (A sample letter you can use to arrange for a name change on title is provided in Section C7, below.)

5. Cancel Credit Cards and Accounts

It may be advisable to cancel credit cards, automatic teller bank cards and charge accounts the conservatee holds to avoid unwieldy bills, but use your discretion. For example, if the conservatee has an account at a local grocery store and is not tallying up unreasonable bills there, it might be convenient to keep it open. (A sample letter to cancel credit cards and other charge accounts is provided in Section C7, below.)

6. Take Precautions If Conservatee Owns a Vehicle

If the conservatee is able to drive safely and has a current driver's license, see to it that both the car and conservatee are adequately insured. (Also see Chapter 11, Section A1, which discusses a conservator's potential liability for allowing a conservatee to drive unsafely.)

If it is unsafe for the conservatee to drive, you may sell her vehicle. A court order must be obtained beforehand if by selling the vehicle you dispose of more than $5,000 of the conservatee's assets in one year. You must also comply with DMV requirements, which include notifying the DMV of the sale no more than five days after the transfer.

If you don't sell the car, obtain the ownership certificate and notify any lender that a conservatorship has been established. Change the title with the DMV into the name of the conservatorship. Do not transfer the title into your own name, or your name as conservator of the estate. That could make you legally responsible if the car were involved in an accident.

If you keep the car, you or anyone else may drive it only for the conservatee's benefit. Keep registration current. If the vehicle is expensive and is not likely to depreciate in value, perhaps an antique car, place it in an insured storage facility.

7. Contact Institutions and Businesses

If you notify institutions, agencies and businesses by mail about the conservatorship, modify the accompanying letter to meet your situation.

SAMPLE LETTER

March 10, 19__

Re: Conservatorship of Barbara Rowdy

To whom it concerns:

On March 6, 19__, I was appointed conservator of the estate of Barbara Rowdy. Enclosed is a certified copy of the Letters of Conservatorship. From now on, please send all correspondence and documents concerning Ms. Rowdy to: Sherman Oyster, Conservator of the Estate of Barbara Rowdy, 2020 Vision Street, San Francisco, CA 94104. I can be reached at (415) 555-1212.

[*To receive benefits*:] Please make Ms. Rowdy's Veterans' Administration [*or other agency benefits*] checks payable to: "Sherman Oyster, Conservator of the Estate of Barbara Rowdy," and send them directly to me. Also, advise me if your agency has any special accounting requirements.

[*For bank accounts*:] Please send me a listing of all accounts held by Ms. Rowdy at the Bank of Berkeley, the manner in which title is held and the balance of each account on March 6, 19__ [*the date the judge signed the Order Appointing Probate Conservator*]. I would also appreciate a copy of the most recent bank statements for accounts held by Ms. Rowdy at the Bank of Berkeley, along with a listing of the interest rate and current balance in each account. I would also like to know if Ms. Rowdy has a safe-deposit box at your institution. This letter advises you that I am revoking any signature authorization on Ms. Rowdy's accounts.

Enclosed is an automatic teller machine card that has been cut in half for account number 99999999. I request that all automatic teller machine cards for this account be canceled effective immediately.

I understand that although there might ordinarily be an early withdrawal penalty, accounts in federally-insured institutions may be withdrawn before the maturation date when a conservatorship is established. Please let me know your institution's policies.

[*For stock transfer:*] Please transfer the stock from Ms. Rowdy's name to "Sherman Oyster, Conservator of the Estate of Barbara Rowdy." Also, let me know how many shares of stock Ms. Rowdy owns, and forward forms to me for the transfer. This letter advises you that Ms. Rowdy is no longer authorized to transact business on any stock accounts held with your company.

[*For canceling credit cards:*] Enclosed is a credit card which has been cut in half for account number 99999999. I request that all credit card accounts held by Ms. Rowdy at your institution be canceled as of the date of this letter. Please send final statements to me.

[*To tenant renting conservatee's property:*] Rental checks should be made payable to: "Sherman Oyster, Conservator of the Estate of Barbara Rowdy," and sent directly to me. Please contact me with any questions or problems about your rental unit.

Sincerely,

Sherman Oyster
Enclosure

D. Bank Accounts, Insurance and Valuables

A CONSERVATOR MUST MANAGE the conservatee's money and assets carefully. This section provides information on how to handle financial accounts, insurance and valuables.

1. Bank Accounts

The conservatee probably has bank accounts, savings and loan or credit union accounts. Either change them into the name of the conservatorship or close them and open conservatorship accounts as needed. All conservatorship accounts should be in your name as conservator of the estate, with no other authorized signators. For example, Joe Evans is conservator of Mary Jones, and the name on the account is "Joe Evans, Conservator of the Estate of Mary Jones."

For accounts that are already open, any signature authorizations on the accounts should be revoked. You will need the balance in the conservatee's open accounts on the date the judge signed the Order Appointing Probate Conservator.[4] Accounts in federally insured institutions may be withdrawn without penalty before the maturation date when a conservatorship is established, but you may need to remind some institutions of this. If you contact financial institutions by letter, modify the sample letter in Section C7 of this chapter.

Always use the conservatee's Social Security number for accounts. If you use your own Social Security number, it may create serious problems with taxes, and may open you to allegations of commingling funds. To establish a conservatorship account, you'll need to provide a certified copy of the Letters of Conservatorship. If you want to establish or remove funds from a blocked account, see Chapter 14.

---

[4]This information is needed to prepare the Inventory and Appraisement covered in Chapter 13, Section C3.

All conservatorship accounts that you set up must be with federally insured financial institutions, and no more than the insured amount—currently $100,000—should be deposited with a single financial institution. Deposit money in accounts that earn the highest possible interest rate, unless you anticipate the need to withdraw money and incur penalties. Large amounts of money should be deposited in interest-bearing accounts such as savings or money market accounts, and funds should be transferred to a low-interest or non-interest bearing checking account as needed. Conservators often find it convenient to keep enough money to handle two or three months' worth of expenses in a checking account.

2. Conservatee's Separate Bank Account

A conservatee may want to maintain a small personal account to help preserve independence and self-esteem. Courts often encourage this. If the conservatee has a personal account, do not be a co-signer on it, and do not include it as part of the conservatorship estate. This set-up is appropriate only if:

- the conservatee will be receiving wages for her work—since her earnings are not part of the estate. (Wages are discussed in Section C2a of this chapter.)

- the court authorized the conservatee to receive an allowance, which could be given directly to the conservatee as cash or deposited into the conservatee's independent account. (Look at Item 31 of the signed Order Appointing Probate Conservator.)

3. Insurance

A conservator is authorized to:

- obtain, change or end policies for medical, hospital, health or disability insurance;

- continue plans for life or annuity insurance or employee welfare plans or benefits; or

- insure the conservatee, conservator or estate against liability to others.

Take steps to protect any valuable estate property against fire, theft or other possible hazards. For example, if the conservatee's estate includes a house and a vehicle, insure both of them. If someone is living in the conservatee's house, or caretakers work in the home, take careful steps to protect the property, especially jewelry and valuable small items that are easily stolen or misplaced. If you aren't sure how to insure or protect the conservatee's property, seek the help of a qualified insurance agent. Check prices and recommendations so you have the correct amount of coverage at a reasonable price.

You may also obtain insurance which covers the conservatee's last major illness and burial expenses. But if that insurance is expensive, secure a court order first.

 Prior court approval is needed before a conservator may:

- elect benefit or payment options, allow a policy to end, change beneficiaries or ownership, assign rights, borrow against a policy or cash in an insurance policy (Probate Code §2459(c));[5] or

- allow a life insurance policy to lapse. The court will probably require that the beneficiaries be informed before granting such an order.

4. Valuables and Safe-Deposit Boxes

Valuable items such as securities, jewelry and stamp or coin collections should be deposited in a safe-deposit box at an insured financial institution or with a trust company authorized to do business in California. Unless a court order designated that certain personal property be placed in a blocked account, it can be removed without permission from the court. (Note that the amount of bond required might decrease if valuables are placed in blocked accounts. See Chapter 14, Section F.)

Larger items of value—such as furs, antiques, artwork and collector's items—may be placed in an insured rental

---

[5] If a conservatee had a practice of borrowing on the loan value of an insurance policy to pay current premiums, the conservator can follow this practice without court approval (Probate Code §2459(d)).

storage space. It's a good idea to photograph valuables for insurance purposes.

E. Organize the Estate

A CONSERVATOR MUST keep extremely accurate financial records. You will use these records to prepare required court documents, and to answer any questions about your management of the estate.[6]

1. Keep Track of Debts and Expenses

Find out what the conservatee owes and whether any payments are overdue. Note any of the conservatee's outstanding bills and regular expenses to assist in making a budget. You may need to go through the conservatee's personal papers and contact banks or companies that hold her mortgage, supply utilities or provide nursing care. If the conservatee has a checkbook register, it may be a helpful information source. You may also need to look through the conservatee's unopened or overlooked mail; you might discover that the rent hasn't been paid and the phone bill is past due.

If the conservatee has debts that were incurred before the conservatorship was set up, make arrangements to pay them. If there are any debts you don't believe the conservatee owes, you may either refuse to pay or return to court for an order authorizing their payment. If you don't pay a debt, it's possible the conservatee could be sued—and you would then need to hire a lawyer. (See Chapter 17.)

 Certain funds, such as welfare, Social Security and VA benefits, should not be used to pay the conservatee's debts, because they are considered exempt from collection. If the conservatee's finances are in shambles, you may want to consult a group such as Consumer Credit

Counselors or seek help from an accountant or financial consultant. It may even be appropriate to seek termination of the conservatorship. (See Chapter 16.)

COMMON DEBTS AND EXPENSES

It may take some digging to figure out what the conservatee owes and what her expenses are likely to be. To help you anticipate potential debts and expenses, here is a list of some common ones:

- Rent or mortgage payments, home maintenance or repair costs
- Utilities (gas and electric, telephone, water)
- Transportation expenses such as car payments and insurance
- Clothing, laundry and cleaning
- Food, personal and household items
- Home care workers
- Nursing and medical care, medication, medical aids and medical supplies
- Insurance premiums (home, life, accident, health)
- Loans (bank or personal), court judgments against the conservatee
- Credit card charges, department store charges
- Bills owing attorneys, accountants, medical professionals
- State, federal or municipal taxes
- Spousal or child support
- Wages due employees

---

2. Set Up Budget

Set up a budget that includes all the conservatee's expected expenses and debts—and the income available to pay them. You may want to get help from a bookkeeper or accountant if you're not familiar with budgeting.

If possible, discuss budgeting with the conservatee. Take into account the size of the estate, the conservatee's lifestyle, age and life expectancy. Don't forget to include possible expenses of handling the estate such as accountants' fees, bond premiums, and conservator's fees, if you are requesting any. (See Section H for information on compensation for your role as conservator.)

---

[6]*Nolo's Personal Recordkeeper* (Nolo Press) is a software program that allows you to organize and keep track of personal and financial records, including insurance, bank documents and other important items.

3. Establish Ongoing Accounting System

Keep detailed records of all money you spend and receive as conservator. Expenditures must be for the support and benefit of the conservatee and any dependents, and should be clearly itemized in the conservatorship check register or passbook. Whenever possible, make payments by check rather than cash to provide a detailed list of all expenses.

For very simple estates, a balanced checkbook with detailed entries will provide most of the information needed. You may want to use a very simple checkbook management program for your computer. For more complex estates you may need a more sophisticated system of accounting may. Before setting up your accounting system, become familiar with the conservatorship documents and information the court requires. (See Chapter 13.)

4. Save Receipts and Statements

You must account to the court for all expenditures you make on behalf of the conservatee or his estate, so keep all receipts, no matter how small the amount. You will need to give the court a breakdown of these expenditures—including costs of the conservatee's food, housing, clothing and medical care. You must also account for expenditures made while managing the estate such as payments for insurance premiums, accountants' fees or claim settlements.

Depending on the court's policies, you may need to produce originals or copies of the receipts. Keep receipts in a safe, organized place such as in an envelope or file folder. Even though the court may never ask to see the original receipts, you're better off safe than sorry.

Keep careful track of all statements, correspondence and other documents from financial institutions. Some courts guard against the possibility of altering documents by requiring you to attach original bank statements to your financial accounts. Keep copies of all financial documents for at least five years.

F. Guidelines for Handling the Estate

FOLLOW THE GENERAL SUGGESTIONS set out in this section for handling the conservatorship estate.

1. Avoid Conflicts of Interest

Never get into transactions in which your own financial interests and those of the estate could conflict without first getting authorization from the court. For example, do not purchase assets from the estate at less than a fair price or purchase life insurance for the conservatee in which you are named the beneficiary.

If you owe the conservatee money—and you wish to have the amount reduced, you must seek court approval (Probate Code §2503(a)-(b)). If you profit by your actions or harm the estate, you could be removed from your role as conservator (Probate Code §2650(f)). (If you have any doubt about a transaction, seek court approval before undertaking it. See Chapter 15.)

2. Keep Estate Separate

All accounts and assets belonging to the conservatee, including those with title, must either be in the name of the estate or in your name specifically as conservator of the estate—and must be kept separate from your property.

The conservatee's Social Security number should always be used. Even if an asset is listed in your name as conservator of the estate, remember that you are handling it for the conservatee's benefit. It does not belong to you.

3.   Maintain Adequate Bond

Bond is a type of financial guarantee under which you arrange to reimburse the estate for stolen or misappropriated estate assets. When you are appointed conservator of the estate, you are usually required to post and maintain the correct amount of bond. (See Chapter 14 for details on bond. Instructions on changing the bond amount are covered in Chapter 15, Section C2.)

4.   Check Estate Planning

Estate planning is the method of designating to whom and how property is to be transferred after death, usually by will. Several other common estate planning arrangements, such as trusts, allow for assets to go directly to another person without having it processed through the time-consuming and costly court procedure known as probate.[7]

If the conservatee is of sound mind and wishes to make estate planning arrangements, that should be done now, before his condition changes. If the conservatee is incapable of making estate planning arrangements, you can't make them for him. As conservator, you have no right to create or change the conservatee's will.[8]

Do not sign the conservatee's estate planning documents as a witness, since that could be used as proof of your undue influence should the conservatee's heirs con-

---

[7] Detailed information and step-by-step instructions on estate planning are contained in *Plan Your Estate with a Living Trust* by Denis Clifford (Nolo Press), *The Simple Will Book* by Denis Clifford (Nolo Press) and, for those with access to a personal computer, *WillMaker* (Nolo Press/ Legisoft) provides software and a manual to take you through the steps of making your own will.

[8] A conservator may create living trusts that are consistent with the conservatee's will and estate planning documents. If you want to do that, consult an attorney. (See Chapter 17.)

test them later. If the conservatee wants to create or change estate planning documents, it may make sense for him to hire his own attorney, which will require prior court approval.

G.   Managing the Estate

THIS SECTION CONTAINS some general suggestions and rules for managing the conservatorship estate. Bear in mind that most complex or potentially risky actions require a court order. (See Chapter 15 for information on returning to court to obtain approval.)

 If you plan to enter into long-term contracts, manage a business or need help handling the estate, consider hiring an accountant, financial advisor or attorney. Court approval may be required beforehand. (See Section A2, above.)

1.   Investments

As conservator, you may buy and sell stocks, bonds and securities listed and purchased on a United States stock or bond exchange, registered money market mutual funds invested in federal obligations,[9] or direct obligations of either California or the federal government that have a remaining maturity of five years or less (Probate Code §2574). If you retain stock, be very careful. Only invest in relatively safe, conservative investments. If the conservatee already has a brokerage account, send a letter to the brokerage house and change title to your name as conservator of the estate. (See the sample letter in Section C7 of this chapter.)

You may continue a dividend reinvestment plan with a corporation or mutual fund that the conservatee set up before the conservatorship. You may also continue plans

---

[9] They must mature no later than five years from the date of investment. Repurchase agreements that are fully collateralized by U.S. government obligations are also allowed.

for annuities, profit-sharing, employee welfare or benefits.[10]

Do not play the stock market or take any investment risks without first getting court approval. If you mishandle any of the estate, you could be held personally liable. And even if a transaction is authorized by law, you may only make it if it is considered a safe investment. Seek the help of a financial advisor or lawyer if you have questions.

 You must obtain court approval to:

- invest in bonds issued by any state other than California, or any city or district in any state;

- elect benefit or payment options, change beneficiaries, or take other steps to alter or end a plan the conservatee already has—such as an annuities, profit-sharing, employee welfare or benefits plan; or

- invest in any type of money fund other than registered money market mutual funds invested in federal obligations.

2. Lending, Giving Away and Selling Property

You may get rid of the conservatee's valueless property, such as broken dishes or furniture, old or torn clothing and other useless items that cannot be sold (Probate Code §2465). Consider donating these items to charity and later claiming deductions on the conservatee's tax returns. Always get a detailed receipt from the organization to which you donate.

If you're not sure whether an item has value, play it safe. Keep it, get it appraised or obtain permission from the court before getting rid of it. Also, make sure property you give away is not co-owned with someone else. Keep

in mind that if you sell property, the conservatee may have to pay taxes because of his increased income.

You may lend money as long as you obtain a reasonable amount of interest. For example, do not make interest-free or low-interest loans to yourself or family members, even if the conservatee might have done so.

No court approval is necessary to sell personal property that will burden the estate if it's retained. For example, perishable property or property that is sitting in storage and depreciating in value could be sold without court authorization. Again, make sure property you sell is not co-owned with someone else.

You may usually sell up to $5,000 worth of personal property per year without getting court permission. However, if you want to sell household furnishings or effects and the conservatee doesn't want them sold, you'll need to obtain a court order.

 Seek court approval before you:

- make gifts of any estate property or income (Probate Code §2580);

- give away extra income that isn't needed to support the conservatee or his dependents, even if the conservatee had a practice of doing that before the conservatorship was established (Probate Code §2423);

- sell real estate, secured or unsecured notes, contracts for mining property or contracts to sell real estate, or securities;[11]

- exchange any estate assets for other property—for example, trading parcels of real estate or exchanging stocks or bonds for different ones (Probate Code §2557);

- sell personal property exceeding $5,000 per year or sell household furnishings or effects that the conservatee doesn't want sold; or

- sell anything that has been left to someone in the conservatee's will or other estate planning documents.

---

[10]Other permissible investments include certain common trust funds (Probate Code §2574(a)(6)), U.S. Treasury bonds redeemable at par value to federal estate taxes when the holder dies—also referred to as Flower Bonds (Probate Code §2574(a)(4)) and eligible securities for the investment of surplus state money (Probate Code §2574(a)(4)).

---

[11]A Judicial Council form, "Ex Parte Petition for Authority to Sell Securities and Order," available from the court and libraries, may be used. With an ex parte petition, no one must be formally notified. (The procedure is beyond the scope of this book.)

In addition to obtaining court permission, you must formally notify the intended beneficiary.

3. Settlements, Compromises and Claims

You may extend, renew or modify loans or judgments held by the conservatee. You may settle or compromise most claims under $25,000, including claims for support. The exception to the $25,000 ceiling is taxes, which aren't limited to the $25,000 amount and don't require court approval. However, all other settlements, compromises and claims require a court order. (See Section G6 of this chapter which discusses compromising unpaid taxes.)

4. Conservatee's Residence and Real Estate

You may handle lease or rental agreements for the conservatee's real estate where the amount involved is $1,500 or less per month, or is month-to-month. You can sign lease or rental agreements if the conservatee rents or is in a care facility.

Arrange to make rent or mortgage payments as well as paying other costs of maintaining the conservatee's residence. If there are utility bills, contact local companies that provide services such as PG&E, water and telephone companies. Make sure the accounts are paid. If the conservatee has a low income or is elderly, find out whether she qualifies for special rates or discounts. Arrange for bills to be sent to you. (Also read Chapter 11, Section C, which gives information about the conservatee's residence for a conservator of the person.)

You may arrange for repairs or maintenance of the home where the conservatee or her dependents live without seeking court approval (Probate Code §2457). However, if you want to make improvements such as adding an additional room or extensively redecorating the house, you must get permission from the court.

You'll need court authorization for most matters concerning real estate, including:

- buying, selling, refinancing or borrowing against property;
- changing ownership of real property, partitioning, granting easements, foreclosing or accepting deeds of trust; or
- arranging for you, a friend or relative to live with the conservatee while paying little or no rent.

5. Business Interests

If the conservatee owns shares in a corporation in California or another state, or is a member of a nonprofit corporation, no court approval is needed for the conservator to:

- vote shares;
- grant proxies to exercise voting rights;
- waive notice or give consent to the holding of shareholders' meetings; or
- authorize, ratify, approve or confirm any action taken by shareholders, members or property owners (Probate Code §2458).

If the conservatee is a partner or sole proprietor of a business, you legally have authority to continue the business. But because businesses often include contracts between owners, dealing with business interests may be complex. You'll need court approval to sell the conservatee's partnership interests and take most other business actions, such as exercising stock options or participating in a corporate merger or dissolution. That is beyond the scope of this book.

6. Taxes and Tax Returns

You are responsible for preparing, signing and filing all tax returns on behalf of the conservatee. These may include federal, state, municipal, property and income taxes. All tax returns should be prepared in the conservatee's name and Social Security number.

Be aware that if the conservatee lives in a nursing home, he may be entitled to special tax credits. You may complete the tax returns yourself, or hire a tax preparer or accountant and pay for these services directly out of the conservatee's estate, without obtaining prior court approval.[12]

If prior taxes weren't paid or filed, you will need to take care of them. Obtain this information from the appropriate taxing authorities, who will probably require a certified copy of the Letters of Conservatorship before releasing copies of tax records. If penalties were assessed because tax returns weren't filed or taxes weren't paid, those penalties probably can be waived if the conservatee was mentally incapable of handling his taxes. Your appointment as conservator is an important basis of proof that the conservatee didn't have the capacity to file his tax returns. If the taxing agency insists on imposing a penalty despite the conservatorship, send a letter explaining the situation, request that penalties be waived and attach copies of tax returns. If the taxing agency is uncooperative and the penalty amount warrants it, hire an attorney. (See Section G3 for information on compromising claims.)

If you hired employees, you are responsible for seeing that employment taxes are paid. If you made any gifts from the estate, you may need to file gift tax returns. (You'll need a court order to make gifts from the estate. See Section G2, above.)

---

[12]Court approval is needed if the tax preparer or accountant performs significant work, such as auditing the conservatee's estate. Unless you are familiar with tax law, you are probably better off hiring a professional to prepare the conservatee's taxes.

TAX REFUNDS AND POSTPONEMENT

If the conservatee is blind, disabled or at least 62 years old and lives in a household with a low annual income—currently $13,200 or less—part of the taxes may be refunded by the State of California. A conservatee living in a convalescent home or residential care facility may also be eligible for this refund. To obtain information on the Homeowners Assistance and Renters Assistance programs, contact the Franchise Tax Board at (800) 852-7050.

If the conservatee is blind, disabled or at least 62 years old, owns at least 20% equity in a home and has an annual household income of less than $24,000, he may be eligible for a property tax postponement. With this arrangement, a lien is placed on the house, and taxes are due when the conservatee sells his house, moves out or dies. Information on this program is available from Property Tax Postponement for Senior Citizens at (800) 952-5661.

7. Finding Additional Cash

Should debts or ongoing expenses exceed the conservatee's income, try to revise the estate budget so you can pay all the bills. Also look into obtaining additional benefits for the conservatee, discussed in Chapter 10. If the income is insufficient to support the conservatee and his dependents or if the conservatee's debts exceed cash on hand, you may need to sell some of his assets. (See Section G2 of this chapter.)

You have no responsibility to support the conservatee financially, unless he is your spouse, child or parent (Civil Code §242). (See the discussion of community property and the spouse's duties in Section C2b of this chapter.) However, conservators sometimes lend money to the conservatorship estate until monthly income is received. If you advance money to the conservatee or her estate, you may reimburse yourself without court approval as long as you don't receive interest or any compensation for your loan. Only with court approval may you receive interest at the legal rate accrued on court judgments (Probate Code §2466).

Court authorization is needed if you want to borrow money on behalf of the estate. But borrowing could be unwise. For example, if the conservatee receives Medi-Cal or other benefits available to those with low incomes, taking out a mortgage may result in her losing needed benefits because a home is considered an exempt asset to these agencies, but cash is not exempt.

Borrowing money may seem like a good idea to get out of an immediate cash bind, but repaying the loan with interest could later be a burden. And if the conservatee dies before the loan is repaid, her estate plan could be significantly affected.

 Consult an attorney if you are interested in taking out a loan, regular mortgage or reverse annuity mortgage. (See Chapter 17.)

REVERSE ANNUITY MORTGAGES

For older conservatees who own their homes, a reverse annuity mortgage may be an excellent way of obtaining funds. This type of mortgage works opposite from a regular mortgage—where a person receives a large sum of money and repays it in monthly payments. With a reverse annuity mortgage, a lender pays monthly payments to the conservatee, who must repay the loan in a lump sum at the end of the loan term. The loan is usually designed to last between three and twelve years, with repayment made from the proceeds of the sale of the house. Reverse annuity mortgages do not affect Social Security benefits, SSI or Medicare eligibility.

A reverse annuity mortgage can be set up so monthly payments increase over time—anticipating inflation and the need for more funds as the conservatee gets older. To qualify for a reverse annuity mortgage, the conservatee generally must be at least 70 years of age, have free and clear title to a single family home, townhouse or condominium and meet low to moderate income and asset guidelines. Only a few financial institutions offer reverse annuity mortgages.

H. Reimbursements and Compensation

WITH COURT APPROVAL, a conservator of the estate or person and estate may be reimbursed for time spent or expenses incurred in taking care of a conservatee or his estate. Generally, courts only approve financial compensation for duties performed as a conservator rather than as a family member. For example, a conservator probably wouldn't be paid for visiting the conservatee, but she might be entitled to be paid for time spent doing bookkeeping for the estate.

1. Court Costs and Bond Premiums

You do not need court approval to reimburse yourself for fees paid to the county clerk to obtain the conservatorship. You can pay yourself back using estate funds, and then show these expenditures on the accounts you later file with the court. You may also reimburse yourself for amounts paid as premiums on your bond, if bonding was obtained through a surety company rather than through private sureties. Remember to keep receipts and records of all expenditures and reimbursements; you'll need them when you prepare accounting documents.

2. Conservatorship Expenses

A conservator of the estate typically is not personally responsible for paying the estate's expenses, unless he's married to the conservatee, or the conservatee is a dependent child or parent in need. The conservator normally is permitted to hire competent help as needed—such as an accountant and perhaps an investment advisor—as long as the expense is reasonably related to the size of the estate. A conservator may also hire an attorney to represent either the conservatee or her estate, but you must first get court approval.

The conservator of the estate or person and estate may be reimbursed from the estate's assets for:

- money of her own which she paid for the benefit of the conservatee (Probate Code §2623). This includes money spent for the conservatee before the conservatorship was established. [13]

---

[13] If you spent your own money supporting the conservatee before your appointment as conservator, the expenditures must have been the type you would have been authorized to make as conservator, and made with the intention that you'd be paid back.

- expenses incurred to maintain and repair the place where the conservatee lives (Probate Code §2457).

- expenses incurred in collecting and managing the conservatee's estate—such as long distance phone calls and extraordinary traveling expenses (Probate Code §2430(a)(4)). However, you cannot be reimbursed for postage, photocopying costs, the cost of your trips to court, or for ordinary mileage. It is presumed those costs will be covered by the conservator's compensation fees, if any.

3. Compensation for a Conservator's Time

You may get compensation from the estate for your services if you spent a lot of time managing the estate. Bear in mind that financial compensation is treated as your income for tax purposes. If you'll be receiving money from the conservatee's estate after he dies, you may choose not to be paid now. An accountant may be able to help you decide what is most prudent financially.

If you want to receive compensation, keep a written record of the time you spent working on the conservatorship. Sometimes courts will not allow compensation for work done as conservator of the person if the conservatee is a close family member. Courts also may not allow compensation if the conservator has put in very little time in his role as conservator, has not acted in the conservatee's best interests or has not followed court procedures—including filing accounts on time.

Local probate rules may govern the amount and procedure for obtaining compensation. Some have set schedules of how much the conservatee may receive, which is usually based on the value of the estate. Check your local probate policy manual.

You must petition the court for an order granting compensation. The amount is typically fixed by local court rule or practice, and usually amounts to a certain percentage of the value of estate. The court may also authorize periodic payments to the conservator for services (Probate Code §2643). The conservator must document items for which compensation should be granted.

You may petition the court for compensation any time after the Inventory and Appraisement is filed (see Chapter 13, Section C3), but it must be no sooner than 90 days after the date Letters of Conservatorship were issued (Probate Code §2640). Many courts will not allow the money to be disbursed until one year after Letters of Conservatorship were issued, after accounting documents have been filed with the court. Some courts have local rules requiring simultaneous filings of a petition for compensation and the conservator's first account.

 Never pay yourself for your services from the estate without first receiving court approval. (Chapter 13, Section E4 shows you how to apply for compensation when you prepare account documents.)

COURT REPORTING REQUIREMENTS
FOR CONSERVATOR OF THE ESTATE

A CONSERVATOR OF THE ESTATE must give the court information about what assets are in the estate and how they are being handled—and must periodically update this information. These records make the conservatorship public; anyone may check the conservator's actions and object to perceived wrongdoing.

All documents are carefully reviewed by the court. When the court approves a conservator's account, the conservator is protected from future liability, provided she gave accurate information and had documents served correctly.

 If you have not obtained a copy of your court's probate policy manual, do so now. Many courts have special procedural requirements for estate conservatorships. Also, some provide preprinted forms for certain documents.

A. Filing Deadlines

THE ACCOMPANYING BOX is a summary of when documents are due at the court. If you do not comply with these deadlines, the court can have you removed as conservator—and may hold you liable for any damages caused by your failure to file documents on time.

If there is a good reason why you can't file your papers on time, you may be able to obtain an extension or revised deadline schedule. However, some courts have a policy of requiring people who don't file documents on time to come to court and prove why they shouldn't be held in contempt. (See Chapter 8, Section C, for information on obtaining a continuance. Chapter 17 discusses attorneys and legal research.)

 Many courts set hearing dates for when documents are due. If you are given due dates from the court, comply with them. These dates may be several weeks or months after the deadline listed in the accompanying chart to allow ample time to gather and prepare documents.

COURT REPORTING REQUIREMENTS FOR CONSERVATORSHIP OF THE ESTATE	
DEADLINE FROM DATE JUDGE SIGNS ORDER APPOINTING PROBATE CONSERVATOR	COURT PAPERS AND REQUIRED ACTION
2 weeks (suggested date)	If required, Application and Order Appointing Probate Referee should be filed.
6 weeks (suggested date)	Send Application and Order and Inventory and Appraisement to the probate referee.
90 days	Inventory and Appraisement must be filed.
90 days	General Plan of Conservator due. (See Chapter 9, Section E)
1 year	First Account due. A Status Report is also due if you are conservator of the person and estate or if required by local rule.
Each 1 to 2 year anniversary	Accounts due. A Status Report is also due if you are conservator of the person and estate or if required by local rule.
When conservator or conservatee moves	Notification to Court of Address of Conservator and Conservatee due.
When conservatorship is no longer needed	Final Account and termination documents due. (See Chapter 16.) A judge must sign an order allowing the conservatorship to end and a hearing may be required.

B. Keeping Track of Estate

TO PREPARE REQUIRED FINANCIAL DOCUMENTS, you'll need detailed information about:

- assets the conservatee owns (see Chapter 12, Section C1);
- the conservatee's present and expected income, including benefits (see Chapter 10 and Chapter 12, Section C1); and
- all transactions you make for the estate (see Chapter 12, Section E).

It is essential that you organize the estate and keep accurate financial records. Throughout this chapter you will rely on those important records. (Chapter 12, Section E, gives suggestions on how to keep the estate organized.)

C. Documents Due Within 90 Days

WITHIN 90 DAYS of the date the judge signs the Order Appointing Probate Conservator, you must file a report with the court listing what the conservatee owns. This section gives an idea of the steps you will take. Allow yourself plenty of time to prepare your papers. It is best to begin the process within two weeks of the date the judge signs the Order Appointing Probate Conservator.

1. How Estate Is Appraised

After a conservator organizes the estate's assets, she arranges for non-cash items to be appraised by an inde-

pendent court-appointed appraiser, called a "probate referee" or an "inheritance tax referee" in some counties.[1] A probate referee is assigned by the court after the conservator completes one or two short forms and files them with the court.

The conservator prepares a detailed list of all estate assets, called the Inventory and Appraisement. If the estate only consists of cash items, the conservator may appraise them by simply listing their values. If there are non-cash items, the conservator forwards the Inventory and Appraisement to the probate referee. The probate referee will appraise and provide values for the non-cash items, complete the Inventory and Appraisement and return it to the conservator for filing with the court. It usually takes four to six weeks for the probate referee to complete the appraisal.

The estate is charged a fee for the appraisal, usually one-tenth of one percent of the total value of the assets appraised with a minimum of $75 and a maximum of $10,000 (Probate Code §§8961, 8963). The referee may also charge the estate for his necessary expenses, such as mileage for driving to inspect property.

2. Application and Order Appointing Probate Referee

If the conservatorship includes real estate or personal property that is not cash, you must usually request that the court appoint a probate referee to appraise those assets. First look at Item 3m of the Order Appointing Probate Conservator. If the judge completed this item, you'll find the name and address of the probate referee—also known as an inheritance tax referee. If so, you may go on to Section C3, below.

If Item 3m is blank, you must complete an Application and Order Appointing Probate Referee. In it, you ask the court to appoint a probate referee to appraise non-cash assets. There is no standard form for this purpose, but most courts have a local form, so check with your court first. Some courts use two forms—one for the application

---

[1] It is possible to use the services of a different appraiser, but that requires a special order from the court. This is beyond the scope of this book.

and the other for the order—but the substance is the same as the sample presented here. [2]

On the application, provide approximate values on the date the conservatorship was established for:

- cash items (cash, uncashed checks issued to the conservatee before the conservatorship was established, accounts in financial institutions, certificates of deposit, U.S. savings bonds and money market funds held by a brokerage house);
- real estate; and
- personal property.

 If any property increased or decreased in value since the date the conservatorship was set up, do not use the present values. Do not list income or property obtained after the date the judge signed the Order Appointing Probate Conservator. Also do not list the conservatee's wages earned for employment, if she receives any.

AVOIDING USE OF PROBATE REFEREE WHEN CONSERVATEE'S BELONGINGS ARE VALUELESS

You can often get around the requirement that personal property be appraised if the conservatee only owns property of basically no value—such as old clothes and worn-out household items.

To do this, complete an Application and Order Appointing Probate Referee. On the application, do not fill in a dollar amount for personal property. Instead, briefly explain why you don't want personal property appraised by a probate referee. For example, "The conservatee owns no personal belongings other than old clothes, toiletries and items of personal value to him such as photographs, letters and old books. It would be an unnecessary expense to the estate to have those items appraised." On the order, type in the words, "No probate referee is required for personal property."

 The Application and Order Appointing Probate Referee should be filed with the court no more than two weeks after the judge signs the Order Appointing Probate Conservator. Make at least three photocopies of the Application and Order and take or send the original and at least two copies to the court along with a self-addressed, stamped envelope. (Instructions for filing documents are set out in Chapter 5, Section D.)

A judge will review your application and appoint a probate referee. It usually takes at least a couple weeks to get it back, because larger courts forward the form to a probate referee coordinator to complete. Either arrange to have the signed order mailed to you or to pick it up at the court. You will need a file-stamped copy of the Order Appointing Probate Referee that lists the probate referee's name and address.

3. Inventory and Appraisement

In the Inventory and Appraisement, list all money, goods and other property that were in the estate on the date you were appointed conservator. The probate referee may need to appraise property other than cash and fill in the amounts on the form. If so, she'll need about four to six weeks to complete the appraisal and return the document to you. Only then may you file the Inventory and Appraisement with the court.

OBTAINING ASSISTANCE FROM PROBATE REFEREE

Probate referees are often very helpful with the appraisal process. Most offices carry a short reference manual titled *Probate Referees' Procedures Guide*. This manual gives guidelines and samples for preparing the Inventory and Appraisement. To obtain a free copy, contact your local probate referee. Or check with the Daily Journal Corporation, 1390 Market Street, Suite 910, San Francisco, California 94102, telephone (415) 558-9888.

---

[2] The form provided in Appendix B is used in the Central District in Los Angeles County.

NAME AND ADDRESS OF ATTORNEY	TELEPHONE NO:	FOR COURT USE ONLY
DONNA GARCIA 900 Any Road Ventura, CA 93009	(805) 555-1212	

NAME OF COURT, OR BRANCH, MAILING AND STREET ADDRESS
Ventura Superior Court
800 S. Victoria Avenue, Ventura, CA 93009

ESTATE OF
MIKE GARCIA

☐ DECEDENT ☐ INCOMPETENT ☑ CONSERVATEE ☐ MINOR

APPLICATION AND ORDER APPOINTING PROBATE REFEREE	CASE NUMBER 088-00-00

It is requested that a Probate Referee be appointed to appraise the assets of the above entitled estate consisting of the following approximate values:

1. CASH $ 45,000

2. REAL ESTATE $ 92,000

3. PERSONAL PROPERTY $ 2,000

REMARKS _____

Donna Garcia
Attorney
In Pro Per

IT IS ORDERED that (name):

a disinterested person, is appointed Probate Referee to appraise the above entitled estate. When a Probate

Referee is appointed, such referee is authorized to fix the clear market value of the estate as of the date of

death of the decedent, or as of the date of appointment if a conservatorship or guardianship, and to appraise

all interest, inheritances, transfers, and property of the estate under the laws of the State of California.

DATED: _____

Judge of the Superior Court

APPLICATION AND ORDER APPOINTING PROBATE REFEREE

229A

76A650Q (Rev. 9-83) 4-84
RP005

PROB C 605

ATTORNEY OR PARTY WITHOUT ATTORNEY *(Name and Address)*:	TELEPHONE NO.:	FOR COURT USE ONLY
HELEN CHEN 90 West Street SW Napa, CA 94559	(707) 555-1212	

ATTORNEY FOR *(Name)*: In Pro Per

SUPERIOR COURT OF CALIFORNIA, COUNTY OF   Napa

STREET ADDRESS: 825 Brown Street

MAILING ADDRESS: P.O. Box 880

CITY AND ZIP CODE: Napa, CA 94559

BRANCH NAME: ---

ESTATE OF (NAME):

JILL N. JACKSON

☐ DECEDENT ☒ CONSERVATEE ☐ MINOR

INVENTORY AND APPRAISEMENT ☒ Complete ☐ Final ☐ Partial No.: ☐ Supplemental ☐ Reappraisal for Sale	CASE NUMBER: 0001
	Date of Death of Decedent or of Appointment of Guardian or Conservator:

APPRAISALS

1. Total appraisal by representative (attachment 1) $ 17,444.42
2. Total appraisal by referee (attachment 2) $ 64,012.00

                                                    TOTAL: $ 81,456.42

DECLARATION OF REPRESENTATIVE

3. Attachments 1 and 2 together with all prior inventories filed contain a true statement of
   ☒ all ☐ a portion of the estate that has come to my knowledge or possession, including particularly all money and all just claims the estate has against me. I have truly, honestly, and impartially appraised to the best of my ability each item set forth in attachment 1.
4. ☐ No probate referee is required ☐ by order of the court dated *(specify)*:

I declare under penalty of perjury under the laws of the State of California that the foregoing is true and correct.

Date: October 31, 19__

....
HELEN CHEN
(TYPE OR PRINT NAME) (Include title if corporate officer)

► *Helen Chen*
(SIGNATURE OF PERSONAL REPRESENTATIVE)

STATEMENT REGARDING BOND
(Complete if required by local court rule)

5. ☒ Bond is waived.
6. ☐ Sole personal representative is a corporate fiduciary.
7. ☐ Bond filed in the amount of: $ ☐ Sufficient ☐ Insufficient
8. ☐ Receipts for: $ have been filed with the court for deposits in a blocked account
   at *(specify institution and location)*:

Date: October 31, 19

► *Helen Chen*
(SIGNATURE OF ATTORNEY OR PARTY WITHOUT ATTORNEY)

DECLARATION OF PROBATE REFEREE

9. I have truly, honestly, and impartially appraised to the best of my ability each item set forth in attachment 2.
10. A true account of my commission and expenses actually and necessarily incurred pursuant to my appointment is

    Statutory commission: $
    Expenses *(specify)*: $
    TOTAL: $

I declare under penalty of perjury under the laws of the State of California that the foregoing is true and correct.

Date:

►

....
(TYPE OR PRINT NAME)

(SIGNATURE OF REFEREE)

(Instructions on reverse)

Form Approved by the
Judicial Council of California
DE-160, GC-040 (Rev. January 1, 1985)

INVENTORY AND APPRAISEMENT
(Probate)

Prob C 600-611,
2610-2616

CAPTION: INVENTORY AND APPRAISEMENT

- Fill in the caption following the general instructions in Chapter 3, Section H2b.
- After the words "Estate of," fill in the conservatee's name. Then check the box before the word "Conservatee."
- Check the box before the word "Complete."
- Under the case number, fill in the date the judge signed the Order Appointing Probate Conservator. This information should be stamped or handwritten next to the judge's signature.

Items 1-2: Leave these items and the "TOTAL," in the lower right of the section, blank. You will list the total appraisal amounts after the form is complete.

Item 3: Check the first box before the word "all."

Item 4: Leave this item blank unless the conservatee's estate consists only of cash, uncashed checks issued to the conservatee before the conservatorship was established, accounts in banks, savings and loan and credit unions, certificates of deposit, U.S. savings bonds and money market funds held by a brokerage house. If that's your situation, check the first box before the words "No probate referee is required."

Fill in the date and type or print your name in the space provided. Then sign your name above the words "Signature of Personal Representative."

Item 5: Look at the Order Appointing Probate Conservator to complete this item. If Item 3d(1) of the Order is checked ("Bond is not required"), then check this item. Otherwise, leave it blank.

Item 6: Skip this item.

Item 7: If you checked Item 5, skip this item. Otherwise, look at the Order Appointing Probate Conservator. If Item 3d(2) of the Order is checked and an amount listed ("Bond is fixed at ..."), check this item and fill in the amount. For now, leave the boxes blank before the words "Sufficient" and "Insufficient." After the probate referee has appraised the estate's property, you must check one of the boxes.

Item 8: This item refers to money or assets in a blocked account. Look at Item 3d(3) of the Order Appointing Probate Conservator to complete this item. If that box is checked ("Deposits shall be made at ..."), check this box. In the spaces provided, fill in the amount deposited in a blocked account, the name of the financial institution and its address. (See Chapter 14, Section E1, for directions on establishing blocked accounts.)

Leave the date and signature lines blank in the "Statement Regarding Bond" section.

Items 9-10: Leave these items blank.

Leave the date and signature lines blank in the Declaration of Probate Referee section. This information will be completed by the probate referee.

a. Attachment 1 (Cash Items)

Make several copies of the Attachment form. If the conservatee owns a substantial amount of property, you may need to complete a number of Attachment pages.

In Chapter 12, Section C1, you gathered information about the conservatee's assets. In Attachment 1, you give information about those cash items you are entitled to appraise:

- cash;
- uncashed checks issued to the conservatee before the conservatorship was established;
- accounts in financial institutions;
- certificates of deposit;
- U.S. savings bonds; and
- money market funds held by a brokerage house.

 If you haven't done so already, contact each financial institution where the conservatee has accounts, and get a signed letter from the bank stating the amount in each account on the date the judge signed the Order Appointing Probate Conservator, and the amount of interest accrued on the appointment date. (See Chapter 12, Section C1.)

ESTATE OF

JILL N. JACKSON

CASE NUMBER

000-9

ATTACHMENT NO: 1

(IN DECEDENTS' ESTATES. ATTACHMENTS MUST CONFORM TO PROBATE CODE 601
REGARDING COMMUNITY AND SEPARATE PROPERTY)

PAGE . . . . . OF . . . . . TOTAL PAGES
(ADD PAGES AS REQUIRED)

Item No.	Description	Appraised value
		$
1.	Savings Account No. 500, Great Bank, 100 California Plaza, San Francisco, CA 94102	
	Principal balance at date of conservatorship:	4,080.00
	Interest accrued at date of conservatorship:	$18.92
2.	Checking Account No. 600, Great Bank, 100 California Plaza, San Francisco, CA 94102	$935.74
3.	Certificate of Deposit No. 700 (blocked account), Best Savings & Loan, North San Francisco Branch, 4140 160th Avenue, San Francisco, CA 94118:	
	Principal balance at date of conservatorship:	$10,000.00
	Interest accrued at date of conservatorship:	$123.00
4.	Cash in conservatee's possession	$93.26
5.	An undivided one-half interest in Checking Account No. 898, Great Bank, 100 California Plaza, San Francisco, CA 94102	$216.00
6.	Uncashed check from granddaughter Marti Marks, dated July 4, 19__, payable to conservatee	$450.00
7.	Uncashed refund check from TV Repair Company dated June 15, 19__, payable to conservatee	$41.50
8.	Uncashed check from Social Security dated July 11, 19__, payable to conservatee	$620.00
9.	Uncashed check from Former Company, Inc., dated August 29, 19__, payable to conservatee	$ 866.00

TOTAL: $17,444.42

Form Approved by the
Judicial Council of California
Effective January 1, 1976

F1306-A

INVENTORY AND APPRAISEMENT (ATTACHMENT)

Prob C 481,
600-605, 784,
1550, 1901

CAPTION: ATTACHMENT 1 TO INVENTORY AND APPRAISEMENT

- After the words "Estate of," fill in the conservatee's full name. Fill in the case number at the far right.
- After the words "Attachment No.," fill in "1."
- Once you have completed the attachments, fill in the page numbers at the top (such as "Page 1 of 4 Total Pages").

Starting with Item No. 1, give a short description and value of each money item owned by the conservatee on the date you were appointed conservator. Be specific, giving certificate, policy and account numbers whenever possible. Give the full name of institutions in which accounts are kept, along with their locations. If any accounts are jointly held, indicate that at the beginning of the description. Don't list community property, as it will be handled by the conservatee's spouse outside of the conservatorship estate.[3]

Some courts—such as those in Los Angeles and Alameda—require that you list the monthly amount received for periodic benefits, and when payments started or are expected to begin. These benefits generally include VA benefits, Social Security and welfare. Check your local probate policy manual.

Once you've listed all the cash assets, add them and fill in the total. Finally, go back to Item 1 of the Inventory and Appraisement you completed in Section C3, above, and fill in the same amount.

b. Attachment 2 (Real Estate and Personal Property)

Before getting started, make sure you have several blank copies of the Attachment form, since you may need to complete several.

In Attachment 2, you list all assets a conservator is not authorized to appraise. This includes stocks and bonds (even if the value is listed on the open stock exchange), jewelry, annuity policies, mutual funds, real estate, vehicles, promissory notes, business interests, coin collections and antiques. Ordinary household and personal possessions are usually grouped together and given the value they would bring at a yard sale. If the conservatee's business is part of the estate, it must also be appraised.

CAPTION: ATTACHMENT 2 TO INVENTORY AND APPRAISEMENT

- After the words "Estate of," fill in the conservatee's full name. Fill in the case number at the far right.
- After the words "Attachment No.," fill in "2."
- After you have completed the attachments, fill in the page numbers (such as "Page 3 of 3 Total Pages").

In Chapter 12, Section C1, you obtained information about what the conservatee owns. Starting with Item No. 1, list each asset owned by the conservatee. Be specific under "Description," giving certificate, policy and account numbers whenever possible. At the right of each asset, type a blank line. The probate referee will fill in the correct amount when she appraises the estate. Triple-space between each numbered item.

---

[3] Portions of community property can be made part of the estate with the spouse's consent or a court order. That is beyond the scope of this book. (See Chapter 12, Section C2b.)

ESTATE OF

    JILL N. JACKSON

CASE NUMBER
000-9

ATTACHMENT NO: 2

(IN DECEDENTS' ESTATES. ATTACHMENTS MUST CONFORM TO PROBATE CODE 601
REGARDING COMMUNITY AND SEPARATE PROPERTY)

PAGE . . . . . OF . . . . . . TOTAL PAGES
(ADD PAGES AS REQUIRED)

Item No.	Description	Appraised value
1.	Real property in the City of San Francisco, County of California, State of California, described as Lot X in Block Y of Tract Z, as per map recorded in Book Q, Page 21 of Maps in the office of the County Recorder of said county. Commonly known as 8280 - 150th Avenue, San Francisco, California (improved with single dwelling); Assessors Parcel No. 000-000-000.	$
2.	Household furnishings and personal effects located at conservatee's residence, 8280 - 150th Avenue, San Francisco, California	
3.	200 shares of common stock of Corporation Inc, N.Y. Stock Exchange	
4.	20 - U.S. Savings Bonds, Series E, $100 each, issued December, 1974	
5.	2 - $4,000 San Francisco Municipal School District of San Francisco County, 1976 School Bond Series X, 4% due December 31, 1996	
6.	Owner of life insurance policy on life of sister Margaret Johnson, Policy No. 1-AOK, Happy Insurance Company, Oakland, California	
7.	1976 Ford Mustang, License XX, Vehicle No. 180S42	
8.	Canadian and U.S. stamp collection, 1966-1990	
9.	$8,000 promissory note dated October 9, 1985, payable to conservatee by John Such, interest at 9%, secured by deed of trust recorded October 15, 1985 in Book 1, Page 1, in Official Records of Alameda County Principal balance at date of conservatorship: Interest accrued at date of conservatorship:	
	TOTAL:	

Form Approved by the
Judicial Council of California
Effective January 1, 1976

F1306-A

INVENTORY AND APPRAISEMENT (ATTACHMENT)

Prob C 481,
600-605, 784,
1550, 1901

If the conservatee owns any property jointly with others, in the beginning of the description indicate the type of ownership and percentage owned—such as a one-half or one-third interest. Do not list community property assets owned with the conservatee's spouse.[4] Different types of joint property ownership (including joint tenancy, tenancy in common and community property) are covered in Chapter 2, Section B2d.

Household furnishings and personal effects such as clothing, jewelry, books, decorative art and household items may be grouped together unless there are special items of value. For vehicles, try to include the model, make, year, license and vehicle identification number. Include business interests as well.

If the conservatee holds a promissory note, leave a blank for the principal balance as well as the accrued interest. If the conservatee holds a mortgage or deed of trust secured by real property, include the recording reference.[5] List trusts where the conservatee is a beneficiary, insurance on the conservatee's own life or life insurance on someone else's life where the conservatee is the beneficiary.

All real property must contain a full and accurate legal description, which gives enough details of the property to allow its identification by a surveyor. You can either retype the legal description in the "Description" column or attach a photocopy of the legal description. If you do not have the legal description, obtain a copy of the deed from the county recorder for a small fee. Or call the customer service department of a title company; many will send you a copy of the deed for free. It's a good idea to include the common street address and the assessor's parcel number, which is listed on property tax bills.

4. Have Property Appraised

Make at least one photocopy of the entire Inventory and Appraisement, including all attachments. About a month before your documents are due in court, you'll need to get all items listed in Attachment 2 appraised by the probate referee. If nothing is listed in Attachment 2, skip to Section C4c.

a   Send Documents to Probate Referee

You're now ready to forward the Inventory and Appraisement and attachments to the probate referee to appraise the items listed in Attachment 2. The referee's name and address are on the Order Appointing Probate Referee, explained in Section C2, above.

Modify the accompanying sample letter, and include an estimated value of the conservatee's household items and personal effects. They generally are grouped together as one item and valued at what they would bring at a yard sale. The referee usually will accept reasonable suggested valuations, and will insert them as the appraised values. But should you have any relatively recent appraisals of the conservatee's assets, include copies.

 Send the documents to the probate referee about six weeks before your documents are due in court. It will take time if there are problems with your documents or the probate referee has a full schedule.

---

[4]Portions of community property can be made part of the estate with a court order. That is beyond the scope of this book. (See Chapter 12, Section C2b.)

[5]If the encumbrance was not recorded, have it recorded at once. You can prepare and record your own deed in California using *The Deeds Book* by Attorney Mary Randolph (Nolo Press).

SAMPLE LETTER

August 14, 19___

Shelly Ham
Probate Referee
601 Appraisal Street
Merced, CA 95340

Re: <u>Conservatorship of Darlene Holmes</u>

Dear Ms. Ham:

You have been appointed probate referee in this conservatorship. Enclosed are:

1) Date-stamped copy of the order appointing you referee;

2) Original and one copy of the Inventory and Appraisement along with Attachments 1 and 2; and

3) Self-addressed, stamped envelope.

Please appraise the assets listed on Attachment 2, complete the Inventory and Appraisement and return it to me by September 15 for filing with the court.

I estimate the value of the conservatee's household furniture, furnishings and personal effects at the date of the conservatorship to be approximately $900.

Sincerely,

Guy Kamola
50 Any Street
Merced, CA 95340
(209) 555-1212

Enclosures

b. Probate Referee Completes Documents

If you haven't received the Inventory and Appraisement a week before it is due at the court, contact the probate referee. When you receive the completed papers from the probate referee, you must then pay the fee charged. Typically, the fee is one-tenth of one percent of the total assets appraised, plus actual costs—a minimum of $75 and no more than $10,000. You may pay the probate referee from a conservatorship account.

Look over the appraisals and if you disagree with them, call the probate referee and explain your concerns. It's likely the probate referee will be willing to change the appraisal amount if your explanation is reasonable—but you cannot make changes to appraisals in Attachment 2 yourself. If you can't come to an agreement, complete and file the Inventory and Appraisement anyhow. You have the right to object in court within 30 days of the date the Inventory and Appraisement is filed (Probate Code §2614).[6]

c. Complete Inventory and Appraisement

Carefully review what the probate referee filled in on the Inventory and Appraisement. You can then complete the document.

Items 1-2: If the appraisal amounts and total are not listed, fill them in now.

Item 7: If bond is required, you should have checked this item. Look at the total amount of the Inventory and Appraisement listed in Item 2. If you are using a surety company or making deposits with the court, the amount of bond should equal the value of all personal property plus the annual estimated income from real and personal property in the estate, excluding cash or other personal property deposited in blocked accounts. The amount of bond is doubled if you are using personal sureties.

If bond is sufficient, check the box before the word "Sufficient." If bond is not high enough, check the box before the word "Insufficient"—and a higher or additional bond will be required by the court. (See Chapter 14, Section F.)

---

[6]If you want to object to the appraisals, or if anyone else objects, see a lawyer.

Fill in the date and sign your name above the words "signature of attorney or party without attorney."

d. File Inventory and Appraisement with Court

Remember that the Inventory and Appraisement must be filed with the court no more than 90 days after the date the judge signed the Order Appointing Probate Conservator. In some courts, you must also show that investigators' fees were paid. (See Chapter 7, Section E.) If you run into problems meeting the deadlines, call the court and ask for a continuance.

Make at least two photocopies of the Inventory and Appraisement and all Attachment pages. If anyone requested special notice, have them served by mail and complete a Proof of Service by Mail. (See Chapter 15, Section B4.) Then file the original and one copy of each document with the court following the instructions in Chapter 5, Section D.

e. If Additional Assets Are Discovered

If you discover additional assets that the conservatee owned when the conservatorship was established, even if you discover them several years later, you must complete a supplemental Inventory and Appraisement. You need not include income or financial benefits received after the conservatorship was set up.

Example: Joe is appointed conservator of the estate of his elderly mother, Mirth. Several months after Joe files an Inventory and Appraisement for the estate, he discovers a box of documents—including passbooks for several savings accounts he'd never known existed, and a deed of trust for an unimproved piece of land. As conservator, Joe contacts the bank and finds out that the accounts are still open. He also verifies that the land still belongs to Mirth. Joe prepares a supplemental Inventory and Appraisement, listing the bank accounts in Attachment 1 and the land in Attachment 2. Joe requests the appointment of a probate referee to appraise the land.

To complete a supplemental Inventory and Appraisement, follow the instructions in Section C3, above, but in the caption check the box before the word "Supplemental." If the new assets fall into the category of Attachment 1, you may appraise them yourself following the instructions in Section C3a, above.

Again, non-cash assets must be appraised by a probate referee. Follow the guidelines in Sections C3 and C4 to have the assets appraised as of the date they were discovered or received. If assets need to be appraised by a probate referee, forward the Inventory and Appraisement to the probate referee you used earlier. Complete the Inventory and Appraisement and file it with the court after serving anyone who requested special notice.

 Additional assets could mean a higher bond is required. (See Chapter 14, Section F.)

5. File General Plan If Required

If a general plan is required, see Chapter 9, Section E.

D. Overview of Accounts

THE COURT REQUIRES periodic accounts that set out the details of your management of the conservatorship estate. Account documents show what income was received and spent during the year, what money and property you are currently handling for the conservatee and any reimbursements or compensation you have received. If you haven't applied for compensation for your work, you may do so. (Information on compensation is in Chapter 12, Section H.)

Local court accounting requirements vary, but all courts insist that you keep detailed and accurate records. Some courts require a receipt for each expenditure; some only for expenditures exceeding a certain amount—often $20 or more. Some courts want original bank statements rather than copies.

A hearing is scheduled for each account, but it is usually just a formal reminder that your papers are due on that date. You should not need to attend unless someone files objections or you need more time to fix errors in the documents. Many courts give pre-grant decisions over the telephone, and allow the conservator time to fix any errors in the account documents.

 Accounts are generally due approximately one year after Letters of Conservatorship are issued and every two years after that. You must prepare several typewritten documents, obtain a hearing date and notify certain people. If no one files written objections to your account papers, you may not need to appear in court for a hearing.

WAIVER OF ACCOUNTS

Courts will generally waive accounts for at least one year— and possibly altogether— if:

- the conservator has not handled any money or assets for the conservatorship estate during the entire account period; or

- the conservatorship is a "small estate" and all income not retained was spent for the benefit of the conservatee (Probate Code §2628). Small estates have a total value of: (1) less than $5,000 in property—excluding the value of the residence in which the conservatee lives; and (2) a monthly income of less than $300, excluding public benefit payments such as welfare.

If you are conservator of a small estate, you may have requested a waiver in Item 1k of the original petition. If the judge did not grant a waiver of accounts in the Order Appointing Probate Conservator, you may either file accounts following the instructions in this book or obtain court approval waiving accounts. (See Chapter 17 for information about lawyers and legal research.)

 You might choose to hire an accountant, probate paralegal or attorney to assist you with accounts. Court permission is needed to hire accountants and attorneys. And with a judge's approval, fees for accountants and attorneys may be paid from the estate. (See Chapter 17 for information on attorneys.)

1. Overview of Procedure and Format

Here is an overview of the steps you'll take to prepare an account:

Step 1. Check local rules, and follow any procedures specific to your court.

Step 2. Prepare the required documents. Each account must include:

- *Account Schedules and Summary of Account.* The schedules give a detailed breakdown of the conservatee's assets, income and expenditures. The Summary of Account briefly summarizes the schedules.

- *Account and Report of Conservator and Petition for Its Settlement and for Allowance of Fees.* This document gives information about how you handled the estate, the status of the conservatee's assets, what services you provided on the conservatee's behalf and whether you want to be compensated for your work.

- *(Proposed) Order Settling Account and Report of Conservator and Allowing Fees.* This proposed order is signed by a judge after the accounts are reviewed by the court. The order confirms that the court approves of your handling of the estate during the account period.

- *Notice of Hearing and Proof of Service.* The Notice of Hearing gives information on when and where a hearing will be held on the account. It must be served on several people. A proof of service shows who was notified about the hearing.

- *Status Report.* Information about the well-being of the conservatee and the status of the estate is always required if you are conservator of the person and estate. Many local rules require a status report even if you are only conservator of the estate.

- *Documents Required by Local Rules.* Some courts require updated address information. They may have preprinted local forms that must be completed.

Step 3. Photocopy the documents and file them with the court.

Step 4. Have those people entitled to notice served. Then prepare proofs of service and file them with the court.

Step 5. If the court contacts you and requests additional documentation, provide it and have copies served on anyone entitled to notice.

Step 6. Several days before the hearing date, find out the tentative decision on your petition.

Step 7. Attend the scheduled hearing if necessary.

Step 8. Obtain a copy of the court order.

2. Periodic Accounts

The first account is due approximately one year after the conservatorship is established. After that, you are responsible for filing accounts until the conservatorship ends, generally every two years.[7] Each account must include current information and the documents described in Section D1, above.

3. Final Account

If the conservatorship is ending because the conservatee has become able to take care of her estate or has died, follow the instructions in Chapter 16, Section C.

E.   How to Prepare Accounts

GIVE YOURSELF AT LEAST A MONTH or two to collect, prepare and have documents served. Follow the instructions in Chapter 3, Section H3, for completing pleadings on lined paper. It's possible that your court will accept handwritten, printed documents; call first and find out if they're acceptable. Use the samples in this chapter as a guide, but don't copy instructions word-for-word onto your documents.

1.   Check Local Court Rules

Some courts assign dates for the accounts at the appointment hearing or by mail. If an account is due and you weren't already assigned a hearing date, time and location, call the probate clerk and arrange to have a hearing scheduled. Find out:

- whether any local forms are required; and
- how many copies of each document the court requires.

If the probate court clerk does not answer your questions, you may be able to find the guidance you need in the local probate policy manual. (See Chapter 17, Section D2, for information on obtaining probate policy manuals.)

2.   Account Schedules

You must prepare five or six account schedules, depending on the requirements set out in your local probate policy manual. All schedules must contain information about the account period. For example, the First Account would begin on the date Letters of Conservatorship were issued and end one year from that date.[8]

To complete the schedules, collect all financial records pertaining to the estate during the account period. This includes checkbook registers, bank passbooks, statements from financial institutions, accounting ledgers or computerized accounting information, vouchers, receipts, records of dividends, sales, purchases and tax returns.

Read the explanation of each schedule and follow the format of the samples provided. If you've made a transaction that isn't self-explanatory, jot down a note on a separate piece of paper; you will need to briefly explain it when you prepare your petition in Section E4, below.

To make sure your figures are correct, prepare a draft of the schedules and Summary of Account and make sure everything balances. If schedules are prepared by an accountant or on a computer, it may be easier to use plain white 8-1/2 by 11 inch paper instead of lined paper. For the schedules only, plain white paper is fine.

---

[7]The court could require accounts more or less frequently. For example, for a large estate with a great deal of investing and expenses, yearly accounts might be required. Small estates with virtually no assets could even have accounts waived.

[8]If the hearing for the account is scheduled close to the ending of the account period, it may be necessary to prepare an account for only ten or eleven months. Check with your court if that situation arises.

If there wasn't any activity in a specific category, you are still required to complete a separate schedule. Title it with the correct heading and type "None" several lines down from the heading.

a. Schedule A (Receipts During Account Period)

This schedule shows what new money or property was received during the account period—including benefit checks, payments from renters, reimbursements from insurance or taxes, interest dividends, personal loan payments, refunds, inheritances and pension checks.

If you sold any of the estate's assets, do not include profits in this schedule. Do not include property that was listed in a filed Inventory and Appraisement and do not include any appreciated value of that property. If you transferred money or assets between accounts, do not list those transfers as receipts.

As shown in the samples, receipts can either be listed chronologically or by category, depending on your preference.

SAMPLE SCHEDULE A, LISTING RECEIPTS CHRONOLOGICALLY

SCHEDULE A: RECEIPTS

Date	Source	Purpose	Amount
19__:			
01/09	Ex Company	Pension	$666.00
02/09	Social Security	Retirement benefits	$500.25
03/01	Ex Company	Pension	$666.00
03/07	Social Security	Retirement benefits	$500.25
03/15	California Bank	Interest	$150.00
03/30	Corporation Inc.	Dividend	$44.22
04/01	Ex Company	Pension	$666.00
04/04	SF Examiner	Refund-newspaper	$12.61
04/07	Social Security	Retirement benefits	$500.25
04/16	Three-Star Home	Refund/overpayment	$450.20
05/01	Ex Company	Pension	$666.00
05/02	IRS	Tax refund	$220.97
05/10	Social Security	Retirement benefits	$500.25
06/02	Ex Company	Pension	$666.00
06/08	Social Security	Retirement benefits	$500.25
06/14	California Bank	Interest	$152.25
06/09	Estate of Anna Roper	Inheritance	$5,000.00
06/28	Corporation Inc.	Dividend	$44.22
[continue listings in chronological order…]			
12/31	Corporation Inc.	Dividend	$44.22

TOTAL RECEIPTS: $ *[fill in total]*

SAMPLE SCHEDULE A, LISTING RECEIPTS BY CATEGORY

```
                        SCHEDULE A: RECEIPTS

Source                       Purpose                                Amount

Social Security              Retirement benefits (12 x $500.25)     $6,003.00
Ex Company                   Pension (12 x $666.00)                 $7,992.00
Corporation Inc.             Dividends (4 x $44.22)                   $176.88
Estate of Anna Roper         Inheritance (06/09/__)                 $5,000.00
California Bank              Interest:
                             03/12/__  ($150.00)
                             06/14/__  ($152.25)
                             09/16/__  ($154.53)
                             12/12/__  ($156.85)                      $613.63
Miscellaneous:
SF Examiner                  Refund - newspaper (04/04/__)             $12.61
Three-Star Home              Refund - overpayment (04/16/__)          $450.20
IRS                          Tax refund (05/02/__)                    $220.97

                                       TOTAL RECEIPTS: $20,469.29
```

b.   Schedule B (Gains on Sales)

This schedule lists the profits gained from the sale of personal property owned by the estate, such as stocks, vehicles or other personal property. For each item sold, list the amount the sale brought in. Then subtract the amount listed in the Inventory and Appraisement and provide that figure as the amount gained from the sale.

For this schedule, use the amount listed in the Inventory and Appraisement to determine the profit, regardless of whether that appraisal accurately reflects the item's current market value. For example, if an antique sells for $4,000 and it was valued on the Inventory and Appraisement at $1,000, the net profit listed in Schedule B is $3,000—regardless of the antique's current value.

SAMPLE SCHEDULE B

```
                 SCHEDULE B: GAINS ON SALES

03/11/93    Sale of 50 shares of XYZ Stock
            @ $40 per share                         2,000.00

            Less total appraisal in Inventory &
            Appraisement filed 2/29/___ (Item 4)   (1,700.00)

                                                          Gain: $300.00
05/18/93    Sale of rolltop desk                      600.00

            Less total appraisal in Inventory
            & Appraisement filed 2/29/___ (Item 7)   (400.00)

                                                          Gain: $200.00

                                    TOTAL GAIN FROM SALES: $500.00
```

c. Schedule C
(Disbursements During Account Period)

Schedule C lists expenditures made on behalf of the conservatee and estate during the account period as well as any property delivered outside of the estate. Include payments for the conservatee's personal and medical care, rent or mortgage payments, utility bills, insurance, bond premiums, taxes, personal items, court costs and any court-ordered allowance for the conservatee. If you gave away or donated any of the estate's assets, list them. If you spent any money before the conservatorship was established and

have reimbursed yourself, include those disbursements. (See Chapter 12, Section H.)

Do not include losses resulting from the sale of the estate's assets, and do not include amounts paid for investments or large items of value, such as a car. If you transferred money or assets between accounts, do not list those transfers as disbursements.

As illustrated in the accompanying samples, disbursements can be listed chronologically or by category, depending on your preference.

SAMPLE SCHEDULE C, LISTING DISBURSEMENTS CHRONOLOGICALLY

SCHEDULE C: DISBURSEMENTS

Date	Check #	Payee and Purpose	Amount
19__ :			
02/11	899	Three-Star Home	$800.00
02/14	900	California Bank: Visa bill	$66.78
02/22	901	Colleen Conservator: reimburse bond premium paid 02/03/___	$105.34
02/22	902	Colleen Conservator: reimburse filing fee paid 12/28/___	$125.00
02/25	903	Dr. Herman Jones: medical care	$50.00
02/26	904	SF Chronicle: newspaper	$8.25
03/01	905	Three-Star Home	$1,250.20
[continue listings in chronological order...]			
12/03	949	Allowance for conservatee	$50.00
		TOTAL RECEIPTS:	$ *[fill in total]*

SAMPLE SCHEDULE C, LISTING DISBURSEMENTS BY CATEGORY

<u>SCHEDULE C:</u> DISBURSEMENTS

<u>Date</u>	<u>Check #</u>	<u>Payee and Purpose</u>	<u>Amount</u>
19__ :			
<u>Board and Care Facility</u>			
02/11	899	Three-Star Home	$800.00
03/01	905	Three-Star Home	$1,250.20
		[continue listings in chronological order...]	
12/02	948	Three-Star Home	<u>$800.00</u>
			$9,250.20
<u>Health Insurance, Medical Bills, Medical Supplies</u>			
03/10	907	Davis Pharmacy: medication	$31.00
05/29	922	Great Health Plan-insur, 6 mos.	$816.00
		[continue listings in chronological order...]	
10/25	944	Dr. Herman Jones: medical care	<u>$55.00</u>
			$1,281.94
<u>Costs of Administering Estate</u>			
02/22	901	Colleen Conservator: reimburse bond premium paid 02/03/__	$105.34
02/22	902	Colleen Conservator: reimburse filing fee paid 12/28/__	$125.00
04/10	915	Accurate Accountant: tax prep	<u>$162.50</u>
			392.84
<u>Allowance for Conservatee</u>			
03/03	906	Allowance for conservatee	$50.00
		[continue listings in chronological order...]	
12/03	949	Allowance for conservatee	<u>$50.00</u>
			$500.00
<u>Miscellaneous</u>			
02/14	900	California Bank: Visa bill	$66.78
02/26	904	SF Chronicle: newspaper	$8.25
03/11	908	Dotty's Department: perfume	$9.87
03/14	909	JC Penny: clothing	$100.80
		[continue listings in chronological order...]	
12/18	950	Dotty's Department: cosmetics	<u>$19.76</u>
			$2,889.02
		TOTAL RECEIPTS: $	*[fill in total]*

d.   Schedule D (Losses on Sales)

This schedule shows any losses resulting from the sale of personal property in the estate, such as stocks. For each item sold, list the amount the sale brought in and subtract the amount listed in the Inventory and Appraisement. That figure is the amount lost from the sale. Always use the amount listed in the Inventory and Appraisement to calculate the loss. For instance, if the conservatee owned a computer that was valued on the Inventory and Appraisement at $3,000 and you sold it for $2,000, the loss is $1,000—even if the computer has depreciated in value and is now worth less than the original $3,000 appraisal.

Losses should also be briefly explained in the petition, so the court can understand the loss and it is made clear that you didn't mismanage the estate. (See Section E4, below.)

SAMPLE SCHEDULE D

	SCHEDULE D: LOSSES	
08/12/___	Sale of Steinway Grand Piano	$14,000.00
	Less total appraisal in Inventory and Appraisement filed February 29, 19___ (Item 3)	($16,000.00)
	TOTAL LOSS FROM SALE:	$2,000.00

e.   Schedule E (Property on Hand)

This schedule shows all assets in the conservatorship estate on the date the account period ends, including:

- everything that was previously itemized in an Inventory and Appraisement that has not been sold, given away or spent.

- investments purchased during the account period, such as stocks or bonds, listing the amount paid—not the current value.

- property purchased during the account period, other than items you've listed as disbursements in Schedule C. (See Section E2c, above.) These are usually large items such as cars, not toiletries or clothing—unless they are extremely valuable, such as furs.

- all bank accounts listing the current balance at the end of the account period. You may want to obtain a letter from the bank giving those amounts, since the end of the account period may not coincide with the bank statements.

List the purchase price of property bought during the account period that the conservatee still owns, regardless of its current market value. List the appraised value of all property itemized in Attachment 2 of the original or a supplemental Inventory and Appraisement for all property the conservatee still owns. It doesn't matter if the item has depreciated or its current market value has increased. For example, a car that was appraised at $8,000 in the Inventory and Appraisement should be listed in this schedule as being worth $8,000, even if it would sell for only $6,500.

Some local rules require that original bank statements or an original, signed letter from the bank be attached to the account.

SAMPLE SCHEDULE E

SCHEDULE E: PROPERTY ON HAND

1. Real property commonly known as 111 Wildwood Court,
   San Francisco, CA 94110 $120,800.00

2. One-quarter interest as joint tenant in real property located
   at 90 California Dr., Anycity, California, appraised at $200,000 $50,000.00

3. Savings Account, Bank of California $4,619.51

4. Savings Account, Bank of Marin $7,071.36

5. Checking Account, Bank of Berkeley $672.36

6. Furniture and personal effects $1,500.00

7. 100 shares of Corpo Corporation $3,000.00

8. Certificate of Deposit, Bank of California $11,500.95

                                                       TOTAL: $199,164.18

3. Summary of Account

The Summary of Account summarizes all schedules you've prepared. It helps you double-check that you have accounted for everything in the estate and listed all items in the correct places. It will be attached to the Account, Report and Petition you will prepare in Section E4, below.

If you have filed accounts previously—for example, you are preparing your Second Account—do not list the amount of the Inventory and Appraisement. Instead, fill in the amount listed in Schedule E (Property on Hand) from your last account.

The total of the first part, titled "Charges" (Inventory and Appraisement plus Schedules A and B) *must* list the total of the second part, titled "Credits" (Schedules C, D and E).[9] If the two parts don't add up, you'll need to do some troubleshooting. (See accompanying sidebar.)

IF "CHARGES" AND "CREDITS" DO NOT BALANCE: COMMON MISTAKES

If you end up with different amounts for the "Charges" and "Credits" totals in the Summary of Account, check your work carefully. Here are some typical mistakes you may have made:

- Items are missing from schedules.
- Items are listed in the wrong schedule.
- Addition is wrong.
- If more than one Inventory and Appraisement was filed, all were not listed on the Summary of Account.
- All items listed on Inventory and Appraisements were not accounted for in schedules.
- If second or subsequent account, the amount listed as chargeable from prior accounts was not Schedule E (Property on Hand) from your last account.
- Appraisal values were not used to calculate profits or losses for items sold—for example, the current market value was used.

---

[9]If your court requires additional schedules, modify the Summary of Account to include those schedules.

[Use lined paper and prepare the caption following the Sample Pleading in Chapter 3, Section H3.]

SUMMARY OF ACCOUNT (EXHIBIT "A"
TO ACCOUNT, REPORT AND PETITION)

The petitioner is chargeable and is entitled to the credits set forth in this Summary of Account. The attached supporting schedules are incorporated by reference.

CHARGES

Amount of Inventory and Appraisement (or, if subsequent account, amount chargeable from prior account)	$196,124.89
Receipts During Account Period (Schedule A)	$20,469.29
Gains on Sales (Schedule B)	$500.00
TOTAL CHARGES:	$217,094.18

CREDITS

Disbursements During Account Period (Schedule C)	$15,930.00
Losses on Sales (Schedule D)	$2,000.00
Property on Hand (Schedule E)	$199,164.18
TOTAL CREDITS:	$217,094.18

4. Account, Report and Petition

This document explains how you handled the estate, and includes information about the conservatee's assets and what services you provided. If you want to be compensated for your work, you may request it. [10] (See Chapter 12, Section H.)

Prepare this document on lined paper using the accompanying sample as a guide. All unusual transactions that aren't readily understandable from the schedules must be explained here (Probate Code §2620(d)). This might include changes in assets such as stock splits and estate property that was sold or given away. Any actions you took that might appear to be a conflict of interest should also be clarified here—for example, if you bought estate assets, explain that transaction.

Obviously, the accounts will be titled "First Account," "Second Account," "Third Account," and so on for each one. The last account must be designated in the title.

[Use lined paper and prepare the caption following the Sample Pleading in Chapter 3, Section H3.]

["FIRST," "SECOND" or subsequent; if final, add "AND FINAL"] ACCOUNT AND REPORT OF CONSERVATOR AND PETITION FOR SETTLEMENT AND FOR ALLOWANCE OF FEES *[if final, add "AND FOR DELIVERY OF ASSETS AND DISCHARGE OF CONSERVATOR"]*

DATE: *[hearing date]*
TIME: *[hearing time]*
DEPT: *[department]*

Petitioner *[your name]* respectfully alleges:

1. Petitioner. *[Your name]* is the petitioner in this *["First," "Second" or subsequent; if final account, add "and Final"]* Account. *[Your name]* was appointed conservator of the *["estate" or "person and estate"]* of *[conservatee's name]* on *[date Order Appointing Probate*

---

[10]This document can be used to request court authorization or to obtain instructions for a variety of actions, such as those described in Chapter 15. That is beyond the scope of this book.

Conservator was signed]. Letters of Conservatorship were issued on *[date Letters were issued].*

2. <u>Account Period</u>. Petitioner's *["First,"* *"Second" or subsequent; if final account, add "and Final"]* Account covers the period beginning *[date Order Appointing* *Probate Conservator was signed or for subsequent accounts, date* *from last account]* and continuing through and including *[one year from date Order Appointing Probate* *Conservator was signed, two years from last account or date* *conservatee died].* Petitioner is chargeable with and is entitled to credits as set forth in the Summary of Account, filed with this account as Exhibit "A" and incorporated by reference.

3. *[If final account only, add:]* <u>Reasons for Final</u> <u>Account</u>. *[Briefly state why you are filing a final account.]*

4. <u>Inventory and Appraisement</u>. An Inventory and Appraisement has been prepared in this case by petitioner. It was filed on *[date Inventory and* *Appraisement was filed with the court. If any supplemental Inventory* *and Appraisements were prepared and filed, state that and give the* *date(s).]*

5. <u>Cash Asset Information</u>. During the period of this account, all of the cash in the possession of the conservator was kept with federally-insured banking institutions in savings and checking accounts, except for cash amounts reasonably necessary for the orderly administration of the estate. *[If different, specify types* *of institutions and other kinds of accounts, such as certificates of* *deposit. If local rules require original bank statements or letters, add:* *"Original bank statements (or letters from bank) are attached as* *Exhibit "1."]*

6. <u>Requests for Special Notice</u>. No person has filed a request for special notice *[if* *requested, add: "except for" and fill in name and address of person* *requesting notice].*

7. <u>Services Rendered by Conservator</u>. During the period of this account, petitioner performed the following duties solely as

conservator, rather than as a family member or friend:

[For conservatorship of the person:] Petitioner as conservator of the person *[state services performed as* *conservator of the person, and include an estimate of how much time* *they took.]*

[For conservatorship of the estate:] Petitioner as conservator of the estate managed the conservatorship property, collected income due, invested income, paid bills of the conservatorship estate and the conservatee, and arranged for benefits and insurance. *[Briefly* *describe services performed as conservator of the estate, and include* *an estimate of how much time they took.]*

8. <u>Compensation</u>. Petitioner has not received compensation for [his/her] duties as conservator. Petitioner waives the right to receive a fee. OR: Petitioner requests compensation in the amount of $*[amount]* as a reasonable fee for services rendered.

[Explain how you calculated the amount requested, and why you *believe it reasonable. If you are a close friend or family member, you* *may choose to reduce the fee. For example: "Petitioner spent* *approximately two hours a week for one year overseeing the* *management of the conservatee. A reasonable rate of compensation* *for such services in this area is $15, amounting to $1,560. Petitioner* *spent more than 60 hours managing the conservatorship estate,* *including sorting through conservatee's financial records, setting up an* *accounting system, contacting the IRS and other tax authorities,* *preparing past due tax returns for the last three years, securing waiver* *of penalties for that time period, and preparing this ["First," "Second"* *or subsequent; if final account, add "and Final."] account. Petitioner* *is a CPA, and regularly charges $40 per hour, but requests only $20* *per hour for services rendered, for a total of $1,200."]*

9. <u>Services Rendered by Attorneys</u>. There were no services rendered by attorneys *[if any were* *rendered, add "except for" and briefly explain those services. Note* *that prior court approval is necessary for hiring an attorney.].*

10. Veterans' Administration. The conservatorship estate *[does/does not]* include money or property acquired in whole or in part from money received from the Veterans' Administration. *[**Note:** If the estate does consist of money or property received from the Veterans' Administration, the VA must receive copies of the account documents.]*

11. Amount and Adequacy of Bond. There is a $*[amount]* bond through *[state name of bonding company, personal sureties, or whether deposits were made with the court, as explained in Chapter 14. If a bonding company was used, add: "Bond premiums have been paid through [date]. A proof of bond was filed with the court on [date]—or is attached to this Status Report as Exhibit "2"—or "3" if there is already an Exhibit "2"].* The amount of bond is *["sufficient" or "insufficient"]*, as the conservatorship estate's amount to $*[amount]*, as shown in the attached schedules.

12. Status Report. A separate *[add "confidential" if you are conservator of the person and estate]* status report is also filed in this case.

13. *[Explain any unusual transactions, such as stock splits, investments, losses, etc.]*

14. *[Supply any information required by local rules—such as whether the conservatee is capable of completing an affidavit of voter registration.]*

15. *[For final account only, explain how you plan to distribute and dispose of the estate property. For example, "I plan to turn all estate assets over to Marvin Smith, the executor of the estate.]*

Petitioner requests an order of this court that:

1. The *["First," "Second" or subsequent; if final account, add "and Final"]* Account of petitioner be settled, allowed and approved as filed;

2. All of the acts and proceedings of petitioner be confirmed and approved;

3. *[If requesting compensation:]* The court authorize and direct petitioner to receive the sum of $*[amount]* as the fee for her services to conservatee.

4. *[If final account only, add:]* The court authorize and direct conservator *[your name]* to deliver the estate property in *[his/her]* possession to *[name of personal representative, conservatee or other person receiving property.* **Note:** *If the conservatee has died and you do not know of a will, and do not know who is entitled to inherit property from the conservatee, insert the words "I know of no will and no heirs. I suggest a probate be opened to determine the distribution of the conservatee's estate."].* When *[your name]* delivers the estate property and files receipts, *[he/she]* shall be discharged and the surety on *[his/her]* bond, if any, shall be discharged.

5. For all other proper orders.

Respectfully submitted,

Dated: *[today's date]*   _____

                                [your name]
                                Conservator In Pro Per

VERIFICATION

[Insert verification from Chapter 3, Section H2d.]

5.   (Proposed) Order Settling Account

The judge will sign an order and settle the account if she approves of your management and paperwork. Use the accompanying sample as a guide.

[Use lined paper and prepare the caption following the Sample Pleading in Chapter 3, Section H3.]

ORDER SETTLING *["FIRST," "SECOND" or subsequent; if final, add "AND FINAL"]* ACCOUNT AND REPORT OF CONSERVATOR AND PETITION FOR SETTLEMENT AND FOR ALLOWANCE OF FEES *[if final, add "AND FOR DELIVERY OF ASSETS AND DISCHARGE OF CONSERVATOR."]*

The petition and *["First," "Second" or subsequent; if final account, add "and Final"]* Account of *[your name]*, conservator of the *["estate" or "person and estate"]* of *[conservatee's name]* was regularly heard on *[hearing date]*. *[Your name]* appeared as petitioner In Pro Per and no one appeared in opposition *[if there is opposition, you will need to see an attorney]*. After examining the petition and hearing the evidence, the court finds that all notices of the hearing have been given as required by law, that all allegations of the petition are true, settles the account and grants the petition. Good cause appearing,

IT IS ORDERED AND ADJUDGED:

1. The conservator has in *[his/her]* possession, after deducting the credits to which *[he/she]* is entitled, a balance of property on hand of $*[fill in the amount listed in Schedule E as the property on hand]*, belonging to the estate of the conservatee.

2. The *["First," "Second" or subsequent; if final account, add "and Final"]* Account and report is approved, allowed and settled as filed and all acts and transactions relating to matters in that account and set forth are ratified, confirmed and approved.

3. *[Complete only if you are seeking compensation for your duties:]* The conservator is entitled to reasonable compensation for services rendered during the period of the account in the amount of $*[fill in amount requested as compensation]*, and is directed to pay *[himself/herself]* that amount.

4. *[If final account, add:]* The conservator, *[your name]*, is directed to deliver the property presently being managed by him as conservator to *[name of personal representative, conservatee or other person receiving property]*.

5. *[If final account, add:]* *[Your name]* is discharged as conservator of the *["estate" or "person and estate"]* of *[conservatee's name]*, and the surety on *[his/her]* bond, if any, is discharged.

6. *[If local rules require information on whether the conservatee is capable of completing an affidavit of voter registration, add:]* The conservatee, *[conservatee's name]* is *["able" or "unable"]* to complete an affidavit of voter registration.

Dated:_____   _____

                                      Judge of the Superior Court

6. Notice of Hearing and Proof of Service

Complete a Notice of Hearing following the instructions in Chapter 4, Section G, with these exceptions:

Item 1: After the words "(representative capacity, if any)," enter the words "conservator of the estate," or "conservator of the person and estate."

Just below this, after the words "has filed (specify)," fill in the full title of the petition, such as "First Account and Report of Conservator and Petition for Its Settlement and for Allowance of Fees." Also fill in the title of any other document filed at the same time other than any orders, such as a Status Report.

Item 3: If you already have the date, time and place of the hearing, fill in that information in the box. Otherwise, the clerk will give this information when you file your papers.

Proof of Service (Page Two): Look at Chapter 15, Section B4, to determine who is entitled to service. Then complete the proof of service by mail. (Instructions are contained in Chapter 6, Section D3.) After the words "Name and Address of Each Person to Whom Notice Was Mailed," fill in the names and addresses of everyone entitled to notice. Do not have the proof of service signed yet.

7. Confidential Status Report

If you are conservator of both the person and estate, you must provide a confidential status report indicating your personal evaluation of the conservatee's health, general well-being and functional level. You must also state any plans you have to significantly change the conservatee's living arrangements or conditions, and any significant changes you intend to make to the estate (Probate Code § 2620.1).

Check your local probate policy manual to see if there are any special requirements for a status report. Some courts provide local preprinted forms.[11] Otherwise, use the accompanying sample as a guide, and conform it to any special local rules.

 Some courts require a status report for all conservators of the estate—not just conservators of the person and estate—that gives detailed information about:

- the conservatee's health and residence;
- the amount of any monthly allowance for the support of the conservatee, the source and whether it is adequate;
- the amount and adequacy of bond; and
- the amount of any outstanding liabilities.

[Use lined paper and prepare the caption following the Sample Pleading in Chapter 3, Section H3.]

["CONFIDENTIAL," if you are conservator of the person and estate]
STATUS REPORT

I, GRACE LACE, declare that I am the conservator of the person and estate of JAIME TUCKER and further declare:

A. <u>Health, Placement and Well-Being of Conservatee</u>

1. Conservatee JAIME TUCKER is presently living at Board and Care Manor, 51 New Boarding Way, Truckee, CA 95734, Telephone (916) 555-1212. Board and Care Manor is a board and care home that has nurses on duty and provides partial nursing care.

---

[11]The Judicial Council may be coming out with a preprinted status report form in 1991; check with your court.

2. Conservatee JAIME TUCKER has Alzheimer's disease. He is sometimes lucid, but frequently he is not. He seems to be content living in the board and care home. He participates in activities organized by the home and enjoys talking with the other residents and employees of the facility.

3. Conservatee JAIME TUCKER's health is relatively good. However, he has had dental problems which made it necessary to extract several teeth. He is sometimes incontinent and requires the help of a nurse's aide in bathing. Because of mobility problems, he needs constant supervision. He is confined to a wheelchair, which he can operate himself.

B. Anticipated Changes

4. I do not plan to significantly change the conservatee's living arrangements or conditions. I do not plan to make any significant changes in handling the conservatorship estate.

C. Amount and Adequacy of Bond

5. There is a $100,000 bond through Bonding Bonds Co. The bond premiums have been paid through December 31, 19__. A proof of bond was filed with the court on June 25, 19__ [or is attached to this Status Report as Exhibit "A"].

D. Amount of Any Outstanding Liabilities

6. Outstanding liabilities are covered in the Summary of Account filed with the ["First" or subsequent] Account, Report and Petition of conservator.

E. Monthly Allowance for the Support of Conservatee.

7. The conservatee receives a monthly allowance in the amount of $75 from the income of the estate. The allowance is deposited in an account at Board and Care Manor. The conservatee uses these funds to purchase personal items such as toiletries, magazines and snacks. As conservator of the person and estate, I pay all expenses for the support of the conservatee from the conservatorship estate.

F. Placement of Conservatee in Locked Mental Health Facility.

[A statement is required by Los Angeles County and possibly other courts as to whether the conservatee was placed in a locked mental health facility—check your local rules.]

8. Since the date I was appointed conservator [or since the date of the last status report, if any] the conservatee has not been placed in a locked mental health treatment facility.

[Note: If conservatee was placed in a locked mental health treatment facility, specify whether the placement was made with his consent. If not, immediately consult an attorney.]

I declare under penalty of perjury under the laws of the State of California that the foregoing is true and correct.

Dated: Sept. 15, 19_   _____
                              GRACE LACE
                              Conservator In Pro Per

8. Documents Required by Local Rules

Many courts require local forms for all accounts—or only in certain circumstances, such as when the conservator requests compensation. Check your local rules. Some forms commonly required are:

- *Summary of Fiduciary's Account.* Courts such as those in Contra Costa and Alameda counties require a short form that summarizes information you supplied in other account documents.

- *Address Information.* Some courts, such as Los Angeles Superior Court, require a form that provides current address information. (This form is similar to the one provided in Chapter 4, Section H2.)

9. How to Obtain Court Order

Take these steps to complete the account process and obtain an order:

- *Copy and File Documents.* Follow the instructions in Chapter 15, Section B3. File your documents at least 25 days before the scheduled hearing date.

- *Service of Papers.* At least 20 days before the scheduled hearing date, follow the instructions in Chapter 15, Section B4. Have the server sign the Proof of Service and file it with the court no later than 10 days before the hearing date.

- *Supplemental or Amended Documents.* If the court contacts you and requests additional or amended documentation, follow the instructions in Chapter 15, Section B5. Have everyone entitled to notice served with copies of the amended documents.

- *Find Out Tentative Decision.* A couple days before the hearing date, follow the guidelines in Chapter 15, Section B6.

- *Attend Hearing if Required.* You shouldn't need to attend the hearing if your petition was tentatively granted. Follow the directions in Chapter 15, Section B7.

- *Obtain Court Order.* Once a judge signs the order settling the account, you'll need to obtain copies. Follow any additional orders the judge granted. See Chapter 15, Section B8.

- *Pay Investigators' Fees if Required.* In some counties, court investigator fees must be paid when you file an account. (See Chapter 7, Sections D and E.)

NOTIFYING INVESTIGATOR OF ACCOUNTS

Depending on local rules, conservators of the estate may need to have copies of accounts served on the court investigator. For conservatorships of the person and estate, if the court investigator does not complete the investigation before the hearing date set for the account, the hearing may be continued to a later date.

F. Court Must Have Current Addresses

YOU MUST NOTIFY THE COURT if either you or the conservatee move. Complete a copy of the Notice to Court of Address of Conservator and Conservatee set out in Chapter 4, Section H2. If anyone filed a Request for Special Notice, have them served by mail following the instructions in Chapter 6, Section D2, complete and file a Proof of Service by Mail with the court.

BOND AND ALTERNATIVES

TO PROTECT THE ESTATE, a conservator must usually obtain bond—a financial guarantee that the estate will be reimbursed if the conservator takes improper actions (Probate Code §2320). Conservators of the person only do not need to read this chapter unless a judge requires that they obtain bond—a highly unlikely situation.

Conservators often reduce or eliminate the need for bond by placing estate assets in special blocked accounts that require a court order before the contents may be withdrawn. Or instead of acquiring bond, they make deposits of their own funds with the court. This chapter discusses bond and its alternatives in detail, and provides information on how to acquire bond or make other arrangements.

A. Bond and Sureties

THE BOND AMOUNT REQUIRED depends on the type and value of the conservatee's assets and income as well as the source of bonding. It may also depend on whether the conservatee requested in writing that bond be waived. It is often possible to reduce or eliminate the amount of bond required.

Bond is acquired from sureties—companies or individuals willing to guarantee the conservator's actions. If the conservatee and estate are damaged, sureties generally may be for up to four to six years after the conservator stops serving (Probate Code §2333). It's likely the sureties would then sue the conservator for reimbursement.

Unfortunately, most surety companies will not bond conservators who represent themselves in court without an attorney. A conservator who needs bond and cannot obtain it from a surety company may:

- obtain bond from personal sureties—such as friends or relatives; or

- deposit money, certificates of deposit or certain bonds with the court clerk or assign an interest in financial accounts to the court clerk.

B.   Blocked Accounts

BLOCKED ACCOUNTS REQUIRE written permission from the court before the conservator can withdraw funds or remove assets. They are set up by entering a special agreement with an insured bank, savings and loan or trust company. Some judges require blocked accounts for most of the estate's assets. Conservators may want them because the amount of bond required is reduced by the sum held in the blocked accounts.[1]

As a practical matter, if the conservator will frequently need to use funds in a blocked account, it can be a real inconvenience. Before taking out money or assets, the conservator must complete several documents, set a court hearing, notify several people by mail and obtain a court order.

> *Example:* Kenneth is seeking conservatorship of the estate of Darlene. The estate consists of $85,000 held in bank accounts. Darlene receives Social Security and minimal benefits. For the last few years, she has withdrawn approximately $500 per month to supplement those benefits. Kenneth wants to keep one year's worth of funds—$6,000—in regular accounts, and the remaining $79,000 in blocked accounts. That way, he will not need to obtain bond for the $79,000. Unless Darlene's expenses increase, Kenneth will not need to obtain a court order allowing him to withdraw funds from the blocked account until the $6,000 runs out in about one year.

1.   Guidelines for Blocked Accounts

Generally, money or securities are what is placed in a blocked account, but valuable personal property is sometimes included. Here are rules for placing assets in blocked accounts:

- Estate money may be deposited with an insured bank, savings and loan or trust company authorized to do business in California.

- Estate assets—such as stocks, bonds, jewelry and fine art—may be placed with an insured bank or trust company authorized to do business in California.

If you want to set up a blocked account as an alternative to bond, you may request this in Item 1c(3) of the Petition Appointing Probate Conservator set out in Chapter 4, Section A. If the money or other assets are already on deposit with an institution, you'll need to set up the blocked accounts at that institution. You'll need the name and address of any institution where you want to set up a blocked account. (Instructions for establishing blocked accounts are contained in Section E1, below.)

C.   Court Deposits

YOU MAY CHOOSE TO deposit assets in the bond amount with the court clerk instead of using a surety to obtain bond. You may not use the estate's assets, since the deposit is designed to protect them. Either use your own assets or obtain them from some other source. When accounts are used, they must be held in federally-insured institutions and cannot exceed the insured amount, generally $100,000. You may deposit (Code of Civil Procedure §995.710):

- money (United States only);[2]

- certificates of deposit that are payable to the court;[3]

- bank savings accounts, savings and loan share accounts or investment certificates assigned to the court clerk;

- credit union certificates for funds or share accounts assigned to the court clerk; or

- bearer bonds or bearer notes of the United States or California. Bearer bonds or notes are payable to the person who has them, rather than to a specific individ-

---

[1] If a surety company is used, annual bond premiums the estate would have to pay would also decrease.

[2] If you wish to deposit money, check with the court to find out the rate of interest. You may choose to make other arrangements to receive higher interest.

[3] A certificate of deposit cannot exceed an institution's federally-insured amount, generally $100,000.

ual. They are typically made out as "payable to bearer" or to "cash."[4]

Money deposited with the court must be held in an interest-bearing trust account (Code of Civil Procedure §995.710(a)(1)). If the court authorizes it, you may receive interest quarterly (Code of Civil Procedure §995.740(a)). If bearer bonds or notes are deposited, you may request either that the interest coupons be delivered as they become due or that annual interest be paid (Code of Civil Procedure §995.740).

 If you make deposits with the court, your money or assets will probably be tied up until the conservatorship ends.

D. How Much Bond Is Required

THE AMOUNT OF BOND depends on how the conservator plans to handle the bond requirement:

- If a surety company is used or deposits made with the court clerk, the bond amount equals the estimated value of the proposed conservatee's personal property, plus the estimated yearly gross income from real estate, personal property and public benefits.

- If the surety is a personal one—such as a friend or relative—the bond equals twice that amount (Probate Code §2320).

The conservator can also take steps to reduce the amount of bond required. (See Section D2, below.)

1. Determine Bond Requirement

If you are petitioning to be appointed conservator, read Sections A, B and C, above, to understand the bond requirement.

To determine how much bond is required, you'll need rough estimates of the value of the proposed conservatee's real estate, personal property and income. These amounts should be approximations only; do not have any of the proposed conservatee's property appraised.[5] (Chapter 12, Section C1, contains a list of common assets that may help you make a rough estimate.)

Fill in the figures on the accompanying worksheet, using the instructions that follow. You'll need these figures to complete the Petition for Appointment of Probate Conservator, so write them on the worksheet or on a separate piece of paper.

WORKSHEET FOR CALCULATING BOND

Personal property: $ _____

Annual gross income from

  real property: _____

  personal property: _____

TOTAL BOND REQUIRED
(if using surety company or
making deposits with clerk)* $ _____

*If personal sureties are used, this amount must be **doubled**.

---

[4]When bearer bonds or notes are used, their value must be determined by agreement between the conservator or the court, or the conservator may file a written application with the court to have the value determined (Probate Code §§995.720(a)-(b)). The court may want to have their value determined by a formula based on the principal amount of the bonds or notes rather than the market value (Probate Code §995.710(b)).

[5]Once a conservatorship is established, a probate referee will be appointed by the court to appraise the conservatee's assets (regardless of any appraisal you've had done already), so you would end up paying to have the property appraised twice. (See Chapter 13, Section C1.)

Personal property: List the total estimated value of the proposed conservatee's assets other than real estate and money or assets you plan to place in blocked accounts. (See Section B in this chapter.) This includes bank accounts, vehicles, securities, jewelry, antiques and all other personal possessions. Do not list property that has value only to the proposed conservatee—such as old clothes or toiletries.

Annual gross income from real property: If the proposed conservatee receives any income from real estate (for example, rent from tenants), list the total yearly amount received before taxes.

Annual gross income from personal property: If the proposed conservatee receives any income from personal property (for example, interest on savings accounts), indicate the total yearly amount received before taxes. Also include the estimated yearly total of any public benefits the proposed conservatee is entitled to receive, such as AFDC, General Assistance, Supplemental Security Income and State Supplemental Program.

Total Bond Required: Add the personal property, real property income and personal property income and enter the total in the space provided. This is the amount of bond required if you make deposits with the court or if bond is obtained from a surety company. If you plan to use personal sureties, twice the amount of bond is required.

2. Reducing or Eliminating Bond

The court has discretion in setting the bond amount. Many courts require that some bond be posted, but some will reduce or waive the amount under certain circumstances.

Conservators may be able to reduce the amount of bond required by depositing estate money or assets in blocked accounts. And a judge can waive the bond requirement if:

- The conservatee signs a written nomination selecting you as conservator and requests that bond be waived (Probate Code §2321).[6] (See instructions for Item

---

[6]A court might also waive the bond requirement if the proposed conservatee named you attorney in fact under a financial durable power of attorney.

1c(1) of the petition contained in Chapter 4, Section A.)

- The conservatee owns less than $5,000 worth of assets—excluding his home, and receives no more than $300 per month—excluding public benefits such as welfare, and all income is either spent, saved or invested for the benefit of the conservatee (Probate Code §2323). (If these conditions are met, request that bond be waived in Item 1c(1) of the petition. Instructions are contained in Chapter 4, Section A.)

3. Provide Bond Information in Petition

After you figure out how much bond is needed, indicate that sum in Item 1c(2) of the Petition for Appointment of Probate Conservator. If you want bond to be reduced or waived, you must provide the court with reasons. Or if you want to use personal sureties—where twice the amount of bond is required—you must give an explanation. (See instructions for Item 1c of the Petition for Appointment of Probate Conservator contained in Chapter 4, Section A.)

E.   After Being Appointed Conservator

THE ORDER APPOINTING Probate Conservator gives information about how much bond is required and what assets must be placed in blocked accounts at specific financial institutions. You must take care of these matters before Letters of Conservatorship will be issued and you take over the responsibility of conservator.

1.   Establish Blocked Accounts

Look at Item 3d of the Order Appointing Probate Conservator that was signed by a judge. If the judge authorized a blocked account as an alternative to all or part of the bond, the name and location of any financial institutions in which you will have the blocked account must be specified on the order.

To establish a blocked account, take a copy of the order to the financial institution. If the institution does not yet have the money, securities or personal property, bring it along. The financial institution must complete some paperwork to designate the account as blocked. Ask for a signed receipt showing the balance or contents of the account and indicating that it is blocked. You must provide this document to the court to prove that the account is blocked. Make several copies of the blocked account receipt before filing it with the court.

If the institution does not have its own blocked account form, prepare one yourself. On a blank piece of paper, title your document "Blocked Account Receipt and Agreement." Then type or neatly print: [name and address of financial institution] has received the following: [specify amount of money or give a detailed description of personal property or securities] in the name of [conservatee's name]. This [specify money, property or securities] will be held in a [specify type of account, or safety-deposit box] by [name of financial institution], and will be released only upon order of the Superior Court of California, County of [specify county and any district in which conservatorship is filed]. Withdrawal of [interest or dividends] ["does" or "does not"] require a court order.

Include date and signature lines for the financial institution's representative. Make several copies of the signed document before filing it with the court.

2.   Make Deposits With Court

Item 3d of the Order Appointing Probate Conservator lists the amount of bond required. The assets that may be used are set out in Section C, above. To make a deposit with the court, contact the court and find out its procedures.

Check with your local court to find out whether it has its own agreement form for authorizing deposits. If you must provide the deposit agreement, prepare one on a blank piece of paper. Title your document "Deposit Agreement (Code of Civil Procedure Section 995.710(c))." Then type or neatly print: This agreement is made between [your name], conservator of the [estate or person and estate] of [conservatee's name] and the officer of the Superior Court of California, County of [county and district]. The officer of the Superior Court of California, County of [county and district], is authorized to collect, sell or otherwise apply the deposit to enforce the liability of [your name], on the deposit. The address at which [your name], may be served with notices, papers and other documents is [your full street address].

Include date and signature lines for you and the "Officer of the Superior Court of [county and district]." Make several copies of the signed document before taking it to the court for signing and filing.

3.   Obtain Bond

When bond is required, it's up to you to find sureties to cover the amount. Look at Item 3d of the Order Appointing Probate Conservator to find out how much bond is needed.

a.   Surety Company

Remember that most surety companies will not bond conservators unless they are represented by an attorney. Surety companies are listed in the yellow pages under

"Bond" or "Surety." If you successfully obtain bond through a surety company, get a completed Bond on Qualifying and Order document from the surety company. You may reimburse yourself from the estate for money you spend out of your own pocket for conservatorship bond premiums. Keep copies of all receipts and documents pertaining to the bond. (Chapter 12, Section H1, gives information on reimbursement for such expenses.)

b. Personal Sureties

To use personal sureties, you must find a minimum of two friends, relatives or business associates willing to serve. You cannot be one of the sureties. All those you select must meet these requirements (Code of Civil Procedure §995.510):

- They must be California residents who own their homes or other real estate in California.

- They cannot be lawyers or officers of a California court.

- For bonds of $10,000 or less, each personal surety's net worth must be at least the amount of required bond in personal property, real estate or both. Their net worth is calculated over and above all debts and liabilities and excludes property exempt from enforcement of a money judgment.[7]

- For bonds over $10,000, three or more personal sureties may be used. Each personal surety's net worth may be less than the amount of bond as long as the total worth of all sureties is twice the amount of bond. Again, net worth is calculated over and above all debts and liabilities and excludes property exempt from enforcement of a money judgment.

---

[7] If there is a money judgment against any of the proposed sureties, you'll need to research exemptions. See *Collect Your Court Judgment* by Gini Scott, Stephen Elias and Lisa Goldoftas (Nolo Press).

FINDING PERSONAL SURETIES

Finding people to serve as personal sureties is similar to finding co-signers on a credit card or loan application. They are probably people who are close to you and trust your judgment. They may also be the conservatee's friends or relatives who want to help out.

People you ask to serve as personal sureties may wisely want to know specific details about your plans to manage the estate. They may also want you to informally keep them updated about how you handle the estate.

Everyone willing to serve should understand that they may be held personally liable for any damages caused by your improper actions—regardless of whether your mistakes were intentional or accidental. Their liability may continue for up to six years after you stop serving as conservator. Although sureties may later seek reimbursement from you, they stand to lose the full amount of bond if you mismanage the estate.

Using the information in this section, discuss the surety's role and potential financial liability with anyone willing to take on the job. Once you're satisfied both with their qualifications and willingness to serve, prepare these documents:

- *Bond (Personal) on Qualifying and Order:* This sets out the surety's willingness to provide bond. It must be signed by a judge before being effective.

- *Declaration of Personal Surety:* A separate declaration must be prepared for each surety. The document gives information about the surety's assets and helps a judge decide if the surety is qualified.

Some courts have local Bond (Personal) on Qualifying and Order forms. Otherwise, type or use a word processor to prepare these documents on lined paper using the following samples as guides. Documents must contain full captions and be double-spaced in the text. (See Chapter 3, Section H3.) Make photocopies of your papers and file them with the court.

 If a judge will not sign the order because he does not approve of the sureties you've selected, either obtain different sureties or consult a lawyer.

[Use lined paper and prepare the caption following the Sample Pleading in Chapter 3, Section H3.]

BOND (PERSONAL) ON
QUALIFYING AND ORDER

I, *[your name]*, as conservator, and *[name of first surety]*, and *[name of second surety]*, as sureties, are bound to the State of California in the sum of $*[bond amount]*. We bind ourselves, our heirs, executors and administrators, jointly and severally, to pay in event of breach of this bond as provided in Probate Code Section 2320.

This bond is being executed under an order of the Superior Court of California for the County of *[county where court is located]*, made on *[date judge signed Order Appointing Probate Conservator]* by which *[your name]* was appointed conservator of the *["estate" or "person and estate"]* of *[conservatee's name]*, and Letters of Conservatorship were directed to be issued to *[your name]* on executing a bond under the laws of California.

If *[your name]*, as Conservator of the *["estate" or "person and estate"]*, faithfully executes the duties of *[his/her]* trust according to law, this obligation shall become void; otherwise, it will remain in effect.

A declaration of qualifications for each surety is attached to and incorporated in this Bond (Personal) on Qualifying.

Dated: *[today's date]* _____

[Your Name]

Dated: *[today's date]* _____

[Name of First Surety]

Dated: *[today's date]* _____

[Name of Second Surety]

ORDER

The above bond is approved.

Dated: _____

Judge of the Superior Court

[Use lined paper and prepare the caption following the Sample Pleading in Chapter 3, Section H3.]

DECLARATION OF PERSONAL SURETY
[NAME OF SURETY]

I, *[name of surety]*, declare:

1. I am one of the sureties named in the bond for the *["estate" or "person and estate"]* of *[conservatee's name]*, to which this declaration is attached.

2. My residence address is *[home address]*. My business address is *[business address]*. My occupation is *[occupation]*.

3. I am a resident of California.

4. I am *["an owner of real property" or "householder"]* in California and am worth, exclusive of property exempt from execution and from enforcement of a money judgment, at least $*[amount]* over and above all my debts and liabilities.

5. *[If bond amount exceeds $5,000 or if required by local rules, add:]* I have an estate or interest in California property as follows, which qualifies me as a surety on the bond:

[For each item, give a description of the property and nature of the conservatee's interest, the best estimate of fair market value and the amount of any charge or lien on the property.]

There are no clouds or impediments known to me on my free right of possession, use, benefit or enjoyment of any of the property described above *[except (state any exceptions)]*.

6. *[If bond amount exceeds $10,000 and three or more sureties are used, a surety may be worth less than the amount of bond. If applicable, state:]* There are *[number of sureties]* on this bond, and the aggregate worth of all sureties executing the bond is at least twice the amount of bond. I am worth $*[amount]*.

I declare under penalty of perjury under the laws of the State of California that the foregoing is true and correct.

Dated: *[today's date]* _____

[Name of Surety]

F.   Maintain Correct Bond Amount

SOMETIMES THE AMOUNT of bond needed changes significantly during the conservatorship. For example, a major illness might use up a large part of the estate, meaning less bond would be necessary. More bond would be required if the conservatee inherits a significant amount of money or wins the lottery. Or the amount of bond required could increase if interest earnings or dividends significantly increased the value of the estate. In situations such as these, the conservator would need to get court approval to change the amount of bond.

If the bond amount is too low, you could be personally liable for the difference and Letters of Conservatorship could be revoked. Having too much bond puts the sureties at unnecessary risk, since they are financially responsible for your errors. When a surety company is used, excessive bond means that the estate would have to pay higher premiums than necessary.

You'll need to go back to court to have a judge approve a change of bond. Instructions are contained in Chapter 15, Section B, and sample documents are in Chapter 15, Section C2.

 Sureties may at any time petition the court for authorization to be released from liability on the bond (Code of Civil Procedure §996.110). If this happens, you must be notified in writing. You would then need to get other sureties to fill in, and file an account with the court. This would probably require a lawyer's help.

G.   Withdrawing Funds From Blocked Account

BECAUSE A BLOCKED ACCOUNT requires a judge's approval before any funds may be withdrawn, you'll need to go back to court to obtain an order. Instructions are contained in Chapter 15, Section B, and sample documents are in Chapter 15, Section C3.

GETTING COURT AUTHORIZATION

THE COURT THAT ESTABLISHES a conservatorship also oversees it. By law, a conservator cannot take certain actions without first obtaining court approval. And a conservator who is uncertain about whether an action is legal or ethical may first obtain permission from the court.

A. When to Seek Court Approval

THIS SECTION EXPLAINS WHEN a conservator is required to obtain court approval, and when she may wish to do so. For details about a conservator's role and information on when to obtain court authorization, conservators of the person should read Chapter 11, and conservators of the estate should read Chapter 12.

1. Mandatory Court Approval

All conservators must go to court and obtain an order to:

- transfer the conservatorship case to a different court (Section C4);

- end the conservatorship, resign or have a new conservator appointed (Chapter 16);

- be appointed the other type of conservator if the conservatorship is only for the person or estate;

- receive compensation or reimbursement for expenses other than bond premiums and court costs and fees; or

- hire a lawyer or authorize the payment of attorneys' fees.

a Conservators of the Person

Conservators of the person must obtain court permission to:

- take the conservatee out of California for four months or more;

- make certain medical decisions; or
- place the conservatee in a locked mental health treatment facility.

(Chapter 11 discusses these requirements in more detail.)

b.   Conservators of the Estate

Conservators of the estate must get court approval for:

- almost all matters involving real estate;
- increases and decreases in bond (Section C2);
- permission to remove funds from blocked accounts (Section C3); and
- all but the simplest, most conservative investments.

(Chapter 12 gives details on what actions require a court order.)

2.   Recommended Court Approval

Although a conservator is entitled to get court authorization any time, it obviously doesn't make sense unless it's really necessary. It's best to get a judge's approval before you take any action which the conservatee, her relatives or heirs are likely to oppose—for example, making a difficult medical decision or selling a family heirloom. You should also get court approval if you feel uncomfortable about making an important decision, or if the action you intend may appear to be a conflict of interest.

3.   What This Chapter Covers

Common situations that require court approval are covered in this chapter:

- requesting instructions where a conservator is uncertain about a given action (Section C1);
- requesting an increase or decrease in the amount of bond required (Section C2);
- seeking permission to withdraw funds from a blocked account (Section C3); and

- seeking authorization to transfer the conservatorship to a different California court (Section C4).

B.   How to Obtain Court Approval

HERE IS AN OVERVIEW of the steps to get an order of approval signed by a judge:

1. Check local rules and follow any procedures specific to your court.

2. Complete the appropriate documents for your situation. If there are no samples provided in Section C of this chapter for your circumstances, you'll need to do your own research or hire an attorney. (See Chapter 17.)

3. Photocopy the documents and file them with the court.

4. Have those people entitled to notice served. Then prepare proofs of service and file them with the court.

5. If the court contacts you and requests additional documentation, provide it and have copies served on anyone entitled to notice.

6. Several days before the hearing date, find out the tentative decision on your petition.

7. Attend any scheduled hearings and obtain a court order.

8. Follow the instructions set out in the court order.

1.   Check Local Court Rules

Before you prepare any documents, check with the court where the conservatorship was set up. Each court has its own special procedures for scheduling hearings and obtaining orders.

If your court has one, call the probate clerk who handles procedural questions. Explain that you are filing a petition and specify what it is for, such as "Petition for Instructions" or "Petition for Decrease of Bond." Then find out:

- whether the type of petition you are filing requires notice to anyone. If not, you must add the words "ex parte" before the document title.[1]
- the days and times the petition may be heard, the location, the judge or commissioner who will hear and decide on it and how you may schedule your petition. If you can get a hearing date over the phone, allow yourself time to prepare your papers and at least 25 days to have everyone served.
- whether there are filing fees. There should only be court filing fees if you are transferring the conservatorship to another court in California.
- how many copies of each document are required.

If the probate court clerk cannot answer your questions, you may be able to find the guidance you need in the local probate policy manual. If you do not already have a copy of your court's probate policy manual, see Chapter 17, Section D2, for information.

2. Complete Required Documents

Type or use a word processor to complete your documents on lined pleading paper following the format in Chapter 3, Section H3. Follow the guidelines of the samples in this chapter.

a. Petition

In the petition, explain what action you want to take, why it is necessary and request a judge's authorization to take the action. The petitions in this chapter should be used to obtain a judge's permission *before* you proceed with an action about which you are uncertain.[2] When preparing your petition, pay attention to these details:

- Place the date, time and location under the title of the document.

---

[1] If anyone filed a Request for Special Notice, the petition cannot be heard ex parte without a special court order dispensing with notice. (See Section B4.)

[2] If you've already gone ahead with the action you're not sure of, you can ask a judge to confirm your act. That is beyond the scope of this book.

- If the petition will be heard ex parte, insert the words "ex parte" before the title of the document.
- Make sure the telephone number you list in the caption is one at which you can be reached during the day, or one with an answering machine or service. Probate court personnel are notorious for calling with picky questions before a hearing—and it may delay the hearing if they can't get through.

b. (Proposed) Order

The proposed order, which must be signed by a judge, gives you permission to proceed with a particular action. Before the judge will sign the order, you must give information about the hearing date and attendance. Prepare the document on lined paper following the guidelines of the samples in this chapter. The blank lines on the samples should simply be copied and left blank. The judge will fill them in at the hearing and make any necessary changes.

c. Notice of Hearing

Skip this section if your petition will be heard ex parte—for which no notice is required. Otherwise, complete a Notice of Hearing following the instructions in Chapter 4, Section G, with these exceptions:

Item 1: If you have been appointed conservator by the court, after the words "(representative capacity, if any)," enter the words "conservator of the person," "conservator of the estate," or "conservator of the person and estate." Just below this, after the words "has filed (specify)," fill in the title of the petition, such as "Petition for Instructions."

Item 3: Fill in the information in the box about the date, time and place of the hearing if you obtained them over the phone. Otherwise, have the clerk fill in this information when you file your papers.

Proof of Service (Page 2): Complete the proof of service by mail. (Instructions are contained in Chapter 6, Section D3.) After the words "Name and Address of Each Person to Whom Notice Was Mailed," fill in the names and addresses of everyone entitled to notice explained in Section 4a of this chapter. Do not have the proof of service signed yet.

3. Copy and File Papers With Court

Make two or three photocopies of each document, depending on whether the court requires an additional copy. In addition, make one copy each of the Notice of Hearing and petition for the conservatee and each person entitled to notice.

Take or send the court the original and copies of documents along with two self-addressed, stamped envelopes.[3] If you obtain a hearing date from the clerk when you file your papers, get one at least 25 days in the future to allow enough time to have the papers served.

Make sure all copies of the Notice of Hearing are marked with the date, time and place listed in Item 3. The clerk should give you the original signed Notice of Hearing. Keep it in a safe place. You will need to file it with the court after everyone entitled to notice has been served.

4. Service of Papers

Skip this section if your petition will be heard ex parte—meaning no notice is required. Note that if anyone has filed a Request for Special Notice in the conservatorship case, that person is entitled to be served, so the petition cannot be filed ex parte.

To serve papers, look at the first page of the Notice of Hearing. At the bottom of the page are the words "This

notice was mailed on (date)." Fill in the date documents are being served. After the words "at (place)," fill in the city where they are being mailed.

At least 20 days before the scheduled hearing date, have copies of the Notice of Hearing served by mail on the conservatee and everyone entitled to notice as described in Section 4a of this chapter. Instructions for having documents served by mail are contained in Chapter 6, Section D2. If you don't have papers served in time, you will need to have the hearing continued. (See Chapter 8, Section C.)

a. Who Must be Served

Several people must get notice of the hearing:

- *Conservatee.* The conservatee must always be mailed copies of documents you file with the court, even if she is incapable of reading or understanding them.

- *Conservatee's Spouse.* If the conservatee is married or separated, the conservatee's spouse must receive notice. If the conservatee is divorced, you don't need to have the ex-spouse served.

- *Court Investigator.* Depending on local rules, the court investigator may be entitled to notice. Check local rules or play it safe and serve the investigator.

- *Veterans' Administration.* For a conservatorship of the estate, the Veterans' Administration must be served if the conservatee is entitled to receive its benefits. If you're not sure whether the proposed conservatee receives or is entitled to receive benefits, serve the Veterans' Administration. (See Chapter 6, Section D1b.)

- *Anyone Who Filed Court Papers or Requested Special Notice.* Everyone who filed papers with the court in the conservatorship case must be served, including anyone who contested the conservatorship.[4] People who want to be updated about the conservatorship generally file a document entitled "Request for Special Notice" with the court and serve a copy on you. The document asks for notification of all hearings and usually of all financial matters, including initial and supplemental Inventory & Appraisements. A Request for Special Notice

---

[3] If you are not required to attend the hearing, a signed copy of the order can be sent back to you if there is an extra envelope, saving you a trip to the courthouse.

[4] If anyone has filed objections to the conservatorship or your role as conservator, consult a lawyer.

stays in effect for three years from the date served, unless it is changed or withdrawn (Probate Code §2701). If you aren't sure whether a Request for Special Notice was filed, call the court. Give the clerk the case name and file number, and ask her to pull the file and check. Get the names and addresses of everyone who filed such a request.

- *Anyone Affected by the Order.* This might be someone who stands to inherit something from the conservatee's estate or who you know wants to purchase estate property that you are planning to sell.

Everyone entitled to notice should be mailed copies of the documents you file in court at least 20 days before the scheduled hearing date.[5] If you need authorization from the court earlier or don't want to serve everyone entitled to notice, consult an attorney or do your own legal research. (See Chapter 17.)

b. Complete and File Proof of Service

Have the person who served the papers sign the proof of service on the back of the original Notice of Hearing. Fill in the date and place of service at the bottom of the first page. Finally, make two or three copies, and take or send them to the court at least ten days before the hearing date.

5. If Additional Documents Are Required

If the court contacts you because a document is incorrect or the judge wants additional information, you will need to prepare supplemental or amended documents.

If you completed your petition incorrectly, follow the instructions in Chapter 3, Section I, to prepare an amended petition. If the judge wants additional information, such as a declaration or copies of financial records, prepare and provide them. (See Chapter 3, Section H2c, for more information about completing declarations.)

---

[5]By law, only 15 days' advance notice is required. To be safe, it is best to have them mailed 20 days beforehand.

 If you need to file additional documents with the court, ask the probate court clerk where you should bring them. In some counties, the file is reviewed by a clerk or judge several days before the hearing, so papers must be taken to that reviewer's office. If your papers are not received in time, the hearing will be continued or taken off calendar and you may have to start the process over.

6. Find Out Tentative Decision

Your petition is sent to the office of the judge or commissioner who will be considering it several days before the scheduled hearing. A clerk reviews your papers to make sure everything is in order. In many counties, the judge makes a tentative ruling on your petition—called a "pre-grant decision"—based solely on the papers you've submitted.

Call the court two days before the hearing is scheduled to find out if the judge has made a pre-grant decision on your petition. In some counties, this information is given on a recorded tape one or two days before the hearing. In other counties, you get the information from a clerk. If the judge wants more information, follow the instructions in Section B5, above.

7. Attend Hearing If Required

You must attend the hearing if:

- the pre-grant decision was not in your favor;
- you have reason to believe the conservatee or someone else will appear to contest your petition;
- someone filed papers opposing your petition; or
- you were told by the probate clerk that you will need to appear.

If you attend the hearing, bring copies of all your documents, including the proofs of service. Let the clerk or bailiff know you are in the courtroom. The judge will decide whether to give you permission to undertake the action you requested. The judge may simply grant and sign the order without asking you any questions. However, the judge may want additional information from you. For example, if you want permission to sell property, the judge may want to know why the conservatorship needs more money. The hearing will be similar to the hearing at which you were appointed conservator. (See Chapter 8.)

 See a lawyer if the judge won't grant your petition and you don't know what steps to take.

8.   Obtain and Follow Court Order

Obtain a copy of the signed order before you leave the court. If you weren't required to attend the hearing, make arrangements to get copies of the order. Once the order has been signed by the judge, you may go ahead with the approved action. Make sure you follow the instructions in the order. If the judge modified the order, you must comply with it as changed. Provide a copy of the order to any institution or agency that requires one.

C.   Sample Petitions and Orders

THIS SECTION GIVES EXAMPLES of four petitions and orders. Using the samples as guides, prepare your own documents on lined pleading paper following the instructions in Chapter 3, Section H3. Follow the instructions in Section B, above, for returning to court.

 If you must obtain authorization that is not covered in this book, you will need to do your own legal research or obtain the help of an attorney. (See Chapter 17.)

1.   Request for Instructions and Authorization

Modify the samples provided to obtain permission from a judge to take an action. Do not use these forms for any

matters that are listed elsewhere in this book as requiring the help of an attorney.

a   Petition for Instructions

[Use lined paper and prepare the caption following the Sample Pleading in Chapter 3, Section H3.]

PETITION OF CONSERVATOR FOR INSTRUCTIONS (Probate Code Section 2403 or Probate Code Section 2359(a))

DATE: *[hearing date]*
TIME: *[hearing time]*
DEPT: *[department]*

Petitioner alleges:

1. Petitioner is conservator of the *["person," "estate" or "person and estate," depending on the type of conservatorship]* of *[conservatee's name]*, and letters were issued on *[date Letters of Conservatorship issued]*.

2. Petitioner believes it is necessary to take the following action: *[describe action]*.

3. Petitioner believes such action is in the best interests of the conservatee *[for conservatorships of the estate, add "and the conservatorship estate"]* because: *[state reason why action is necessary and in the best interests of the conservatee; attach copies of any supporting documentation]*.

4. No person has filed a request for special notice *[if requested, add: "except for" and fill in name and address of person requesting notice]*.

5. Petitioner requests the court make an order authorizing the action described in Item 2, above.

Respectfully Submitted,

Dated: *[today's date]*   _____

                              [your name]
                              Conservator In Pro Per

                    VERIFICATION
[Insert verification from Chapter 3, Section H2d.]

b. Proposed Order Authorizing Conservator

[Use lined paper and prepare the caption following the Sample Pleading in Chapter 3, Section H3.]

ORDER AUTHORIZING CONSERVATOR
TO ACT

The Petition for *[exact title of petition]* came on for hearing on _____ at ____:___ ___.M. in Dept. _____ of the Superior Court of California, County of *[name of court]*, the Honorable _____ presiding. *[Your name]* appeared as petitioner In Pro Per and no one appeared in opposition *[if there is opposition, you will need to see an attorney]*.

After examining the Petition for *[exact title of petition]* and hearing the evidence,

THE COURT FINDS:

1. All notices required by law have been given.

2. It is in the best interests of the conservatee *[if you are conservator of the estate add: "and the estate"]* for the conservator to take the following action: *[briefly describe requested action]*.

THE COURT ORDERS that the conservator has authorization to take the following action: *[briefly describe requested action]*.

Dated: _____
                         Judge of the Superior Court

2. Increase or Decrease in Bond

If you want to change the amount of bond required, read Chapter 14, Section F. Then prepare a petition and order using the accompanying samples as guides.

 As discussed in Section B4, some courts may hear petitions for an increase or decrease of bond ex parte—in which case you need not serve documents on anyone. Check local practices.

a. Petition for Change in Bond

[Use lined paper and prepare the caption following the Sample Pleading in Chapter 3, Section H3.]

PETITION FOR *["INCREASE" or "DECREASE"]* OF BOND *["AND FOR PLACEMENT OF FUNDS IN BLOCKED ACCOUNT"]*

DATE: *[hearing date]*
TIME: *[hearing time]*
DEPT: *[department]*

Petitioner respectfully represents:

1. Petitioner is the conservator of the *["estate" or "person and estate"]* of *[conservatee's name]*.

2. Petitioner has filed a bond in the amount of $*[amount]*, as required by law.

3. The existing bond amount is *["excessive" or "insufficient"]* for these reasons: *[explain why the bond amount is too high or low, such as, "The conservatee received an inheritance of $15,000 cash," or "the conservator paid a claim for federal taxes in the amount of $19,400."]*.

4. The character and estimated value of the property of the estate is:

Personal property:	$*[amount]*
Annual gross income from	
real property:	$*[amount]*
personal property:	$*[amount]*
Total:	$*[amount]*
Real Property:	$*[amount]*

5. No person has filed a request for special notice *[if requested, add: "except for" and fill in name and address of person requesting notice]*.

6. Petitioner requests an order *["increasing" or "decreasing"]* the amount of bond, and fixing bond in the amount of $*[amount]*.

7. *[If applicable: "Petitioner further requests that deposits in the amount of $(amount) shall be made in a blocked account at (specify name and address of institution) and receipts filed."]*

Respectfully Submitted,

Dated: *[today's date]* _____

[your name]
Conservator In Pro Per

VERIFICATION
[Insert verification from Chapter 3, Section H2d.]

b. (Proposed) Order Changing Bond

*[Use lined paper and prepare the caption following the Sample
Pleading in Chapter 3, Section H3.]*

ORDER FOR *["INCREASE" or
"DECREASE"]* OF BOND *["AND
ORDER FOR PLACEMENT OF
FUNDS IN BLOCKED ACCOUNT"]*

The Petition for *[exact title of petition]* came on for
hearing on _____ at ___:___
___.M. in Dept._____ of the Superior Court
of California, County of *[county]*, the Honorable
_____ presiding. *[Your name]*
appeared as petitioner In Pro Per and no one
appeared in opposition *[if there is opposition, you will need
to see an attorney]*.

After examining the Petition for *[exact title of
petition]* and hearing the evidence, the court
finds:

1. All notices required by law have been
given.

2. *["Increase" or "Decrease"]* of bond is in the best
interests of the conservatee.

THE COURT ORDERS:

1. Bond is *["increased" or "decreased"]* and shall be
fixed at the amount of $*[amount]*, effective as of
the date of this order *[or, if deposits will be made in a
blocked account, "effective as of the date the conservator files receipts
for the blocked account, which must be no later than (date) "]*.

2. *[If applicable: Deposits shall be made in a blocked account at
(specify name and address of institution) in the amount of $(amount)
and receipts filed.]*

Dated: _____

Judge of the Superior Court

3. Withdrawing Funds from Blocked Account

If funds or personal property are in a blocked account, you
must obtain a court order before removing them. The
court might require receipts or other documentation
proving that the expenses and withdrawal are necessary.
Bear in mind that the amount of required bond may
change if you withdraw money or property from a blocked
account. If so, see Section C2, above, and Chapter 14,
Section F.

 As discussed in Section B4, some courts may
hear these petitions ex parte—in which case,
you need not serve documents on anyone.
And local preprinted forms may even be
available. Check local practices.

a. Petition to Withdraw from Blocked Account

[Use lined paper and prepare the caption following the Sample Pleading in Chapter 3, Section H3.]

PETITION FOR AUTHORITY TO REMOVE
FUNDS FROM BLOCKED ACCOUNT

DATE: *[hearing date]*
TIME: *[hearing time]*
DEPT: *[department]*

Petitioner respectfully represents:

1. Petitioner is the conservator of the *["estate" or "person and estate"]* of *[conservatee's name]*.

2. In accordance with this court's order of *[date judge signed Order Appointing Conservator or other order to place funds in blocked account]*, the amount of *[$ amount—or specify personal property]* was placed in a blocked account, number *[account number]* at *[specify name and address of institution]*. Court approval is needed to make withdrawals from this account.

3. It is necessary to withdraw *[$ amount—or specify personal property]* from the account *[specify reasons, such as "to pay for the conservatee's medical care" or "to make repairs to the conservatee's house, including installing an alarm system"]*.

4. Petitioner has given a bond in the amount of $*[amount]*. After withdrawing funds *[or personal property]* from the blocked account, the character and estimated value of the property of the estate is:

Personal property: $*[amount]*

Annual gross income from

    real property: $*[amount]*

    personal property: $*[amount]*

        Total: $*[amount]*

Real Property: $*[amount]*

5. No person has filed a request for special notice *[if requested, add: "except for" and fill in name and address of person requesting notice]*.

Petitioner requests an order allowing *[your name]*, conservator of the *["estate" or "person and estate"]* of *[conservatee's name]* authorization to withdraw *[specify amount or personal property]* from *[name and address of institution]*.

Respectfully Submitted,

Dated: *[today's date]* _____

[your name]
Conservator In Pro Per

VERIFICATION

[Insert verification from Chapter 3, Section H2d.]

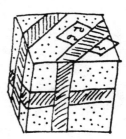

b. (Proposed) Order for Withdrawal from Blocked Account

[Use lined paper and prepare the caption following the Sample Pleading in Chapter 3, Section H3.]

ORDER FOR AUTHORITY TO REMOVE
FUNDS FROM BLOCKED ACCOUNT

The Petition for *[exact title of petition]* came on for hearing on _____ at ___:___ __.M. in Dept. _____ of the Superior Court of California, County of *[county]*, the Honorable _____ presiding. *[Your name]* appeared as petitioner In Pro Per and no one appeared in opposition *[if there is opposition, you will need to see an attorney]*.

After examining the PETITION FOR AUTHORITY TO REMOVE FUNDS FROM BLOCKED ACCOUNT and hearing the evidence, the court finds:

1. All notices required by law have been given.

2. In accordance with this court's order of [*date judge signed Order Appointing Conservator or other order to place funds in blocked account*], the amount of [*$ amount—or specify personal property*] was placed in a blocked account, number [*account number*] at [*specify name and address of institution*]. Court approval is needed to make withdrawals from this account.

3. The withdrawal of funds [*or specify personal property*] from a blocked account is in the best interests of the conservatee.

4. Additional bond [*is/is not*] required.

THE COURT ORDERS:

1. [*Your name*], conservator of the [*"estate" or "person and estate"*] is authorized to withdraw [*specify amount or personal property*] from [*name and address of institution*].

2. Additional bond [*is/is not*] required [*in the amount of $(amount)*].

Dated: _____

Judge of the Superior Court

4. Transfer to Different California Court

You are entitled by law to have the conservatorship transferred to another court as long as it is in the best interests of the conservatee and her estate. A case may be transferred either before or after a conservator has been appointed by the court.

Conservatorship cases are typically transferred if the conservatee moves to a different county. A judge may also allow a transfer if the conservator moved or the conservatee's major assets are located in a different county from her residence.

Call the court from which you are transferring the case—not the new court to which you want the case moved. Explain that you're filing a petition to have the conservatorship proceeding transferred. Find out the fees the old court charges for transferring your case—about $14—and when those fees must be paid.

Another fee must also be paid to the new court when your papers are transferred. The receiving court's fees will be approximately the same as the original filing fee. Call the new court and find out the fee charged to have a case transferred there. If you are conservator of the estate, the fees for transferring the case will be paid out of the estate. Prepare the papers and obtain court approval following the instructions in Section B, above.

After an order is granted, the old court will arrange to have the file transferred to the new court, and transferring fees will be charged to the conservatee's estate (Probate Code §2216(b)). A few days after the order is granted, call the clerk of the old court to find out when the transfer will be complete.

After the date the transfer should have taken place, call the clerk of the new court to verify that the case was transferred, and make arrangements to pay the new court's filing fee.[6] Ask if you will be sent a document in the mail giving you the new case number, or if you can get it over the phone. You will need the new case number for any further contact you may have with the new court.

---

[6]If you want to have those fees waived because you and the estate can't afford them, you'll have to fill out documents and file them with the new court. (See Chapter 5, Section B.)

You may have to follow up with clerks at both courts to make sure the file is transferred. The actual transfer of files notoriously falls through the cracks.

a Petition for Transfer of Proceedings

[Use lined paper and prepare the caption following the Sample Pleading in Chapter 3, Section H3.]

PETITION FOR TRANSFER OF
CONSERVATORSHIP PROCEEDING

DATE: *[hearing date]*
TIME: *[hearing time]*
DEPT: *[department]*

Petitioner alleges:

1. Petitioner is the *["proposed"]* conservator of the *["person," "estate" or "person and estate,"]* of *[conservatee's name]*.

2. Petitioner requests that this conservatorship proceeding be transferred to the Superior Court of the State of California, County of *[new county where you want case transferred; if the new court has a district or branch name, put it after the name of the county]*. This transfer would be in the best interests of the *["proposed"]* conservatee for the following reason(s): *[give reasons why a transfer is needed—for example: "Andrew Smith and I moved to Santa Clara County in May 19___. I applied for welfare benefits on his behalf, and was informed that I cannot obtain benefits unless the conservatorship is transferred to this county. It would be in the conservatee's best interests for me to obtain welfare benefits to help support him"]*.

3. *[Complete this item only if you are the proposed or acting conservator of the estate or person and estate.]* Petitioner is the *["proposed"]* conservator of the estate in this proceeding. The character, value, and location of the estate's property is as follows: *[Briefly list the estate's assets, approximate value and where they are located. You may refer to the Inventory and Appraisement in Chapter 13, Section C3 for this information. If there isn't enough room, provide the information in an Attachment 3.]*

4. The *["proposed"]* conservator's name and address are: *[your name and home address]*.

5. The *["proposed"]* conservatee's name and address are: *[conservatee's name and home address]*.

6. The names, residence addresses and relationships of the *["proposed"]* conservatee's relatives within the second degree so far as known to petitioner are as follows: *[fill in the names and addresses of relatives you listed in Part 1 of the Conservatorship Worksheet (see Chapter 3, Section F1)]*.

7. No person has filed a request for special notice *[if requested, add: "except for" and fill in name and address of person requesting notice]*.

Petitioner requests an order transferring this proceeding to the Superior Court of the State of California, County of *[new county where you want case transferred]*.

Respectfully Submitted,

Dated: *[today's date]* _____

[your name]
Conservator In Pro Per

VERIFICATION
[Insert verification from Chapter 3, Section H2d.]

b.   (Proposed) Order for Transfer of Proceedings

[Use lined paper and prepare the caption following the Sample Pleading in Chapter 3, Section H3.]

ORDER FOR TRANSFER OF
CONSERVATORSHIP PROCEEDING

The Petition for Transfer of Conservatorship Proceeding came on for hearing on _____ at _____:_____ __.M. in Dept. _____ of the Superior Court of California, County of *[name of court]*, the Honorable _____ presiding. *[Your name]* appeared as petitioner In Pro Per and no one appeared in opposition *[if there is opposition, you will need to see an attorney]*.

After examining the Petition for Transfer of Conservatorship Proceeding and hearing the evidence, THE COURT FINDS:

Transfer of the Conservatorship of *[conservatee's name]*, Case Number *[case number from old court]* from this court to the Superior Court of the State of California, County of *[new county where you want case transferred; if the new court has a district or branch name, put it after the name of the county]* is in the best interests of the conservatee.

THE COURT ORDERS that this proceeding be transferred to the Superior Court of the State of California, County of *[new county where you want case transferred]*.

Dated: _____

Judge of the Superior Court

CHAPTER 16

HOW TO END A CONSERVATORSHIP

AS A COURT-APPOINTED conservator, you are responsible for serving until the court issues an order relieving you from those responsibilities. This may happen if:

- the conservatorship is no longer needed—so it is ended altogether;[1] or

- you become unable or unwilling to handle the responsibility. If so, the conservatorship itself does not end, but a new person may take over the role. (Section D of this chapter discusses this situation, but instructions are beyond the scope of this book.)

A. Reasons to End a Conservatorship

A CONSERVATORSHIP TYPICALLY ends when the conservatee dies. However, it may end sooner if a judge determines the conservatorship is no longer necessary. Reasons that would justify ending a conservatorship include:

- *The estate is used up.* Conservatorships of the estate may end if there are no more assets in the estate (Probate Code §2626). All of the assets should have been used for the support and benefit of the conservatee.[2]

---

[1]Technically, the conservatorship ends automatically if the conservatee dies (Probate Code §1860(a)). However, a conservator of the estate must obtain a court order releasing her from her duties. A conservator of the person should also obtain such a court order.

[2]With prior court approval, a conservator of the estate can transfer conservatorship assets out of state and end the California conservatorship (Probate Code §2808). Those procedures are beyond the scope of this book.

Example: Herman is conservator of the person and estate of his friend, Johnny. When Herman obtained the conservatorship, Johnny's estate consisted of approximately $35,000 cash. After several years, the estate is used up on Johnny's living expenses, housing and medical bills. Following the instructions in this chapter, Herman terminates the conservatorship of the estate. He continues as the conservator of Johnny's person.

- *The conservatee's condition improves.* If a conservatee's physical and mental abilities improve, he may be able to permanently resume caring for himself or handling his own money. A court order to end the conservatorship is needed.

  Example: Barbara is conservator of the person of her adult daughter, Cathy. Barbara obtained the conservatorship when Cathy was in a coma following a serious automobile accident. Although Cathy's doctors said she would never get better, she came out of the coma and recovered remarkably. Because Cathy is again able to care for herself, a conservatorship is no longer necessary. Barbara goes to court and ends the conservatorship following the instructions in this book.

- *The conservatorship is contested.* The conservatee, court investigator, his friends or relatives could file documents claiming that a conservatorship isn't needed.

  Example: Andrew is conservator of the person and estate of his elder sister, Patty, who has many physical ailments. Andrew is in his 70s, and is also beginning to have serious health problems. Andrew's younger sister, who is in her early 60s, discovers valid durable powers of attorney that authorize her to handle Patty's finances and make medical decisions. She suggests that Andrew end the conservatorship, but he is unwilling to do that. Andrew's younger sister then files court documents to end the conservatorship.

Note: Regardless of why a conservatorship ends, another conservatorship proceeding may be initiated (Probate Code §1863(d)). For example, this might happen if a conservatee gets better for some time and then takes a turn for the worse. This book may be used to initiate new proceedings, which require new documents, another initial filing fee and a different case number.

B. Your Role If Conservatee Dies

THE LOSS OF THE CONSERVATEE may evoke mixed feelings—sadness at losing someone dear to you and relief that you have fewer responsibilities. Although the conservatee's death ends your role as conservator, you'll need to take some steps to bring your job to an official end.

Depending on the circumstances, you may be coordinating your efforts with the person responsible for distributing estate property and paying estate taxes. This person is generally appointed by a court located in the county where the conservatee lived at the time of his death. If the conservatee left a will, that person is called the personal representative or executor. If there was no will, she is known as the administrator.[3] In this book, the person handling the estate of a conservatee who has died is referred to as the "personal representative."

When a conservatee dies, you may face difficult, painful tasks: arranging for the disposition of the bodily remains,[4] paying doctor and hospital bills; and if the conservatee lived in a care facility, arranging to pick up his possessions. Do not throw out or give away anything without first contacting the personal representative, family or close friends.

---

[3] An administrator is appointed according to a priority list containing approximately a dozen and a half entries. A conservator who is not closely related to the deceased conservatee ranks near the bottom of the priority list (Probate Code §8461).

[4] Bodily remains may be cremated or buried, or the body may be donated to a medical school for research—or certain body organs or tissues donated to transplant facilities. (See Appendix A for information on donating body organs or tissues.)

IF CONSERVATEE DIES BEFORE A CONSERVATORSHIP IS ESTABLISHED

Sometimes a conservatee dies shortly after conservatorship proceedings have begun. This may be before the conservatorship hearing date, or after the hearing but before Letters of Conservatorship have been issued. To stop the process, follow your court's local rules.

A proposed conservator of the person who has not obtained issued Letters of Conservatorship may usually call or send a letter to the court indicating that the conservatee has died. The court may require a certified copy of the death certificate.

A proposed conservator of the estate can usually follow the same procedures unless he has possession of some of the proposed conservatee's money or property. If so, he'll need to give that property to the personal representative handling the probate estate and possibly file an account with the personal representative. The personal representative must obtain a court order in the probate estate case if such an account is necessary.

1. Obtain Copies of Death Certificate

When a person dies in California, an official death certificate is filed in the county health department or vital statistics office of the county where the death occurred. The death certificate lists personal information about the deceased, such as her Social Security number, occupation and dates of birth and death.

You'll need to provide the court with a certified copy of the death certificate. If funeral home or cemetery personnel are involved, you can ask them to obtain certified copies for you. They will generally charge for this service. If you prefer, you may order certified copies from the health department or vital statistics office in the county where the conservatee died. Copies will also be available from the County Recorder's office a month or so after the date of death. Call the appropriate office to get the address and cost. Then send a check to cover the fee, and include in your request the name of the deceased as well as the date and city of death.

2. How to Handle Conservatorship Estate

Skip this section unless you are conservator of the estate or person and estate.

After the conservatee's death, you must continue managing the estate until you turn it over to someone designated in a court order (Probate Code §2467). This is usually the personal representative who is authorized to handle the estate. It may take several months to complete the process. During that time, you must wrap up the estate following the guidelines below.

- *Maintain the Estate.* You must maintain the estate until it is turned over to the personal representative handling the estate (Probate Code §2467). Pay conservatorship expenses incurred before or after the conservatee's death, such as rent or costs of home health care. Do not cash any benefit checks, such as Social Security, that were issued in the month the conservatee died or afterwards. If anyone files a claim for expenses that you didn't contract for, you'll need court approval before you can pay the claim (Probate Code §2631(c)). You'll also need court approval to pay your own fees or attorneys' fees. If there are any complicated investments or transactions in progress, seek an attorney's help. (See Chapter 17.)

- *Pay for Burial or Cremation.* You may pay a reasonable sum for the disposition of the conservatee's remains (Probate Code §2631(a)).[5] Unless family members all agree, do not make extravagant burial arrangements without prior court approval.

- *Pay for Last Illness.* You may pay doctor's bills and hospital fees for the conservatee's last illness (Probate Code §2631(a)). If there was insurance to cover these costs, you may contact the insurance company and arrange for payment.

Note: If you can't pay the expenses to cover the conservatee's last illness and burial, you may petition the court for an order allowing you to liquidate the estate if the remaining estate value is less than $10,000 (Probate Code §2631(b)).[6] That is beyond the scope of this book.

---

[5]For resources that can provide information on donating body organs and tissues, see Appendix A.

[6]This procedure may be followed when there is no executor named in the conservatee's will who is acting in that capacity.

a   Contact Personal Representative

You may become responsible for settling the conservatee's estate, or will need to contact the person who is responsible, referred to in this book as the "personal representative."[7] Depending on whether the conservatee had an estate plan, this may be the:

- executor (if one was named in a will and is able to serve);

- administrator (if there was no will and a person was appointed to this position by the probate court;

- person filing a small estate affidavit under California Probate Code § 13100 (for estates under $60,000); or

- trustee (if the conservatee had a living trust).

Obtain copies of any documents filed in the court that show the personal representative has authority to act in this role. Do not turn over assets to the personal representative before obtaining an authorizing court order.

 If there is no personal representative and no probate has been opened, you will need to ask the court for guidance. (See Account, Report and Petition in Chapter 13, Section E4.)

C.   How to End a Conservatorship

IF YOU WISH TO END the conservatorship, read Section A of this chapter and make sure you have an appropriate reason for doing so. Generally, this would be where the conservatee has died, his situation has changed and he can resume taking care of himself or managing his own estate, or—for a conservatorship of the estate—the estate has been used up. If you plan to end the conservatorship, do so quickly. Otherwise, you and the sureties will continue to have liability for the estate.

Follow the instructions in this section only if the conservatee and his estate will not be in any danger if the conservatorship ends. Here is an overview of the steps you'll take to end the conservatorship and be relieved of your duties as conservator:

1. Check local rules, and follow any procedures specific to your court.

2. Complete these documents:

- *Petition for Termination of Conservatorship.* Here you request that a judge allow the conservatorship to end.

- *(Proposed) Order Terminating Conservatorship.* This proposed order is signed by a judge after he reviews your request to end the conservatorship.

- *Final Account (Estate Conservatorship).* Conservators of the estate or person and estate must prepare final account documents following the instructions in Chapter 13, Section E.

- *Notice of Hearing and Proof of Service.* This form gives information on when and where a hearing will be held. It must be served on a number of people. A proof of service shows who was notified about the hearing.

- *Documents Required by Local Rules.* Check local rules to find out if you must complete preprinted local forms or other documents.

3. Photocopy the documents and file them with the court.

4. Have those people entitled to notice served. Then prepare proofs of service and file them with the court.

5. Pay fees for the court investigation.

6. If the court contacts you and requests additional documentation, provide it and have copies served on anyone entitled to notice.

7. Several days before the hearing date, find out the tentative decision on your petition.

8. Attend the scheduled hearing if necessary.

9. Obtain a copy of the court order.

10. If you are conservator of the estate, you must prepare several documents and arrange to transfer the estate property to the personal representative or conservatee. You then file the documents with the court and obtain a discharge of both you and the sureties.

---

[7]Detailed information about settling estates is covered in *How to Probate an Estate*, by Julia Nissley (Nolo Press).

1. Check Local Court Rules

Many courts have their own procedures for ending conservatorships. Before you prepare any documents, check with the court where the conservatorship was set up. Explain that you are filing a petition to end a conservatorship and find out:

- the days and times the petition may be heard, the location, the judge or commissioner who will hear and decide on it and how you may schedule your petition. If you can get a hearing date over the phone, allow time to prepare your papers and at least 20 days to have everyone served.

- whether any local forms are required.

- how many copies of each document the court requires.

    If the probate court clerk does not answer your questions, you may be able to find the guidance you need in the local probate policy manual. (See Chapter 17, Section D2, for information on obtaining probate policy manuals.)

2. Complete Required Documents

Use a typewriter or word processor to prepare your documents on lined pleading paper following the format in Chapter 3, Section H3. Follow the guidelines of the samples in this chapter.

a. Petition for Termination

In this petition, you tell why the court should allow the conservatorship to end. If the conservatee has died, attach a certified copy of the death certificate to the petition.

[Use lined paper and prepare the caption following the Sample Pleading in Chapter 3, Section H3.]

PETITION FOR TERMINATION
OF CONSERVATORSHIP

DATE: *[hearing date]*
TIME: *[hearing time]*
DEPT: *[department]*

Petitioner respectfully represents:

1. Petitioner is the conservator of the *["person," "estate" or "person and estate"]* of *[conservatee's name]*.

2. Petitioner has been acting as conservator since *[date Letters of Conservatorship were originally issued]*.

3. At the time of appointment, a conservatorship was necessary for the following reason(s): *[briefly state why a conservatorship was necessary. For example: "The conservatee was in a coma following an automobile accident and was unable to take care of her personal needs or manage her own finances."]*.

4. A conservatorship is no longer necessary for the conservatee for the following reason(s): *[state why a conservatorship is no longer needed. For example: "The conservatee has recovered fully, and is now able to care for herself (and her finances). Copies of written statements by her doctor and psychologist are attached to this petition as Exhibit A," or "The conservatee died on March 19, 19___. A certified copy of the death certificate is attached as Exhibit A," or "The conservatorship estate has been used up."]*.

5. *[If the conservatee is still living:]* The best interests of the conservatee require termination of the conservatorship for the following reason(s): *[state why ending the conservatorship is best for the conservatee. For example: "The conservatee is now fully recovered, and wants the conservatorship to end so she may handle her finances independently," or "The conservatorship estate has been used up and it would be an unnecessary burden and expense to continue a conservatorship of the estate."]*.

6. The names, residence addresses and relationships of the conservatee's relatives within the second degree so far as known to petitioner are as follows: *[fill in the names and addresses of relatives you listed in Part 1 of the Conservatorship Worksheet (see Chapter 3, Section F1)]*.

7. No person has filed a request for special notice *[if requested, add: "except for" and fill in name and address of person requesting notice]*.

8. The conservatorship estate *[does/does not]* include money or property acquired in whole or in part from money received from the Veterans' Administration. *[Note: If the estate does consist of money or property received from the Veterans' Administration, the VA must receive copies of the termination documents.]*

Petitioner requests an order of this court that:

1. The conservatorship of the *["person," "estate" or "person and estate"]* of *[conservatee's name]* be terminated.

2. *[If conservatorship of the person or person and estate, add:]* The conservator of the person, *[your name]*, be discharged.

3. For all other proper orders.

Respectfully Submitted,

Dated: *[today's date]*   _____

                            [your name]
                            Conservator In Pro Per

VERIFICATION

[Insert verification from Chapter 3, Section H2d.]

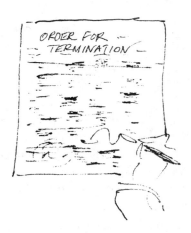

b. (Proposed) Order for Termination

On the scheduled hearing date, a judge should sign an order that allows the conservatorship to end and releases the conservator from her duties. However, a conservator of the estate must take several more steps before being fully discharged. (See Section C10 of this chapter.)

[Use lined paper and prepare the caption following the Sample Pleading in Chapter 3, Section H3.]

ORDER FOR TERMINATION
OF CONSERVATORSHIP

The Petition for Termination of Conservatorship came on for hearing on _____ at _____ _____.M. in Dept. _____ of the Superior Court of California, County of *[county]*, the Honorable _____ presiding. *[Your name]* appeared as petitioner In Pro Per and no one appeared in opposition *[if there is opposition, you will need to see an attorney]*.

After examining the Petition for Termination of Conservatorship and hearing the evidence, the court finds:

1. All notices required by law have been given.

2. Termination of the Conservatorship of the *["person," "estate" or "person and estate"]* of *[conservatee's*

name] is in the best interests of the conservatee.

THE COURT ORDERS:

1. The conservatorship of the *["person," "estate" or "person and estate"]* of *[conservatee's name]* is terminated effective _____.

2. *[If conservatorship of the person or person and estate:]* The conservator of the person, *[your name]*, is discharged.

3. *[If conservatorship of the estate or person and estate:]* The conservator has filed a final account and report of *[his/her]* acts as conservator. On settlement of the account, the conservator shall surrender the estate's assets to *[name of personal representative, conservatee or other person receiving property. (See final account in Chapter 13, Section E4.)]*.

Dated: _____

        Judge of the Superior Court

c. Final Account (Conservator of the Estate)

If you are conservator of the estate or person and estate, it is essential that you present a final account of the conservatee's money and assets to the court. You will then be discharged—that is, relieved—of your duties and liabilities as conservator. Without this court-ordered discharge, you and your sureties could be liable to the conservatee or his heirs for anything that happens to the estate.

If the conservatee has died, follow the guidelines in Section B2 of this chapter for handling the estate. If the conservatee is still living, pay those bills and expenses necessary to support the conservatee. Do not take unusual steps, such as making investments or selling real estate.

Prepare a final account following the guidelines in Chapter 13, Section E, and include all sample paragraphs pertaining to a final account. Many courts have local rules about the final account which are set out in probate policy manuals.

IF INVENTORY AND APPRAISEMENT WAS NOT FILED

No more than 90 days after the conservatorship of the estate is established, the conservator is responsible for filing an Inventory and Appraisement with the court. (Inventory and Appraisements are covered in Chapter 13, Section C3.)

If the conservatorship ends before you file the Inventory and Appraisement—generally because the conservatee has died—the court can waive the filing requirement (Probate Code §2633). This situation requires additional research or the help of an attorney. (See Chapter 17.)

d. Notice of Hearing

Complete a Notice of Hearing following the instructions in Chapter 4, Section G, with these exceptions:

Item 1: Enter the words "conservator of the person," "conservator of the estate," or "conservator of the person and estate." Just below this, after the words "has filed (specify)," fill in the full title of all documents you are filing, such as "Petition for Termination of Conservatorship" and any account documents.

Item 3: Fill in the information in the box about the date, time and place of the hearing if you obtained these over the phone. Otherwise, ask the clerk to fill in this information when you file your papers.

Proof of Service (Page 2): Complete the proof of service by mail. (Instructions are contained in Chapter 6, Section D3.) After the words "Name and Address of Each Person to Whom Notice Was Mailed," fill in the names and addresses of everyone entitled to notice set out in Chapter 15, Section B4. Do not have the proof of service signed yet.

e. Local Forms

Check with the court to find out whether local forms must be filed with the Petition for Termination or final account. For example, some counties may require proof of payment of the court investigator's fees. If the conservatee has died, you may need to complete a form notifying the court or investigator of the death.

3. Copy and File Papers With Court

Make two or three photocopies of each document, depending on whether the court requires an additional copy. In addition, make one copy each of the Notice of Hearing, petition and any final account for the conservatee and each person entitled to notice.

Take or send the court the original and copies of documents along with two self-addressed, stamped envelopes. If you obtain a hearing date from the clerk when you file your papers, get one at least 25 days in the future to allow enough time to have the papers served.

Make sure all copies of the Notice of Hearing are marked with the date, time and place listed in Item 3. The clerk should give you the original signed Notice of Hearing, unless local rules mandate that the clerk keeps it. (See Chapter 5, Section D1b.) If you are given the original Notice of Hearing, keep it in a safe place. You will need to file it with the court after everyone entitled to notice has been served.

4. Service of Papers

At least 20 days before the scheduled hearing date, have copies of the Notice of Hearing and Petition served by mail on everyone entitled to notice as described in Chapter 15, Section B4.[8] Instructions for having documents served by mail are contained in Chapter 6, Section D2. If you don't have papers served in time, you will need to have the hearing continued. (See Chapter 8, Section C.)

Make sure the date and place of service at the bottom of the first page is filled in. Have the person who served the papers sign the proof of service on the back of the original Notice of Hearing.

Finally, make two or three copies, and take or send them to the court at least ten days before the hearing date following the instructions in Chapter 5, Section D.

---

[8]By law, only 15 days' advance notice is required. To be safe, it is best to have the documents mailed 20 days beforehand.

5. Pay Fees for Investigation

Most counties require that fees for the investigations be paid before the hearing for termination. Each investigation costs around $200. Check with the court clerk and arrange to pay the fees. If you are conservator of the estate, you may either pay fees for the investigations from the conservatorship estate or pay from your own funds and reimburse yourself. If the estate cannot afford the fees, you may apply for a waiver of those fees. (See Chapter 5, Section B.)

Each court has its own rules for how payment of investigations is handled. In some counties, such as San Francisco County, you must complete preprinted forms and obtain an order from the court before paying the investigator's fees. Check with the court investigator's office.

6. If Additional Documents Are Required

If the court contacts you because a document is incorrect or the judge wants additional information, you will need to prepare supplemental or amended documents. Follow the instructions for preparing and serving additional documents in Chapter 15, Section B5.

7. Find Out Tentative Decision

Your petition is sent to the office of the judge or commissioner several days before the scheduled hearing. A clerk reviews your papers to make sure everything is in order. In many counties, the judge makes a tentative ruling on your petition—called a "pre-grant decision"—based solely on the papers you've submitted.

Call the court two days before the hearing is scheduled to find out if the judge has made a pre-grant decision on your petition. In some counties, this information is given on a recorded tape either one or two days before the hearing. In other counties, you get the information from a clerk.

If the judge tentatively granted your petition, ask the clerk whether you need to attend the hearing. In some counties, petitions granted by the judge ahead of time are not called at the hearing unless someone shows up to contest them.

8. Attend Hearing If Required

If the pre-grant decision was in your favor, you need not attend the hearing unless:

- you have reason to believe someone will show up to contest your petition;
- someone filed papers objecting to your petition; or
- you were told by the probate clerk that you will need to appear.

If you attend the hearing, bring copies of all your documents, including the proofs of service. Let the clerk or bailiff know you are in the courtroom. The conservatee should also attend if the conservatorship is ending because he can care for himself again.

At the hearing, the judge will decide whether to end the conservatorship. The judge may simply grant and sign the order without asking you any questions. Or the judge may want to ask you a few additional questions. The hearing will be similar to the hearing at which you were appointed conservator. (See Chapter 8.) Depending on the court's schedule, your hearing may be pushed to the end of the scheduled hearings, or your case may even be continued to another date.

See a lawyer if someone objects to your petition or the judge won't grant it.

9. Obtain Court Order

Obtain a copy of the signed order before you leave the court. If you weren't required to attend the hearing, arrange to get copies of the order. Make sure you follow the instructions in the order. If the judge modified it, you must comply with those instructions.

10.   Additional Requirements for Conservators of the Estate

As conservator of the estate, you must distribute the estate's assets according to the order settling the final account that was signed by a judge. (See Chapter 13, Section E4.)

Distribution is usually either to the conservatee or, if the conservatee has died, to the conservatee's personal representative. You must then file several documents with the court to be released from your duties. The rest of this section takes you through those important steps.

a   Receipt on Transfer of Conservatorship Assets

The document used to show that assets were distributed is called a Receipt on Transfer of Conservatorship Assets. The person receiving the assets will sign it when she receives the estate's assets. If more than one person was specified in the order settling the final account that was signed by a judge, prepare a separate document on lined paper for each.

[Use lined paper and prepare the caption following the Sample Pleading in Chapter 3, Section H3.]

RECEIPT ON TRANSFER OF
CONSERVATORSHIP ASSETS

RECEIVED FROM *[your name],* conservator of the *["estate" or "person and estate"]* of *[conservatee's name],* the following assets of the conservatorship, as ordered by this court on *[date judge signed Order for Termination of Conservatorship]*: *[specify assets to be given to person named in court order].*

Dated: _____

_____
[Name of person receiving assets]

_____
[Capacity, such as "executor of the estate of," followed by conservatee's name"]

b.   Declaration for Final Discharge and Order

After you've distributed the assets and received a signed receipt from the conservatee or the estate's personal representative, you will apply for a final discharge from the court relieving you of your duties as conservator of the estate and releasing the sureties from liability. Some courts have local preprinted forms. Otherwise, prepare a document on lined paper following this sample, and date and sign the declaration.

[Use lined paper and prepare the caption following the Sample Pleading in Chapter 3, Section H3.]

DECLARATION FOR FINAL
DISCHARGE AND ORDER

I, *[your name],* declare that I am the conservator of the *["estate" or "person and estate"]* of *[conservatee's name].* I have performed all acts required of me as conservator, including paying all money due from me as conservator, delivering all of the estate property as specified in this order of the court dated *[date judge signed Order for Termination of Conservatorship],* and filing receipt(s) with this court.

I declare under penalty of perjury under the laws of the State of California that the foregoing is true and correct.

Dated: *[today's date]*

_____
[your name]
Conservator In Pro Per

ORDER FOR FINAL DISCHARGE

IT IS ORDERED THAT *[your name]* is discharged as conservator of the *["estate" or "person and estate"]* of *[conservatee's name],* and the surety *[or sureties]* on *[his/her]* bond, if any, *[is/are]* discharged and released from all liability to be incurred in the future.

Dated: _____

_____
Judge of the Superior Court

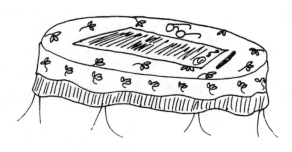

c. How to Obtain Final Discharge

Contact whoever is authorized to receive the estate assets, as set out in the order settling the final account that was signed by a judge. Arrange to turn over everything specified in that order. You may need to sign over title documents and provide bank books, keys to the safety-deposit box and personal property.

Once the person has received everything specified in the order settling the final account, ask him to date and sign the Receipt on Transfer of Conservatorship Assets. Again, if you distribute assets to more than one person, obtain signed copies of a receipt from each one.

Make photocopies of the Receipt on Transfer of Conservatorship Assets and Declaration for Final Discharge and Order for filing with the court. Then take or send your documents to court and obtain a signed copy of the order from the judge.

Finally, provide copies of the Declaration for Final Discharge and Order that was signed by the judge to everyone serving as a surety. They are then formally released from their liability.[9]

D. Change of Conservators

ONCE YOU'VE BEEN APPOINTED conservator, you can't simply decide to stop serving in that capacity, even if the conservatee agrees with the decision or the estate's assets are used up. Sometimes a change in conservators is necessary because you can no longer handle the job or someone else is better suited. A change in conservators would also be needed if the original conservator has died. In all of these situations, a judge must approve the new conservator and release the old one from the job. Throughout the process, the conservatorship remains intact.

---

[9]Although the liability for the conservatorship ends with a judge's discharge, someone could still file suit for damages to the estate that occurred during the conservatorship. Generally, a lawsuit may be filed against the conservator or surety no more than four years after discharge (Probate Code §2333(b)).

1. Resignation of Conservator

If you wish to stop serving as conservator, you must get an order from the court allowing you to resign. If you stop acting as conservator without a court's approval, you are still responsible for all the duties and liabilities of a conservator and may be prosecuted for failing to perform. However, when you resign with court approval, the conservatorship continues and the court names a new person to step in and take over the conservator's duties. If you are conservator of the estate, you must file a final account with the court.

Judges do not generally let conservators resign without good reason. For example, a conservator might seek court permission from the court to resign if the conservatee prefers someone else to serve in the role of conservator. A conservator might need to resign if he can't handle the job any longer because of poor health. Or perhaps the conservator's life has changed, making it difficult to continue with the responsibility, and someone else is better suited and willing to take on the job.

Although a conservator is not responsible for finding someone else to step in, a judge will probably be reluctant to let you resign unless someone else is available to take over. If you must resign quickly, such as after being quickly stricken by a disabling illness, a temporary conservator is sometimes named to take over until the next permanent conservator can be appointed. In very rare, extreme cases where no one can take over and it would be detrimental for the conservatee to stay with the present conservator, the court might order the Public Guardian or Public Conservator to take over.

The process of resigning as conservator is beyond the scope of this book and will require that you do your own research or obtain the help of an attorney. (See Chapter 17.)

2. Death of Conservator

When a conservator dies, the conservatorship continues and a new person must take over the conservatorship duties. For a conservatorship of the estate, a final account must be filed by the person handling the deceased conservator's estate or by an attorney. Those procedures are beyond the scope of this book.

3. Removal (Contested Cases)

A conservator may be removed from her position by a court order—meaning she is no longer authorized to serve as conservator. When a conservator is removed, the conservatorship continues, but the court appoints a successor conservator. For conservatorships of the estate, a final account must be filed.

Pending a hearing on whether the conservator is to be removed, a conservator's powers may be suspended—meaning she does not have the legal right to act as conservator. Or the court can require the conservator of an estate to turn over the estate assets to someone designated by the court. Occasionally, a temporary conservator is appointed to take over while the dispute is being resolved.

A proceeding to remove a conservator can be initiated by the conservatee, a relative or any interested person such as a court investigator, social service agency or hospital. Common reasons for removing someone from her position as conservator include:

- *The conservatee wants someone else to serve as conservator.* The conservatee's wishes are almost always followed, unless there is good reason not to. For example, the conservatee's choice might not be followed if he does not have the mental capacity to decide on a conservator.

- *The conservator is not doing an adequate job or has a conflict of interest.* For example, a conservator of the person might be removed for neglecting or failing to arrange for adequate care of the conservatee. Or a

conservator of the estate might be removed if he did not arrange for the support of the conservatee, didn't keep track of how money was spent or mismanaged the estate. A conservator who becomes incapacitated, and perhaps has a conservator appointed for him, would be removed since he would not be able to perform his duties.

- *The conservator fails to provide required court documents.* For a conservatorship of the estate, this would include the required Inventory and Appraisement and periodic financial accounts.

- *The conservator takes unauthorized actions.* For a conservatorship of the person, this includes involuntarily placing the conservatee in a mental health facility, subjecting her to involuntary medical treatment, allowing experimental drugs or convulsive treatment without obtaining prior court approval. For a conservatorship of the estate, this might mean selling real estate or significant estate assets without prior court approval.

- *The conservator might harm the conservatee or estate.* For example, a conservatee might be in danger if the conservator was convicted of a felony either prior to or during his time acting as conservator. A conservator whose actions are considered immoral—such as being involved in serious drug use, physically or psychologically abusing the conservatee or embezzling the conservatee's money—may be removed. A conservator of the estate who declares bankruptcy or insolvency might also be removed.

The process of removing a conservator begins when someone files and serves the conservator with a petition for removal. The procedures for defending against this are beyond the scope of this book. If someone tries to have you removed or suspended as conservator, consult a lawyer. (See Chapter 17.)

LEGAL HELP BEYOND THE BOOK

THIS CHAPTER PROVIDES GUIDANCE if you need to hire a lawyer or other legal professional, or if you need to do legal research beyond the scope of this book. As noted several times, it is best to consult an attorney if the conservatorship is contested at any point or if an attorney is representing the conservatee. An experienced lawyer will probably be more skillful than you are in arguing why you should be appointed or retained as conservator. Additionally, the loser of a contested conservatorship can be held liable for the opposing party's legal fees, so you're probably better off having some assistance.

If your conservatorship is not contested, and you just want someone to prepare legal forms or check your work—but not provide legal advice—you may be able to save considerable money by hiring an independent paralegal instead of a lawyer. (See Section B in this chapter.)

A. Free or Low-Cost Legal Help

MANY PROGRAMS THAT USED to offer free legal help have dwindled in the past few years. But if you and the conservatee have a low income, you may be able to find free or low-cost legal help with your conservatorship. The definitions of "low income" vary depending on the county, but eligibility for free legal help is likely when someone qualifies for public assistance.

1. Legal Aid Offices

Most counties have a legal aid office (often called legal services or legal assistance) available to low-income people for free or low-cost advice, consultation and sometimes representation. Not all legal aid offices handle conservatorship cases, but you may get a referral from them for free legal assistance, or to attorneys who offer reasonably priced services. To find a legal aid office in your area, check in the telephone book's white pages under "Legal Aid" or "Legal Services," the yellow pages under "Attorneys" or ask the clerk at your court.

2. County Bar Associations (Volunteer Legal Service Programs)

Some county bar associations have established their own legal service programs or corporations to help low-income people with legal problems by providing free or low-cost legal services. Check with your local bar association for information on available legal services and to find out whether you qualify for assistance. To find a listing for the bar association in your county, check in the phone book or with directory assistance.

B.   Independent Paralegals

A NUMBER OF BUSINESSES known as "independent paralegals" or "typing services" assist people in filling out legal forms. Relatively simple procedures such as uncontested divorces, bankruptcies, guardianships and conservatorships are all routinely handled by independent paralegals at a substantially lower cost than lawyers would charge.

Typing services are very different from lawyers in that they can't give legal advice or represent you in court—by law, only lawyers are allowed to do those things. They can, however:

- provide instructions and refer you to legal information needed to handle your own conservatorship;
- provide the appropriate forms; and
- type your papers so they'll be accepted by a court.

As a general matter, the longer a typing service has been in business, the better. People at a typing service should be up front with you about not being attorneys and not providing legal advice.

A recommendation from someone who has used a particular typing service is the best way to find a reputable one in your area. The services often advertise in classified sections of local newspapers or in local throwaway papers like the *Classified Flea Market* or *Giant Nickel*. They also may be listed in the yellow pages under "typing services" or "paralegals."

HIRING PROFESSIONAL CONSERVATORS AS CONSULTANTS

People in the business of serving as conservators to conservatees unrelated by blood or marriage are referred to as "professional private conservators." Many are not lawyers. Experienced professional private conservators may be good consultants, since they know the ropes of conservatorships.

If you're interested in locating a local professional private conservator, start by asking the local court investigator or probate examiner for recommendations. You may want to check with several professional private conservators before selecting one.

C.   Finding and Hiring a Lawyer

LAWYERS—ALSO CALLED ATTORNEYS—are the only people allowed to give legal advice in California. When you hire a lawyer, find someone with experience in handling conservatorships.

If you've already been appointed conservator of the estate, you'll need to obtain court approval before you can hire a lawyer. If the lawyer doesn't know this, it's a bad sign.

1.   What a Lawyer Can Do

There are a variety of ways you can choose to use a lawyer's services, depending on your needs.

- *Consultation and Advice:* You can often meet with a lawyer to discuss a problem and determine whether the lawyer can help with it. Frequently these initial consultations are free or relatively reasonably priced. At the consultation, a lawyer should listen to the details of your situation, analyze it for you and advise you on your best plan of action. Bring a list of questions you want answered, and make sure the lawyer answers them in a way you understand. Ideally, she will give you more than just conclusions, but will educate you about your whole situation and the legal alternatives from which you can make your own choices. If you are willing to put in some time and work of your own, using a lawyer as a consultant may be worthwhile.

- *Checking Your Work:* Some people are comfortable preparing all their own conservatorship papers following the instructions in this book, but want the security that comes with having someone experienced check the work. You may be able to find a lawyer to do this, but that will probably require shopping around a bit. If you find a lawyer who is experienced in conservatorships and is willing to check your work, make sure you agree on an hourly rate or flat fee in advance.

- *Contested and Complex Conservatorships:* If the conservatorship is contested, you will need to hire a lawyer to represent you. If you are dealing with an estate that requires numerous courtroom appearances, you may wish to hire a lawyer. The lawyer can make the courtroom procedures less baffling by helping you understand what happens there and why. Some lawyers encourage willing clients to help out with some of the legwork of a case, such as gathering and organizing documents, which can keep legal fees down.

2. Finding a Lawyer

If you seek help from a lawyer, make sure you find one who has handled conservatorships before. Or you could consult a probate attorney who has handled a number of guardianships, since the forms and procedures for guardianships and conservatorships are very similar.

Here are some suggestions for how to find lawyers. You may need to check around until you find someone you feel comfortable hiring.

- *Personal Referrals:* If you know someone who was pleased with a lawyer, check with that person. If the lawyer can't take on your case, she might be willing to recommend someone else who is experienced, competent and available.

- *Probate Examiner or Investigator:* In many courts, a probate examiner reviews accounts and other conservatorship documents. Someone at that office may be able to steer you to a good attorney. Or the local court investigator may be able to give you a good recommendation.

- *Group Legal Practices:* Some unions, employers and consumer action organizations offer plans to their members or employees for legal work at rates substantially lower than is available through most private practitioners. If you're a member of such a plan, check with it for a lawyer, especially if your problem is covered for free. However, beware of plans which do no more than refer you to a local attorney who will supposedly give you a good price.

- *Legal Clinics:* Legal clinics such as Hyatt Legal Services and Jacoby and Meyers loudly advertise their low initial consultation fees. This generally means that a basic consultation is inexpensive—often about $20— but anything beyond that isn't so cheap. Not all legal clinics handle conservatorships. If you're comfortable with the lawyer you talk with and the representation, it may be worthwhile to hire him. But be sure that the advertised or quoted price includes everything you think it does.

- *Pre-Paid Legal Insurance:* "Legal insurance" plans are marketed by companies such as Bank of America, Montgomery Ward and Amway.[1] These plans often are offered by mail to credit card customers and in some cases are sold door-to-door. Many of these plans offer several free legal consultations, a simple will and some

---

[1] It's a misnomer to refer to these programs as "legal insurance." The programs provide an initial level of service for a low fee and then charge specific fees for additional or different work. Thus, most pre-paid plans are marketing devices for the participating lawyers rather than insurance plans. As with any consumer transaction, check out the plan carefully before signing up.

letter writing for a monthly charge of less than $10. There's no guarantee that the lawyers available through these plans are of the best caliber; sometimes they aren't.

- *Lawyer Referral Panels:* Most county bar associations maintain services that will give you the names of some attorneys who practice in your area. Usually, you can get a referral to an attorney who specializes in the area you need, and an initial consultation for a low fee. A problem with the panels is that they usually provide minimal screening for the attorneys listed, which means those who participate may not be the most experienced or competent. It may be possible to find a skilled attorney willing to work for a reasonable fee following this approach, but take time to check out the credentials and experience of the person to whom you are referred.

- *Yellow Pages:* The yellow pages in every telephone book have an extensive number of lawyers listed under "Attorneys" both by specialty and by alphabetical order. Some of the ads quote initial consultation rates. If all else fails, call several law offices and briefly explain your situation and the kind of help you want. Try to talk to a lawyer to get an idea of how friendly and sympathetic he is to your concerns.

3. Agreeing on Legal Fees

Whether you simply hire an attorney to check your paperwork or to handle the case from beginning to end, you and he should agree on the fee to be charged before any work begins. You might be able to set a flat fee for setting up the conservatorship, rather than paying an hourly rate. That way, if the attorney is slow in preparing documents or you have to wait at court, your wallet won't be slowly emptying as the clock ticks on.

Regardless of the fee arrangement, you must pay for court fees, service of process and other fees such as costs of an investigation.[2] Either the attorney will ask you to pay these costs up front, or will advance the costs and bill you

later for reimbursement. Most conservatorships will require well over $150 in costs to set up the conservatorship, since the court filing fees are often over $100. In addition, fees for the court investigation and service of process will be an additional expense.

Make sure you understand what law office costs you will be expected to pay. For example, some lawyers charge clients for the costs of each photocopy made for a case, as well as postage and long distance telephone calls, while other lawyers include these office costs in their hourly fees.

Lawyers sometimes require a retainer fee before they'll start working on your case—usually of at least several hundred dollars. When costs and lawyers' fees are billed, they are deducted from this retainer. If fees exceed the retainer, you are billed for the excess. But if the retainer is more money than the legal fees and costs, you are given a refund. You should be sent bills regularly, regardless of whether or not you give the lawyer a retainer fee. If you have any questions about fees, ask the attorney for copies of all bills and records of time spent on your case.

In California, an attorney must give you an agreement in writing if the total amount you pay, including all attorneys' fees, is likely to be more than $1,000. There's a good chance you will exceed this amount for a conservatorship of the estate, even if it is uncontested. Regardless, it is always a good idea to get the fee arrangement in writing. The law also requires that the written contract clearly explain all charges and services, and that it set out both the lawyer's and client's responsibilities.

Fees tend to be the biggest cause for misunderstanding between a lawyer and client, and a written agreement can go a long way in preventing problems. Make sure you understand the fee agreement before you sign it. In addition to the lawyers' fees, get a clear picture of what costs you will be paying.

---

[2]Court costs and bond premiums may be reimbursed by the conservatee's estate. Costs for the investigation are paid out of the estate.

D. Doing Your Own Legal Research

DURING THE COURSE of obtaining a conservatorship, you may have questions this book does not answer. If you want additional legal information, can't get the answer from a court clerk and don't wish to consult a lawyer, you will need to do some research on your own.

1. Citations in This Book

This book includes many numbered references to California law. These are called "citations," and most refer to a set of statutes called the California Probate Code. Citations are included in this book so that you can look them up in the law library if you want. The accompanying box lists most citations used in this book.

LEGAL CITATIONS

Civil Code

Code of Civil Procedure

California Rules of Court

Government Code

Probate Code

Welfare & Institutions Code

United States Code

---

2. Probate Policy Manuals or Memoranda

Although all probate courts follow the basic procedures outlined in the Probate Code, most counties have some special rules of their own. Many counties have small printed pamphlets called probate policy manuals or memoranda. These pamphlets tell you things such as when particular forms must be presented to the court, what must be included in court documents and where to call for information. In addition to covering conservatorships, most probate policy manuals contain information on estates of people that have died as well as guardianships.

Call the court clerk and find out if the probate policy manual is available through the court. More often than not, you'll need to go to the library to look at one. You can consult a book which contains probate policy manuals for counties throughout California, such as:

- *California Local Probate Rules* (published by California Continuing Education of the Bar); or

- *Court Rules* (published by Daily Journal Corporation). Superior Court rules for all counties are contained in this multi-volume set. Most—but not all—counties include probate rules in their Superior Court rules.

Make sure that you look at the current probate policy manual for the specific county in which you are filing the conservatorship. You don't need to be concerned with other counties' rules.

3. How to Do Legal Research

This section provides an overview of the steps you'll take to do legal research. For more complicated research, you'll likely need to consult additional sources.

a. Find a Law Library

Each California county must have a law library that is open to the public without charge. In most libraries, you will find law librarians willing and even pleased to give you a hand, as long as you don't ask them to answer legal questions or interpret what you find in the books, since this might be considered practicing law. If you encounter any difficulty because you are not a lawyer, you may need to give a gentle reminder that the California constitution requires public access.

 Some local public libraries also have quite extensive collections of law and legal research books. Before making a special trip to the law library, you may first want to check with the public library.

b. Consult Background Resources

If you do not have a particular legal citation, or need help with documents or procedures not covered in this book, look in background materials which provide general information about the law. These include encyclopedias, form books and practice manuals.

NOLO RESOURCES FOR
LEGAL RESEARCH

If you decide to delve into the world of legal research, see *Legal Research: How to Find and Understand the Law,* by Stephen Elias and Susan Levinkind (Nolo Press). This hands-on guide to the law library addresses the research methods discussed here in much more detail and will answer most of the questions that are likely to arise in the course of your research.

If you want a guided tour through the basics of legal research, you'll be interested in *Legal Research Made Easy: A Roadmap Through the Law Library Maze,* a 2-1/2 hour video by Nolo Press and Legal Star Communications.

Here are several background resources which you can consult when you begin researching the law and procedures of conservatorships:

- *California Conservatorships and Guardianships* (William S. Johnstone, Jr. and Susan T. House, published by California Continuing Education of the Bar). This book covers all aspects of conservatorships and provides many sample forms. Periodic supplements give updates on the law.

- *California Family Law Practice and Procedure* (Christian E. Markey, Jr., Editorial Consultant, published by Matthew Bender). This book provides information and samples of conservatorship forms and procedures. Look in Volumes 5 and 5A.

- *California Forms of Pleading and Practice* (published by Matthew Bender). If you want guidance on a procedure not covered in this book, turn to this attorneys' form book. Look in Volume 7B ("Guardianship and Conservatorship") of this multi-volume set.

- *California Probate Procedure* (by Arthur K. Marshall, published by Parker & Sons Publications, Inc.). This three-volume set gives a wide variety of information and forms. Volume 1 provides an overview of conserva-

torship law, and provides citations to statutes and case law. It is somewhat dense, but still quite readable. Volume 2 contains Probate Policy Manuals for many counties. If you use this resource, make sure they are the most up-to-date. Volume 3 provides checklists and local forms for use in many counties. Again, make sure these forms are the most current.

c. Read the Law

Background resources, including this book, are only discussions about law and procedure, not the law itself. But many background resources provide you with citations to relevant statutes (laws passed by the California legislature) and court interpretations of these laws. In California, conservatorships are governed by a group of statutes called the Probate Code.

You may find statutes in a single volume of the California Probate Code, or in a section of a book which consists of the California Probate Code along with several other codes. You usually can find these books in a public library.

There also are multi-volume annotated book sets which give the statutes and information about each statute. They have information about the history of each statute—when it was first passed and when different sections were amended. You may find that reading statutes leaves you less than fully enlightened. They tend to be difficult to understand and are sometimes purposely ambiguous. You'll also find citations of cases and very short summaries of cases in which courts interpreted the statute. The case law summaries are by no means complete, and it's hard to tell from them whether they're related to the particular issue you're researching, so read the case yourself rather than relying on the annotation.

d. Read Cases

Case law refers to judges' published opinions about a dispute that was resolved in court. These decisions give important information about how a law has been interpreted. If you can find a case decision in which the facts were similar to your situation, you can get some guidance on how a court might decide your case.

RESOURCES AND INFORMATION

AGING AND THE ELDERLY

**California Department on Aging
(Central Office)** (916) 322-5290

Every county is served by an agency that coordinates services for the elderly. Check the government pages of your telephone book under "Aging," "Area Agency on Aging," "Senior Citizens Services" or a similar heading, or call the central office.

HEALTH MATTERS

You may want to contact an organization to learn more about the conservatee's physical condition, to find out about local resources or to join a support group.

AIDS National Hotline	**(800) 342-AIDS**
Alzheimers Association	**(800) 621-0379**
American Cancer Society	**(800) 227-2345**
American Kidney Fund	**(800) 638-8299**
American Parkinson Disease Association	**(800) 223-2732**
Cancer Information Service	**(800) 237-1225**
Family Caregiver Alliance (Resource for caregivers of brain-impaired adults)	**(800) 445-8106**
Huntington's Disease Society of America	**(800) 345-HDSA**
Lou Gehrig's Disease (Amyotrophic Lateral Sclerosis)	**(800) 782-4747**
Medicare Telephone Hotline	**(800) 638-6833**
National Head Injury Foundation	**(800) 444-NHIF**
National Health Information Center	**(800) 336-4797**
National Kidney Foundation, Inc.	**(800) 622-9010**
National Parkinson Foundation Inc.	**(800) 327-4545**
National Spinal Cord Injury Association	**(800) 962-9629**
Spinal Cord Injury Hotline (American Paralysis Association)	**(800) 526-3456**

HOME CARE AND CAREGIVER SUPPORT

**California Association for
Health Services at Home** (916) 443-8055

This organization provides information about specific home care providers in a given area and gives referrals to local home care organizations, which can in turn give even more detailed information and referrals.

Children of Aging Parents (215) 945-6900

This nonprofit organization gives support and information to family and friends of the dependent elderly. It maintains a directory of self-help support groups for caregivers and puts out helpful publications. Send $1 and a self-addressed, stamped envelope with any request for information to: 1609 Woodbourne Rd., Suite 302A, Levittown, PA 19057-1511.

Family Caregiver Alliance (Resource for caregivers of brain-impaired adults) (800) 445-8106

This nonprofit organization provides referrals and information about brain disorders. For Bay Area residents, it can also provide support groups and consultations for friends and family, as well as in-home care services for brain-damaged adults. Services are free, low-cost or set on a sliding-scale system.

**Licensing and Certification
of Health Services** (916) 445-2070

This agency establishes standards to be met by home health care agencies and individual health care providers such as independent home health care workers. It can give information regarding whether a health care provider is licensed or certified in California and what state standards must be met for that license or certification.

HOSPICES

Hospices are at-home programs or live-in facilities that provide services to people who are in the last stages of a terminal illness. Hospices also arrange to help family members obtain emotional support and practical assistance.

Hospice Link: Information and Referral **(800) 331-1620**
Hospice Help Line **(800) 658-8898**

INSURANCE
(HEALTH AND LONG-TERM CARE)

National Insurance Consumer Helpline **(800) 942-4242**

This organization provides free literature on long-term care insurance, Medicare supplemental insurance, companies marketing long-term care insurance, and information about disability and health insurance.

Health Insurance Counseling Advocacy Program (HICAP), Central Office **(916) 323-7315**

These agencies provide free information about Medicare, private insurance, supplemental insurance and long-term medical care coverage. Local agencies are listed in the white pages or are available from a local senior information line or Medicare number.

California State Department of Insurance **(800) 927-4357**

This government agency regulates the sale of insurance and maintains records about companies that are authorized to sell long-term care insurance in California. It can provide you with a pamphlet about long-term care insurance.

NURSING AND LONG-TERM CARE FACILITIES

If you are looking for a care facility or wish to lodge a complaint against a facility, one of these agencies should be able to help.

American Association of Homes for the Aging **(202) 783-2242**

AAHA is a national association of nonprofit nursing facilities and senior independent living centers. It will provide information and a list of member facilities in California.

American Health Care Association **(202) 842-4444**

AHCA is a national association of both profit and nonprofit accredited nursing facilities. It will provide a list of its member facilities in California. It also distributes pamphlets on long-term care.

California Advocates for Nursing Home Reform **(415) 474-5171**

This nonprofit grassroots advocacy organization works on the local, state and national levels for the rights of nursing home residents.

California Department on Aging, Ombudsman Office **(800) 231-4024**

This 24-hour crisis line is for reporting problems at long-term care facilities. The long-term care ombudsman also responds to complaints about abuse at long-term care facilities and can mediate disputes between residents and the facilities. There is no charge for services.

Licensing and Certification of Health Services **(916) 445-2070**

This agency establishes standards to be met by nursing facilities. It can give information regarding whether a facility is licensed or certified in California and what state standards must be met for that license or certification.

Nursing Home Licensure Office **(916) 445-3281**

This office inspects nursing facilities, issues state licenses and Medicare and Medi-Cal certifications. You can check the record of any nursing facility in the state through this office.

ORGAN AND TISSUE DONATION

Living Bank Organ Donor Registry and Referral **(800) 528-2971**
National Kidney Foundation, Inc. **(800) 622-9010**
United Network for Organ Sharing **(800) 24-DONOR**

FORMS FOR OBTAINING A COURT-ORDERED CONSERVATORSHIP

Chapter	Form Name
4	Petition for Appointment of Probate Conservator
4	Declaration of Medical or Accredited Practitioner
4	Confidential Supplemental Information
4	Order Appointing Court Investigator
4	Order Appointing Probate Conservator
4, 6	Citation for Conservatorship
4, 6	Notice of Hearing
4	Notification to Court of Address of Conservator and Conservatee
6	Order Dispensing Notice
8	Duties of Conservator (and Acknowledgment of Receipt of Handbook)
9	Proof of Service by Mail of Order Appointing Conservator
9	Letters of Conservatorship
9	Proof of Service by Mail
13	Application and Order Appointing Probate Referee
13	Inventory and Appraisement
13	Attachment to Inventory and Appraisement
General	Lined Paper (Blank)

ATTORNEY OR PARTY WITHOUT ATTORNEY *(Name and Address)*:

ATTORNEY FOR *(Name)*:

TELEPHONE NO.:

FOR COURT USE ONLY

SUPERIOR COURT OF CALIFORNIA, COUNTY OF

STREET ADDRESS:

MAILING ADDRESS:

CITY AND ZIP CODE:

BRANCH NAME:

CONSERVATORSHIP OF (NAME):

PROPOSED CONSERVATEE

PETITION FOR APPOINTMENT OF PROBATE CONSERVATOR OF THE

☐ **PERSON** ☐ **ESTATE** ☐ **Limited Conservatorship**

CASE NUMBER:

1. PETITIONER *(name)*: 　　　　　　　　　　　　REQUESTS THAT

   a. *(name and address)*: 　　　　　　　　　　　　*(telephone)*:

   be appointed ☐ conservator ☐ limited conservator   of the PERSON of the proposed conservatee and Letters issue upon qualification.

   b. *(name and address)*: 　　　　　　　　　　　　*(telephone)*:

   be appointed ☐ conservator ☐ limited conservator   of the ESTATE of the proposed conservatee and Letters issue upon qualification.

   c. (1) ☐ bond not be required for the reasons stated in Attachment 1c.
   　　(2) ☐ bond be fixed at: $　　　　　　　　　 to be furnished by an authorized surety company or as otherwise provided by law. *(Specify reasons if the amount is different from the minimum required by section 2320 of the Probate Code.)*
   　　(3) ☐ deposits at *(specify institution)*:
   　　　　 in the amount of: $　　　　　　　　be allowed. Receipts will be filed.

   d. ☐ authorization be granted under section 2590 of the Probate Code to exercise independently the powers specified in Attachment 7.

   e. ☐ orders relating to the capacity of the proposed conservatee under sections 1873 or 1901 of the Probate Code be granted. *(Specify orders, facts, and reasons in Attachment 1e.)*

   f. ☐ orders relating to the powers and duties of the proposed conservator of the person under sections 2351-2358 of the Probate Code be granted. *(Specify orders, facts, and reasons in Attachment 1f.)*

   g. ☐ the proposed conservatee be adjudged to lack the capacity to give informed consent for medical treatment or healing by prayer and that the proposed conservator of the person be granted the powers specified in section 2355 of the Probate Code.

   h. ☐ *(for limited conservatorship only)* orders relating to the powers and duties of the proposed limited conservator of the person under section 2351.5 of the Probate Code be granted. *(Specify powers and duties in Attachment 1h.)*

   i. ☐ *(for limited conservatorship only)* orders relating to the powers and duties of the proposed limited conservator of the estate under section 1830(b) of the Probate Code be granted. *(Specify powers and duties in Attachment 1i.)*

   j. ☐ *(for limited conservatorship only)* orders limiting the civil and legal rights of the proposed limited conservatee be granted. *(Specify limitations in Attachment 1j.)*

   k. ☐ other orders be granted. *(Specify in Attachment 1k.)*

(Continued on reverse)

Page one of four

Form Approved by the
Judicial Council of California
GC-310 [Rev. July 1, 1990]

PETITION FOR APPOINTMENT OF PROBATE CONSERVATOR

Do NOT use this form for a temporary conservatorship.

Probate Code, §§ 1820, 1821

CONSERVATORSHIP OF (NAME):

	CASE NUMBER:

PROPOSED CONSERVATEE

2. Proposed conservatee is (name):

(present address):   (telephone):

3. a. JURISDICTIONAL FACTS   The proposed conservatee has no conservator within California and is a

  (1) ☐ resident of California and
- ☐ a resident of this county.
- ☐ not a resident of this county but commencement of the conservatorship in this county is in the best interests of the proposed conservatee. *(Specify reasons in Attachment 3a.)*

  (2) ☐ nonresident of California but
- ☐ is temporarily living in this county, or
- ☐ has property in this county, or
- ☐ commencement of the conservatorship in this county is in the best interests of the proposed conservatee. *(Specify reasons in Attachment 3a.)*

b. Petitioner

  (1) ☐ is ☐ is not a **creditor** or agent of a creditor of the proposed conservatee.

  (2) ☐ is ☐ is not a **debtor** or agent of a debtor of the proposed conservatee.

c. Proposed conservator is

  (1) ☐ a nominee. *(Affix nomination as Attachment 3c.)*

  (2) ☐ related to proposed conservatee as *(specify)*:

  (3) ☐ a private professional conservator as defined in Probate Code section 2341 who has filed with the county clerk the information statement required by Probate Code section 2342.

  (4) ☐ other *(specify)*:

d. Petitioner is

  (1) ☐ the proposed conservatee.

  (2) ☐ the spouse of the proposed conservatee.

  (3) ☐ a relative of the proposed conservatee *(specify relationship)*:

  (4) ☐ a state or local public entity, officer, or employee.

  (5) ☐ a bank ☐ other entity authorized to conduct the business of a trust company.

  (6) ☐ an interested person or friend of the proposed conservatee.

  (7) ☐ a private professional conservator who has filed the information statement (Prob. Code, § 2342).

  (8) ☐ the guardian of the proposed conservatee.

e. Character and estimated value of the property of the estate

  (1) Personal property: $ . . . . $

  (2) Annual gross income from

    (i) ☐ real property: $ . . . . $

    (ii) ☐ personal property: $ . . . . . $

      Total: $ . . . . . $

  (3) Real Property: $

4. Proposed conservatee

  a. Proposed conservatee ☐ is ☐ is not a patient in or on leave of absence from a state institution under the jurisdiction of the State Department of Mental Health or the State Department of Developmental Services *(specify state institution)*:

  b. Proposed conservatee ☐ is neither receiving nor entitled to receive ☐ is receiving or entitled to receive benefits from the Veterans Administration *(estimate amount of monthly benefit payable)*: $

  c. Proposed conservatee ☐ is ☐ is not able to complete an affidavit of voter registration.

(Continued on next page)

CONSERVATORSHIP OF (NAME):	CASE NUMBER:
PROPOSED CONSERVATEE	

5. a. Proposed conservatee

(1) ☐ is an adult.

(2) ☐ will be an adult on the effective date of the order (date):

(3) ☐ is a married minor.

(4) ☐ is a minor whose marriage has been dissolved.

b. Proposed conservatee requires a conservator and is

(1) ☐ unable properly to provide for his or her personal needs for physical health, food, clothing, or shelter.
Supporting facts are ☐ specified in Attachment 5b(1) ☐ as follows:

(2) ☐ substantially unable to manage his or her financial resources or resist fraud or undue influence.
Supporting facts are ☐ specified in Attachment 5b(2) ☐ as follows:

c. ☐ **Proposed conservatee** voluntarily requests the appointment of a conservator. (Specify facts showing good cause in Attachment 5(c).)

d. ☐ **Confidential Supplement Information** (Judicial Council form GC-312) is filed with this petition. (All petitioners must file this form except banks and other entities authorized to do business as a trust company.)

e. **Proposed conservatee** ☐ is ☐ is not developmentally disabled as defined in section 1420 of the Probate Code (specify the nature and degree of the alleged disability in Attachment 5e). Petitioner is aware of the requirements of section 1827.5 of the Probate Code.

(Continued on reverse)

6. ATTENDANCE AT HEARING **Proposed conservatee**

    a. ☐ will attend the hearing AND ☐ is the petitioner ☐ is not the petitioner
        AND ☐ has ☐ has not nominated the proposed conservator.

    b. ☐ is able but unwilling to attend the hearing AND ☐ does ☐ does not wish to contest the establishment of a
        conservatorship AND ☐ does ☐ does not object to the proposed conservator
        AND ☐ does ☐ does not prefer that another person act as conservator.

    c. ☐ is unable to attend the hearing because of medical inability. An affidavit or certificate of a licensed medical practitioner
        or an accredited religious practitioner is affixed as Attachment 6c.

    d. ☐ is not the petitioner, is out of state, and will not attend the hearing.

7. ☐ Granting the proposed conservator of the estate powers to be exercised independently under section 2590 of the Probate Code
    would be to the advantage and benefit and in the best interest of the conservatorship estate. Powers and reasons are specified
    in Attachment 7.

8. ☐ a. There is no form of medical treatment for which the proposed conservatee has the capacity to give an informed consent.

       b. Attached to this petition is a declaration executed by a licensed physician stating that the proposed conservatee lacks
       the capacity to give informed consent for any form of medical treatment and giving reasons and the factual basis for
       this conclusion. *(Label as Attachment 8.)*

       c. Proposed conservatee ☐ is ☐ is not an adherent of a religion that relies on prayer alone for healing as
       defined in section 2355(b) of the Probate Code.

9. ☐ Filed with this petition is a Petition for Appointment of Temporary Conservator *(Judicial Council form GC-110)*.

10. ☐ The names, residence addresses, and relationships of the spouse and all relatives within the second degree of the proposed
     conservatee so far as known to petitioner are

     a. ☐ listed below ☐ listed in Attachment 10

     b. ☐ not known, so relatives under Probate Code section 1821(b)(1)-(4) are ☐ listed below ☐ listed in Attach-
       ment 10.

           RELATIONSHIP AND NAME   RESIDENCE ADDRESS

(1) Spouse:

(2)

11. ☐ Filed with this petition is a proposed Order Appointing Court Investigator *(see Judicial Council form GC-330)*.

12. ☐ Number of pages attached: _____

Date: _____

▶ _____
                       (SIGNATURE OF PETITIONER)

I declare under penalty of perjury under the laws of the State of California that the foregoing is true and correct.
Date:

. . . .   ▶ _____
        (TYPE OR PRINT NAME)   (SIGNATURE OF PETITIONER)

SUPERIOR COURT OF CALIFORNIA, COUNTY OF

STREET ADDRESS:

MAILING ADDRESS:

CITY AND ZIP CODE:

BRANCH NAME:

CONSERVATORSHIP OF THE ☐ PERSON ☐ ESTATE OF (NAME):

Proposed Conservatee

DECLARATION OF MEDICAL OR ACCREDITED PRACTITIONER

CASE NUMBER:

I, (name): , hereby state:

1. a. ☐ I am a duly licensed medical practitioner, and the proposed conservatee is under my treatment. My office is located at (address):

   b. ☐ I am an accredited practitioner of a religion whose tenets and practices call for reliance on prayer alone for healing, which religion is adhered to by the proposed conservatee. The proposed conservatee is under my treatment. My office is located at (address):

2. The proposed conservatee is unable to attend the court hearing on the petition for appointment of a conservator set for (date): and will continue to be unable to attend a court hearing
   ☐ until (date): ☐ for the foreseeable future because of medical inability. Supporting facts are ☐ stated below ☐ stated in attachment 2.

I declare under penalty of perjury under the laws of the State of California that the foregoing is true and correct and that this declaration is executed on (date): . . . . at (place): . . . .

_____
(Signature of declarant)

Emotional or psychological instability shall not be considered good cause for the absence unless, by reason of the instability, attendance at the hearing is likely to cause serious and immediate physiological damage to the proposed conservatee.

Form Approved by the
Judicial Council of California
Revised Effective January 1, 1981
GC-335(81)

**DECLARATION OF MEDICAL OR
ACCREDITED PRACTITIONER**

CONFIDENTIAL (DO NOT ATTACH TO PETITION)

ATTORNEY OR PARTY WITHOUT ATTORNEY *(Name and Address)*:

TELEPHONE NO.:

FOR COURT USE ONLY

ATTORNEY FOR *(Name)*:

SUPERIOR COURT OF CALIFORNIA, COUNTY OF

STREET ADDRESS:

MAILING ADDRESS:

CITY AND ZIP CODE:

BRANCH NAME:

CONSERVATORSHIP OF (NAME):

PROPOSED CONSERVATEE

CONFIDENTIAL SUPPLEMENTAL INFORMATION
(Probate Conservatorship)

Conservatorship of ☐ Person ☐ Estate ☐ Limited Conservatorship

CASE NUMBER:

HEARING DATE:

DEPT.:   TIME:

1. a. **Proposed conservatee** *(name)*:
   b. Date of birth:
   c. Social Security No.:

2. ☐ **UNABLE TO PROVIDE FOR PERSONAL NEEDS*** The following facts support petitioner's allegation that the proposed conservatee is unable to provide properly for his or her needs for physical health, food, clothing, and shelter *(specify in detail. Enlarge upon the reasons stated in the petition. Provide specific examples from the proposed conservatee's daily life showing significant behavior patterns)*: ☐ Specified in Attachment 2.

(Continued on reverse)

Page one of four

Form Adopted by the
Judicial Council of California
GC-312 [New July 1, 1990]

CONFIDENTIAL SUPPLEMENTAL INFORMATION
(Probate Conservatorship)

*If this item is not applicable, complete item 8.
Probate Code, § 1821

CONSERVATORSHIP OF *(NAME)*:	CASE NUMBER:
PROPOSED CONSERVATEE	

3. ☐ UNABLE TO MANAGE FINANCIAL RESOURCES* The following facts support petitioner's allegation that the proposed conservatee is substantially unable to manage his or her financial resources or to resist fraud or undue influence *(specify in detail. Enlarge upon the reasons stated in the petition. Provide specific examples from the proposed conservatee's daily life showing significant behavior patterns.)*: ☐ Specified in Attachment 3.

4. RESIDENCE *("Residence" means the place usually described as "home"; for example, owned real property or long-term rental)*
   a. The proposed conservatee is **located** at *(street address, city, state)*:

   b. The proposed conservatee's **residence is*** ☐ the address in item 4a ☐ other *(street address, city, state)*:

(Continued on next page)

CONFIDENTIAL SUPPLEMENTAL INFORMATION
(Probate Conservatorship)

CONFIDENTIAL

CONSERVATORSHIP OF (NAME):	CASE NUMBER:
PROPOSED CONSERVATEE	

4. RESIDENCE (continued)

c. **Ability to live in residence*** The proposed conservatee is

(1) ☐ **living** in his or her residence and

    (i) ☐ will continue to live there unless circumstances change.

    (ii) ☐ will need to be moved after a conservator is appointed (specify supporting facts below in 4c(3)).

    (iii) ☐ other (specify and give supporting facts below in 4c(3)).

(2) ☐ **not living** in his or her residence and

    (i) ☐ will return by (date):   (specify supporting facts below in 4c(3)).

    (ii) ☐ will not return to live there (specify supporting facts below).

    (iii) ☐ other (specify and give supporting facts below in 4c(3)).

(3) ☐ Supporting facts (specify if required): ☐ Specified in Attachment 4.

5. ALTERNATIVES TO CONSERVATORSHIP*

Petitioner has considered the following alternatives to conservatorship and found them to be unsuitable or unavailable to the proposed conservatee (specify alternatives considered and reasons each is unsuitable or unavailable): ☐ Reasons specified in Attachment 5.

a. Voluntary acceptance of informal or formal assistance (reason unsuitable or unavailable):

b. Special or limited power of attorney (reason unsuitable or unavailable):

c. General power of attorney (reason unsuitable or unavailable):

d. Durable power of attorney for ☐ health care ☐ estate management (reason unsuitable or unavailable):

e. Trust (reason unsuitable or unavailable):

f. Other alternatives considered (specify and give reason each is unsuitable or unavailable):

(Continued on reverse)

CONFIDENTIAL SUPPLEMENTAL INFORMATION
(Probate Conservatorship)

*If this item is not applicable, complete item 8.

CONFIDENTIAL

CONSERVATORSHIP OF *(NAME)*:	CASE NUMBER:
PROPOSED CONSERVATEE	

6. SERVICES PROVIDED* *(complete a or b, or both a and b)*

   a. ☐ During the year before this petition was filed,

      (1) **health services** ☐ were provided ☐ were not provided to the proposed conservatee *(explain)*:
      ☐ Explained in Attachment 6a(1).

      (2) **social services** ☐ were provided ☐ were not provided to the proposed conservatee *(explain)*:
      ☐ Explained in Attachment 6a(2).

      (3) **estate management assistance** ☐ was provided ☐ was not provided to the proposed conservatee *(explain)*:
      ☐ Explained in Attachment 6a(3).

   b. ☐ Petitioner has **no knowledge** of what ☐ social services ☐ health services ☐ estate management assistance were provided to the proposed conservatee during the year before this petition was filed. Petitioner has no reasonable means of determining what services were provided.

7. SUPPORTING FACTS (AFFIDAVITS) The information provided above is stated

   a. Item 1: ☐ on petitioner's own knowledge ☐ in an affidavit (declaration) by another person attached as Attachment 1a.
   b. Item 2: ☐ on petitioner's own knowledge ☐ in an affidavit (declaration) by another person attached as Attachment 2a.
   c. Item 3: ☐ on petitioner's own knowledge ☐ in an affidavit (declaration) by another person attached as Attachment 3a.
   d. Item 4: ☐ on petitioner's own knowledge ☐ in an affidavit (declaration) by another person attached as Attachment 4a.
   e. Item 5: ☐ on petitioner's own knowledge ☐ in an affidavit (declaration) by another person attached as Attachment 5a.
   f. Item 6: ☐ on petitioner's own knowledge ☐ in an affidavit (declaration) by another person attached as Attachment 6a.

8. ITEMS NOT APPLICABLE The following items on this form were not applicable to the proposed conservatee:
   ☐ 2 ☐ 3 ☐ 4b ☐ 4c ☐ 5 ☐ 6 *(specify reasons each item is not applicable)*:
   ☐ Reasons specified in Attachment 8.

9. ☐ Number of pages attached: _____

10. DECLARATION I declare under penalty of perjury under the laws of the State of California that the foregoing is true and correct.

Date:

. . . . ▶ _____
       (TYPE OR PRINT NAME)   (SIGNATURE OF PETITIONER)

ATTORNEY OR PARTY WITHOUT ATTORNEY *(Name and Address)* :

TELEPHONE NO.:

FOR COURT USE ONLY

ATTORNEY FOR *(Name)* :

SUPERIOR COURT OF CALIFORNIA, COUNTY OF

STREET ADDRESS:

MAILING ADDRESS:

CITY AND ZIP CODE:

BRANCH NAME:

CONSERVATORSHIP OF THE ☐ **PERSON** ☐ **ESTATE OF** *(NAME)* :

☐ CONSERVATEE ☐ PROPOSED CONSERVATEE

CASE NUMBER:

ORDER APPOINTING COURT INVESTIGATOR
☐ **Conservatorship** ☐ **Limited Conservatorship**

TO *(name)* :

You are hereby appointed Court Investigator in the matter entitled above.

1. ☐ **Prior to appointment of a conservator** YOU ARE DIRECTED TO

a. personally interview and inform the proposed conservatee of the contents of the citation, the nature, purpose, and effect of the proceedings, and of the right to oppose the proceeding, attend the hearing, have the matter tried by jury, be represented by counsel, and have legal counsel appointed by the court if unable to retain an attorney.

b. determine

(1) whether it appears that the proposed conservatee is unable or unwilling to attend the hearing.

(2) whether the proposed conservatee wishes to contest the establishment of the conservatorship; and whether the proposed conservatee objects to the proposed conservator, or whether he or she prefers another person to act as conservator.

(3) whether the proposed conservatee wishes to be represented by counsel, and if so, whether counsel has been retained, and if not, the name of an attorney the proposed conservatee wishes to retain.

(4) whether the proposed conservatee desires the court to appoint legal counsel if the proposed conservatee has not retained an attorney.

(5) whether the appointment of legal counsel would be helpful to the resolution of the matter or is necessary to protect the interests of the proposed conservatee if the proposed conservatee does not plan to retain legal counsel and has not requested the court to appoint legal counsel.

(6) whether the proposed conservatee is capable of completing an affidavit of voter registration.

c. review (i) the allegations of the petition as to why the appointment of a conservator is required and (ii) the statements in the **Confidential Supplemental Information** *(form No. GC-312)* and refer to the supplemental information in making your determinations.

d. at least five days before the hearing, report your findings in writing to the court, including in your report the proposed conservatee's express communications concerning the following:

(1) representation by legal counsel;

(2) whether the proposed conservatee is not willing to attend the hearing, does not wish to contest the establishment of the conservatorship, and does not object to the proposed conservator or prefer that another person act as conservator.

e. at least five days before the date set for hearing, mail a copy of your report to all of the following:

(1) the attorney, if any, for the petitioner;

(2) the attorney, if any, for the proposed conservatee;

(3) ☐ other persons ordered by the court *(specify names and addresses in Attachment 1e)*.

f. ☐ other *(specify in Attachment 1f)*.

2. ☐ **Before the court grants an order relating to medical consent under section 1880 of the Probate Code**

☐ **Before the court grants an order under section 2253 of the Probate Code authorizing the temporary conservator to change the residence of the temporary conservatee**

YOU ARE DIRECTED TO

a. personally interview and inform the conservatee of the contents of the petition, the nature, purpose, and effect of the proceedings, and of the right to oppose the petition, attend the hearing, and be represented by legal counsel.

(Continued on reverse)

Form Approved by the
Judicial Council of California
GC-330 [Rev. July 1, 1990]

ORDER APPOINTING COURT INVESTIGATOR
(Probate Conservatorship)

Probate Code, §§ 1454,
1826, 1851

CONSERVATORSHIP OF (NAME):	CASE NUMBER:
☐ CONSERVATEE ☐ PROPOSED CONSERVATEE	

2. *(continued)*

   b. determine

     (1) whether it appears that the conservatee is unable or unwilling to attend the hearing.

     (2) whether the conservatee wishes to contest the petition.

     (3) whether the conservatee wishes to be represented by counsel, and if so, whether counsel has been retained, and if not, the name of an attorney the conservatee wishes to retain.

     (4) whether the conservatee desires the court to appoint legal counsel if the conservatee has not retained an attorney.

     (5) whether the appointment of legal counsel would be helpful to the resolution of the matter or is necessary to protect the interests of the conservatee if the conservatee does not plan to retain legal counsel and has not requested the court to appoint legal counsel.

     (6) *(for change of residence only)* determine whether the proposed change of place of residence is required to prevent irreparable harm to the conservatee and whether no means less restrictive of the conservatee's liberty will suffice to prevent the harm.

   c. at least five days before the hearing on medical consent or at least two days before the hearing on change of residence, report your findings in writing to the court, including the conservatee's express communications concerning representation by legal counsel and whether the conservatee is not willing to attend the hearing and whether he or she does not wish to contest the petition.

   d. at least five days before the date set for hearing on medical consent or at least two days before the hearing on change of residence, mail a copy of your report to all of the following:

     (1) the attorney, if any, for the petitioner;

     (2) the attorney, if any, for the conservatee;

     (3) ☐ other persons and addresses ordered by the court *(specify names and addresses in Attachment 2d).*

   e. ☐ other *(specify in Attachment 2e).*

3. ☐ **Duties after appointment of conservator** YOU ARE DIRECTED TO

   a. visit and personally inform the conservatee that he or she is under a conservatorship and of the name of the conservator.

   b. determine whether the conservatee wishes to petition the court for termination of the conservatorship.

   c. determine whether the conservatee is still in need of the conservatorship.

   d. determine whether the conservatee is capable of completing an affidavit of voter registration.

   e. determine whether the conservator is acting in the best interests of the conservatee.

   f. inform the court immediately if you are unable at any time to locate the conservatee.

   g. as may be necessary, visit personally with the conservator and other persons to determine whether the conservator is acting in the best interest of the conservatee.

   h. ☐ *(for conservatorships existing on December 31, 1980, in which the conservatee has not been adjudged incompetent)* determine whether an order should be made under section 1873 of the Probate Code broadening the capacity of the conservatee.

   i. ☐ determine whether the present condition of the conservatee is such that the terms of the court order under sections 1873 or 1901 of the Probate Code should be modified or that the order should be revoked.

   j. ☐ determine whether the conservatee still lacks the capacity to give informed consent for any form of medical treatment.

   k. ☐ *(for limited conservatorship only)* make a recommendation regarding the continuation or termination of the limited conservatorship.

   l. ☐ mail at the same time your report is certified to the court a copy to the conservator, to the attorneys of record for the conservator and conservatee, and to any other persons as ordered by the court *(specify names and addresses in Attachment 3l).*

   m. ☐ other *(specify in Attachment 3m).*

The visit and investigation under item 3 shall be so conducted that it is completed and your findings are certified in writing to the court not less than 15 days before the expiration of one year from the date the conservator was appointed. Visits and investigations shall be made biennially thereafter, with written findings certified to the court not less than 15 days before the date of biennial court review.

4. Number of pages attached: _____

Date: _____

_____
JUDGE OF THE SUPERIOR COURT

ATTORNEY OR PARTY WITHOUT ATTORNEY *(Name and Address)* :

TELEPHONE NO.:

FOR COURT USE ONLY

ATTORNEY FOR *(Name)* :

SUPERIOR COURT OF CALIFORNIA, COUNTY OF

STREET ADDRESS:

MAILING ADDRESS:

CITY AND ZIP CODE:

BRANCH NAME:

CONSERVATORSHIP OF THE ☐ **PERSON** ☐ **ESTATE OF** *(NAME)* :

CONSERVATEE

ORDER APPOINTING PROBATE CONSERVATOR
☐ **Limited Conservatorship**

CASE NUMBER:

1. The petition for appointment of conservator came on for hearing as follows *(check boxes c, d, e, and f to indicate **personal presence**)* :
   a. Judge *(name)* :

   b. Hearing date: Time: ☐ Dept.:   ☐ Room:
   c. ☐ Petitioner *(name)* :
   d. ☐ Attorney for petitioner *(name)* :
   e. ☐ Attorney for person cited *(name, address, and telephone)* :

   f. Person cited was ☐ present ☐ unable to attend ☐ able but unwilling to attend ☐ out of state.

2. THE COURT FINDS
   a. All notices required by law have been given.
   b. *(Name)* :
      (1) ☐ is unable properly to provide for his or her personal needs for physical health, food, clothing, or shelter.
      (2) ☐ is substantially unable to manage his or her financial resources or to resist fraud or undue influence.
      (3) ☐ has voluntarily requested appointment of a conservator and good cause has been shown for the appointment.
   c. **Conservatee**
      (1) ☐ is an adult.
      (2) ☐ will be an adult on the effective date of this order.
      (3) ☐ is a married minor.
      (4) ☐ is a minor whose marriage has been dissolved.
   d. ☐ There is no form of medical treatment for which the conservatee has the capacity to give an informed consent.
      ☐ Conservatee is an adherent of a religion defined in section 2355(b) of the Probate Code.
   e. ☐ Granting the conservator powers to be exercised independently under section 2590 of the Probate Code is to the advantage and benefit and in the best interest of the conservatorship estate.
   f. ☐ Conservatee is not capable of completing an affidavit of voter registration.
   g. ☐ Attorney *(name)* :   has been appointed by the court as legal counsel to represent the conservatee in these proceedings. The cost for representation is: $
      The conservatee has the ability to pay ☐ all ☐ none ☐ a portion of this sum *(specify)* : $
   h. ☐ Conservatee need not attend the hearing.
   i. ☐ The appointed court investigator is *(name, address, and telephone)* :

   j. ☐ *(for limited conservatorship only)* The limited conservatee is developmentally disabled as defined in section 1420 of the Probate Code.
   k. ☐ The conservator is a private professional conservator as defined by Probate Code section 2341 who has filed with the county clerk the confidential statement required by Probate Code section 2342.

(Continued on reverse)

Form Approved by the
Judicial Council of California
GC-340 [Rev. July 1, 1990]

**ORDER APPOINTING
PROBATE CONSERVATOR**
(Probate Conservatorship)

Do NOT use this form for a temporary conservatorship.

Probate Code, § 1830

CONSERVATORSHIP OF (NAME):	CASE NUMBER:
CONSERVATEE	

3. THE COURT ORDERS

a. *(Name)*:

   (Address):   *(Telephone)*:

   is appointed [ ] conservator [ ] limited conservator of the PERSON of *(name)*:
   and Letters shall issue upon qualification.

b. *(Name)*:

   (Address):   *(Telephone)*:

   is appointed [ ] conservator [ ] limited conservator of the ESTATE of *(name)*:
   and Letters shall issue upon qualification.

c. [ ] Conservatee need not attend the hearing.

d. (1) [ ] Bond is not required.

   (2) [ ] Bond is fixed at: $ to be furnished by an authorized surety company or as otherwise provided by law.

   (3) [ ] Deposits shall be made at *(specify institution)*:

       in the amount of: $ and receipts filed.

e. [ ] For legal services rendered, [ ] conservatee [ ] conservatee's estate [ ] parents of the minor [ ] minor's estate shall pay to *(name)*:   the sum of: $

   [ ] forthwith [ ] as follows *(specify terms, including any combination of payors)*:

f. [ ] Conservatee is disqualified from voting.

g. [ ] Conservatee lacks the capacity to give informed consent for medical treatment and the conservator of the person is granted the powers specified in section 2355 of the Probate Code. [ ] The treatment shall be performed by an accredited practitioner of the religion defined in section 2355(b) of the Probate Code.

h. [ ] The conservator of the estate is granted authorization under section 2590 of the Probate Code to exercise independently the powers specified in Attachment 3h [ ] subject to the conditions provided.

i. [ ] Orders relating to the capacity of the conservatee under sections 1873 or 1901 of the Probate Code as specified in Attachment 3i are granted.

j. [ ] Orders relating to the powers and duties of the conservator of the person under sections 2351-2358 of the Probate Code as specified in Attachment 3j are granted.

k. [ ] Orders relating to the conditions imposed under section 2402 of the Probate Code upon the conservator of the estate as specified in Attachment 3k are granted.

l. [ ] Other orders as specified in Attachment 3l are granted.

m. [ ] The inheritance tax referee appointed is *(name and address)*:

n. [ ] *(for limited conservatorship only)* Orders relating to the powers and duties of the limited conservator of the person under section 2351.5 of the Probate Code as specified in Attachment 3n are granted.

o. [ ] *(for limited conservatorship only)* Orders relating to the powers and duties of the limited conservator of the estate under section 1830(b) of the Probate Code as specified in Attachment 3o are granted.

p. [ ] *(for limited conservatorship only)* Orders limiting the civil and legal rights of the limited conservatee as specified in Attachment 3p are granted.

q. [ ] This order is effective on the [ ] date signed [ ] date minor attains majority *(date)*:

4. Number of boxes checked in item 3: _____

5. [ ] Number of pages attached: _____

Date: _____

                                   _____
                                     JUDGE OF THE SUPERIOR COURT
                                     [ ] SIGNATURE FOLLOWS LAST ATTACHMENT.

**ORDER APPOINTING
PROBATE CONSERVATOR**
(Probate Conservatorship)

ATTORNEY FOR (NAME):

SUPERIOR COURT OF CALIFORNIA, COUNTY OF

STREET ADDRESS:

MAILING ADDRESS:

CITY AND ZIP CODE:

BRANCH NAME:

CONSERVATORSHIP OF THE ☐ PERSON ☐ ESTATE OF (NAME):

Proposed Conservatee

CITATION FOR CONSERVATORSHIP
☐ Limited Conservatorship

CASE NUMBER:

THE PEOPLE OF THE STATE OF CALIFORNIA,

To (name):

1. You are hereby cited and required to appear at a hearing in this court

   on (date):   at (time):   in ☐ Dept: ☐ Div: ☐ Rm.:

   located at (street address and city):

   and to give any legal reason why, according to the verified petition filed with this court, you should not be found to be ☐ unable to provide for your personal needs ☐ unable to manage your financial resources and by reason thereof, why the following person should not be appointed ☐ conservator ☐ limited conservator of your ☐ person ☐ estate (name):

2. A conservatorship of the person may be created for a person who is unable properly to provide for his or her personal needs for physical health, food, clothing or shelter. A conservatorship of the property (estate) may be created for a person who is unable to resist fraud or undue influence, or who is substantially unable to manage his or her own financial resources. "Substantial inability" may not be proved solely by isolated incidents of negligence or improvidence.

3. At the hearing a conservator may be appointed for your ☐ person ☐ estate. The appointment may affect or transfer to the conservator your right to contract, to manage and control your property, to give informed consent for medical treatment, to fix your place of residence, and to marry. You may also be disqualified from voting if you are found to be incapable of completing an affidavit of voter registration. The judge or the court investigator will explain to you the nature, purpose, and effect of the proceedings and answer questions concerning the explanation.

4. You have the right to appear at the hearing and oppose the petition. You have the right to hire an attorney of your choice to represent you. The court will appoint an attorney to represent you if you are unable to retain one. You must pay the cost of that attorney if you are able. You have the right to a jury trial if you wish.

5. *(for limited conservatorship only)* You have the right to oppose the petition in part by objecting to any or all of the requested duties or powers of the limited conservator.

Dated: . . . . Clerk, by _____ , Deputy

SEAL

(Proof of service on reverse)

**CITATION FOR CONSERVATORSHIP
AND PROOF OF SERVICE**

CONSERVATORSHIP OF (NAME):

Proposed Conservatee

CASE NUMBER:

PROOF OF SERVICE   Page 2
(Citation for Conservatorship)

1. I served the citation and petition as follows:

   a. Person cited (name):

   b. Person served (name):

   c. [ ] By delivery at [ ] home [ ] business
      (1) date:
      (2) time:
      (3) address:

   d. [ ] By mailing (1) date:
      (2) place:

2. Manner of service (check proper box)

   a. [ ] **Personal service.** By personally delivering copies to the person served. (CCP 415.10)

   b. [ ] **Mail and acknowledgment service. By mailing** (by first-class or airmail) copies to the person served, together with two copies of the form of notice and acknowledgment and a return envelope, postage prepaid, addressed to the sender. (CCP 415.30) **(Attach completed acknowledgment of receipt.)**

   c. [ ] **Service on person outside state** (CCP 415.40) (specify manner of service):

   d. [ ] **Other manner authorized by court** [ ] specified below [ ] specified in attachment 2d.

3. At the time of service I was at least 18 years of age and not a party to this proceeding.

4. Fee for service: $

5. Person serving

   a. [ ] Not a registered California process server.

   b. [ ] Registered California process server.

   c. [ ] Employee or independent contractor of a registered California process server.

   d. [ ] Exempt from registration under Bus. & Prof. Code 22350(b).

   e. [ ] California sheriff, marshal, or constable.

   f. Name, address and telephone number and, if applicable, county of registration and number:

I declare under penalty of perjury under the laws of the State of California that the foregoing is true and correct and that this declaration is executed on (date):
at (place):

(For California sheriff, marshal, or constable use only)
I certify that the forgoing is true and correct and that this certificate is executed on (date): . . . . California.
at (place):

_____   _____
(Signature)   (Signature)

ATTORNEY FOR (NAME):

SUPERIOR COURT OF CALIFORNIA, COUNTY OF

STREET ADDRESS:

MAILING ADDRESS:

CITY AND ZIP CODE:

BRANCH NAME:

☐ GUARDIANSHIP ☐ CONSERVATORSHIP OF THE ☐ PERSON ☐ ESTATE OF
(NAME):

☐ Minor ☐ Conservatee

NOTICE OF HEARING

☐ **Guardianship** ☐ **Conservatorship** ☐ **Limited Conservatorship**

CASE NUMBER:

This notice is required by law. This notice does not require you to appear in court, but you may attend the hearing if you wish.

1. NOTICE is given that (name):
   (representative capacity, if any):
   has filed (specify):

   reference to which is made for further particulars.

2. ☐ The petition includes an application for the independent exercise of powers under section 2590 of the Probate Code. Powers requested are ☐ specified below ☐ specified in attachment 2.

3. A hearing on the matter will be held

   | on (date): | at (time): | in ☐ Dept: | ☐ Div: | ☐ Rm.: |

   located at (address of court):

   Dated: . . . . ☐ Clerk, by _____ , Deputy

   ☐ Attorney _____
   (Signature)

   This notice was mailed on (date): . . . . , at (place): . . . ., California.

(Continued on reverse)

Form Approved by the
Judicial Council of California
Revised Effective January 1, 1981
GC-020(81)

**NOTICE OF HEARING
GUARDIANSHIP OR CONSERVATORSHIP**

| GUARDIANSHIP ☐ CONSERVATORSHIP OF (NAME): ☐ Minor ☐ Conservatee | CASE NUMBER: |

NOTICE OF HEARING—GUARDIANSHIP OR CONSERVATORSHIP
CLERK'S CERTIFICATE OF ☐ POSTING ☐ MAILING

I certify that I am not a party to this cause and that a true copy of the foregoing Notice of Hearing—Guardianship or Conservatorship

1. ☐ *(for sales under section 2543(c) of the Probate Code only)* was posted at (address):

2. ☐ was mailed, first class, postage fully prepaid, ☐ with a copy of the petition (title):

   in a sealed envelope addressed to each person whose name and address is given below.
I certify that the notice was posted or mailed and this certificate was executed on (date):. . . . .
at (place): . . . ., California.

Clerk, by ———————————————— , Deputy

PROOF OF SERVICE BY MAIL

I am over the age of 18 and not a party to this cause. I am a resident of or employed in the county where the mailing occurred. My residence or business address is:

I served the foregoing Notice of Hearing—Guardianship or Conservatorship ☐ with a copy of the petition (title):

by enclosing a true copy in a sealed envelope addressed to each person whose name and address is given below and depositing the envelope in the United States mail with the postage fully prepaid.

(1) Date of deposit: (2) Place of deposit (city and state):

I declare under penalty of perjury under the laws of the State of California that the foregoing is true and correct and that this declaration is executed on (date):. . . . . .at (place): . . . .

. . . .   ————————————————————
(Type or print name)   (Signature of declarant)

NAME AND ADDRESS OF EACH PERSON TO WHOM NOTICE WAS MAILED

☐ List of names and addresses continued on attachment.

<table>
<tr><td>PARTY WITHOUT AN ATTORNEY (Name and Address):

In Pro Per</td><td>TELEPHONE NO:</td><td rowspan="3">FOR COURT USE ONLY</td></tr>
<tr><td colspan="2">NAME OF COURT:
STREET ADDRESS:
MAILING ADDRESS:
CITY AND ZIP CODE:
BRANCH NAME:</td></tr>
<tr><td colspan="2">CONSERVATORSHIP OF THE ☐ PERSON ☐ ESTATE OF (NAME):

CONSERVATEE</td></tr>
<tr><td>NOTIFICATION TO COURT OF ADDRESS OF
CONSERVATOR AND CONSERVATEE</td><td>CASE NUMBER</td><td></td></tr>
</table>

1. INFORMATION ABOUT CONSERVATOR

NAME OF CONSERVATOR:

STREET ADDRESS:

CITY: STATE: ZIP:

MAILING ADDRESS (If different):

CITY: STATE: ZIP:

PHONE NUMBER (Include area code):   (   )

2. INFORMATION ABOUT CONSERVATEE

NAME OF CONSERVATEE:

STREET ADDRESS:

CITY: STATE: ZIP:

MAILING ADDRESS (If different):

CITY: STATE: ZIP:

PHONE NUMBER (Include area code):   (   )

3. INFORMATION ABOUT COMPLETION OF THIS FORM:

NAME:

CAPACITY (e.g., Conservator):

STREET ADDRESS:

CITY: STATE: ZIP:

MAILING ADDRESS (If different):

CITY: STATE: ZIP:

PHONE NUMBER (Include area code):   (   )

Date:

....
(TYPE OR PRINT NAME)   (SIGNATURE OF PERSON WHO SERVED PAPERS)

ATTORNEY OR PARTY WITHOUT ATTORNEY (NAME AND ADDRESS):	TELEPHONE NO.:	FOR COURT USE ONLY
ATTORNEY FOR (NAME):		

SUPERIOR COURT OF CALIFORNIA, COUNTY OF

STREET ADDRESS:

MAILING ADDRESS:

CITY AND ZIP CODE:

BRANCH NAME:

☐ GUARDIANSHIP ☐ CONSERVATORSHIP OF (NAME):

☐ Minor ☐ Conservatee

ORDER DISPENSING NOTICE	CASE NUMBER:

1. THE COURT FINDS that a petition for *(specify)*:
has been filed and

  a. ☐ all persons entitled to notice of hearing have ☐ waived notice ☐ consented to the appointment of the proposed ☐ guardian ☐ conservator.

  b. ☐ *(for guardianship only)* the following persons cannot with reasonable diligence be given notice (names):

  c. ☐ *(for guardianship only)* the giving of notice to the following persons is contrary to the interest of justice (names):

  d. ☐ good cause exists for dispensing with notice to the following persons referred to in section 1460(b) of the Probate Code (names):

  e. ☐ other *(specify)*:

2. THE COURT ORDERS that notice of hearing on the petition for (specify):

  a. ☐ is not required except to persons requesting special notice under section 2700 of the Probate Code.
  b. ☐ is dispensed with to the following persons (names):

Dated: . . . . _____

Judge of the Superior Court

Form Approved by the
Judicial Council of California
Effective January 1, 1981
GC-021(81)

ORDER DISPENSING WITH NOTICE
GUARDIANSHIP OR CONSERVATORSHIP

TO COURT CLERK: This form is CONFIDENTIAL if local rule requires the Acknowledgment of Receipt to have a Social Security or driver's license number.

ATTORNEY OR PARTY WITHOUT ATTORNEY *(Name and Address)*:	TELEPHONE NO.:	*FOR COURT USE ONLY*

ATTORNEY FOR *(Name)*:

SUPERIOR COURT OF CALIFORNIA, COUNTY OF

STREET ADDRESS:

MAILING ADDRESS:

CITY AND ZIP CODE:

BRANCH NAME:

CONSERVATORSHIP OF (NAME):

DUTIES OF CONSERVATOR and Acknowledgment of Receipt of Handbook	CASE NUMBER:

DUTIES OF CONSERVATOR

When you have been appointed by the court as a conservator, you become responsible to the court and assume certain duties and obligations. All of your actions as conservator are subject to review by the court. An attorney is best qualified to advise you about these matters. You should clearly understand the information on this form. You will find additional information in the **Judicial Council *Handbook for Conservators***, which you are required by law to possess.

I. THE CONSERVATEE'S RIGHTS

A conservatee does not lose all rights or all voice in important decisions affecting his or her way of life. All conservatees have the right to be treated with understanding and respect, the right to have their wishes considered, and the right to be well cared for by you. A conservatee generally keeps the right to (1) control his or her own salary, (2) make or change a will, (3) marry, (4) receive personal mail, (5) be represented by a lawyer, (6) ask a judge to change conservators, (7) ask a judge to end the conservatorship, (8) vote, unless a judge decides the conservatee isn't capable of exercising this right, (9) control personal spending money, if a judge has authorized an allowance, and (10) make his or her own medical decisions, unless a judge has taken away that right and given it to you. Ask your attorney what rights the conservatee does not have and consult your attorney when you are in doubt.

II. ☐ CONSERVATOR OF THE PERSON

As conservator of the person, you will arrange for the conservatee's care and protection, decide where the conservatee will live, and make arrangements for the conservatee's health care, meals, clothing, personal care, housekeeping, transportation, and recreation.

1. ASSESS THE CONSERVATEE'S NEEDS AND DEVELOP A GENERAL PLAN
You must assess the conservatee's needs and show how you plan to meet them in a *General Plan of Conservatorship* and file your plan with the court within 90 days after your appointment.

2. DECIDE WHERE THE CONSERVATEE WILL LIVE
You may decide where the conservatee will live, but you must choose the "least restrictive, appropriate" living situation that is safe and comfortable and allows the conservatee as much independence as possible. You must not move the conservatee from the state or place the conservatee involuntarily in a mental health treatment facility without permission of the court. You must notify the court of each change of the conservatee's address and your address.

3. PROVIDE MEDICAL CARE TO THE CONSERVATEE
You are responsible for ensuring the conservatee's health needs are met. You may not, however, give or withhold consent for medical treatment over the conservatee's objection *unless* the court has given you exclusive authority to consent because the conservatee has lost the ability to make sound medical choices.

4. FILE A STATUS REPORT
If you are conservator of the estate as well as conservator of the person, you must file with the court a *Status Report* on the conservatee's condition one year after your appointment and at least every two years after that.

(Continued on reverse)

Page one of four

Form Adopted by the
Judicial Council of California
GC-348 [New January 1, 1992]

**DUTIES OF CONSERVATOR
and Acknowledgment of Receipt of Handbook
(Probate Conservatorship)**

Probate Code, § 1834

II. CONSERVATOR OF THE PERSON (continued)

5. WORK WITH THE CONSERVATOR OF THE ESTATE
If someone else is handling the conservatee's assets, the two of you must work together to be sure the conservatee can afford the care you arrange. Purchases you make for the conservatee must be approved by the conservator of the estate or you may not be reimbursed.

6. CONSULT YOUR ATTORNEY AND OTHER RESOURCES
Your attorney will advise you on your duties, the limits of your authority, the rights of the conservatee, and your dealings with the court. If you have legal questions, check with your attorney, not the court staff. Other questions may be answered better and less expensively by calling on local community resources. (To find these resources, see the *Handbook for Conservators* and the local supplement distributed by the court.)

III. ☐ CONSERVATOR OF THE ESTATE

As conservator of the estate, you will manage the conservatee's finances, protect the conservatee's income and assets, make an inventory of the conservatorship estate's assets, develop a *General Plan* to ensure the conservatee's needs are met, make sure the conservatee's bills are paid, invest the conservatee's money, see that the conservatee is receiving all the income and benefits he or she is entitled to, ensure that tax returns are filed on time, keep accurate financial records, and regularly report your financial accounts to the court. (NOTE: The assets and finances of the conservatee are known as "the estate.")

1. MANAGING THE ESTATE'S ASSETS

a. Prudent investments
You must manage the estate assets with the care of a prudent person dealing with someone else's property. This means you must be cautious and you may not make any speculative investments.

b. Keep estate assets separate from anyone else's
You must keep the money and property in this estate separate from anyone else's, including your own. When you open a bank account for the estate, the account name must indicate that it is a *conservatorship* account and not your personal account. Never deposit estate funds in your personal account or otherwise mix them with yours or anyone else's property, even for brief periods. Securities in the estate must be held in a name that shows they are estate property and not your personal property.

c. Interest-bearing accounts and other investments
Except for checking accounts intended for ordinary administration expenses, estate accounts must earn interest. You may deposit estate funds in insured accounts in financial institutions, but you should not put more than $100,000 in any one institution. Consult with an attorney before making other investments.

d. Other restrictions
There are many other restrictions on your authority to deal with estate assets. Without prior order of the court, you may not pay fees to yourself or to your attorney, make a gift of estate assets, or borrow from the estate. If you do not obtain the court's permission when it is required, you may be removed as conservator or you may be required to reimburse the estate from your own personal funds, or both. You should consult with an attorney concerning the legal requirements affecting sales, leases, mortgages, and investments of estate property.

2. INVENTORY OF ESTATE PROPERTY

a. Locate the estate's property
You must locate, take possession of, and protect all the conservatee's income and assets that will be administered in the estate. You should change the ownership of most assets into the conservatorship estate's name. For real estate, you must record a copy of your Letters with the county recorder in each county where the conservatee owns real property.

b. Determine the value of the property
You must arrange to have a court-appointed referee determine the value of the property unless the appointment is waived by the court. You, rather than the referee, must determine the value of certain "cash items." An attorney can advise you about how to do this.

c. File an inventory and appraisal
Within 90 days after your appointment as conservator, you must file with the court an inventory and appraisal of all the assets in the estate.

(Continued on next page)

III. CONSERVATOR OF THE ESTATE *(continued)*

3. GENERAL PLAN FOR THE CONSERVATORSHIP

Within 90 days after your appointment, you must file a detailed *General Plan* describing how you will manage the estate.

4. INSURANCE

You should determine that there is appropriate and adequate insurance covering the assets and risks of the estate. Maintain the insurance in force during the entire period of the administration (except for assets after they are sold).

5. RECORD KEEPING

a. Keep an accounting

You must keep complete and accurate records of each financial transaction affecting the estate. The checkbook for the conservatorship checking account is your indispensable tool for keeping records of income and expenditures. You will have to prepare an accounting of all money and property you have received, what you have spent, the date of each transaction, and its purpose. You must describe in detail what you have left after you pay the estate's expenses.

b. Court review of your records

You must file a petition requesting the court to review and approve your accounting one year after your appointment and at least every two years after that. Save your receipts because the court may ask to review them also. If you do not file your accountings as required, the court will order you to do so. You may be removed as conservator if you fail to comply.

6. CONSULTING AN ATTORNEY

Your attorney will advise you and help prepare your inventories, accountings, and petitions to the court. If you have questions, check with your attorney, not the court staff. You should cooperate with your attorney at all times. **When in doubt, contact your attorney.**

IV. ☐ LIMITED CONSERVATOR (for the developmentally disabled only)

1. AUTHORITY SPECIFIED IN YOUR LETTERS

As limited conservator, you have authority to take care of *ONLY* those aspects of the conservatee's life and financial affairs specified in your Letters of Conservatorship and the court's order appointing you. The conservatee retains all other legal and civil rights. Although most of the information in parts I–III of this form also applies to limited conservatorships (especially the duties of the conservator of the person), you should clarify with your attorney exactly which information applies in your case.

2. DUTY TO HELP CONSERVATEE DEVELOP SELF-RELIANCE

You must secure for the limited conservatee treatment, services, and opportunities that will assist him or her to develop maximum self-reliance and independence. This assistance may include training, education, medical and psychological services, social opportunities, vocational opportunities, and other appropriate help.

V. ☐ TEMPORARY CONSERVATOR

As temporary conservator, you have generally the same duties and authority as general conservators *except* the conservatorship will end on the date specified in your Letters of Temporary Conservatorship. Most of the information in parts I–III of this form also applies to temporary conservatorships, but you must consult your attorney about which duties you will *not* perform because of the limited time. A temporary conservator should avoid making long-term decisions or changes that could safely wait until a general conservator is appointed. As temporary conservator, however, you may not move a conservatee from his or her home or sell or give away the conservatee's home or any other assets without court approval.

Sign the Acknowledgment of
Receipt on the reverse.

(Continued on reverse)

CONSERVATORSHIP OF *(NAME)*:	CASE NUMBER:

ACKNOWLEDGMENT OF RECEIPT
of Duties of Conservator and *Handbook for Conservators*
(Probate Code, § 1834)

1. A petition has been filed with the court requesting that I be appointed as a conservator.
2. I acknowledge that I have received the following:
   a. ☐ A copy of this statement of the duties and liabilities of the office of conservator *(Duties of Conservator form)*.
   b. ☐ The *Handbook for Conservators* adopted by the Judicial Council *(check one)*:
      (1) ☐ and the *local court supplement* to ''How to Find and Use Community Resources.''
      (2) ☐ no *local court supplement* is now available. I shall acquire a copy when it becomes available.

I declare under penalty of perjury under the laws of the State of California that the foregoing acknowledgment is true and correct.

Date:

. . . .
(TYPE OR PRINT NAME)

▶ _____
(SIGNATURE OF PETITIONER)

*Social Security No.: _____   *Driver's License No.: _____

Date:

. . . .
(TYPE OR PRINT NAME)

▶ _____
(SIGNATURE OF PETITIONER)

*Social Security No.: _____   *Driver's License No.: _____

Date:

. . . .
(TYPE OR PRINT NAME)

▶ _____
(SIGNATURE OF PETITIONER)

*Social Security No.: _____   *Driver's License No.: _____

*Supply your Social Security number and driver's license number ONLY if required to do so by local court rule. The law requires the court to keep this information CONFIDENTIAL. (Probate Code, § 1834(b).)

NOTICE
This statement of duties and liabilities is a summary and is not a complete statement of the law. Your conduct as a conservator is governed by the law itself and not by this summary or by the Judicial Council *Handbook for Conservators*. When in doubt, consult your attorney.

GC-348 [New January 1, 1992]   **DUTIES OF CONSERVATOR**
and Acknowledgment of Receipt of Handbook
(Probate Conservatorship)   Page four of four

ATTORNEY OR PARTY WITHOUT ATTORNEY (NAME AND ADDRESS):	TELEPHONE NO.:	FOR COURT USE ONLY

ATTORNEY FOR (NAME):

SUPERIOR COURT OF CALIFORNIA, COUNTY OF

STREET ADDRESS:

MAILING ADDRESS:

CITY AND ZIP CODE:

BRANCH NAME:

☐ GUARDIANSHIP ☐ CONSERVATORSHIP OF THE ☐ PERSON ☐ ESTATE
OF (NAME):

☐ Minor ☐ Conservatee

PROOF OF SERVICE BY MAIL OF ORDER APPOINTING ☐ GUARDIAN ☐ CONSERVATOR	CASE NUMBER:

PROOF OF SERVICE BY MAIL
(Personal delivery also permitted. Probate Code, § 1466)

I am over the age of 18 and not a party to this cause. I am a resident of or employed in the county where the mailing occurred. My residence or business address is:

I served the Order Appointing ☐ Guardian ☐ Conservator by enclosing a true copy in a sealed envelope addressed to each person whose name and address is given below and depositing the envelope in the United States mail with the postage fully prepaid.

(1) Date of deposit: (2) Place of deposit (city and state):

I declare under penalty of perjury under the laws of the State of California that the foregoing is true and correct and that this declaration is executed on (date): . . . . at (place): . . . .

. . . . _____
(Type or print name)   (Signature of declarant)

NAME AND ADDRESS OF EACH PERSON TO WHOM NOTICE WAS MAILED

a. ☐ Ward 14 years of age or older:

b. ☐ Conservatee:

c.

☐ List of names and addresses continued in attachment.

Do NOT use this form for personal delivery permitted in lieu of mailing by section 1466 of the Probate Code.

Form Approved by the
Judicial Council of California
Revised Effective January 1, 1981
GC-030(81)

**PROOF OF SERVICE BY MAIL
OF ORDER APPOINTING
GUARDIAN OR CONSERVATOR**

☐ IF RECORDED RETURN TO:

ATTORNEY FOR (Name):

SUPERIOR COURT OF CALIFORNIA, COUNTY OF

STREET ADDRESS:

MAILING ADDRESS:

CITY AND ZIP CODE:

BRANCH NAME:

CONSERVATORSHIP OF (NAME):

Conservatee

| **LETTERS OF CONSERVATORSHIP**
☐ **Person** ☐ **Estate** ☐ **Limited Conservatorship** | CASE NUMBER: |

FOR RECORDER'S USE ONLY

STATE OF CALIFORNIA, COUNTY OF

1. ☐ (Name):　　　　　　　　　　　　　　　　is the appointed
   ☐ conservator ☐ limited conservator of the ☐ person ☐ estate of
   (name):

2. ☐ *(for conservatorship that was on December 31, 1980, a guardianship of an adult or of the person of a married minor)* (name):
   was appointed the guardian of the ☐ person ☐ estate by order
   dated:　　　　　　　　　　　　　and is now the conservator of the
   ☐ person ☐ estate of (name):

3. ☐ Other powers have been granted or conditions imposed as follows:
   a. ☐ exclusive authority to give consent for and to require the conservatee to receive medical treatment that the conservator in good faith based on medical advice determines to be necessary even if the conservatee objects, subject to the limitations stated in section 2356 of the Probate Code.
   ☐ This treatment shall be performed by an accredited practitioner of the religion whose tenets and practices call for reliance on prayer alone for healing of which the conservatee was an adherent prior to the establishment of the conservatorship.
   ☐ *(applicable only if the court order limits the duration)* This medical authority terminates on (date):

   b. ☐ powers to be exercised independently under section 2590 of the Probate Code as specified in attachment 3b *(specify powers, restrictions, conditions, and limitations).*
   c. ☐ conditions relating to the care and custody of the property under section 2402 of the Probate Code as specified in attachment 3c.
   d. ☐ conditions relating to the care, treatment, education, and welfare of the conservatee under section 2358 of the Probate Code as specified in attachment 3d.
   e. ☐ *(for limited conservatorship only)* powers of the limited conservator of the person under section 2351.5 of the Probate Code as specified in attachment 3e.
   f. ☐ *(for limited conservatorship only)* powers of the limited conservator of the estate under section 1830(b) of the Probate Code as specified in attachment 3f.
   g. ☐ other *(specify):*

SEAL

Dated: . . . .

Clerk, by ———————————————————— , Deputy

☐ Number of pages attached:
(Continued on reverse)

This form may be recorded as notice of the establishment of a conservatorship of the estate as provided in section 1875 of the Probate Code.

Form Approved by the
Judicial Council of California
Effective January 1, 1981
GC-350(81)

LETTERS OF CONSERVATORSHIP

CONSERVATORSHIP OF (NAME):	CASE NUMBER:
Conservatee	

LETTERS OF CONSERVATORSHIP   Page 2

AFFIRMATION

I solemnly affirm that I will perform the duties of ☐ conservator ☐ limited conservator according to law.

Executed on (date): . . . . , at (place) . . . .

_____
(Signature of appointee)

CERTIFICATION

I certify that this document and any attachments is a correct copy of the original on file in my office, and that the letters issued to the person appointed above have not been revoked, annulled, or set aside, and are still in full force and effect.

Dated: . . . .   Clerk, by _____ , Deputy

SEAL

PARTY WITHOUT AN ATTORNEY (*(Name and Address):*	TELEPHONE NO.:	FOR COURT USE ONLY

In Pro Per

NAME OF COURT:
STREET ADDRESS:
MAILING ADDRESS:
CITY AND ZIP CODE:
BRANCH NAME:

CONSERVATORSHIP OF THE ☐ PERSON ☐ ESTATE OF (NAME):

CONSERVATEE

PROOF OF SERVICE BY MAIL	CASE NUMBER:

I declare that:

1. At the time of service I was at least 18 years of age and not a party to this legal action.
2. I am a resident of or employed in the county where the mailing occurred.
3. My business or residence address is _____

4. I served copies of the following paper(s) in the manner shown [list exact titles of paper(s)]:

5. Manner of service: by placing true copies in a sealed envelope addressed to each person whose name and address is given below and depositing the envelopes in the United States Mail with the postage fully prepaid.
   a. Date of deposit: _____
   b. Place of deposit (city and state): _____

6. Name and address of each person to whom documents were mailed:

☐ Additional names and addresses on reverse.

I declare under penalty of perjury under the laws of the State of California that the foregoing is true and correct.

Date:

....
(TYPE OR PRINT NAME)   (SIGNATURE OF PERSON WHO SERVED PAPERS)

NP

PROOF OF SERVICE BY MAIL

NAME AND ADDRESS OF ATTORNEY	TELEPHONE NO:	FOR COURT USE ONLY

NAME OF COURT, OR BRANCH, MAILING AND STREET ADDRESS

ESTATE OF

☐ DECEDENT ☐ INCOMPETENT ☐ CONSERVATEE ☐ MINOR

APPLICATION AND ORDER APPOINTING PROBATE REFEREE

CASE NUMBER

It is requested that a Probate Referee be appointed to appraise the assets of the above entitled estate consisting of the following approximate values:

1. CASH $ _____

2. REAL ESTATE $ _____

3. PERSONAL PROPERTY $ _____

REMARKS _____

_____

_____

Attorney

IT IS ORDERED that (name):

a disinterested person, is appointed Probate Referee to appraise the above entitled estate. When a Probate Referee is appointed, such referee is authorized to fix the clear market value of the estate as of the date of death of the decedent, or as of the date of appointment if a conservatorship or guardianship, and to appraise all interest, inheritances, transfers, and property of the estate under the laws of the State of California.

DATED: _____

Judge of the Superior Court

_____

APPLICATION AND ORDER APPOINTING PROBATE REFEREE

ATTORNEY OR PARTY WITHOUT ATTORNEY *(Name and Address)*:

TELEPHONE NO.:

FOR COURT USE ONLY

ATTORNEY FOR *(Name)*:

SUPERIOR COURT OF CALIFORNIA, COUNTY OF

STREET ADDRESS:

MAILING ADDRESS:

CITY AND ZIP CODE:

BRANCH NAME:

ESTATE OF (NAME):

☐ DECEDENT ☐ CONSERVATEE ☐ MINOR

INVENTORY AND APPRAISEMENT

CASE NUMBER:

☐ Complete   ☐ Final

☐ Partial No.:   ☐ Supplemental

☐ Reappraisal for Sale

Date of Death of Decedent or of Appointment of Guardian or Conservator:

APPRAISALS

1. Total appraisal by representative (attachment 1) $
2. Total appraisal by referee (attachment 2) $

TOTAL: $

DECLARATION OF REPRESENTATIVE

3. Attachments 1 and 2 together with all prior inventories filed contain a true statement of
☐ all ☐ a portion of the estate that has come to my knowledge or possession, including particularly all money and all just claims the estate has against me. I have truly, honestly, and impartially appraised to the best of my ability each item set forth in attachment 1.

4. ☐ No probate referee is required ☐ by order of the court dated *(specify)*:

I declare under penalty of perjury under the laws of the State of California that the foregoing is true and correct.

Date:

▶

. . . .
(TYPE OR PRINT NAME) (Include title if corporate officer)

(SIGNATURE OF PERSONAL REPRESENTATIVE)

STATEMENT REGARDING BOND

(Complete if required by local court rule)

5. ☐ Bond is waived.
6. ☐ Sole personal representative is a corporate fiduciary.
7. ☐ Bond filed in the amount of: $ ☐ Sufficient ☐ Insufficient
8. ☐ Receipts for: $ have been filed with the court for deposits in a blocked account
at *(specify institution and location)*:

Date:

▶

(SIGNATURE OF ATTORNEY OR PARTY WITHOUT ATTORNEY)

DECLARATION OF PROBATE REFEREE

9. I have truly, honestly, and impartially appraised to the best of my ability each item set forth in attachment 2.
10. A true account of my commission and expenses actually and necessarily incurred pursuant to my appointment is

Statutory commission: $

Expenses *(specify)*: $

TOTAL: $

I declare under penalty of perjury under the laws of the State of California that the foregoing is true and correct.

Date:

▶

. . . .
(TYPE OR PRINT NAME)

(SIGNATURE OF REFEREE)

(Instructions on reverse)

Form Approved by the
Judicial Council of California
DE-160, GC-040 (Rev. January 1, 1985)

INVENTORY AND APPRAISEMENT
(Probate)

Prob C 600-611,
2610-2616

INSTRUCTIONS

See Probate Code, §§ 604, 608, 609, 611, 2610-2616 for additional instructions.

If required in a decedent's estate proceeding by local court rule, furnish an extra copy for the clerk to transmit to the assessor (Probate Code, § 600).

See Probate Code, §§ 600-602 for items to be included.

If the minor or conservatee is or has been during the guardianship or conservatorship confined in a state hospital under the jurisdiction of the State Department of Mental Health or the State Department of Developmental Services, mail a copy to the director of the appropriate department in Sacramento (Probate Code, § 2611).

The representative shall list on attachment 1 and appraise as of the date of death of the decedent or date of appointment of the guardian or conservator at fair market value moneys, currency, cash items, bank accounts and amounts on deposit with any financial institution (as defined in Probate Code, § 605), and the proceeds of life and accident insurance policies and retirement plans payable upon death in lump sum amounts to the estate, except items whose fair market value is, in the opinion of the representative, an amount different from the ostensible value or specified amount.

The representative shall list on attachment 2 all other assets of the estate which shall be appraised by the referee.

If joint tenancy and other assets are listed for appraisal purposes only and not as part of the probate estate, they must be separately listed on additional attachments and their value excluded from the total valuation of attachments 1 and 2.

Each attachment should conform to the format approved by the Judicial Council (see form Inventory and Appraisement (Attachment) (DE-161, GC-041) and Cal. Rules of Court, rule 201).

ESTATE OF:

ATTACHMENT NO:

(IN DECEDENTS' ESTATES, ATTACHMENTS MUST CONFORM TO PROBATE CODE 601
REGARDING COMMUNITY AND SEPARATE PROPERTY)

PAGE . . . . . OF . . . . . TOTAL PAGES
(ADD PAGES AS REQUIRED)

Item No.   Description   Appraised value
1. $

Form Approved by the
Judicial Council of California
Effective January 1, 1976

INVENTORY AND APPRAISEMENT (ATTACHMENT)

Prob C 481,
600-605, 784,
1550, 1901

F1306-A

1

2

3

4

5

6

7

8

9

10

11

12

13

14

15

16

17

18

19

20

21

22

23

24

25

26

27

28

GET 25% OFF
YOUR NEXT PURCHASE

RECYCLE YOUR OUT-OF-DATE BOOKS

It's important to have the most current legal information. Because laws and legal procedures change often, we update our books regularly. To help keep you up-to-date we are extending this special offer. Cut out and mail the title portion of the cover of any old Nolo book with your next order and we'll give you a 25% discount off the retail price of ANY new Nolo book you purchase directly from us. For current prices and editions call us at 1-800-992-6656.

This offer is to individuals only.

Nim's Island

MOVIE STORYBOOK

Adapted by Sonia Sander
Based on the screenplay by Joseph Kwong & Paula Mazur
and Mark Levin & Jennifer Flackett
Based on characters by Wendy Orr

Scholastic Inc.
New York   Toronto   London   Auckland   Sydney
Mexico City   New Delhi   Hong Kong   Buenos Aires

ISBN-13: 978-0-545-08169-6
ISBN-10: 0-545-08169-6

Published by Scholastic Inc.
SCHOLASTIC and associated logos are trademarks and/or registered trademarks of Scholastic Inc.

www.walden.com/nimsisland

12 11 10 9 8 7 6 5 4 3 2 1   8 9 10 11 12/0

Printed in the U.S.A.
First printing, May 2008

Nim Rusoe was an eleven-year-old girl who lived a very unusual life.

She and her dad, Jack, lived all alone on a beautiful tropical island. The island wasn't on any maps. And it was all theirs.

They built themselves a home and had everything they needed to live a happy and comfortable life.

Even though Nim and Jack were the only people on the island, Nim wasn't lonely at all. She had lots of friends. Many of them came from the insides of books. One of Nim's best friends was Alice from the story *Alice in Wonderland*. Alice was a true friend to Nim and helped keep her out of trouble.

Another of her friends was Huck Finn from the book *Adventures of Huckleberry Finn*. Huck was fun to be around and always had a trick up his sleeve. He and Nim would often race each other through the forest. Huck usually won, except that he nearly always cheated.

But not all of Nim's friends came from books . . . some of them were animals from the island! Selkie was one of Nim's best friends. He was a big, friendly sea lion who often swam with Nim. Another of Nim's friends was Galileo, a sharp-eyed pelican who flew above the ocean all day long catching fish.

Nim was also friends with a green iguana named Fred and a great big sea turtle named Chica. Nim loved her animal friends, and they loved her, too. But her best friend wasn't an animal from the island OR a character from a book.

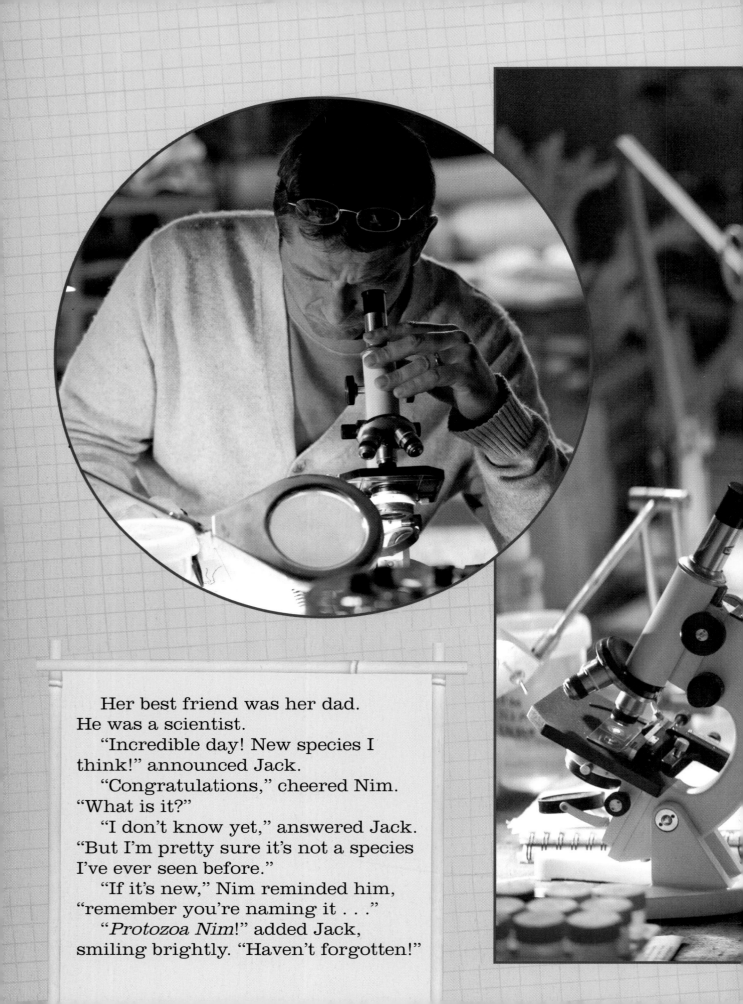

Her best friend was her dad. He was a scientist.

"Incredible day! New species I think!" announced Jack.

"Congratulations," cheered Nim. "What is it?"

"I don't know yet," answered Jack. "But I'm pretty sure it's not a species I've ever seen before."

"If it's new," Nim reminded him, "remember you're naming it . . ."

"*Protozoa Nim*!" added Jack, smiling brightly. "Haven't forgotten!"

Every once in a while, a big ship would come to their island, bringing them supplies. Nim loved when new books came on the ship — especially books about the adventure hero Alex Rover.

"The new Alex Rover book! Excellent!" cried Nim, as she pulled the latest novel out of a large crate. She tore open the book and eagerly began to read it. She couldn't wait to find out what Alex Rover was up to next!

Alex Rover was an adventurer who was always getting himself in danger, and Nim loved reading his action-packed stories.

But what Nim didn't know was that there was a *real* Alex Rover. And the real Alex Rover couldn't have been more different from the character.

The *real* Alex Rover was actually named *Alexandra*. She was an author living in San Francisco, and she was afraid of *everything* — including germs, people, and the outdoors. In fact, Alexandra was so afraid, she hadn't left her apartment in months.

Back on the island, Jack was packing up for a trip. He was going away for two days on a scientific expedition. He wanted Nim to come along, but she had other things in mind.

"Chica's eggs are about to hatch," said Nim. "I need to protect the baby turtles from the sand crabs. Chica only saved one last year."

"Are you sure you'll be all right?" he asked. He and Nim had never been apart for more than one night before; he was worried about leaving her alone on the island.

"I've got Selkie and Fred and Chica and the new Alex Rover book," said Nim. "I'll be excellent."

So Jack loaded his gear onto his ship and set sail, hopeful to find some new discoveries on his trip.

Soon after he left, an e-mail came for Jack. Nim eagerly clicked it open . . . and could hardly believe her eyes.

"Dear Jack Rusoe," the e-mail began. "I need a bit of help on my newest adventure. Might you be able to answer a few questions for me? Alex Rover."

Alex Rover!?

She quickly wrote back: "Dear Alex Rover, I am sure Jack would love to help you with your newest adventure. He will be back on Thursday. He's a great fan of yours. We both are! From Nim."

"It was incredible, Jack!" gushed Nim that night as she spoke to her dad on her satellite telephone. "I saved all Chica's babies from the crabs!"

"I wish you could be here, Nim," said Jack, holding up a glowing jar labeled *Protozoa Nim*.

"Did you find any new species?" asked Nim.

"I'm not sure yet, but I have a good feeling about it," he said proudly. "Now go to sleep. We'll talk in the morning."

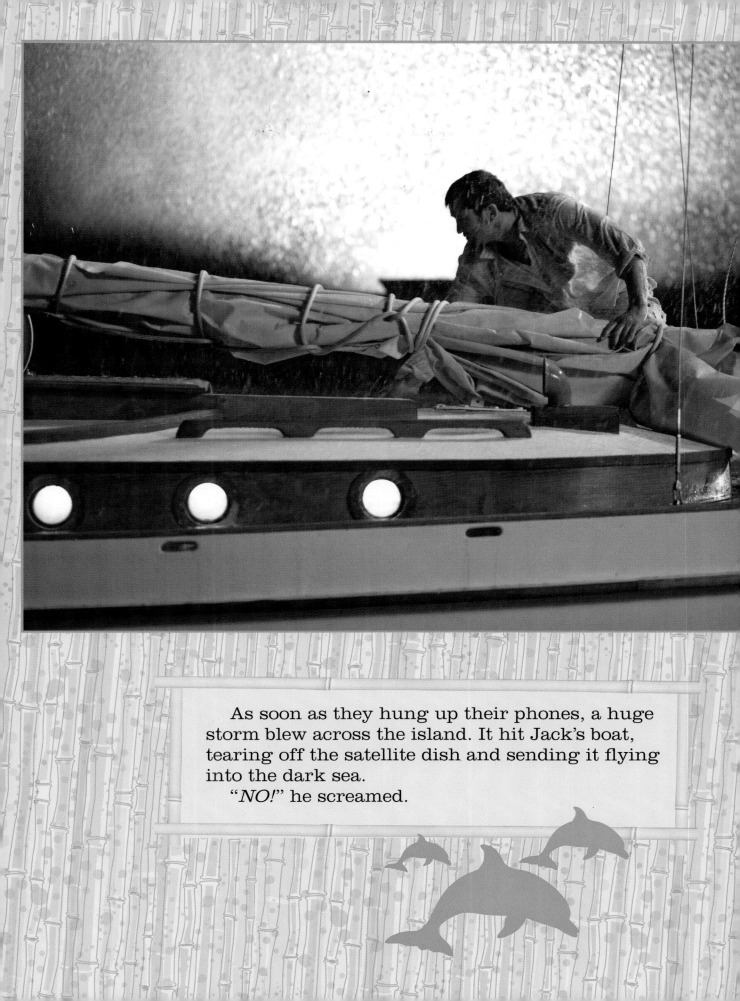

As soon as they hung up their phones, a huge storm blew across the island. It hit Jack's boat, tearing off the satellite dish and sending it flying into the dark sea.

"*NO!*" he screamed.

The storm hit the island hard as well, and Nim did her best to protect their home. She covered their computer with plastic and shut all the windows. She was scared, but luckily she wasn't alone. She had Selkie and Fred close by her side. They cuddled up close and got through the storm together.

The next morning, Nim was relieved to find that their computer still worked. And she was surprised to see that she had received another e-mail from Alex Rover! He asked her about the volcano on their island, which they called Fire Mountain, and wondered what it looked like inside.

"Dear Alex Rover," Nim wrote, a plan forming in her head, "I'm not sure what it looks like inside a volcano, but I'll let you know soon."

Nim knew what she had to do: climb Fire Mountain. So she suited up in her climbing gear and began to scale the rocky peak.

It was hard, but Nim finally reached the top. And when she got there, she saw something very strange. Across the horizon, there was a giant ship with the word *Buccaneer* written across it — and it was heading straight toward her island! Nim scrambled down the rocks quickly — badly cutting her leg in the process.

Nim was hurt and scared. She needed help, but who would come all the way to her remote island to rescue her? There was only one person who was brave enough for the job: the world's greatest adventurer, Alex Rover.

"Dear Alex Rover," Nim wrote. "My volcano expedition didn't go well at all. I fell down the face of the mountain and got a nasty gash on my leg. I'm all alone, and my father's gone! Our island is twenty degrees south, a hundred and sixty-two degrees west in the South Pacific Sea . . ." she wrote. "*COME!* I can't do this all alone. I need *you*, Alex Rover. Please help me."

Alexandra knew she had to go rescue Nim. But how would she ever get to Nim's Island? She could barely even leave her house!

Meanwhile, Nim had to figure out how to keep the *Buccaneer* off her island. But she couldn't do it all alone, so she gathered Alice and Huck to help her form a plan.

With her trusty tool belt at her side, Nim started to work on her plan. Suddenly, Galileo appeared in the sky. He dived down straight for Nim's tool belt and swooped back into the air with it in his mouth.

"No, Galileo! No! No!" Nim cried out to the pelican. "My tools! Galileo! I need those! Come back!"

But Galileo refused to come back. Instead he flew off toward someone who needed the tools even more than Nim — Jack.

Jack's ship was in very bad shape from the storm; he wasn't sure if he'd ever make it home to Nim. He suddenly heard a loud *SPLASH!* and peered into the water beside his boat. A tool belt had fallen from the sky! Then he saw Galileo lying on the deck, heaving for breath.

"Galileo? Thank you!" cried Jack. "There's hope for me yet!"

Meanwhile, in San Francisco, Alexandra was having problems of her own. "I . . . I can't leave," she said. "Can't do it . . ."

"Frankly, I'm amazed you made it *this* far," teased her creation, Alex Rover, who had suddenly come to life out of the pages of her book. "Probably best you don't go anyway. I mean, Nim didn't ask for *you*, did she? She asked for *me*."

"Unfortunately, you aren't real," insisted Alexandra.

The taxi honked impatiently as Alex Rover began wrestling with Alexandra. He was trying to pull Alexandra outside, while she fought to stay in her apartment. The taxi driver could hardly believe his eyes as he stared at the strange scene of a lady fighting with someone who was completely invisible.

Finally, Alexandra made her way to the waiting car, but her journey was only just beginning. . . . She had a long, long way to go before she even got *somewhat* close to Nim.

Nim's Island wasn't exactly easy to get to. Alexandra traveled by land, air, and sea to reach her destination. . .

. . . And she was terrified nearly every step of the way.

Back on the island, the tourists from the *Buccaneer* had just landed on Nim's beach. Now was the time for Nim to put her plan into action. Using a tree as a catapult, she launched Fred and the other iguanas over the trees and into the air toward the beach.

Then Nim raced to the volcano and climbed to its top. She started a fire in its large crater. *CRACK!* Sparks flew as she fanned the flames to rage as big and hot as they could.

"Come on, now," she encouraged the fire. "Smoke! Burn!"

Next Nim loosened some boulders so they fell into the volcano's pit, sending up a huge cloud of ash! The tourists on the beach were terrified and hurried back onto the *Buccaneer*.

Closer to Nim than ever, and clenching her seat as she rattled around in a tiny helicopter, Alexandra found herself smack dab in the middle of a terrible storm.

"Storm's changing course!" announced the pilot. "This is bad! We have to find someplace to land!" Spotting the *Buccaneer*, the pilot hoped he'd be able to land the helicopter safely on its decks.

But Alexandra was not warmly greeted by the crew after they landed. She needed to get to Nim's Island, but they would not take her.

"We've just been there," yelled the captain of the ship. "Trust us, no human being could survive in that place!"

So Alexandra took matters into her own hands. She released one of the *Buccaneer*'s lifeboats into the choppy ocean below.

The storm was hitting Jack hard as well. But thanks to the tools Galileo brought him, Jack was able to build himself a makeshift wind-powered engine. With heavy rains and winds raging around him, Jack put his new engine to the test. And very slowly, he moved forward.

"Blow, wind! Blow! Blow me home!" cried Jack, desperately. "Come on, Mother Nature! Get me to Nim!"

But as the storm raged on, Jack's boat ripped apart piece by piece.

"I will not give up, Nim! I will never give up! I *will* get back to you! I promise!" cried Jack as yet another wave crashed over him.

Back on the island, Nim huddled in a corner as the storm lashed out. Suddenly, through the rain and thunder, Nim heard a distant cry.

"Daddy?" she whispered.

Nim peered out at the churning ocean. "Is there something out there?" she asked.

It was a boat! Convinced that it was her father, Nim ran through the pouring rain to the beach. In the distance, the small boat was being tossed violently onto the rocks.

Without a second thought, Nim hung onto Selkie's back as the sea lion carried her through the surf and out to the sinking boat. Once out there, Nim bravely dived into the water to save her dad.

Only it wasn't her father she ended up saving. It was a woman.

"Who are you?" asked Nim.

"I'm Alex Rover."

"That's impossible. Alex Rover is a *man*. He's a hero. He *saves* people. He doesn't need saving," cried Nim.

"I know," replied Alexandra, feeling a little embarrassed. "I'm the real Alex Rover. I'm the *writer*. I created him."

"You have to go," said Nim. "You can't be here. You have to go before my dad gets back. This is *our* island. We don't want anyone else here!"

With that, Nim ran off into the forest, leaving Alexandra all alone on the beach.

"But she needs you, Nim," said Alice softly after Nim had returned to her home. "Go get her."

"But this is my island, right, Huck?" asked Nim, planting her feet firmly on the ground.

"That's kinda why you gotta go get her," said Huck.

Nim couldn't believe Huck was agreeing with Alice. She'd been outvoted and overruled. She sighed deeply, grabbed a lantern, and headed back to the beach to rescue Alexandra all over again.

Nim went to the beach to find Alexandra. She brought her back to her house and made her some food.

The next morning, Alexandra awoke to find Nim sadly staring out at the ocean. Nim was crying.

"If his boat was afloat, he'd be home right now," Nim stammered, fighting back her tears. "Y-You found your way all the way from San Francisco and you don't know how to do anything. H-He would be back by now if he was still alive. He's not coming back, Alexandra," Nim sobbed.

Alexandra hugged Nim in her arms. "I promise, you will be okay," Alexandra said. "I will make sure of that. Be it here or anywhere. You will not be alone."

Then Alexandra spotted something on the horizon. Looking up, Nim spotted it, too — it was a boat! And . . . on the boat was a person. It was Jack!

"It's him! It's him! Daddy!" cried Nim, waving her arms excitedly before jumping onto the zip line and flying through the forest down to the beach.

"You're home! You're alive!" Nim cried, happily greeting her father.

"I told you I'd be back," said a very weak, chapped, and sunburned Jack.

He then looked at Alexandra and was startled and confused by her presence. *Who was this beautiful woman — and how did she get on their beach?* Jack looked to Nim for an answer.

"This is Alex Rover, Dad. She wrote the books," said Nim. "Or, well, what I mean is, this is *Alexandra* Rover, the *writer*."

"I-I'm sorry," said Jack, shaking his head in disbelief. "I just imagined Alex Rover so . . . differently."

It was love at first sight between Jack and Alexandra, and before long, Jack, Nim, and Alexandra had formed a family. The three of them couldn't have been happier together.

Alexandra never imagined the adventure her life would become — until she let it become one. And so began a new story: the writer, the scientist, and the child living together on Nim's Island.